THE
OFFICIAL
FOOTBALL
ASSOCIATION
YEARBOOK

1995-96

THE FOOTBALL ASSOCIATION

THE
OFFICIAL
FOOTBALL
ASSOCIATION
YEARBOOK

1995-96

PAN BOOKS

This edition published 1995 by Pan Books
an imprint of Macmillan Publishers Limited
25 Eccleston Place, London SW1W 9NF
and Basingstoke

Associated companies throughout the world

ISBN 0-330-34582-6

1 3 5 7 9 8 6 4 2

A CIP catalogue record for this book is available from the British Library

Typeset by Spottiswoode Ballantyne Printers Ltd
Printed and bound in Great Britain by BPC Hazell Books Ltd
A member of The British Printing Company Ltd

CONTENTS

1 ● CHIEF EXECUTIVE'S REPORT

It is astonishing to me that, after a period in which The Football Association has experienced quite dramatic change, there remain so many big challenges ahead.

The structure of the professional game has altered irrevocably with the establishment of The F.A. Premier League. Grounds have been transformed. We now see top foreign players more often choosing to further their career in England. Our own star players are less inclined to emigrate. The development of young players has been revolutionised by the expansion of the Centres of Excellence Programme; our best young players are now playing fewer games, as their development is more closely monitored. The F.A.'s commercial programme has realised new money in excess of £20 million in 1995 to date, money which is re-invested in the game's development. And hooliganism, so long the scourge of football, is on the wane, squeezed out by a vast concentration of effort and resources.

However, is it right that at our Wembley finals we still experience obscene chants and gestures among rival supporters? I'm not referring to the Cup Final itself, but to the less well supported finals supposedly affording the smaller teams' fans a one-off treat at Wembley. Why cannot somebody isolate and remove the instigators and ringleaders? After all, they're clearly identifiable to anyone who takes the trouble to look.

Why cannot these nasty people leave the decent supporters to enjoy the game and their day out in peace? It is to counter such unpleasantness that The Football Association is launching this season a new campaign targeting racism and intimidation in the game. We will be involving all football bodies, supporters and local authorities in a concerted effort to improve the atmosphere at matches.

We will also be impressing upon clubs the importance of good behaviour in public by highly-paid professional players. Incidents are few and far between, but when they do occur they attract tremendous adverse publicity and reflect badly upon the decent professionals in the game. The Professional Footballers' Association has accepted that players are professionals virtually 24 hours a day, 7 days a week and 52 weeks a year and that, if clubs themselves do not clearly take firm action over public misbehaviour away from the actual game, then the F.A. should step in.

Although The F.A. Premier League has been spectacularly successful there is a widespread worry that the gap between it and The Football League will become unbridgable. When The F.A. Premier League was set up, transitional financial arrangements were made. The Football Association pays The Football League £2 million p.a. and The F.A. Premier League contributes 3% of the gate money plus their revenue from the pools contract. The Football League was also able to negotiate a fruitful contract with Independent Television. The ITV contract expires in 1996 and the other deals run out in 1997. There will need to be some imaginative and realistic negotiations if the present structure of full time professional football in 92 towns and cities is to be preserved.

The Centres of Excellence revolution has given us a sound base for the future. But this will be worthless if other issues central to the technical development of top class players are ignored. Are there failings in development between the ages of 16 and 21? Can our coaches be better qualified and more knowledgeable? Do we play too much and practise too little? Is the Football Association National School the best method of investing over £500,000 p.a. in attempting to develop international players of the future? We are moving quickly to address such questions, but anyone who has seen the young players of such emerging countries as Japan or Oman or Nigeria will know that throughout the world the level of skill is improving all the time.

There have been a number of high-profile cases involving financial irregularities. The football authorities are reacting by bringing in tough new rules to ensure compliance with financial regulations, control of the activities of agents and prohibition of inducements to young players. The new rules will be backed by wide-ranging codes of conduct and clear disciplinary procedures designed to punish anyone who transgresses in future. With the new financial power of football comes responsibility, and we must not shirk it.

The Football Association has demonstrated vigour and dynamism in moving the game forward in the nineties. I believe we will need those qualities in abundance to tackle the issues that remain. Whatever the difficulties we experienced in the 1994–95 season, we faced up to them and handled them promptly and efficiently. We will continue to be upfront.

Graham Kelly

2 ● WORLD CUP FINALS 1930–1994

Year	Venue	Winner		Runner-up	Result	
1930	Montevideo	Uruguay	v	Argentina	4–2	
1934	Rome	Italy	v	Czechoslovakia	2–1	*
1938	Paris	Italy	v	Hungary	4–2	
1950	Rio de Janeiro	Uruguay	v	Brazil	2–1	
1954	Berne	West Germany	v	Hungary	3–2	
1958	Stockholm	Brazil	v	Sweden	5–2	
1962	Santiago	Brazil	v	Czechoslovakia	3–1	
1966	Wembley	England	v	West Germany	4–2	*
1970	Mexico City	Brazil	v	Italy	4–1	
1974	Munich	West Germany	v	Holland	2–1	
1978	Buenos Aires	Argentina	v	Holland	3–1	*
1982	Madrid	Italy	v	West Germany	3–1	
1986	Mexico City	Argentina	v	West Germany	3–2	
1990	Rome	West Germany	v	Argentina	1–0	
1994	Los Angeles	Brazil	v	Italy	0–0	†

* after extra time
† won on penalty-kicks

3 ● EUROPEAN CHAMPIONSHIP FINALS 1960–1992

Year	Venue	Winner		Runner-up	Result	
1960	Paris	USSR	v	Yugoslavia	2–1	
1964	Madrid	Spain	v	USSR	2–1	
1968	Rome	Italy	v	Yugoslavia	2–0	†
1972	Brussels	West Germany	v	USSR	3–0	
1976	Belgrade	Czechoslovakia	v	West Germany	2–2	††
1980	Rome	West Germany	v	Belgium	2–1	
1984	Paris	France	v	Spain	2–0	
1988	Munich	Holland	v	USSR	2–0	
1992	Gothenburg	Denmark	v	Germany	2–0	

† *after 1–1 draw*
†† *won on penalty-kicks*

4 ● EUROPEAN CHAMPION CLUBS' CUP WINNERS 1956–1995

Year	Venue	Winner		Runners-up	Result	
1956	Paris	Real Madrid	v	Stade de Rheims	4–3	
1957	Madrid	Real Madrid	v	AC Fiorentina	2–0	
1958	Brussels	Real Madrid	v	AC Milan	3–2	*
1959	Stuttgart	Real Madrid	v	Stade de Rheims	2–0	
1960	Glasgow	Real Madrid	v	Eintracht Frankfurt	7–3	
1961	Berne	Benfica	v	Barcelona	3–2	
1962	Amsterdam	Benfica	v	Real Madrid	5–3	
1963	Wembley	AC Milan	v	Benfica	2–1	
1964	Vienna	Inter-Milan	v	Real Madrid	3–1	
1965	Madrid	Inter-Milan	v	Benfica	1–0	
1966	Brussels	Real Madrid	v	Partizan Belgrade	2–1	
1967	Lisbon	Celtic	v	Inter-Milan	2–1	
1968	Wembley	Manchester United	v	Benfica	4–1	*
1969	Madrid	AC Milan	v	Ajax Amsterdam	4–1	
1970	Milan	Feyenoord	v	Celtic	2–1	*
1971	Wembley	Ajax Amsterdam	v	Panathinaikos	2–0	
1972	Rotterdam	Ajax Amsterdam	v	Inter-Milan	2–0	
1973	Belgrade	Ajax Amsterdam	v	Juventus	1–0	
1974	Brussels	Bayern Munich	v	Atletico Madrid	1–1	
	Brussels	Bayern Munich	v	Atletico Madrid	4–0	
1975	Paris	Bayern Munich	v	Leeds United	2–0	
1976	Glasgow	Bayern Munich	v	St Etienne	1–0	
1977	Rome	Liverpool	v	Borussia Mönchengladbach	3–1	
1978	Wembley	Liverpool	v	FC Bruges	1–0	
1979	Munich	Nottingham Forest	v	Malmö	1–0	
1980	Madrid	Nottingham Forest	v	Hamburg	1–0	
1981	Paris	Liverpool	v	Real Madrid	1–0	
1982	Rotterdam	Aston Villa	v	Bayern Munich	1–0	
1983	Athens	Hamburg	v	Juventus	1–0	
1984	Rome	Liverpool	v	Roma	1–1	**
1985	Brussels	Juventus	v	Liverpool	1–0	
1986	Seville	Steaua Bucharest	v	Barcelona	0–0	**
1987	Vienna	Porto	v	Bayern Munich	2–1	
1988	Stuttgart	PSV Eindhoven	v	Benfica	0–0	**
1989	Barcelona	AC Milan	v	Steaua Bucharest	4–0	
1990	Vienna	AC Milan	v	Benfica	1–0	
1991	Bari	Red Star Belgrade	v	Marseille	0–0	**
1992	Wembley	Barcelona	v	Sampdoria	1–0	*
1993	Munich	Marseille	v	AC Milan	1–0	
1994	Athens	AC Milan	v	Barcelona	4–0	
1995	Vienna	Ajax Amsterdam	v	AC Milan	1–0	

* *after extra time*
** *won on penalty-kicks*

5 ● EUROPEAN CUP WINNERS' CUP WINNERS 1961–1995

Year	Venue	Winner		Runners-up	Result	
1961		AC Fiorentina	v	Glasgow Rangers	4–1	†
1962	Glasgow	Atletico Madrid	v	AC Fiorentina	1–1	
	Stuttgart	Atletico Madrid	v	AC Fiorentina	3–0	
1963	Rotterdam	Tottenham Hotspur	v	Atletico Madrid	5–1	
1964	Brussels	Sporting Lisbon	v	MTK Budapest	3–3	*
	Antwerp	Sporting Lisbon	v	MTK Budapest	1–0	
1965	Wembley	West Ham United	v	Munich 1860	2–0	
1966	Glasgow	Borussia Dortmund	v	Liverpool	2–1	*
1967	Nuremberg	Bayern Munich	v	Rangers	1–0	*
1968	Rotterdam	AC Milan	v	Hamburg	2–0	
1969	Basle	Slovan Bratislava	v	Barcelona	3–2	
1970	Vienna	Manchester City	v	Gornik Zabrze	2–1	
1971	Athens	Chelsea	v	Real Madrid	1–1	*
	Athens	Chelsea	v	Real Madrid	2–1	
1972	Barcelona	Glasgow Rangers	v	Moscow Dynamo	3–2	
1973	Salonika	AC Milan	v	Leeds United	1–0	
1974	Rotterdam	Magdeburg	v	AC Milan	2–0	
1975	Basle	Dynamo Kiev	v	Ferencvaros	3–0	
1976	Brussels	Anderlecht	v	West Ham United	4–2	

Ian Wright on the ball during the Cup Winners' Cup Final in Paris.

Year	Venue	Winner		Runners-up	Result	
1977	Amsterdam	Hamburg	v	Anderlecht	2-0	
1978	Paris	Anderlecht	v	Austria Vienna	4-0	
1979	Basle	Barcelona	v	Fortuna Düsseldorf	4-3	*
1980	Brussels	Valencia	v	Arsenal	0-0	**
1981	Düsseldorf	Dynamo Tbilisi	v	Carl Zeiss Jena	2-1	
1982	Barcelona	Barcelona	v	Standard Liège	2-1	
1983	Gothenburg	Aberdeen	v	Real Madrid	2-1	*
1984	Basle	Juventus	v	Porto	2-1	
1985	Rotterdam	Everton	v	Rapid Vienna	3-1	
1986	Lyon	Dynamo Kiev	v	Atletico Madrid	3-0	
1987	Athens	Ajax Amsterdam	v	Lokomotiv Leipzig	1-0	
1988	Strasbourg	Mechelen	v	Ajax Amsterdam	1-0	
1989	Berne	Barcelona	v	Sampdoria	2-0	
1990	Gothenburg	Sampdoria	v	Anderlecht	2-0	*
1991	Rotterdam	Manchester United	v	Barcelona	2-1	
1992	Lisbon	Werder Bremen	v	Monaco	2-0	
1993	Wembley	Parma	v	Royal Antwerp	3-1	
1994	Copenhagen	Arsenal	v	Parma	1-0	
1995	Paris	Real Zaragoza	v	Arsenal	2-1	*

† *aggregate over two legs*
* *after extra time*
** *won on penalty-kicks*

6 ● UEFA CUP WINNERS 1958-1995

Known also as the Inter Cities Fairs' Cup until 1971. Two-leg finals except in 1964 and 1965.
Aggregate scores.

Year	Winner		Runners-up	Result	
1958	Barcelona	v	London	8-2	
1960	Barcelona	v	Birmingham	4-1	
1961	Roma	v	Birmingham	4-2	
1962	Valencia	v	Barcelona	7-3	
1963	Valencia	v	Dynamo Zagreb	4-1	
1964	Real Zaragoza	v	Valencia	2-1	
1965	Ferencvaros	v	Juventus	1-0	
1966	Barcelona	v	Real Zaragoza	4-3	
1967	Dynamo Zagreb	v	Leeds United	2-0	
1968	Leeds United	v	Ferencvaros	1-0	
1969	Newcastle United	v	Ujpest Dozsa	6-2	
1970	Arsenal	v	Anderlecht	4-3	
1971	Leeds United	v	Juventus	3-3	*
1972	Tottenham Hotspur	v	Wolverhampton Wanderers	3-2	
1973	Liverpool	v	Borussia Mönchengladbach	3-2	
1974	Feyenoord	v	Tottenham Hotspur	4-2	
1975	Borussia Mönchengladbach	v	Twente Enschede	5-1	
1976	Liverpool	v	FC Bruges	4-3	
1977	Juventus	v	Bilbao	2-2	*
1978	PSV Eindhoven	v	Bastia	3-0	
1979	Borussia Mönchengladbach	v	Red Star Belgrade	2-1	
1980	Eintracht Frankfurt	v	Borussia Mönchengladbach	3-3	*
1981	Ipswich Town	v	AZ 67 Alkmaar	5-4	
1982	IFK Gothenburg	v	Hamburg	4-0	
1983	Anderlecht	v	Benfica	2-1	
1984	Tottenham Hotspur	v	Anderlecht	2-2	†
1985	Real Madrid	v	Videoton	3-1	
1986	Real Madrid	v	Cologne	5-3	
1987	IFK Gothenburg	v	Dundee United	2-1	
1988	Bayer Leverkusen	v	Espanol	3-3	†
1989	Napoli	v	Stuttgart	5-4	
1990	Juventus	v	AC Fiorentina	3-1	
1991	Inter-Milan	v	Roma	2-1	
1992	Ajax Amsterdam	v	Torino	2-2	*
1993	Juventus	v	Borussia Dortmund	6-1	
1994	Inter-Milan	v	Casino Salzburg	2-0	
1995	Parma	v	Juventus	2-1	

* *won on away goals rule*
† *won on penalty-kicks*

7 ● REVIEW OF THE EUROPEAN SEASON 1994–1995

The European champion of champions were Ajax of Amsterdam who beat holders AC Milan with a late goal in the 40th European Cup Final, played on 24 May at the Ernst Happel Stadium in Vienna. Ajax, winning the Final for the fourth time but for the first since 1973, had already overcome their Italian opponents twice in the competition – at the "Champions League" stage. Their credentials were further enhanced by having just won the Dutch title for the 25th time: if they went on to avoid defeat in the season's last League fixture at the following weekend, they would become the first to remain unbeaten throughout the campaign.

Ajax deserved their success in Vienna for a spirited second-half performance and it was an 18-year-old substitute, Patrick Kluivert, who forced in the winning goal on 84 minutes when extra time looked very much on the cards. Rijkaard, 33 and about to retire, put the Amsterdam-born teenager clear in the box and he held off Boban's challenge to stretch a long left leg forward and stab the ball past Rossi. It provided the 14th 1–0 scoreline in the history of the Final. If Milan had won, they would have equalled Real Madrid's record of six Final victories. As it was, a worldwide TV audience of half a billion saw Ajax skipper Danny Blind – who almost made it 2–0 in the last minute – receive the huge trophy from UEFA President Lennart Johansson.

Italian clubs were again successful in all three UEFA competitions. In addition to Milan featuring in the Champions' Final, Sampdoria made it to the Cup Winners' Cup semi-finals and two Italian giants – Parma and Juventus – contested the UEFA Cup Final. The Genoa club lost out to Arsenal, and goalkeeper David Seaman in particular, in a shootout. Then the "Gunners" were themselves beaten by Real Zaragoza in the Final in Paris on 10 May, when ex-Tottenham player Nayim's 50-yard punt in the dying seconds of extra time deceived a back-pedalling

Seaman and won it 2–1 for the Spaniards. Arsenal were that close to becoming the first club in Cup Winners' Cup history to retain the trophy.

Another London side, Chelsea, did well in the competition. An exciting 2–1 aggregate win over Bruges brought them a semi-final tie with Zaragoza, but a 3–0 reverse in Spain in the first leg left them with the proverbial mountain to climb at the Bridge. To have two English clubs in the last four had been greatly encouraging: generally, though, there was disappointment in Europe for our teams. Manchester United, fresh from a "double" season, began their sequence of six Champions League matches with a 4–2 success against Gothenburg at Old Trafford. But there were comprehensive defeats at Barcelona and in the Swedish return and the door to the quarter-finals was slammed shut.

Parma drew 1–1 with their Italian rivals, Juventus, in the second leg of the UEFA Cup Final played at Milan's San Siro and won the trophy 2–1 on aggregate. Gianluca Vialli blasted Juventus in front with a left-foot volley on 33 minutes, but then Dino Baggio – scorer of Parma's goal in the first leg – headed a brave equaliser nine minutes into the second half. Parma, second in Serie A, were seven points behind Juve: they failed to make up the difference. But they had appeared in a European final in three consecutive seasons – and won twice.

England's three UEFA Cup representatives were Blackburn Rovers and Newcastle United, by virtue of League position, and Coca-Cola Cup winners Aston Villa. Rovers went out to a little-known Swedish side, Trelleborgs, in the first round. Newcastle conceded two goals in their home leg against Athletic Bilbao and the Spaniards took full advantage. Villa triumphed over Inter-Milan before their season took a turn for the worse. They barely preserved their Premier League status.

QUALIFYING COMPETITION

Group 1

	P	W	D	L	F	A	Pts
1 ROMANIA	7	5	2	0	15	6	17
2 France	6	2	4	0	6	0	10
3 Poland	6	3	1	2	12	7	10
4 Israel	7	2	3	2	11	10	9
5 Slovakia	6	1	2	3	8	15	5
6 Azerbaijan	6	0	0	6	2	16	0

Israel	2-1	Poland
Slovakia	0-0	France
Romania	3-0	Azerbaijan
France	0-0	Romania
Israel	2-2	Slovakia
Poland	1-0	Azerbaijan
Romania	3-2	Slovakia
Poland	0-0	France
Azerbaijan	0-2	Israel
Azerbaijan	0-2	France
Israel	1-1	Romania
Romania	2-1	Poland
Israel	0-0	France
Slovakia	4-1	Azerbaijan
Poland	4-3	Israel
France	4-0	Slovakia
Azerbaijan	1-4	Romania
Poland	5-0	Slovakia
Romania	2-1	Israel

16.08.95 France v Poland
16.08.95 Azerbaijan v Slovakia
06.09.95 France v Azerbaijan
06.09.95 Slovakia v Israel
06.09.95 Poland v Romania
11.10.95 Romania v France
11.10.95 Israel v Azerbaijan
11.10.95 Slovakia v Poland
15.11.95 Slovakia v Romania
15.11.95 Azerbaijan v Poland
15.11.95 France v Israel

Group 2

	P	W	D	L	F	A	Pts
1 SPAIN	7	6	1	0	15	3	19
2 Belgium	7	3	2	2	13	9	11
3 Denmark	6	3	2	1	10	6	11
4 FYR Macedonia	7	1	3	3	7	12	6
5 Cyprus	7	1	2	4	4	12	5
6 Armenia	6	0	2	4	2	9	2

Cyprus	1-2	Spain
FYR Macedonia	1-1	Denmark
Belgium	2-0	Armenia
Armenia	0-0	Cyprus
Denmark	3-1	Belgium
FYR Macedonia	0-2	Spain
Belgium	1-1	FYR Macedonia
Spain	3-0	Denmark
Cyprus	2-0	Armenia
Belgium	1-4	Spain
FYR Macedonia	3-0	Cyprus
Spain	1-1	Belgium
Cyprus	1-1	Denmark
Armenia	0-2	Spain
Belgium	2-0	Cyprus
Denmark	1-0	FYR Macedonia
Armenia	2-2	FYR Macedonia
Denmark	4-0	Cyprus
FYR Macedonia	0-5	Belgium
Spain	1-0	Armenia

16.08.95 Armenia v Denmark
06.09.95 Belgium v Denmark
06.09.95 Spain v Cyprus
06.09.95 FYR Macedonia v Armenia
07.10.95 Armenia v Belgium
11.10.95 Denmark v Spain
11.10.95 Cyprus v FYR Macedonia
15.11.95 Spain v FYR Macedonia
15.11.95 Cyprus v Belgium
15.11.95 Denmark v Armenia

Group 3

	P	W	D	L	F	A	Pts
1 TURKEY	5	3	1	1	12	6	10
2 Switzerland	5	3	1	1	10	7	10
3 Sweden	6	2	1	3	7	8	7
4 Hungary	5	1	2	2	6	8	5
5 Iceland	5	1	1	3	3	9	4

Iceland	0-1	Sweden
Hungary	2-2	Turkey
Turkey	5-0	Iceland
Switzerland	4-2	Sweden
Switzerland	1-0	Iceland
Sweden	2-0	Hungary
Turkey	1-2	Switzerland
Turkey	2-1	Sweden
Hungary	2-2	Switzerland
Hungary	1-0	Sweden
Switzerland	1-2	Turkey
Sweden	1-1	Iceland
Iceland	2-1	Hungary

16.08.95 Iceland v Switzerland
06.09.95 Sweden v Switzerland
06.09.95 Turkey v Hungary
11.10.95 Switzerland v Hungary
11.10.95 Iceland v Turkey
11.11.95 Hungary v Iceland
15.11.95 Sweden v Turkey

Group 4

	P	W	D	L	F	A	Pts
1 CROATIA	7	5	1	1	12	2	16
2 Italy	6	4	1	1	11	4	13
3 Lithuania	6	3	1	2	6	5	10
4 Ukraine	7	3	1	3	5	8	10
5 Slovenia	7	2	2	3	9	8	8
6 Estonia	7	0	0	7	2	18	0

Estonia	0–2	Croatia
Slovenia	1–1	Italy
Ukraine	0–2	Lithuania
Croatia	2–0	Lithuania
Estonia	0–2	Italy
Ukraine	0–0	Slovenia
Ukraine	3–0	Estonia
Slovenia	1–2	Lithuania
Italy	1–2	Croatia
Italy	4–1	Estonia
Croatia	4–0	Ukraine
Slovenia	3–0	Estonia
Ukraine	0–2	Italy
Lithuania	0–0	Croatia
Lithuania	0–1	Italy
Croatia	2–0	Slovenia
Estonia	0–1	Ukraine
Lithuania	2–1	Slovenia
Estonia	1–3	Slovenia
Ukraine	1–0	Croatia

16.08.95 Estonia v Lithuania
03.09.95 Croatia v Estonia
06.09.95 Italy v Slovenia
06.09.95 Lithuania v Ukraine
08.10.95 Croatia v Italy
11.10.95 Slovenia v Ukraine
11.10.95 Lithuania v Estonia
11.11.95 Italy v Ukraine
15.11.95 Slovenia v Croatia
15.11.95 Italy v Lithuania

Group 5

	P	W	D	L	F	A	Pts
1 NORWAY	7	6	1	0	16	1	19
2 Netherlands	7	3	2	2	15	5	11
3 Czech Republic	6	3	2	1	13	5	11
4 Belarus	6	2	1	3	6	10	7
5 Luxembourg	7	2	0	5	2	18	6
6 Malta	7	0	2	5	2	15	2

Czech Republic	6–1	Malta
Luxembourg	0–4	Netherlands
Norway	1–0	Belarus
Malta	0–0	Czech Republic
Belarus	2–0	Luxembourg
Norway	1–1	Netherlands
Belarus	0–4	Norway
Netherlands	0–0	Czech Republic
Malta	0–1	Norway
Netherlands	5–0	Luxembourg
Malta	0–1	Luxembourg
Czech Republic	4–2	Belarus
Luxembourg	0–2	Norway
Netherlands	4–0	Malta
Belarus	1–1	Malta
Czech Republic	3–1	Netherlands
Norway	5–0	Luxembourg
Belarus	1–0	Netherlands
Luxembourg	1–0	Czech Republic
Norway	2–0	Malta

16.08.95 Norway v Czech Republic
06.09.95 Czech Republic v Norway
06.09.95 Luxembourg v Malta
06.09.95 Netherlands v Belarus
07.10.95 Belarus v Czech Republic
11.10.95 Malta v Netherlands
11.10.95 Luxembourg v Belarus
12.11.95 Malta v Belarus
15.11.95 Czech Republic v Luxembourg
15.11.95 Netherlands v Norway

Group 6

	P	W	D	L	F	A	Pts
1 PORTUGAL	6	5	0	1	17	5	15
2 Rep. of Ireland	7	4	2	1	14	4	14
3 Austria	6	4	0	2	20	4	12
4 Northern Ireland	7	3	1	3	10	11	10
5 Latvia	7	2	0	5	6	16	6
6 Liechtenstein	7	0	1	6	1	28	1

N. Ireland	4–1	Liechtenstein
Liechtenstein	0–4	Austria
N. Ireland	1–2	Portugal
Latvia	0–3	Rep. of Ireland
Latvia	1–3	Portugal
Austria	1–2	N. Ireland
Rep. of Ireland	4–0	Liechtenstein
Portugal	1–0	Austria
Liechtenstein	0–1	Latvia
N. Ireland	0–4	Rep. of Ireland
Portugal	8–0	Liechtenstein
Rep. of Ireland	1–1	N. Ireland
Austria	5–0	Latvia
Rep. of Ireland	1–0	Portugal
Latvia	0–1	N. Ireland
Austria	7–0	Liechtenstein
Portugal	3–2	Latvia
Liechtenstein	0–0	Rep. of Ireland
N. Ireland	1–2	Latvia
Rep. of Ireland	1–3	Austria

15.08.95 Liechtenstein v Portugal
17.08.95 Latvia v Austria
03.09.95 Portugal v N. Ireland
06.09.95 Austria v Rep. of Ireland
06.09.95 Latvia v Liechtenstein
11.10.95 Rep. of Ireland v Latvia
11.10.95 Austria v Portugal
11.10.95 Liechtenstein v N. Ireland
15.11.95 Portugal v Rep. of Ireland
15.11.95 N. Ireland v Austria

Group 7

	P	W	D	L	F	A	Pts
1 BULGARIA	6	6	0	0	18	4	18
2 Germany	6	4	1	1	12	6	13
3 Georgia	7	4	0	3	9	5	12
4 Albania	7	2	0	5	8	11	6
5 Moldova	7	2	0	5	7	18	6
6 Wales	7	1	1	5	6	16	4

Wales	2−0	Albania
Georgia	0−1	Moldova
Moldova	3−2	Wales
Bulgaria	2−0	Georgia
Albania	1−2	Germany
Georgia	5−0	Wales
Bulgaria	4−1	Moldova
Albania	0−1	Georgia
Wales	0−3	Bulgaria
Moldova	0−3	Germany
Germany	2−1	Albania
Georgia	0−2	Germany
Bulgaria	3−1	Wales
Albania	3−0	Moldova
Germany	1−1	Wales
Moldova	0−3	Bulgaria
Georgia	2−0	Albania
Bulgaria	3−2	Germany
Wales	0−1	Georgia
Moldova	2−3	Albania

06.09.95 Germany v Georgia
06.09.95 Wales v Moldova
06.09.95 Albania v Bulgaria
07.10.95 Bulgaria v Albania
08.10.95 Germany v Moldova
11.10.95 Wales v Germany
11.10.95 Georgia v Bulgaria
15.11.95 Germany v Bulgaria
15.11.95 Albania v Wales
15.11.95 Moldova v Georgia

Group 8

	P	W	D	L	F	A	Pts
1 FINLAND	7	5	0	2	17	8	15
2 Russia	6	4	2	0	18	1	14
3 Scotland	7	4	2	1	12	3	14
4 Greece	6	4	0	2	13	6	12
5 Faroe Islands	7	1	0	6	5	24	3
6 San Marino	7	0	0	7	1	24	0

Finland	0−2	Scotland
Faroe Islands	1−5	Greece
Scotland	5−1	Faroe Islands
Greece	4−0	Finland
Russia	4−0	San Marino
Scotland	1−1	Russia
Greece	2−0	San Marino
Finland	5−0	Faroe Islands
Finland	4−1	San Marino
Greece	1−0	Scotland
Russia	0−0	Scotland
San Marino	0−2	Finland
San Marino	0−2	Scotland
Greece	0−3	Russia
Faroe Islands	0−4	Finland
Russia	3−0	Faroe Islands
Faroe Islands	3−0	San Marino
Faroe Islands	0−2	Scotland
San Marino	0−7	Russia
Finland	2−1	Greece

16.08.95 Scotland v Greece
16.08.95 Finland v Russia
06.09.95 Scotland v Finland
06.09.95 Faroe Islands v Russia
06.09.95 San Marino v Greece
11.10.95 Russia v Greece
11.10.95 San Marino v Faroe Islands
15.11.95 Scotland v San Marino
15.11.95 Russia v Finland
15.11.95 Greece v Faroe Islands

SCHEDULE FOR FINALS

England will host the final stages, from 8 to 30 June 1996. England, as hosts, qualify automatically for the finals, but the holders, Denmark, do not. The eight group winners qualify, as do the six best second-placed teams. The other two second-placed teams will play off at a neutral venue in December. The six best runners-up will be determined by results achieved against the first, third and fourth-placed teams in each group, rather than the lower-placed teams. Three points, for the first time, are awarded for a win in the qualifying groups. The final will be at Wembley on 30 June 1996.

Group A – play at Wembley and Villa Park
Group B – play at Elland Road and St James' Park
Group C – play at Old Trafford and Anfield
Group D – play at Hillsborough and City Ground

1	Saturday 8th June	A1−A2	Wembley
2	Sunday 9th June	B1−B2	Elland Road
3		C1−C2	Old Trafford
4		D1−D2	Hillsborough
5	Monday 10th June	A3−A4	Villa Park
6		B3−B4	St James' Park

7	Tuesday 11th June	C3–C4	Anfield
8		D3–D4	City Ground
9	Thursday 13th June	A2–A3	Villa Park
10		B2–B3	St James' Park
11	Friday 14th June	C2–C3	Anfield
12		D2–D3	City Ground
13	Saturday 15th June	A4–A1	Wembley
14		B4–B1	Elland Road
15	Sunday 16th June	C4–C1	Old Trafford
16		D4–D1	Hillsborough
17	Tuesday 18th June	A4–A2	Villa Park
18		B4–B2	St James' Park
19		A3–A1	Wembley
20		B3–B1	Elland Road
21	Wednesday 19th June	C4–C2	Anfield
22		D4–D2	City Ground
23		C3–C1	Old Trafford
24		D3–D1	Hillsborough
25	Saturday 22nd June	1B–2A	Anfield
26		2B–1A	Wembley
27	Sunday 23rd June	1C–2D	Old Trafford
28		2C–1D	Villa Park
29	Wednesday 26th June	1 v 4	Old Trafford
30		2 v 3	Wembley
31	Sunday 30th June	Final	Wembley

9 ● ENGLAND'S FULL INTERNATIONAL RECORD 1872–1995

(Up to and including 11th June 1995)

	HOME						AWAY					
	P	W	D	L	F	A	P	W	D	L	F	A
Albania	1	1	0	0	5	0	1	1	0	0	2	0
Argentina	5	3	2	0	10	6	5	1	2	2	5	5
Australia	–	–	–	–	–	–	5	3	2	0	5	2
Austria	5	3	1	1	18	9	10	5	2	3	36	16
Belgium	4	3	1	0	17	3	14	10	3	1	50	21
Bohemia	–	–	–	–	–	–	1	1	0	0	4	0
Brazil	8	2	4	2	10	10	10	1	3	6	6	15
Bulgaria	2	1	1	0	3	1	3	2	1	0	4	0
Cameroon	1	1	0	0	2	0	1	1	0	0	3	2
Canada	–	–	–	–	–	–	1	1	0	0	1	0
Chile	1	0	1	0	0	0	3	2	1	0	4	1
Colombia	1	0	1	0	1	1	1	1	0	0	4	0
Cyprus	1	1	0	0	5	0	1	1	0	0	1	0
Czechoslovakia	5	4	1	0	13	6	7	3	2	2	12	9
Denmark	6	5	0	1	9	3	8	4	4	0	18	8
Ecuador	–	–	–	–	–	–	1	1	0	0	2	0
Egypt	–	–	–	–	–	–	2	2	0	0	5	0
FIFA	1	0	1	0	4	4	–	–	–	–	–	–
Finland	2	2	0	0	7	1	7	6	1	0	27	5
France	8	6	2	0	23	4	14	9	1	4	39	23
Germany, East	2	2	0	0	4	1	2	1	1	0	3	2
Germany (and West)	8	5	0	3	15	9	13	4	4	5	22	19
Greece	3	2	1	0	8	0	3	3	0	0	7	1
Holland	6	2	3	1	14	8	6	2	2	2	4	6
Hungary	7	6	0	1	18	9	11	6	1	4	29	18
Iceland	–	–	–	–	–	–	1	0	1	0	1	1
Ireland, Northern	49	40	6	3	169	36	47	34	10	3	150	44
Ireland, Republic of	6	3	2	1	11	6	7	2	4	1	8	6
Israel	–	–	–	–	–	–	2	1	1	0	2	1
Italy	6	3	2	1	9	5	11	3	3	5	16	17
Japan	1	1	0	0	2	1	–	–	–	–	–	–
Kuwait	–	–	–	–	–	–	1	1	0	0	1	0
Luxembourg	3	3	0	0	18	1	4	4	0	0	20	2
Malaysia	–	–	–	–	–	–	1	1	0	0	4	2
Malta	1	1	0	0	5	0	1	1	0	0	1	0
Mexico	2	2	0	0	10	0	4	1	1	2	4	3
Morocco	–	–	–	–	–	–	1	0	1	0	0	0
New Zealand	–	–	–	–	–	–	2	2	0	0	3	0
Nigeria	1	1	0	0	1	0	–	–	–	–	–	–
Norway	4	2	2	0	9	1	5	3	0	2	17	6
Paraguay	–	–	–	–	–	–	1	1	0	0	3	0
Peru	–	–	–	–	–	–	2	1	0	1	5	4
Poland	5	3	2	0	10	2	6	2	3	1	6	4
Portugal	6	5	1	0	12	4	9	3	4	2	23	13
Rest of Europe	1	1	0	0	3	0	–	–	–	–	–	–
Rest of the World	1	1	0	0	2	1	–	–	–	–	–	–

	HOME						AWAY					
	P	W	D	L	F	A	P	W	D	L	F	A
Romania	4	0	4	0	3	3	5	2	2	1	4	2
San Marino	1	1	0	0	6	0	1	1	0	0	7	1
Saudi Arabia	–	–	–	–	–	–	1	0	1	0	1	1
Scotland	53	25	11	17	115	87	54	18	13	23	73	81
Spain	6	5	0	1	19	6	11	5	2	4	16	14
Sweden	5	2	2	1	12	9	10	4	3	3	15	10
Switzerland	5	3	2	0	12	3	10	7	0	3	25	9
Tunisia	–	–	–	–	–	–	1	0	1	0	1	1
Turkey	2	2	0	0	13	0	3	2	1	0	9	0
USA	1	1	0	0	2	0	6	4	0	2	29	7
USSR (and CIS)	4	2	1	1	10	5	8	3	3	2	11	10
Uruguay	4	1	2	1	3	3	5	1	1	3	5	9
Wales	49	32	9	8	126	46	48	30	12	6	113	44
Yugoslavia	7	4	3	0	15	7	7	1	2	4	8	13
TOTAL	306	195	68	43	788	301	406	210	99	97	876	458

GRAND TOTAL

Played	Won	Drawn	Lost	Goals For	Against
712	405	167	140	1664	759

The England squad for the match against Uruguay.

10 ● ENGLAND'S GOALSCORERS 1946–1995

(Up to and including 11th June 1995)

49	Charlton, R	5	Baily	2	Froggatt, J
48	Lineker	5	Brooking	2	Froggatt, R
44	Greaves	5	Carter	2	Haines
30	Finney	5	Edwards	2	Hancocks
30	Lofthouse	5	Hitchens	2	Hunter
26	Platt	5	Latchford	2	Ince
26	Robson, B	5	Neal	2	Lee, S
24	Hurst	5	Pearson, S C (Stan)	2	Moore
23	Mortensen	5	Pearson, J S (Stuart)	2	Perry
21	Channon	5	Pickering, F	2	Pointer
21	Keegan	5	Shearer	2	Royle
20	Peters	5	Wright, I	2	Smith, A
18	Haynes	4	Adams	2	Taylor, P
18	Hunt, R	4	Barnes, P	2	Tueart
16	Lawton	4	Bull	2	Wignall
16	Taylor, T	4	Dixon, K	2	Worthington
16	Woodcock	4	Hassall	1	A'Court
13	Chivers	4	Pearce	1	Astall
13	Mariner	4	Revie	1	Beattie
13	Smith, R	4	Robson, R	1	Bowles
12	Francis, T	4	Steven	1	Bradford
11	Douglas	4	Watson, D	1	Bridges
11	Mannion	4	Webb	1	Chamberlain
11	Barnes, J	3	Anderton	1	Crawford
10	Clarke, A	3	Baker	1	Dixon, L
10	Flowers, R	3	Blissett	1	Goddard
10	Lee, F	3	Butcher	1	Hirst
10	Milburn	3	Currie	1	Hughes, E
10	Wilshaw	3	Elliott	1	Kay
9	Beardsley	3	Ferdinand	1	Keown
9	Bell	3	Francis, G	1	Kidd
9	Bentley	3	Grainger	1	Langton
9	Hateley	3	Kennedy, R	1	Lawler
8	Ball	3	McDermott	1	Lee, J
8	Broadis	3	Matthews, S	1	Lee, R
8	Byrne, J	3	Morris	1	Le Saux
8	Hoddle	3	O'Grady	1	Mabbutt
8	Kevan	3	Peacock	1	Marsh
7	Connelly	3	Ramsey	1	Medley
7	Coppell	3	Sewell	1	Melia
7	Paine	3	Wilkins	1	Merson
6	Charlton, J	3	Wright, W	1	Mullery
6	Gascoigne	2	Allen, R	1	Nicholls
6	Johnson	2	Anderson	1	Nicholson
6	Macdonald	2	Bradley	1	Palmer
6	Mullen	2	Broadbent	1	Parry
6	Rowley	2	Brooks	1	Sansom
6	Waddle	2	Cowans	1	Shackleton
5	Atyeo	2	Eastham	1	Sheringham

● **15**

1 Stiles
1 Summerbee
1 Tambling
1 Thompson, P B (Phil)

1 Viollet
1 Wallace
1 Walsh
1 Weller

1 Wise
1 Withe
1 Wright, M

11 ● ENGLAND CAPS 1872–1995

(Up to and including 11th June 1995)

1	Abbott W (Everton)		1	Ball J (Bury)
5	A'Court A (Liverpool)		1	Balmer W (Everton)
35	Adams T (Arsenal)		1	Bamber J (Liverpool)
5	Adcock H (Leicester City)		3	Bambridge A (Swifts)
1	Alcock C (Wanderers)		18	Bambridge E C (Swifts)
1	Alderson J (C Palace)		1	Bambridge E H (Swifts)
2	Aldridge A (WBA, Walsall Town Swifts)		73	Banks G (Leicester, Stoke)
3	Allen A (Stoke)		1	Banks H (Millwall)
1	Allen A (Aston Villa)		6	Banks T (Bolton)
5	Allen C (QPR, Spurs)		2	Bannister W (Burnley, Bolton)
5	Allen H (Wolves)		3	Barclay R (Sheff Wed)
2	Allen J (Portsmouth)		2	Bardsley D (QPR)
5	Allen R (WBA)		2	Barham M (Norwich City)
1	Alsford W (Spurs)		5	Barkas S (Man City)
2	Amos A (Old Carthusians)		11	Barker J (Derby County)
1	Anderson R (Old Etonians)		1	Barker R (Herts Rangers)
2	Anderson S (Sunderland)		1	Barker R R (Casuals)
30	Anderson V (Nottm Forest, Arsenal,		1	Barlow R (WBA)
	Man Utd)		2	Barmby N (Spurs)
9	Anderton D (Spurs)		78	Barnes J (Watford, Liverpool)
1	Angus J (Burnley)		22	Barnes P (Man City, WBA, Leeds Utd)
43	Armfield J (Blackpool)		1	Barnet H (Royal Engineers)
1	Armitage G (Charlton)		3	Barrass M (Bolton)
3	Armstrong D (Middlesbrough, Southampton)		1	Barrett A (Fulham)
1	Armstrong K (Chelsea)		3	Barrett E (Oldham, Aston Villa)
1	Arnold J (Fulham)		1	Barrett J (West Ham Utd)
7	Arthur J (Blackburn)		5	Barry L (Leicester City)
3	Ashcroft J (Woolwich Arsenal)		1	Barson F (Aston Villa)
1	Ashmore G (WBA)		1	Barton J (Blackburn)
1	Ashton C (Corinthians)		7	Barton P (Birmingham)
5	Ashurst W (Notts County)		3	Barton W (Wimbledon, Newcastle)
2	Astall G (Birmingham)		16	Bassett W (WBA)
5	Astle J (WBA)		1	Bastard S (Upton Park)
17	Aston J (Man Utd)		21	Bastin C (Arsenal)
12	Athersmith W (Aston Villa)		17	Batty D (Leeds Utd, Blackburn)
6	Atyeo J (Bristol City)		2	Baugh R (Stafford Road, Wolves)
1	Austin S (Man City)		1	Bayliss A (WBA)
			3	Baynham R (Luton)
1	Bach P (Sunderland)		57	Beardsley P (Newcastle, Liverpool)
7	Bache J (Aston Villa)		2	Beasant D (Chelsea)
5	Baddeley T (Wolves)		1	Beasley A (Huddersfield)
1	Bagshaw J (Derby County)		2	Beats W (Wolves)
2	Bailey G (Man Utd)		9	Beattie K (Ipswich)
5	Bailey H (Leicester Fosse)		2	Becton F (Preston, Liverpool)
2	Bailey M (Charlton)		2	Bedford H (Blackpool)
19	Bailey N (Clapham Rovers)		48	Bell C (Man City)
9	Baily E (Spurs)		2	Bennett W (Sheff Utd)
1	Bain J (Oxford Univ)		1	Benson R (Sheff Utd)
1	Baker A (Arsenal)		12	Bentley R (Chelsea)
2	Baker B (Everton, Chelsea)		1	Beresford J (Aston Villa)
8	Baker J (Hibernian, Arsenal)		1	Berry A (Oxford Univ)
72	Ball A (Blackpool, Everton, Arsenal)		4	Berry J (Man Utd)

● 17

1	Bestall J (Grimsby)	2	Brown A S (Sheff Utd)
1	Betmead H (Grimsby)	9	Brown G (Huddersfield, Aston Villa)
1	Betts M (Old Harrovians)	5	Brown J (Blackburn)
1	Betts W (Sheff Wed)	6	Brown J H (Sheff Wed)
3	Beverley J (Blackburn)	1	Brown K (West Ham)
1	Birkett R H (Clapham Rovers)	1	Brown T (WBA)
1	Birkett R (Middlesbrough)	1	Brown W (West Ham)
2	Birley F (Oxford Univ, Wanderers)	3	Bruton J (Burnley)
3	Birtles G (Nottm Forest)	1	Bryant W (Clapton)
4	Bishop S (Leicester City)	6	Buchan C (Sunderland)
3	Blackburn F (Blackburn)	1	Buchanan W (Clapham Rovers)
1	Blackburn G (Aston Villa)	1	Buckley F C (Derby County)
26	Blenkinsop E (Sheff Wed)	13	Bull S (Wolves)
1	Bliss H (Spurs)	1	Bullock F E (Huddersfield)
14	Blissett L (Watford)	3	Bullock N (Bury)
1	Blockley J (Arsenal)	4	Burgess H (Man City)
23	Bloomer S (Derby County, Middlesbrough)	4	Burgess H (Sheff Wed)
5	Blunstone F (Chelsea)	1	Burnup C (Cambridge Univ)
8	Bond R (Preston, Bradford City)	3	Burrows H (Sheff Wed)
7	Bonetti P (Chelsea)	1	Burton F E (Nottm Forest)
2	Bonsor A (Wanderers)	2	Bury L (Cambridge Univ, Old Etonians)
1	Booth F (Man City)	77	Butcher T (Ipswich, Rangers)
2	Booth T (Blackburn, Everton)	1	Butler J (Arsenal)
2	Bould S (Arsenal)	1	Butler W (Bolton)
6	Bowden E (Arsenal)	2	Byrne G (Liverpool)
5	Bower A (Corinthians)	11	Byrne J J (C Palace, West Ham)
3	Bowers J (Derby County)	33	Byrne R (Man Utd)
5	Bowles S (QPR)		
1	Bowser S (WBA)	4	Callaghan I (Liverpool)
1	Boyer P (Norwich)	1	Calvey J (Nottm Forest)
3	Boyes W (WBA, Everton)	8	Campbell A (Blackburn, Huddersfield)
1	Boyle T (Burnley)	9	Camsell, G (Middlesbrough)
3	Brabrook P (Chelsea)	1	Capes A (Stoke)
3	Bracewell P (Everton)	2	Carr J (Middlesbrough)
1	Bradford G (Bristol Rovers)	2	Carr J (Newcastle)
12	Bradford J (Birmingham)	1	Carr W H (Owlerton)
3	Bradley W (Man Utd)	13	Carter H S (Sunderland, Derby County)
1	Bradshaw F (Sheff Wed)	3	Carter J H (WBA)
1	Bradshaw T (Liverpool)	5	Catlin A E (Sheff Wed)
4	Bradshaw W (Blackburn)	2	Chadwick A (Southampton)
3	Brann G (Swifts)	7	Chadwick E (Everton)
2	Brawn W (Aston Villa)	8	Chamberlain M (Stoke)
6	Bray J (Man City)	8	Chambers H (Liverpool)
1	Brayshaw E (Sheff Wed)	46	Channon M (Southampton, Man City)
4	Bridges B (Chelsea)	2	Charles G (Nottm Forest)
11	Bridgett A (Sunderland)	35	Charlton J (Leeds Utd)
2	Brindle T (Darwen)	106	Charlton R (Man Utd)
5	Brittleton J (Sheff Wed)	1	Charnley R (Blackpool)
9	Britton C (Everton)	1	Charnsley C (Small Heath)
7	Broadbent P (Wolves)	8	Chedgzoy S (Everton)
14	Broadis I (Man City, Newcastle)	3	Chenery C (C Palace)
1	Brockbank J (Cambridge Univ)	27	Cherry T (Leeds Utd)
3	Brodie J B (Wolves)	2	Chilton A (Man Utd)
5	Bromilow T G (Liverpool)	1	Chippendale H (Blackburn)
2	Bromley-Davenport W E (Oxford Univ)	24	Chivers M (Spurs)
18	Brook E (Man City)	1	Christian E (Old Etonians)
47	Brooking T (West Ham)	4	Clamp E (Wolves)
3	Brooks J (Spurs)	1	Clapton D (Arsenal)
7	Broome F H (Aston Villa)	4	Clare T (Stoke)
3	Brown A (Aston Villa)	19	Clarke A (Leeds Utd)

1	Clarke H (Spurs)
4	Clay T (Spurs)
35	Clayton R (Blackburn)
1	Clegg J (Sheff Wed)
2	Clegg W (Sheff Wed, Sheff Albion)
61	Clemence R (Liverpool, Spurs)
5	Clement D (QPR)
2	Clough B (Middlesbrough)
14	Clough N (Nottm Forest)
4	Coates R (Burnley, Spurs)
9	Cobbold W (Cambridge Univ, Old Carthusians)
2	Cock J (Huddersfield, Chelsea)
13	Cockburn H (Man Utd)
37	Cohen G (Fulham)
1	Colclough H (C Palace)
1	Cole A (Man Utd)
1	Coleman E (Dulwich Hamlet)
1	Coleman J (Woolwich Arsenal)
2	Collymore S (Nottm Forest)
3	Common A (Sheff Utd, Middlesbrough)
2	Compton L H (Arsenal)
1	Conlin J (Bradford City)
20	Connelly J (Burnley, Man Utd)
1	Cook T E (Brighton)
2	Cooper C (Nottm Forest)
1	Cooper N C (Cambridge Univ)
15	Cooper T (Derby County)
20	Cooper T (Leeds Utd)
42	Coppell S (Man Utd)
20	Copping W (Leeds Utd, Arsenal)
1	Corbett B (Corinthians)
1	Corbett R (Old Malvernians)
3	Corbett W (Birmingham)
9	Corrigan J (Manchester C.)
7	Cottee A (West Ham, Everton)
4	Cotterill G (Cambridge Univ, Old Brightonians)
1	Cottle J (Bristol City)
3	Cowan S (Man City)
10	Cowans G (Aston Villa, Bari)
1	Cowell A (Blackburn)
3	Cox J (Liverpool)
1	Cox J D (Derby County)
14	Crabtree J (Burnley, Aston Villa)
1	Crawford J F (Chelsea)
2	Crawford R (Ipswich)
10	Crawshaw T (Sheff Wed)
8	Crayston W (Arsenal)
1	Creek N (Corinthians)
7	Cresswell W (South Shields, Sunderland, Everton)
41	Crompton R (Blackburn)
26	Crooks S (Derby County)
1	Crowe C (Wolves)
2	Cuggy F (Sunderland)
12	Cullis S (Wolves)
2	Cunliffe A (Blackburn)
1	Cunliffe D (Portsmouth)
1	Cunliffe J (Everton)

6	Cunningham L (WBA, Real Madrid)
3	Curle K (Man City)
2	Currey E (Oxford Univ)
17	Currie A (Sheff Utd, Leeds Utd)
6	Cursham A (Notts County)
8	Cursham H (Notts County)
5	Daft H (Notts County)
7	Daley A (Aston Villa)
1	Danks T (Nottm Forest)
2	Davenport J (Bolton)
1	Davenport P (Nottm Forest)
2	Davis G (Derby County)
3	Davis H (Sheff Wed)
1	Davison J (Sheff Wed)
2	Dawson J (Burnley)
3	Day S (Old Malvernians)
16	Dean W (Everton)
3	Deane B (Sheffield Utd)
2	Deeley N (Wolves)
2	Devey J (Aston Villa)
8	Devonshire A (West Ham)
9	Dewhurst F (Preston)
1	Dewhurst G (Liverpool Ramblers)
48	Dickinson J (Portsmouth)
3	Dimmock J (Spurs)
6	Ditchburn E (Spurs)
1	Dix R (Derby County)
1	Dixon J (Notts County)
8	Dixon K (Chelsea)
21	Dixon L (Arsenal)
4	Dobson A (Notts County)
1	Dobson C (Notts County)
5	Dobson M (Burnley, Everton)
1	Doggart A (Corinthians)
15	Dorigo T (Chelsea, Leeds Utd)
4	Dorrell A (Aston Villa)
36	Douglas B (Blackburn)
1	Downs R (Everton)
5	Doyle M (Manchester C.)
5	Drake E (Arsenal)
6	Ducat A (Woolwich Arsenal, Aston Villa)
4	Dunn A T (Cambridge Univ, Old Etonians)
1	Duxbury M (Man Utd)
2	Earle S (Clapton, West Ham)
19	Eastham G (Arsenal)
1	Eastham G R (Bolton)
17	Eckersley W (Blackburn)
18	Edwards D (Man Utd)
1	Edwards J (Shropshire Wanderers)
16	Edwards W (Leeds Utd)
2	Ellerington W (Southampton)
3	Elliott G (Middlesbrough)
5	Elliott W (Burnley)
4	Evans R (Sheff Utd)
2	Ewer F (Casuals)
1	Fairclough P (Old Foresters)
1	Fairhurst D (Newcastle)
1	Fantham J (Sheff Wed)

2 Fashanu J (Wimbledon)
1 Felton W (Sheff Wed)
1 Fenton M (Middlesbrough)
20 Fenwick T (QPR, Spurs)
7 Ferdinand L (QPR)
2 Field E (Clapham Rovers)
76 Finney T (Preston)
11 Fleming H (Swindon)
2 Fletcher A (Wolves)
49 Flowers R (Wolves)
7 Flowers T (Southampton, Blackburn)
9 Forman F (Nottm Forest)
3 Forman F R (Nottm Forest)
11 Forrest J (Blackburn)
1 Fort J (Millwall)
5 Foster R (Oxford Univ, Corinthians)
3 Foster S (Brighton & Hove Albion)
1 Foulke W (Sheff Utd)
1 Foulkes W (Man Utd)
1 Fox F (Gillingham)
12 Francis G (QPR)
52 Francis T (Birmingham, Nottm Forest,
   Man City, Sampdoria)
27 Franklin C (Stoke)
5 Freeman B (Everton, Burnley)
13 Froggatt J (Portsmouth)
4 Froggatt R (Sheff Wed)
1 Fry C (Corinthians)
1 Furness W (Leeds Utd)

2 Galley T (Wolves)
2 Gardner T (Aston Villa)
1 Garfield B (WBA)
1 Garratty W (Aston Villa)
3 Garrett T (Blackpool)
32 Gascoigne P (Spurs, Lazio)
2 Gates E (Ipswich)
3 Gay L (Cambridge Univ, Old Brightonians)
2 Geary F (Everton)
1 Geaves R (Clapham Rovers)
3 Gee C (Everton)
4 Geldard A (Everton)
1 George C (Derby County)
3 George W (Aston Villa)
2 Gibbins W (Clapton)
1 Gidman J (Aston Villa)
3 Gillard I (QPR)
1 Gilliat W (Old Carthusians)
1 Goddard P (West Ham)
25 Goodall F (Huddersfield)
14 Goodall J (Preston, Derby County)
3 Goodhart H (Old Etonians)
1 Goodwyn A (Royal Engineers)
1 Goodyer A (Nottm Forest)
5 Gosling R (Old Etonians)
1 Gosnell A (Newcastle)
1 Gough H (Sheff Utd)
14 Goulden L (West Ham)
2 Graham L (Millwall)
2 Graham T (Nottm Forest)

7 Grainger C (Sheff Utd, Sunderland)
1 Gray A (Crystal Palace)
57 Greaves J (Chelsea, Spurs)
8 Green G (Sheff Utd)
1 Green T (Wanderers)
2 Greenhalgh E (Notts County)
18 Greenhoff B (Man Utd, Leeds Utd)
2 Greenwood D (Blackburn)
6 Gregory J (QPR)
6 Grimsdell A (Spurs)
3 Grosvenor A (Birmingham)
2 Gunn W (Notts County)
1 Gurney R (Sunderland)

3 Hacking J (Oldham)
1 Hadley N (WBA)
1 Hagan J (Sheffield U.)
1 Haines J (WBA)
1 Hall A (Aston Villa)
10 Hall G (Spurs)
17 Hall J (Birmingham)
1 Halse H (Man Utd)
1 Hammond H (Oxford Univ)
3 Hampson J (Blackpool)
4 Hampton H (Aston Villa)
3 Hancocks J (Wolves)
30 Hapgood E (Arsenal)
1 Hardinge H (Sheff Utd)
4 Hardman H (Everton)
13 Hardwick G (Middlesbrough)
1 Hardy H (Stockport County)
21 Hardy S (Liverpool, Aston Villa)
2 Harford M (Luton Town)
3 Hargreaves F (Blackburn)
2 Hargreaves J (Blackburn)
1 Harper E (Blackburn)
1 Harris G (Burnley)
2 Harris P (Portsmouth)
6 Harris S (Cambridge Univ,
   Old Westminsters)
2 Harrison A (Old Westminsters)
2 Harrison G (Everton)
2 Harrow J (Chelsea)
8 Hart E (Leeds Utd)
1 Hartley F (Oxford City)
1 Harvey A (Wednesbury Strollers)
1 Harvey C (Everton)
5 Hassall H (Huddersfield, Bolton)
32 Hateley M (Portsmouth, AC Milan,
   Monaco, Rangers)
5 Hawkes R (Luton)
5 Haworth G (Accrington)
2 Hawtrey J (Old Etonians)
1 Haygarth E (Swifts)
56 Haynes J (Fulham)
2 Healless H (Blackburn)
2 Hector K (Derby County)
1 Hedley G (Sheff Utd)
4 Hegan K (Corinthians)
2 Hellawell M (Birmingham)

5 Henfrey A (Cambridge Univ, Corinthians)	28 Hunter N (Leeds Utd)
1 Henry R (Spurs)	49 Hurst G (West Ham)
1 Heron F (Wanderers)	
5 Heron G (Uxbridge, Wanderers)	16 Ince P (Man Utd)
1 Hibbert W (Bury)	2 Iremonger J (Nottm Forest)
25 Hibbs H (Birmingham)	
2 Hill F (Bolton)	9 Jack D (Bolton, Arsenal)
6 Hill G (Man Utd)	1 Jackson E (Oxford Univ)
11 Hill J (Burnley)	3 Jarrett B (Cambridge Univ)
3 Hill R (Luton)	2 Jefferis F (Everton)
1 Hill R H (Millwall)	2 Jezzard B (Fulham)
1 Hillman J (Burnley)	8 Johnson D (Ipswich, Liverpool)
1 Hills A (Old Harrovians)	2 Johnson E (Saltley Coll, Stoke)
8 Hilsdon G (Chelsea)	5 Johnson J (Stoke)
6 Hine E (Leicester City)	5 Johnson T (Man City, Everton)
3 Hinton A (Wolves, Nottm Forest)	6 Johnson W (Sheff Utd)
3 Hirst D (Sheff Wed)	10 Johnston H (Blackpool)
7 Hitchens G (Aston Villa, Inter-Milan)	3 Jones A (Walsall Swifts, Great Lever)
2 Hobbis H (Charlton)	6 Jones H (Blackburn)
53 Hoddle G (Spurs, Monaco)	1 Jones H (Nottm Forrest)
24 Hodge S (Aston Villa, Spurs, Nottm Forest)	3 Jones M (Sheffield U, Leeds Utd)
6 Hodgetts D (Aston Villa)	8 Jones R (Liverpool)
5 Hodgkinson A (Sheffield U)	1 Jones W (Bristol City)
3 Hodgson G (Liverpool)	2 Jones W (Liverpool)
3 Hodkinson J (Blackburn)	1 Joy B (Casuals)
3 Hogg W (Sunderland)	
2 Holdcroft G (Preston)	3 Kail E (Dulwich Hamlet)
5 Holden A (Bolton)	1 Kay T (Everton)
4 Holden G (Wednesbury OA)	9 Kean F (Sheff Wed, Bolton)
2 Holden-White C (Corinthians)	63 Keegan K (Liverpool, SV Hamburg,
1 Holford T (Stoke)	Southampton)
10 Holley G (Sunderland)	4 Keen E (Derby County)
3 Holliday E (Middlesbrough)	14 Kelly R (Burnley, Sunderland, Huddersfield)
1 Hollins J (Chelsea)	2 Kennedy Λ (Liverpool)
7 Holmes R (Preston)	17 Kennedy R (Liverpool)
10 Holt J (Everton, Reading)	1 Kenyon-Slaney W (Wanderers)
14 Hopkinson E (Bolton)	11 Keown M (Everton, Arsenal)
2 Hossack A (Corinthians)	14 Kevan D (WBA)
7 Houghton W (Aston Villa)	2 Kidd B (Man Utd)
5 Houlker A (Blackburn, Portsmouth,	1 King R (Oxford Univ)
Southampton)	1 Kingsford R (Wanderers)
5 Howarth R (Preston, Everton)	1 Kingsley M (Newcastle)
23 Howe D (WBA)	4 Kinsey G (Wolves, Derby County)
3 Howe J (Derby)	3 Kirchen A (Arsenal)
1 Howell L (Wanderers)	1 Kirton W (Aston Villa)
2 Howell R (Sheff Utd, Liverpool)	1 Knight A (Portsmouth)
1 Howey S (Newcastle)	4 Knowles C (Spurs)
2 Hudson A (Stoke)	
1 Hudson J (Sheffield)	26 Labone B (Everton)
1 Hudspeth F (Newcastle)	2 Lampard F (West Ham)
6 Hufton A (West Ham)	3 Langley J (Fulham)
62 Hughes E (Liverpool, Wolves)	11 Langton R (Blackburn, Preston, Bolton)
3 Hughes L (Liverpool)	12 Latchford R (Everton)
9 Hulme J (Arsenal)	2 Latheron E (Blackburn)
1 Humphreys P (Notts County)	4 Lawler C (Liverpool)
3 Hunt G (Spurs)	23 Lawton T (Everton, Chelsea, Notts County)
2 Hunt Rev. K (Leyton)	2 Leach T (Sheff Wed)
34 Hunt R (Liverpool)	5 Leake A (Aston Villa)
2 Hunt S (WBA)	1 Lee E (Southampton)
7 Hunter J (Sheff Heeley)	27 Lee F (Manchester C.)

1 Lee J (Derby)	1 Maskrey H (Derby County)
2 Lee R (Newcastle)	3 Mason C (Wolves)
14 Lee S (Liverpool)	5 Matthews R (Coventry)
1 Leighton J (Nottm Forest)	54 Matthews S (Stoke, Blackpool)
10 Le Saux G (Blackburn)	2 Matthews V (Sheff Utd)
6 Le Tissier M (Southampton)	2 Maynard W (1st Surrey Rifles)
1 Lilley H (Sheff Utd)	1 Meadows J (Man City)
2 Linacre H (Nottm Forest)	6 Medley L (Spurs)
13 Lindley T (Cambridge Univ, Nottm Forest)	1 Meehan T (Chelsea)
4 Lindsay A (Liverpool)	2 Melia J (Liverpool)
1 Lindsay W (Wanderers)	2 Mercer D (Sheff Utd)
80 Lineker G (Leicester, Everton,	5 Mercer J (Everton)
Barcelona, Spurs)	23 Merrick G (Birmingham)
7 Lintott E (QPR, Bradford City)	14 Merson P (Arsenal)
1 Lipsham H (Sheff Utd)	2 Metcalfe V (Huddersfield)
1 Little B (Aston Villa)	1 Mew J (Man Utd)
4 Lloyd L (Liverpool, Nottm Forest)	1 Middleditch B (Corinthians)
1 Lockett A (Stoke)	13 Milburn J (Newcastle)
5 Lodge L (Cambridge Univ, Corinthians)	1 Miller B (Burnley)
7 Lofthouse J (Blackburn, Accrington)	1 Miller H (Charlton)
33 Lofthouse N (Bolton)	3 Mills G (Chelsea)
5 Longworth E (Liverpool)	42 Mills M (Ipswich)
1 Lowder A (Wolves)	14 Milne G (Liverpool)
3 Lowe E (Aston Villa)	1 Milton A (Arsenal)
3 Lucas T (Liverpool)	4 Milward A (Everton)
2 Luntley E (Nottm Forest)	5 Mitchell C (Upton Park)
1 Lyttelton Hon A (Cambridge Univ)	1 Mitchell J (Man City)
1 Lyttelton Hon E (Cambridge Univ)	1 Moffat H (Oldham)
	4 Molyneux G (Southampton)
16 Mabbutt G (Spurs)	7 Moon W (Old Westminsters)
1 Macauley R (Cambridge Univ)	2 Moore H (Notts County)
14 Macdonald M (Newcastle)	1 Moore J (Derby County)
6 Macrae S (Notts County)	108 Moore R (West Ham)
5 McCall J (Preston)	1 Moore W (West Ham)
25 McDermott T (Liverpool)	2 Mordue J (Sunderland)
8 McDonald C (Burnley)	1 Morice C (Barnes)
28 McFarland R (Derby County)	6 Morley A (Aston Villa)
4 McGarry W (Huddersfield)	1 Morley H (Notts County)
2 McGuinness W (Man Utd)	1 Morren T (Sheff Utd)
1 McInroy A (Sunderland)	2 Morris F (WBA)
17 McMahon S (Liverpool)	3 Morris J (Derby)
3 McManaman S (Liverpool)	3 Morris W (Wolves)
4 McNab R (Arsenal)	1 Morse H (Notts County)
2 McNeal R (WBA)	3 Mort T (Aston Villa)
9 McNeil M (Middlesbrough)	1 Morten A (C Palace)
1 Maddison F (Oxford Univ)	25 Mortensen S (Blackpool)
24 Madeley P (Leeds Utd)	1 Morton J (West Ham)
5 Magee T (WBA)	9 Mosforth W (Sheff Wed, Sheff Albion)
4 Makepeace H (Everton)	4 Moss F (Arsenal)
19 Male G (Arsenal)	5 Moss F (Aston Villa)
26 Mannion W (Middlesbrough)	2 Mosscrop E (Burnley)
35 Mariner P (Ipswich, Arsenal)	3 Mozley B (Derby)
1 Marsden J (Darwen)	12 Mullen J (Wolves)
3 Marsden W (Sheff Wed)	35 Mullery A (Spurs)
9 Marsh R (QPR, Manchester C)	
2 Marshall T (Darwen)	50 Neal P (Liverpool)
17 Martin A (West Ham)	16 Needham E (Sheff Utd)
1 Martin H (Sunderland)	2 Neville G (Man Utd)
3 Martyn N (Crystal Palace)	27 Newton K (Blackburn, Everton)
1 Marwood B (Arsenal)	2 Nicholls J (WBA)

1 Nicholson W (Spurs)
5 Nish D (Derby)
23 Norman M (Spurs)
3 Nuttall H (Bolton)

16 Oakley W (Oxford Univ, Corinthians)
3 O'Dowd J (Chelsea)
2 O'Grady M (Huddersfield, Leeds Utd)
1 Ogilvie R (Clapham Rovers)
1 Oliver L (Fulham)
2 Olney B (Aston Villa)
4 Osborne F (Fulham, Spurs)
1 Osborne R (Leicester City)
4 Osgood P (Chelsea)
11 Osman R (Ipswich)
2 Ottaway C (Oxford Univ)
1 Owen J (Sheffield)
3 Owen S (Luton)

7 Page L (Burnley)
19 Paine T (Southampton)
18 Pallister G (Middlesbrough, Man Utd)
18 Palmer C (Sheff Wed)
1 Pantling H (Sheff Utd)
3 Paravacini P J de (Cambridge Univ)
19 Parker P (QPR, Man Utd)
1 Parker T (Southampton)
1 Parkes P (QPR)
2 Parkinson J (Liverpool)
1 Parr P (Oxford Univ)
3 Parry E (Old Carthusians)
2 Parry R (Bolton)
2 Patchitt B (Corinthians)
2 Pawson F (Cambridge Univ, Swifts)
1 Payne J (Luton)
6 Peacock A (Middlesbrough, Leeds Utd)
3 Peacock J (Middlesbrough)
59 Pearce S (Nottm Forest)
1 Pearson H (WBA)
1 Pearson J H (Crewe)
15 Pearson J S (Stuart) (Man Utd)
8 Pearson S C (Stan) (Man Utd)
1 Pease W (Middlesbrough)
1 Pegg D (Man Utd)
4 Pejic M (Stoke)
3 Pelly F (Old Foresters)
25 Pennington J (WBA)
5 Pentland F (Middlesbrough)
3 Perry C (WBA)
1 Perry T (WBA)
3 Perry W (Blackpool)
1 Perryman S (Spurs)
67 Peters M (West Ham, Spurs)
1 Phelan M (Man Utd)
3 Phillips L (Portsmouth)
3 Pickering F (Everton)
1 Pickering J (Sheff Utd)
1 Pickering N (Sunderland)
1 Pike T (Cambridge Univ)
1 Pilkington B (Burnley)

1 Plant J (Bury)
55 Platt D (Aston Villa, Bari, Juventus, Sampdoria)
1 Plum S (Charlton)
3 Pointer R (Burnley)
1 Porteous T (Sunderland)
1 Priest A (Sheff Utd)
1 Prinsep J (Clapham Rovers)
2 Puddefoot S (Blackburn)
1 Pye J (Wolves)
3 Pym R (Bolton)

4 Quantrill A (Derby County)
5 Quixall A (Sheffield W.)

2 Radford J (Arsenal)
4 Raikes G (Oxford Univ)
32 Ramsey A (Southampton, Spurs)
1 Rawlings A (Preston)
2 Rawlings W (Southampton)
1 Rawlinson J (Cambridge Univ)
1 Rawson H (Royal Engineers)
2 Rawson W (Oxford Univ)
1 Read A (Tufnell Park)
1 Reader J (WBA)
3 Reaney P (Leeds Utd)
2 Reeves K (Norwich, Man City)
5 Regis C (WBA, Coventry)
13 Reid P (Everton)
6 Revie D (Manchester C.)
8 Reynolds J (WBA, Aston Villa)
1 Richards C (Nottm Forest)
1 Richards G (Derby County)
1 Richards J (Wolves)
2 Richardson J (Newcastle)
1 Richardson K (Aston Villa)
1 Richardson W (WBA)
1 Rickaby S (WBA)
5 Rigby A (Blackburn)
4 Rimmer E (Sheff Wed)
1 Rimmer J (Arsenal)
1 Ripley S (Blackburn)
17 Rix G (Arsenal)
1 Robb G (Spurs)
3 Roberts C (Man Utd)
4 Roberts F (Man City)
6 Roberts G (Spurs)
1 Roberts H (Arsenal)
1 Roberts H (Millwall)
3 Roberts R (WBA)
2 Roberts W (Preston)
4 Robinson J (Sheff Wed)
11 Robinson J W (Derby County, New Brighton Tower, Southampton)
90 Robson B (WBA, Man Utd)
20 Robson R (WBA)
14 Rocastle D (Arsenal)
5 Rose W (Wolves, Preston)
2 Rostron T (Darwen)
1 Rowe A (Spurs)

6	Rowley J (Man Utd)
2	Rowley W (Stoke)
6	Royle J (Everton, Manchester C)
3	Ruddlesdin H (Sheff Wed)
1	Ruddock N (Liverpool)
6	Ruffell J (West Ham)
1	Russell B (Royal Engineers)
11	Rutherford J (Newcastle)
4	Sadler D (Man Utd)
2	Sagar C (Bury)
4	Sagar E (Everton)
5	Salako J (Crystal Palace)
1	Sandford E (WBA)
5	Sandilands R (Old Westminsters)
1	Sands J (Nottm Forest)
86	Sansom K (C Palace, Arsenal)
1	Saunders F (Swifts)
1	Savage A (C Palace)
1	Sayer J (Stoke)
3	Scales J (Liverpool)
1	Scattergood E (Derby County)
3	Schofield J (Stoke)
17	Scott L (Arsenal)
1	Scott W (Brentford)
17	Seaman D (QPR, Arsenal)
6	Seddon J (Bolton)
5	Seed J (Spurs)
6	Settle J (Bury, Everton)
6	Sewell J (Sheffield W.)
1	Sewell W (Blackburn)
5	Shackleton L (Sunderland)
2	Sharp J (Everton)
8	Sharpe L (Man Utd)
1	Shaw G E (WBA)
5	Shaw G L (Sheff Utd)
2	Shea D (Blackburn)
17	Shearer A (Southampton, Blackburn)
1	Shellito K (Chelsea)
6	Shelton A (Notts County)
1	Shelton C (Notts Rangers)
2	Shepherd A (Bolton, Newcastle)
9	Sheringham T (Spurs)
125	Shilton P (Leicester, Stoke, Nottm Forest, Southampton, Derby County)
1	Shimwell E (Blackpool)
1	Shutt G (Stoke)
3	Silcock J (Man Utd)
3	Sillett P (Chelsea)
1	Simms E (Luton)
8	Simpson J (Blackburn)
12	Sinton A (QPR)
12	Slater W (Wolves)
1	Smalley T (Wolves)
5	Smart T (Aston Villa)
3	Smith A (Nottm Forest)
1	Smith A K (Oxford Univ)
13	Smith A M (Arsenal)
2	Smith B (Spurs)
1	Smith C E (C Palace)

20	Smith G O (Oxford Univ, Old Carthusians, Corinthians)
4	Smith H (Reading)
2	Smith J (WBA)
5	Smith Joe (Bolton)
2	Smith J C R (Millwall)
3	Smith J W (Portsmouth)
1	Smith Leslie (Brentford)
6	Smith Lionel (Arsenal)
15	Smith R A (Spurs)
1	Smith S (Aston Villa)
1	Smith S C (Leicester City)
2	Smith T (Birmingham)
1	Smith T (Liverpool)
3	Smith W H (Huddersfield)
1	Sorby T (Thursday Wanderers)
3	Southworth J (Blackburn)
3	Sparks F (Herts Rangers, Clapham Rovers)
2	Spence J (Man Utd)
2	Spence R (Chelsea)
2	Spencer C (Newcastle)
6	Spencer H (Aston Villa)
7	Spiksley F (Sheff Wed)
3	Spilsbury B (Cambridge Univ)
1	Spink N (Aston Villa)
1	Spouncer W (Nottm Forest)
33	Springett R (Sheffield W.)
11	Sproston B (Leeds Utd, Spurs, Man City)
3	Squire R (Cambridge Univ)
1	Stanbrough M (Old Carthusians)
8	Staniforth R (Huddersfield)
2	Starling R (Sheff Wed, Aston Villa)
3	Statham D (WBA)
6	Steele F (Stoke)
1	Stein B (Luton)
1	Stephenson C (Huddersfield)
3	Stephenson G (Derby County, Sheff Wed)
2	Stephenson J (Leeds Utd)
1	Stepney A (Man Utd)
1	Sterland M (Sheffield Wed)
36	Steven T (Everton, Rangers, Marseille)
7	Stevens G A (Spurs)
46	Stevens G (Everton, Rangers)
3	Stewart J (Sheff Wed, Newcastle)
3	Stewart P (Spurs)
28	Stiles N (Man Utd)
3	Stoker J (Birmingham)
2	Storer H (Derby County)
19	Storey P (Arsenal)
1	Storey-Moore I (Nottm Forest)
20	Strange A (Sheff Wed)
1	Stratford A (Wanderers)
1	Streten B (Luton)
2	Sturgess A (Sheff Utd)
8	Summerbee M (Man City)
1	Sunderland A (Arsenal)
5	Sutcliffe J (Bolton, Millwall)
19	Swan P (Sheffield Wed)
6	Swepstone H (Pilgrims)
19	Swift F (Manchester C)

1	Tait G (Birmingham Excelsior)
6	Talbot B (Ipswich, Arsenal)
3	Tambling R (Chelsea)
3	Tate J (Aston Villa)
1	Taylor E (Blackpool)
8	Taylor E H (Huddersfield)
2	Taylor J (Fulham)
3	Taylor P H (Liverpool)
4	Taylor P J (C Palace)
19	Taylor T (Man Utd)
1	Temple D (Everton)
2	Thickett H (Sheff Utd)
2	Thomas D (Coventry)
8	Thomas D (QPR)
9	Thomas G (Crystal Palace)
2	Thomas M (Arsenal)
16	Thompson P (Peter) (Liverpool)
42	Thompson P (Phil) (Liverpool)
2	Thompson T (Aston Villa, Preston)
8	Thomson R (Wolves)
4	Thornewell G (Derby County)
1	Thornley I (Man City)
4	Tilson S (Man City)
2	Titmuss F (Southampton)
27	Todd C (Derby)
2	Toone G (Notts County)
1	Topham A (Casuals)
2	Topham R (Wolves, Casuals)
3	Towers A (Sunderland)
2	Townley W (Blackburn)
2	Townrow J (Clapton Orient)
1	Tremelling D (Birmingham)
2	Tresadern J (West Ham)
6	Tueart D (Man City)
7	Tunstall F (Sheff Utd)
1	Turnbull R (Bradford City)
2	Turner A (Southampton)
2	Turner H (Huddersfield)
3	Turner J (Bolton, Stoke, Derby County)
1	Tweedy G (Grimsby)
1	Ufton D (Charlton)
2	Underwood A (Stoke)
1	Unsworth D (Everton)
4	Urwin T (Middlesbrough, Newcastle)
1	Utley G (Barnsley)
5	Vaughton O (Aston Villa)
6	Veitch C (Newcastle)
1	Veitch J (Old Westminsters)
2	Venables T (Chelsea)
2	Venison B (Newcastle)
1	Vidal R (Oxford Univ)
2	Viljoen C (Ipswich)
2	Viollet D (Man Utd)
2	Von Donop P (Royal Engineers)
3	Wace H (Wanderers)
62	Waddle C (Newcastle, Spurs, Marseille)
9	Wadsworth S (Huddersfield)

1	Wainscoat W (Leeds Utd)
5	Waiters A (Blackpool)
2	Walden F (Spurs)
59	Walker D (Nottm Forest, Sampdoria, Sheff Wed)
18	Walker W (Aston Villa)
7	Wall G (Man Utd)
3	Wallace C (Aston Villa)
1	Wallace D (Southampton)
5	Walsh P (Luton)
9	Walters A (Cambridge Univ, Old Carthusians)
1	Walters M (Rangers)
13	Walters P (Oxford Univ, Old Carthusians)
1	Walton N (Blackburn)
1	Ward J (Blackburn Olympic)
1	Ward P (Brighton and Hove Albion)
2	Ward T (Derby County)
5	Waring T (Aston Villa)
1	Warner C (Upton Park)
22	Warren B (Derby County, Chelsea)
1	Waterfield G (Burnley)
12	Watson D (Norwich, Everton)
65	Watson D (Sunderland, Man City, Werder Bremen, Southampton, Stoke)
5	Watson V (West Ham)
3	Watson W (Burnley)
4	Watson W (Sunderland)
3	Weaver S (Newcastle)
2	Webb G (West Ham)
26	Webb N (Nottm Forest, Man Utd)
3	Webster M (Middlesbrough)
26	Wedlock W (Bristol City)
2	Weir D (Bolton)
2	Welch R de C (Wanderers, Harrow Chequers)
4	Weller K (Leicester)
3	Welsh D (Charlton)
3	West G (Everton)
6	Westwood R (Bolton)
2	Whateley O (Aston Villa)
1	Wheeler J (Bolton)
4	Wheldon G (Aston Villa)
1	White D (Man City)
1	White T (Everton)
2	Whitehead J (Accrington, Blackburn)
1	Whitfield H (Old Etonians)
1	Whitham M (Sheff Utd)
7	Whitworth S (Leicester)
1	Whymark T (Ipswich)
1	Widdowson S (Nottm Forest)
2	Wignall F (Nottm Forest)
5	Wilkes A (Aston Villa)
84	Wilkins R (Chelsea, Man Utd, AC Milan)
1	Wilkinson B (Sheff Utd)
1	Wilkinson L (Oxford Univ)
24	Williams B (Wolves)
2	Williams O (Clapton Orient)
6	Williams S (Southampton)
6	Williams W (WBA)
2	Williamson E (Arsenal)

Darren Anderton sprints away from USA's Agoos.

	United States	Romania	Nigeria	Republic of Ireland	Uruguay	Japan	Sweden	Brazil
D. Seaman (Arsenal)	1	1		1				
R. Jones (Liverpool)	2	2	2		2			
G. Le Saux (Blackburn R)	3	3	3	3	3		3	8
B. Venison (Newcastle U)	4				4			
T. Adams (Arsenal)	5	5		5	5			
G. Pallister (Man. United)	6	6		6	6		6	
D. Platt (Sampdoria)	7		7	7	7	7	7	7
J. Barnes (Liverpool)	8	10	10		10		4	
A. Shearer (Blackburn R)	9	9	9	9		9	9	9
T. Sheringham (Tottenham H)	10	8*	9*		9	10*	10	10
D. Anderton (Tottenham H)	11			11	11	11	11	11
L. Ferdinand (QPR)	9*							
I. Wright (Arsenal)	10*	8						
P. Ince (Man. United)		4		4				
R. Lee (Newcastle U)		7	4					
M. Le Tissier (Southampton)		11	8*	10				
S. Pearce (Nottm. Forest)		2*					3	3
D. Wise (Chelsea)		7*	11					
T. Flowers (Blackburn R)			1		1	1	1	1
S. Howcy (Newcastle U)			5					
N. Ruddock (Liverpool)			6					
P. Beardsley (Newcastle U)			8	8	8	8	8	
S. McManaman (Liverpool)			4*		3*	4*		
W. Barton (Wimbledon and Newcastle United)				2			2	6*
N. Barmby (Tottenham H)					8*		8*	
A. Cole (Man. United)					9*			
G. Neville (Man. United)						2		2
D. Batty (Blackburn R)						4		4
J. Scales (Liverpool)						5	6*	6
D. Unsworth (Everton)						6		
S. Collymore (Nottm. Forest)						10		10*
P. Gascoigne (Lazio)						8*	4*	4*
C. Cooper (Nottm. Forest)							5	5

substitute

● 27

13 ● UNDER-21 INTERNATIONAL MATCHES 1976–1995

UQ   UEFA Competition Qualifier
UF   UEFA Competition Finals

v Albania

| 1989 | 7/3 | Shkoder | W | 2–1 | UQ |
| 1989 | 25/4 | Ipswich | W | 2–0 | UQ |

v Angola

| 1995 | 10/6 | La Seyne | W | 1–0 | |

v Austria

| 1994 | 11/10 | Kapfenberg | W | 3–1 | UQ |

v Belgium

| 1994 | 5/6 | Berre | W | 2–1 | |

v Brazil

| 1993 | 11/6 | Draguignan | D | 0–0 | |
| 1995 | 6/6 | Toulon | L | 0–2 | |

v Bulgaria

1979	5/6	Pernik	W	3–1	UQ
1979	20/11	Leicester	W	5–0	UQ
1989	5/6	Toulon	L	2–3	

v Czech Republic

| 1993 | 9/6 | Saint Cyr | D | 1–1 | |

v Czechoslovakia

| 1990 | 27/4 | Toulon | W | 2–1 | |
| 1992 | 26/5 | Toulon | L | 1–2 | |

v Denmark

1978	19/9	Hvidovre	W	2–1	UQ
1979	11/9	Watford	W	1–0	UQ
1982	21/9	Hvidovre	W	4–1	UQ
1983	20/9	Norwich	W	4–1	UQ
1986	12/3	Copenhagen	W	1–0	UF
1986	26/3	Manchester City	D	1–1	UF
1988	13/9	Watford	D	0–0	
1994	8/3	Brentford	W	1–0	

v Finland

1977	26/5	Helsinki	W	1–0	UQ
1977	12/10	Hull	W	8–1	UQ
1984	16/10	Southampton	W	2–0	UQ
1985	21/5	Mikkeli	L	1–3	UQ

v France

1984	28/2	Sheffield Wed	W	6–1	UF
1984	28/3	Rouen	W	1–0	UF
1987	11/6	Toulon	L	0–2	
1988	13/4	Besançon	L	2–4	UF
1988	27/4	Arsenal	D	2–2	UF
1988	12/6	Toulon	L	2–4	
1990	23/5	Aix en Provence	W	7–3	
1991	3/6	Toulon	W	1–0	
1992	28/5	Aubagne	D	0–0	
1993	15/6	Toulon	W	1–0	
1994	31/5	Aubagne	L	0–3	
1995	12/6	Cannes	L	0 2	

v East Germany

| 1980 | 16/4 | Sheffield Wed | L | 1–2 | UF |
| 1980 | 23/4 | Jena | L | 0–1 | UF |

v West Germany

1982	21/9	Sheffield United	W	3–1	UF
1982	12/10	Bremen	L	2–3	UF
1987	8/9	Lüdenscheid	L	0–2	

v Germany

| 1991 | 10/9 | Scunthorpe | W | 2–1 | |

v Greece

1982	16/11	Piraeus	L	1–0	UQ
1983	29/3	Portsmouth	W	2–1	UQ
1989	7/2	Patras	L	0–1	

v Holland

| 1993 | 27/4 | Portsmouth | W | 3–0 | UQ |
| 1993 | 12/10 | Utrecht | D | 1–1 | UQ |

v Hungary

1981	5/6	Keszthely	W	2–1	UQ
1981	17/11	Nottingham	W	2–0	UQ
1983	26/4	Newcastle	W	1–0	UQ
1983	11/10	Nyiregyhaza	W	2–0	UQ
1990	11/9	Southampton	W	3–1	
1992	12/5	Vac	D	2–2	

v Israel

| 1985 | 27/2 | Tel Aviv | W | 2–1 | |

v Italy

1978	8/3	Manchester City	W	2–1	UF
1978	5/4	Rome	D	0–0	UF
1984	18/4	Manchester City	W	3–1	UF
1984	2/5	Florence	L	0–1	UF
1986	9/4	Pisa	L	0–2	UF
1986	23/4	Swindon	D	1–1	UF

v Latvia

1995	25/4	Riga	W	1–0	UQ
1995	7/6	Burnley	W	4–0	UQ

v Malaysia

1995	8/6	Six-Fours	W	2–0	

v Mexico

1988	5/6	Toulon	W	2–1	
1991	29/5	Vitrolles	W	6–0	
1992	24/5	Six-Fours	D	1–1	

v Morocco

1987	7/6	Toulon	W	2–0	
1988	9/6	Toulon	W	1–0	

v Norway

1977	1/6	Bergen	W	2–1	UQ
1977	6/9	Brighton	W	6–0	UQ
1980	9/9	Southampton	W	3–0	
1981	8/9	Drammen	D	0–0	
1992	13/10	Peterborough	L	0–2	UQ
1993	1/6	Stavanger	D	1–1	UQ

v Poland

1982	17/3	Warsaw	W	2–1	UF
1982	7/4	West Ham	D	2–2	UF
1989	2/6	Plymouth	W	2–1	UQ
1989	10/10	Jastrzebie Zdroj	W	3–1	UQ
1990	16/10	Tottenham	L	0–1	UQ
1991	12/11	Pila	L	1–2	UQ
1993	28/5	Jastrzebie Zdroj	W	4–1	UQ
1993	7/9	Millwall	L	1–2	UQ

v Portugal

1987	13/6	Sollies-Pont	D	0–0	
1990	21/5	Six-Fours	L	0–1	
1993	7/6	Miramas	W	2–0	
1994	7/6	Toulon	W	2–0	
1994	6/9	Leicester	D	0–0	UQ

v Republic of Ireland

1981	25/2	Liverpool	W	1–0	
1985	25/3	Portsmouth	W	3–2	
1989	9/6	Six-Fours	D	0–0	
1990	13/11	Cork	W	3–0	UQ
1991	26/3	Brentford	W	3–0	UQ
1994	15/11	Newcastle	W	1–0	UQ
1995	27/3	Dublin	W	2–0	UQ

v Romania

1980	14/10	Ploesti	L	0–4	UQ
1981	28/4	Swindon	W	3–0	UQ
1985	30/4	Brasov	D	0–0	UQ
1985	9/9	Ipswich	W	3–0	UQ

v Russia

1994	29/5	Bandol	W	2–0

v San Marino

1993	16/2	Luton	W	6–0	UQ
1993	17/11	San Marino	W	4–0	UQ

v Scotland

1977	27/4	Sheffield United	W	1–0	
1980	12/2	Coventry	W	2–1	UF
1980	4/3	Aberdeen	D	0–0	UF
1982	19/4	Glasgow	W	1–0	UF
1982	28/4	Manchester City	D	1–1	UF
1988	16/2	Aberdeen	W	1–0	UF
1989	22/3	Nottingham	W	1–0	UF
1993	13/6	La Ciotat	W	1–0	

v Senegal

1989	7/6	Sainte-Maxime	W	6–1
1991	27/5	Arles	W	2–1

v Spain

1984	17/5	Seville	W	1–0	UF
1984	24/5	Sheffield United	W	2–0	UF
1987	18/2	Burgos	W	2–1	
1992	8/9	Burgos	W	1–0	

v Sweden

1979	9/6	Vasteras	W	2–1	
1986	9/9	Oestersund	D	1–1	
1988	18/10	Coventry	D	1–1	UQ
1989	5/9	Uppsala	L	0–1	UQ

v Switzerland

1980	18/11	Ipswich	W	5–0	UQ
1981	31/5	Neuenburg	D	0–0	UQ
1988	28/5	Lausanne	D	1–1	

v Turkey

1984	13/11	Bursa	D	0–0	UQ
1985	15/10	Bristol	W	3–0	UQ
1987	28/4	Izmir	D	0–0	UQ
1987	13/10	Sheffield	D	1–1	UQ
1991	30/4	Izmir	D	2–2	UQ
1991	15/10	Reading	W	2–0	UQ
1992	17/11	Leyton	L	0–1	UQ
1993	30/3	Izmir	D	0–0	UQ

v USA

1989	11/6	Toulon	L	0–2
1994	2/6	Arles	W	3–0

v USSR

1987	9/6	La Ciotat	D	0–0
1988	7/6	Six-Fours	W	1–0
1990	25/5	Toulon	W	2–1
1991	31/5	Aix-en-Provence	W	2–1

v Wales

1976	15/12	Wolverhampton	D	0–0
1979	6/2	Swansea	W	1–0
1990	5/12	Tranmere	D	0–0

v Yugoslavia

1978	19/4	Novi Sad	L	1–2	UF
1978	2/5	Manchester City	D	1–1	UF
1986	11/11	Peterborough	D	1–1	UQ
1987	10/11	Zemun	W	5–1	UQ

14 ● ENGLAND UNDER-21 CAPS 1976–1995

(Up to and including 12th June 1995)

1	Ablett G (Liverpool)
1	Adams N (Everton)
5	Adams T (Arsenal)
8	Allen B (QPR)
2	Allen C (Oxford Utd)
3	Allen C (QPR, C Palace)
2	Allen M (QPR)
3	Allen P (West Ham, Spurs)
1	Anderson V (Nottm Forest)
12	Anderton D (Spurs)
1	Andrews I (Leicester City)
10	Ardley N (Wimbledon)
6	Atkinson B (Sunderland)
1	Atherton P (Coventry)
9	Awford A (Portsmouth)
14	Bailey G (Man Utd)
2	Baker G (Southampton)
1	Bannister G (Sheff Wed)
4	Barker S (Blackburn)
3	Barmby N (Spurs)
2	Barnes J (Watford)
9	Barnes P (Man City)
4	Barrett E (Oldham)
14	Bart-Williams C (Sheff Wed)
7	Batty D (Leeds Utd)
1	Bazeley D (Watford)
2	Beagrie P (Sheff Utd)
5	Beardsmore R (Man Utd)
4	Beckham D (Man Utd)
1	Beeston C (Stoke)
3	Bertschin K (Birmingham)
2	Birtles G (Nottm Forest)
6	Blackwell D (Wimbledon)
8	Blake M (Aston Villa)
4	Blissett L (Watford)
2	Booth A (Huddersfield)
13	Bracewell P (Stoke, Sunderland, Everton)
4	Bradshaw P (Wolves)
2	Breacker T (Luton Town)
5	Brennan M (Ipswich)
4	Brightwell I (Man City)
4	Brock K (Oxford Utd)
5	Bull S (Wolves)
7	Burrows D (WBA, Liverpool)
7	Butcher T (Ipswich)
3	Butt N (Man Utd)
3	Butters G (Spurs)
8	Butterworth I (Coventry City, Nottm Forest)
3	Caesar G (Arsenal)
9	Callaghan N (Watford)
4	Campbell K (Arsenal)
9	Campbell S (Spurs)
1	Carr C (Fulham)
9	Carr F (Nottm Forest)
1	Casper C (Man Utd)
14	Caton T (Man City, Arsenal)
4	Chamberlain M (Stoke)
1	Chapman L (Stoke City)
4	Charles G (Nottm Forest)
12	Chettle S (Nottm Forest)
11	Clark L (Newcastle)
15	Clough N (Nottm Forest)
8	Cole A (Arsenal, Bristol City, Newcastle)
4	Coney D (Fulham)
1	Connor T (Brighton & Hove Albion)
1	Cooke R (Spurs)
8	Cooper C (Middlesbrough)
3	Corrigan J (Man City)
8	Cottee T (West Ham)
3	Couzens A (Leeds Utd)
5	Cowans G (Aston Villa)
6	Cox N (Aston Villa)
5	Cranson I (Ipswich Town)
4	Croft G (Grimsby)
4	Crooks G (Stoke City)
3	Crossley M (Nottm Forest)
3	Cundy J (Chelsea)
6	Cunningham L (WBA)
1	Curbishley A (Birmingham)
7	Daniel P (Hull City)
1	Davis K (Luton)
11	Davis P (Arsenal)
2	D'Avray M (Ipswich)
7	Deehan J (Aston Villa)
3	Dennis M (Birmingham)
1	Dickens A (West Ham)
4	Dicks J (West Ham)
5	Digby F (Swindon)
1	Dillon K (Birmingham)
1	Dixon K (Chelsea)
4	Dobson T (Coventry City)
8	Dodd J (Southampton)
3	Donowa L (Norwich City)
11	Dorigo T (Aston Villa)
9	Dozzell J (Ipswich)
3	Draper M (Notts County)
7	Duxbury M (Man Utd)
6	Dyer B (C Palace)

4 Dyson P (Coventry City)	2 Ince P (West Ham United)
2 Eadie D (Norwich)	10 Jackson M (Everton)
14 Ebbrell J (Everton)	10 James D (Watford)
3 Edghill R (Man City)	2 James J (Luton)
15 Ehiogu U (Aston Villa)	1 Jemson N (Nottm Forest)
3 Elliott P (Luton, Aston Villa)	8 Joachim J (Leicester)
7 Fairclough C (Nottm Forest, Spurs)	7 Johnson T (Notts County, Derby)
1 Fairclough D (Liverpool)	2 Johnston C (Middlesbrough)
11 Fashanu Justin (Norwich, Nottm Forest)	1 Jones C (Spurs)
3 Fear P (Wimbledon)	1 Jones D (Everton)
1 Fenton G (Aston Villa)	2 Jones R (Liverpool)
11 Fenwick T (QPR)	1 Keegan G (Oldham)
5 Fereday W (QPR)	1 Kenny W (Everton)
10 Flitcroft G (Man City)	8 Keown M (Aston Villa)
3 Flowers T (Southampton)	1 Kerslake D (QPR)
4 Forster N (Brentford)	2 Kilcline B (Notts County)
1 Forsyth M (Derby County)	2 King A (Everton)
1 Foster S (Brighton & Hove Albion)	7 Kitson P (Leicester, Derby)
6 Fowler R (Liverpool)	2 Knight A (Portsmouth)
2 Froggatt S (Aston Villa)	2 Knight I (Sheff Wed)
11 Futcher P (Luton, Man City)	5 Lake P (Man City)
2 Gabbiadini M (Sunderland)	1 Langley T (Chelsea)
1 Gale T (Fulham)	10 Lee D (Chelsea)
3 Gallen K (QPR)	2 Lee R (Charlton)
13 Gascoigne P (Newcastle)	6 Lee S (Liverpool)
3 Gayle H (Birmingham)	4 Le Saux G (Chelsea)
17 Gerrard P (Oldham)	2 Lowe D (Ipswich)
1 Gernon I (Ipswich)	7 Lukic J (Leeds Utd)
5 Gibbs N (Watford)	3 Lund G (Grimsby)
1 Gibson C (Aston Villa)	7 Mabbutt G (Bristol Rovers, Spurs)
11 Gilbert W (C Palace)	6 McCall S (Ipswich)
8 Goddard P (West Ham)	5 McDonald N (Newcastle)
11 Gordon D (C Palace)	1 McGrath L (Coventry City)
4 Gordon D (Norwich)	3 Mackenzie S (WBA)
2 Gray A (Aston Villa)	1 McLeary A (Millwall)
1 Haigh P (Hull)	6 McMahon S (Everton, Aston Villa)
11 Hall R (Southampton)	7 McManaman S (Liverpool)
2 Hardyman P (Portsmouth)	5 Makin C (Oldham)
10 Hateley M (Coventry City, Portsmouth)	1 Marriott A (Nottm Forest)
3 Hayes M (Arsenal)	1 Marshall A (Norwich)
1 Hazell R (Wolves)	2 Martin L (Man Utd)
6 Heaney N (Arsenal)	11 Martyn N (Bristol Rovers)
8 Heath A (Stoke, Everton)	3 Matteo D (Liverpool)
7 Hendon I (Spurs)	9 Matthew D (Chelsea)
7 Hesford I (Blackpool)	1 May A (Man City)
9 Hilaire V (C Palace)	4 Merson P (Arsenal)
4 Hill D (Spurs)	3 Middleton J (Nottm Forest, Derby County)
1 Hillier D (Arsenal)	4 Miller A (Arsenal)
1 Hinchcliffe A (Man City)	2 Mills G (Nottm Forest)
2 Hinshelwood P (C Palace)	3 Mimms R (Rotherham, Everton)
7 Hirst D (Sheff Wed)	6 Minto S (Charlton)
12 Hoddle G (Spurs)	2 Moran S (Southampton)
8 Hodge S (Nottm Forest, Aston Villa)	2 Morgan S (Leicester)
7 Hodgson D (Middlesbrough, Liverpool)	2 Mortimer P (Charlton)
1 Holdsworth D (Watford)	8 Moses R (WBA, Man Utd)
1 Holland C (Newcastle)	1 Mountfield D (Everton)
4 Holland P (Mansfield)	1 Muggleton C (Leicester City)
5 Horne B (Millwall)	1 Mutch A (Wolves)
2 Hucker P (QPR)	4 Myers A (Chelsea)
1 Impey A (QPR)	8 Nethercott S (Spurs)

4	Neville P (Man Utd)
4	Newell M (Luton Town)
2	Newton E (Chelsea)
1	Nicholls A (Plymouth)
5	Oakes M (Aston Villa)
1	Oldfield D (Luton)
10	Olney I (Aston Villa)
3	Ord R (Sunderland)
7	Osman R (Ipswich)
22	Owen G (Man City, WBA)
1	Painter I (Stoke)
4	Palmer C (Sheff Wed)
6	Parker G (Hull, Nottm Forest)
8	Parker P (Fulham)
1	Parkes P (QPR)
5	Parkin S (Stoke City)
12	Parlour R (Arsenal)
6	Peach D (Southampton)
1	Peake A (Leicester City)
2	Pearce I (Blackburn)
1	Pearce S (Nottm Forest)
15	Pickering N (Sunderland, Coventry City)
3	Platt D (Aston Villa)
1	Pollock J (Middlesbrough)
12	Porter G (Watford)
1	Pressman K (Sheff Wed)
4	Proctor M (Middlesbrough, Nottm Forest)
3	Ramage C (Derby County)
10	Ranson R (Man City)
18	Redknapp J (Liverpool)
14	Redmond S (Man City)
10	Reeves K (Norwich, Man City)
6	Regis C (WBA)
6	Reid N (Man City)
6	Reid P (Bolton)
4	Richards D (Wolves)
2	Richards J (Wolves)
5	Rideout P (Aston Villa, Bari)
8	Ripley S (Middlesbrough)
1	Ritchie A (Brighton & Hove Albion)
7	Rix G (Arsenal)
3	Roberts A (Millwall)
6	Robins M (Man Utd)
7	Robson B (WBA)
6	Robson S (Arsenal, West Ham)
14	Rocastle D (Arsenal)
4	Rodger G (Coventry City)
4	Rosario R (Norwich)
1	Rowell G (Sunderland)
4	Ruddock N (Southampton)
1	Ryan J (Oldham Athletic)
3	Ryder S (Walsall)
5	Samways V (Spurs)
8	Sansom K (Crystal Palace)
10	Seaman D (Birmingham)
11	Sedgley S (Coventry City, Spurs)
3	Sellars S (Blackburn)
3	Selley I (Arsenal)
8	Sharpe L (Man Utd)
7	Shaw G (Aston Villa)

11	Shearer A (Southampton)
1	Shelton G (Sheff Wed)
1	Sheringham T (Millwall)
16	Sheron M (Man City)
4	Sherwood T (Norwich City)
4	Shipperley N (Chelsea, Southampton)
5	Simpson P (Man City)
10	Sims S (Leicester City)
12	Sinclair T (QPR)
1	Sinnott L (Watford)
3	Slater S (West Ham)
12	Small B (Aston Villa)
10	Smith D (Coventry City)
5	Smith M (Sheff Wed)
1	Smith M (Sunderland)
4	Snodin I (Doncaster)
3	Statham B (Spurs)
6	Statham D (WBA)
3	Stein B (Luton)
7	Sterland M (Sheff Wed)
2	Steven T (Everton)
1	Stevens G (Everton)
7	Stevens G (Brighton & Hove Albion, Spurs)
1	Stewart P (Man City)
5	Stuart G (Chelsea)
10	Suckling P (Coventry City, Man City, C Palace)
3	Summerbee N (Swindon)
1	Sunderland A (Wolves)
4	Sutch D (Norwich)
13	Sutton C (Norwich)
1	Swindlehurst D (C Palace)
1	Talbot B (Ipswich)
7	Thomas D (Coventry City, Spurs)
12	Thomas M (Arsenal)
3	Thomas M (Luton)
1	Thomas R (Watford)
1	Thompson A (Bolton)
6	Thompson G (Coventry City)
5	Thorn A (Wimbledon)
13	Tiler C (Barnsley, Nottm Forest)
5	Unsworth D (Everton)
10	Venison B (Sunderland)
12	Vinnicombe C (Rangers)
1	Waddle C (Newcastle)
7	Walker D (Nottm Forest)
9	Walker I (Spurs)
14	Wallace D (Southampton)
4	Wallace Ray (Southampton)
11	Wallace Rod (Southampton)
2	Walsh G (Man Utd)
4	Walsh P (Luton Town)
9	Walters M (Aston Villa)
2	Ward P (Brighton & Hove Albion)
8	Warhurst P (Oldham, Sheff Wed)
4	Watson D (Barnsley)
7	Watson D (Norwich)
2	Watson G (Sheff Wed)
11	Watson S (Newcastle)
3	Webb N (Portsmouth, Nottm Forest)

2	Whelan N (Leeds Utd)	14	Williams S (Southampton)
3	Whelan P (Ipswich)	1	Winterburn N (Wimbledon)
6	White D (Man City)	1	Wise D (Wimbledon)
4	Whyte C (Arsenal)	2	Woodcock A (Nottm Forest)
1	Wicks S (QPR)	6	Woods C (Nottm Forest, QPR, Norwich)
1	Wilkins R (Chelsea)	2	Wright A (Blackburn)
4	Wilkinson P (Grimsby, Everton)	4	Wright M (Southampton)
4	Williams P (Charlton)	6	Wright W (Everton)
6	Williams P (Derby County)	5	Yates D (Notts County)

15 ● ENGLAND UNDER-21 CAPS 1994–95

	Portugal	Austria	Rep. of Ireland	Rep. of Ireland	Latvia	Brazil	Latvia	Malaysia	Angola	France
P. Gerrard (Oldham A)	1	1	1	1	1		1			
S. Watson (Newcastle U)	2	4	2	2	2		2			
D. Gordon (C. Palace)	3	3	3	3	3		3			
T. Sinclair (QPR)	4		8	11	11					
S. Campbell (Tottenham)	5	5	5							
D. Unsworth (Everton)	6	6	6	6	6					
J. Redknapp (Liverpool)	7	7								
N. Barmby (Tottenham H)	8	11*								
R. Fowler (Liverpool)	9	9								
C. Bart-Williams (Sheff W)	10	10	10	10	10		10			
J. Joachim (Leicester C)	11	11	11			9		9	9	9
B. Dyer (C. Palace)	8*									
R. Edghill (Man. City)		2								
R. Parlour (Arsenal)		8								
N. Whelan (Leeds U)		10*	9							
N. Butt (Man. United)			4	7	7					
G. Fenton (Aston Villa)			7							
J. Pollock (Middlesbrough)			9*							
M. Smith (Sunderland)			10*							
I. Pearce (Blackburn R)				4			4			
A. Roberts (Millwall)				5	5		5			
K. Gallen (QPR)				8	8		8			
N. Shipperley (Southampton)				9	9		9			
S. Nethercott (Tottenham)					4		6			
A. Booth (Huddersfield T)					8*		8*			
D. Watson (Barnsley)						1				1
P. Neville (Man. United)						2		2	2	2
D. Richards (Wolverhampton W)						3		3	3	3
S. Ryder (Walsall)						4			4	4
G. Croft (Grimsby Town)						5		5	5	5
D. Hill (Tottenham H)						6		6	6	6
D. Beckham (Man. United)						7		7	7	7
P. Holland (Mansfield T)						8		8	8	8
N. Forster (Brentford)						10		10	10	10
A. Myers (Chelsea)						11		11	11*	11
C. Allen (Oxford United)						11*				4*
C. Holland (Newcastle U)							7			
A. Thompson (Bolton Wand)							11			
A. Marshall (Norwich City)								1		
C. Casper (Manchester United)								4		
A. Couzens (Leeds United)								6*	11	8*
K. Davis (Luton Town)									1	

*substitute

● 35

16 ● ENGLAND B INTERNATIONAL MATCHES 1949–1995

v Algeria

1990	11/12	Algiers	D	0–0

v Australia

1980	17/11	Birmingham	W	1–0

v CIS

1992	28/4	Moscow	D	1–1

v Czechoslovakia

1978	28/11	Prague	W	1–0
1990	24/4	Sunderland	W	2–0
1992	24/3	Ceske Budejovice	W	1–0

v Finland

1949	15/5	Helsinki	W	4–0

v France

1952	22/5	Le Havre	L	1–7
1992	18/2	QPR	W	3–0

v West Germany

1954	24/3	Gelsenkirchen	W	4–0
1955	23/3	Sheffield	D	1–1
1978	21/2	Augsburg	W	2–1

v Holland

1949	18/5	Amsterdam	W	4–0
1950	22/2	Newcastle	W	1–0
1950	17/5	Amsterdam	L	0–3
1952	26/3	Amsterdam	W	1–0

v Iceland

1989	19/5	Reykjavik	W	2–0
1991	27/4	Watford	W	1–0

v Italy

1950	11/5	Milan	L	0–5
1989	14/11	Brighton	D	1–1

v Luxembourg

1950	21/5	Luxembourg	W	2–1

v Malaysia

1978	30/5	Kuala Lumpur	D	1–1

v Malta

1987	14/10	Ta'Qali	W	2–0

v New Zealand

1978	7/6	Christchurch	W	4–0
1978	11/6	Wellington	W	3–1
1978	14/6	Auckland	W	4–0
1979	15/10	Leyton Orient	W	4–1
1984	13/11	Nottingham Forest	W	2–0

v Northern Ireland

1994	10/5	Sheffield	W	4–2

v Norway

1989	22/5	Stavanger	W	1–0

v Republic of Ireland

1990	27/3	Cork	L	1–4
1994	13/12	Liverpool	W	2–0

v Scotland

1953	11/3	Edinburgh	D	2–2
1954	3/3	Sunderland	D	1–1
1956	29/2	Dundee	D	2–2
1957	6/2	Birmingham	W	4–1

v Singapore

1978	18/6	Singapore	W	8–0

v Spain

1980	26/3	Sunderland	W	1–0
1981	25/3	Granada	L	2–3
1991	18/12	Castellon	W	1–0

v Switzerland

1950	18/1	Sheffield	W	5–0
1954	22/5	Basle	L	0–2
1956	21/3	Southampton	W	4–1
1989	16/5	Winterthur	W	2–0
1991	20/5	Walsall	W	2–1

v USA

1980	14/10	Manchester	W	1–0

v Wales

1991	5/2	Swansea	W	1–0

v Yugoslavia

1954	16/5	Ljubljana	L	1–2
1955	19/10	Manchester	W	5–1
1989	12/12	Millwall	W	2–1

17 ● ENGLAND B CAPS 1978–1995

(Up to and including 13th December 1994)

1	Ablett G (Liverpool)	1	Edghill R (Manchester City)
4	Adams T (Arsenal)	1	Ehiogu U (Aston Villa)
7	Anderson V (Nottingham Forest)	1	Elliott P (Celtic)
1	Armstrong C (Crystal Palace)	3	Elliott S (Sunderland)
2	Armstrong D (Middlesbrough)	3	Eves M (Wolves)
1	Atkinson D (Sheffield Wednesday)	1	Fairclough C (Tottenham)
2	Bailey G (Manchester United)	1	Fairclough D (Liverpool)
1	Bailey J (Everton)	1	Fashanu J (Nottingham Forest)
1	Barmby N (Tottenham)	3	Flanagan M (Charlton and Crystal Palace)
1	Barnes P (WBA)	3	Ford T (WBA)
4	Barrett E (Oldham Athletic)	1	Forsyth M (Derby County)
3	Barton W (Wimbledon)	1	Fowler R (Liverpool)
1	Bart-Williams C (Sheffield Wednesday)	2	Fox R (Newcastle)
3	Batson B (WBA)	1	Gabbiadini M (Sunderland)
5	Batty D (Leeds United)	1	Gallagher J (Birmingham)
2	Beagrie P (Everton)	4	Gascoigne P (Tottenham)
2	Beardsley P (Liverpool)	1	Geddis D (Ipswich Town)
7	Beasant D (Wimbledon)	1	Gibson C (Aston Villa)
2	Beresford J (Newcastle)	2	Gidman J (Aston Villa)
1	Birtles G (Nottingham Forest)	1	Goddard P (West Ham United)
1	Bishop I (West Ham United)	2	Gordon D (Norwich City)
1	Blissett L (Watford)	1	Greenhoff B (Manchester United)
2	Bond K (Norwich and Manchester City)	1	Harford M (Luton Town)
1	Borrows B (Coventry City)	1	Hazell R (Wolves)
1	Bould S (Arsenal)	1	Heath A (Everton)
1	Brock K (QPR)	1	Hilaire V (Crystal Palace)
1	Bruce S (Norwich City)	6	Hill G (Manchester Utd and Derby County)
5	Bull S (Wolves)	3	Hirst D (Sheffield Wednesday)
3	Burrows D (Liverpool)	2	Hoddle G (Tottenham)
1	Butcher T (Ipswich Town)	2	Hodge S (Nottingham Forest)
1	Callaghan N (Watford)	1	Holdsworth D (Wimbledon)
1	Campbell K (Arsenal)	5	Hollins J (QPR)
1	Campbell S (Tottenham)	3	Hurlock T (Millwall)
1	Chapman L (Leeds United)	1	Ince P (Manchester United)
3	Clough N (Nottingham Forest)	1	James D (Liverpool)
1	Cole A (Newcastle)	2	Jobson R (Oldham)
10	Corrigan J (Manchester City)	1	Johnston C (Liverpool)
1	Coton T (Manchester City)	2	Joseph R (Wimbledon)
2	Cowans G (Aston Villa)	7	Kennedy A (Liverpool)
1	Crook I (Norwich City)	1	Keown M (Everton)
1	Cunningham L (WBA)	1	King P (Sheffield Wednesday)
4	Curle K (Wimbledon and Manchester City)	1	Lake P (Manchester City)
6	Daley S (Wolves)	3	Langley T (Chelsea)
1	Daley T (Aston Villa)	1	Laws B (Nottingham Forest)
1	Davenport P (Nottingham Forest)	1	Lee R (Newcastle)
1	Davis P (Arsenal)	2	Le Saux G (Chelsea)
3	Deane B (Sheffield United)	5	Le Tissier M (Southampton)
1	Devonshire A (West Ham United)	1	Lineker G (Leicester City)
2	Dicks J (West Ham)	4	Linighan A (Norwich City)
4	Dixon L (Arsenal)	1	Lukic J (Leeds United)
7	Dorigo T (Chelsea, Leeds United)	1	Lyons M (Everton)
1	Ebbrell J (Everton)	1	McCall S (Ipswich Town)

1 McDermott T (Liverpool)
3 McLeary A (Millwall)
2 McMahon S (Aston Villa and Liverpool)
9 Mabbutt G (Tottenham)
3 Mackenzie S (Manchester City and Charlton)
7 Mariner P (Ipswich Town)
2 Martin A (West Ham United)
6 Martyn N (Bristol Rovers and C Palace)
3 Merson P (Arsenal)
1 Money R (Liverpool)
2 Morley T (Aston Villa)
3 Mortimer D (Aston Villa)
1 Mountfield D (Everton)
3 Mowbray T (Middlesbrough)
3 Mutch A (Wolves)
3 Naylor S (WBA)
6 Needham D (Nottingham Forest)
2 Newell M (Everton)
2 Osman R (Ipswich Town)
7 Owen G (Manchester City)
9 Pallister G (Middlesbrough, Manchester Utd)
5 Palmer C (Sheffield Wednesday)
1 Parker G (Nottingham Forest)
3 Parker P (QPR)
2 Parkes P (West Ham United)
1 Peach D (Southampton)
3 Platt D (Aston Villa)
1 Power P (Manchester City)
3 Preece D (Luton Town)
2 Pressman K (Sheffield Wednesday)
1 Redknapp J (Liverpool)
3 Reeves K (Manchester City)
3 Regis C (WBA)
3 Richards J (Wolves)
3 Rix G (Arsenal)
1 Roberts G (Tottenham)
3 Robson B (WBA, Manchester United)
2 Rocastle D (Arsenal)
5 Roeder G (Orient and QPR)
1 Ruddock N (Liverpool)
2 Sansom K (Crystal Palace)

2 Scales J (Wimbledon, Liverpool)
6 Seaman D (QPR)
1 Sharpe L (Manchester United)
1 Shearer A (Southampton)
1 Sherwood T (Blackburn)
1 Sims S (Leicester City)
3 Sinton A (QPR)
2 Slater S (West Ham United)
4 Smith A (Arsenal)
2 Snodin I (Everton)
4 Speight M (Sheffield United)
2 Spink N (Aston Villa)
2 Statham D (WBA)
3 Sterland M (Sheffield Wednesday, Leeds)
1 Stevens G (Everton)
5 Stewart P (Tottenham)
1 Stubbs A (Bolton)
1 Summerbee N (Swindon)
7 Sunderland A (Arsenal)
2 Sutton C (Norwich, Blackburn)
8 Talbot B (Ipswich and Arsenal)
3 Thomas G (Crystal Palace)
5 Thomas M (Liverpool)
1 Thomas M (Tottenham Hotspur)
1 Thompson P (Liverpool)
1 Waldron M (Southampton)
1 Wallace D (Manchester United)
1 Wallace R (Southampton)
1 Walters M (Rangers)
2 Ward P (Nottingham Forest)
4 Webb N (Manchester United)
1 White D (Manchester City)
1 Wilcox J (Blackburn)
3 Williams P (Charlton Athletic)
4 Williams S (Southampton)
3 Winterburn N (Arsenal)
3 Wise D (Wimbledon)
1 Woodcock T (Cologne)
2 Woods C (Norwich, Rangers)
2 Wright B (Everton)
3 Wright I (Crystal Palace)

18 ● ENGLAND'S INTERNATIONAL MATCH REPORTS 1994–1995

England 0   Portugal 0   (Under-21)

6th September 1994, Leicester

England Under-21s were crowned European champions in 1982 and 1984 but had not reached the final stages of the UEFA Championship since 1988. So the current crop of international hopefuls – who also had Austria, Latvia and the Republic of Ireland in their qualifying group – would be hoping to change matters as part of the new Venables era. But the defensive Portuguese held on for a 0–0 draw, despite having Litos red-carded for a late tackle on Joachim midway through the second half.

Dave Sexton's England could have started the 18-month campaign for the European title more successfully if Liverpool's Robbie Fowler had not been ruled offside when he had the ball in the net in the first period. Television replays indicated clearly that he had received local boy Julian Joachim's pass and dispatched the ball into the far corner in an entirely legitimate way.

Fowler, the Premiership's top scorer with five goals in his club's opening three fixtures, was denied again because club-mate Jamie Redknapp had taken a free-kick too quickly for the Italian referee's liking. Chances were missed as Dean Gordon and then Chris Bart-Williams blasted over the top and, with Litos' dismissal not disrupting the visitors' defensive strategy, England failed to achieve the breakthrough.

England: Gerrard, Watson, Gordon, Sinclair, Campbell, Unsworth, Redknapp, Barmby (Dyer), Fowler, Bart-Williams, Joachim.

Portugal: Custinha, Andrade, Jorge, Litos, Costa, Peixe, Calado, Poejo, Bambo (Vieira), Kenedy, Simao (Afonso).

Referee: G. Cesari (Italy)
Attendance: 6,487

England 2   United States 0

7th September 1994, Wembley

England comprehensively beat USA at Wembley in the opening match of the season to banish to some extent the memory of the previous year's debacle. Sterner challenges lay ahead during the season's series of friendly fixtures, but Coach Terry Venables' four-match unbeaten run – without a goal against – was starting to put a smile back on England supporters' faces.

The American visitors, whose World Cup showing had been better than anticipated, gave the impression at Wembley that they were chiefly concerned with keeping the score to a respectable level. Athletic but largely unadventurous, they managed a solitary shot on target and presented awkward opposition only when defending. Even that defence was breached twice inside eight minutes during the first half. Alan Shearer's double strike virtually rendered the second half academic.

Goals from Thomas Dooley and Alexi Lalas in Boston had brought England an unexpected, perhaps even humiliating, defeat fifteen months before. Now the American pair were standing defiant – for 32 minutes at least – to remind the home players of that fateful day. Then Lalas opted to back off as Shearer brought the ball under control on the edge of the box and the Blackburn striker had time in which to drill a low right-footer to Friedel's left. Seven minutes later Graeme Le Saux, released by Teddy Sheringham, hit a rising cross in from the left and Shearer gave Lalas the slip again to head his fifth England goal in eleven internationals.

England: Seaman, Jones, Le Saux, Venison, Adams, Pallister, Platt, Barnes, Shearer (Ferdinand), Sheringham (Wright), Anderton.

United States: Friedel (Sommer), Agoos (Lapper), Balboa, Caligiuri, Lalas, Dooley, Jones, Sorber, Reyna (Moore), Perez (Wynalda), Stewart (Klopas).

Referee: A. J. Lopez Nieto (Spain)
Attendance: 38,629

Austria 1   England 3   (Under-21)

11th October 1994, Kapfenberg

England Under-21s – and captain Jamie Redknapp in particular – triumphed high in the Alps in their second UEFA Championship qualifier. But, on the down side, Redknapp's Liverpool colleague Robbie Fowler was shown the red card two minutes from time for unwisely prolonging an argument with the Russian referee.

The Liverpool connection had worked well before that late indiscretion, with one of their famous old boys Kevin Keegan managing the side in the absence of the indisposed Dave Sexton and Fowler setting up scoring chances for hat-trick man Redknapp.

The Austrians, however, had caught England cold at the start when Haas powered in a header after just six minutes. The equaliser came on 39 minutes as Fowler's hard left-footer was beaten away by

Alan Shearer heads England's second goal against USA.

Robert Lee scores on his England debut against Romania.

Krassnitzer for Redknapp to pounce. Within a minute England were in front, Redknapp heading in from Fowler's excellent cross.

A couple of minutes after a clearly upset Fowler had been led away after complaining to the referee about the treatment he was receiving from home defenders, the elegant and always confident-looking Redknapp completed his hat-trick with a superb strike from a free-kick.

Austria: Krassnitzer, Hiden, Grassler, Leitner, Dietrich, Panis, Purk, Schopp (Wagner), Kraiger (Obrecht), Schiener, Haas.

England: Gerrard, Edghill, Gordon, Watson, Campbell, Unsworth, Redknapp, Parlour, Fowler, Bart-Williams (Whelan), Joachim (Barmby).

Referee: A. Boutenko (Russia)

Attendance: 2,000

England 1   Romania 1

12th October 1994, Wembley

Terry Venables was looking for opposition to stretch his team and tactics and Romania, World Cup quarter-finalists, duly obliged at Wembley. It was certainly beneficial to meet such a skilful team in one of the preparatory matches for Euro 96. In European terms Romania were one of the strongest outfits that England could hope to measure themselves against.

Romania's defence provided the perfect springboard for counter-attacks and Gheorghe Hagi, a genuine world-class performer, was their guiding force. With a more attacking line-up than had been employed in the previous weekend's 0–0 draw in France, Anghel Iordanescu's side passed the ball around confidently and accurately. For all that they didn't trouble David Seaman too often in England's goal but did take the lead on 37 minutes.

Matthew Le Tissier, slotting in behind the front two (Wright and Shearer) and quickly displaying his Southampton form, almost scored after nine minutes with a dipping shot from an outrageous distance. Then Rob Jones and Alan Shearer went close before Romania scored a bad goal from England's point of view. Petrescu, then at Sheffield Wednesday, chipped a tantalising centre into the box which eluded Tony Adams and set up Tottenham's Dumitrescu for a shot from twelve yards that flew past Seaman.

England responded in a spirited fashion and drew level just before the break. Full-back Graeme Le Saux arrowed a cross towards club-mate Shearer and his knock-down provided Robert Lee, winning his first cap, with an opportunity to control the ball before slipping it past Stelea. With the great Hagi retiring from the fray at half-time, England took the initiative and only a blatant "professional foul" by Popescu on Shearer stopped the Blackburn striker's clear run on goal. The Romanian merely received a yellow card.

England: Seaman, Jones (Pearce), Le Saux, Ince, Adams, Pallister, Lee (Wise), Wright (Sheringham), Shearer, Barnes, Le Tissier.

Romania: Stelea (Prunea), Petrescu, Prodan, Belodedice, Lupescu, Popescu, Lacatus (Cirstea), Dumitrescu, Raducioiu (Timofte), Hagi (Selymes), Munteanu.

Referee: J. Quiniou (France)

Attendance: 48,754

England 1   Republic of Ireland 0   (Under-21)

15th November 1994, Newcastle

Kevin Keegan, stand-in boss once more, declared himself disappointed that his England side had failed to do the record-breaking crowd justice as the fervour that had gripped Newcastle (they were then top of the Premiership) spread to the Under-21s' narrow win over the Republic of Ireland at St James' Park. But at least England got the points – and still headed Group Six.

The only goal of the game arrived midway through the first half. A short free-kick saw Nicky Butt drive in a powerful, diagonal cross which Noel Whelan headed emphatically home. The strapping Leeds youngster, beginning his first full game at Under-21 level, enjoyed an impressive debut.

Previously both Whelan and Graham Fenton had apparently goal-bound efforts inadvertently blocked by another England player and Dean Gordon's surging runs from left-back had caused the visitors considerable problems. The second half offered little in the way of excitement, though home goalkeeper Paul Gerrard had to make a smart diving save to deny Kennedy with eight minutes left on the clock.

England: Gerrard, Watson, Gordon, Butt, Campbell, Unsworth, Fenton, Sinclair, Whelan (Pollock), Bart-Williams (Smith M.), Joachim.

Republic of Ireland: Givens, Carr, Woods, Greene, Breen, Boland, Kavanagh, Moore (Scully), Perkins (Launders), Kennedy, Turner.

Referee: T. Hollung (Norway)

Attendance: 25,863

England 1   Nigeria 0

16th November 1994, Wembley

For the third month in a row England were in action at Wembley and victory over the spirited African champions made it arguably the most satisfying result of Terry Venables' six-match unbeaten tenure as national coach. England may have been chasing shadows for the opening twenty minutes, as the quality of the Nigerians' passing and intelligent use of the width of the Wembley pitch surprised even those who remembered that the visitors had come within a minute of knocking out eventual finalists Italy at USA '94. But captain David Platt's 24th goal in 50

David Platt heads the goal that beat Nigeria.

Darren Anderton keeps control with the Uruguayan defence close by.

internationals – a sensational scoring rate for a player usually deployed in midfield – brought a win that was just reward for England's performance over the ninety minutes.

Tim Flowers' saves denied Yekini and Amokachi – the latter quick to show glimpses of his World Cup class – in those early fretful minutes. Then came an England revival precipitated by Dennis Wise, which was not checked when Robert Lee injured his left hand in a tumble after failing to convert Alan Shearer's knock-down. Steve McManaman replaced him, winning his first cap, but it was an inspirational Wise who continued to drive England forward.

The all-important goal arrived five minutes before half-time. Wise's free-kick following a foul on Graeme Le Saux caused consternation in the retreating Nigerian defence, eluding Neil Ruddock's leap but not Platt's – the Sampdoria midfielder had the requisite yard of space in which to steer his header past an exposed Rufai. Platt had now scored as many England goals as Geoff Hurst.

England kept up the pressure after the break, Peter Beardsley shooting into the side-netting and Wise narrowly missing with a diving header. With the home side committed to attack, there was an occasional gap at the back which Nigeria sought to exploit. A late scare saw Flowers save brilliantly from Adepoju.

England: Flowers, Jones, Le Saux, Lee (McManaman), Howey, Ruddock, Platt, Beardsley (Le Tissier), Shearer (Sheringham), Barnes, Wise.

Nigeria: Rufai, Okafor, Eguavon, Okechukwu, Iroha, George, Adepoju (Kanu), Okocha, Amunike, Amokachi (Ikpeba), Yekini (Ekoku).

Referee: L. Sundell (Sweden)
Attendance: 37,196

England "B" 2   Republic of Ireland "B" 0

13th December 1994, Liverpool

Andy Cole, a prolific scorer for his club (68 goals in 78 appearances for Newcastle United), struck a goal for England after 14 minutes of the only "B" international of the season to do no harm at all to his chances of promotion to Terry Venables' senior squad. Even after Cole had left the action with thirteen minutes remaining, there was no respite for the Irish: Robbie Fowler replaced him and scored on his home ground.

The home team, with only one full international cap between them, handled the vastly more experienced Irish side with relative ease and several players improved their prospects of joining the seniors before too long. One of these – Blackburn skipper Tim Sherwood – set the tone for the match with a thumping shot against the frame of the goal in only the second minute.

Twelve minutes further into the match Cole collected Chris Sutton's pass from the left, tricked his way past Daish and hit a low shot under Branagan's dive to confirm England's early supremacy. Cole was menacing throughout: on one occasion in the second half he twisted and turned in the penalty area and had three Irish defenders falling over themselves in clumsy attempts to block his progress.

The visitors certainly had no opportunity to relax after Cole and Sutton had departed. Barmby and Fowler proved to be as much of a handful and in the closing minutes England might well have added more goals. Just one materialised, Fowler drilling home a fierce shot with the last kick to provide a fitting conclusion to an encouraging night.

England: Pressman (James), Barton, Beresford, Campbell (Redknapp), Scales (Ehiogu), Ruddock, Fox, Sherwood, Cole (Fowler), Sutton (Barmby), Wilcox.

Republic of Ireland: Branagan, Cunningham, Kenna, Babb, Daish, Townsend, McAteer, Whelan (Milligan), Coyne, Kelly (Coyle), McLoughlin.

Referee: H. Dallas (Scotland)
Attendance: 7,431

Republic of Ireland 0   England 2   (Under-21)

27th March 1995, Dublin

Once England began to impose their authority and superior experience before an all-ticket 6,000 crowd at Dalymount Park, an England victory was never in doubt. QPR's Trevor Sinclair and Neil Shipperley of Southampton, formerly with Chelsea, scored the goals that gave England a two-point advantage in their European Championship qualifying group.

Dave Sexton's team struggled to find space to play before the break as a lively home side took up the running. Then England's Kevin Gallen, an impressive teenage regular in QPR's first team, latched onto a weak Irish clearance to rap a drive against an upright. Gallen had opted to play for the country of his birth, though his family hails from Donegal, and he proved unpopular with home supporters as a result.

England's midfield surged forward after the break. On 52 minutes Shipperley nodded on Steve Watson's long throw and Sinclair swivelled to notch his fourth goal for the Under-21s. Shipperley made it 2–0, controlling the ball well before shooting just inside a post.

Republic of Ireland: Givens, Carr, Breen, Greene, Hardy, Durkan, Savage, Boland (Farrelly), Woods, Kennedy, Turner (Launders).

England: Gerrard, Watson, Gordon, Pearce, Roberts, Unsworth, Butt, Gallen, Shipperley, Bart-Williams, Sinclair.

Referee: P. Leduc (France)

England 0   Uruguay 0

29th March 1995, Wembley

Uruguay were making their first appearance at Wembley since a 2–1 scoreline, in their favour, in a warm-up match three weeks before Italia '90. That had put an end to an unbeaten run at Wembley for the home team stretching back six years and, as a further illustration of the difficulty of achieving a satisfactory result against the original World Cup winners, England had not won against Uruguay since the 1960s. Now, in the first completed international for four months, Terry Venables' team found them frustrating opponents once again and had to settle for a goalless draw.

Uruguay were not overly ambitious: they showed Latin skill and mastery of the ball as they flicked it around to a slow rhythm, but Tim Flowers was rarely tested in the home goal. The visitors were without Inter Milan striker Sosa, injured, and their one out-and-out front player – Roma's multi-million-pound Fonseca – made virtually no impact. In fact, when Lopez overlapped down the right before crossing to him early in the match, his attempt at an overhead scissor-kick missed by a mile. Surely he had never done that on "Football Italia".

England gradually got the measure of the match and strove to break the deadlock, yet Ferro's first genuine save didn't arrive until the 54th minute. Rob Jones and substitute Steve McManaman combined with Teddy Sheringham, playing in the normal somewhat isolated Shearer role, to give Darren Anderton some precious space on the right side of the box. His shot was hard and true but the Uruguayan goalkeeper reacted quickly to divert the ball round a post with his right foot. Then two further England substitutes were introduced – first Nicky Barmby, then Andy Cole six minutes later, both graduates of the FA National School and the first ones to be capped at senior level.

The latter, something of a goalscoring legend already, almost unlocked the door. McManaman linked up with Anderton on the right, the Tottenham winger's high cross was headed invitingly back into the goalmouth by Tony Adams and a lurking Cole sent an instant header flashing past Ferro. But the ball thudded against the bar and bounced to safety.

England: Flowers, Jones, Le Saux (McManaman), Venison, Adams, Pallister, Platt, Beardsley (Barmby), Sheringham (Cole), Barnes, Anderton.

Uruguay: Ferro, Aguirregaray, Gutierrez, Lopez, Dorta, Montero, Cedres, Bengoechea, Fonseca, Francescoli (Debray), Poyet.

Referee: H. Krug (Germany)
Attendance: 34,849

Latvia 0   England 1   (Under-21)

25th April 1995, Riga

Trevor Sinclair enhanced his England senior ambitions with a late winner for the Under-21s in Riga. The QPR winger struck after 80 minutes with his fifth goal in twelve appearances at Under-21 level to leave Dave Sexton's unbeaten team top of their European Championship qualifying group. He seized onto Andy Booth's header to finish expertly from a difficult angle.

It had looked to be one of those games where a goal simply wouldn't come. Chances in the first half fell consistently to the England front players, particularly to Kevin Gallen, but Sinclair's QPR team-mate saw his best effort – a first-time volley – brilliantly saved at point-blank range by the Latvian goalkeeper.

Three minutes into the second period Neil Shipperley got his head to Chris Bart-Williams' centre but saw his header bounce on top of the crossbar. Then Gallen turned to flash another volley inches wide of a post. England had compiled almost twenty scoring attempts when Sinclair's unstoppable shot broke the deadlock.

Latvia: Kolinko, Isakovs, Lisjakovs, Lidaks, Dolgopolovs, Voskans (Iljins), Rudenko, Bleidelis, Vucans, Semjonovs (Zverugo), Pahars.

England: Gerrard, Watson, Gordon, Nethercott, Roberts, Unsworth, Butt, Gallen (Booth), Shipperley, Bart-Williams, Sinclair.

Referee: B. Benediks (Slovakia)
Attendance: 300

England 4   Latvia 0   (Under-21)

7th June 1995, Burnley

Dave Sexton's England Under-21s stretched their lead at the top of the UEFA Championship group to five points with an emphatic win over Latvia at Turf Moor. After a tentative start the England team – with Pearce, Holland and Shipperley providing the strength through the middle – virtually set up camp in the Latvian half.

Close-range strikes from Chris Bart-Williams and Neil Shipperley put a confident England well in control before Steve Watson and Andy Booth both headed home for a final scoreline of 4–0. Sheffield Wednesday's Bart-Williams, winning his 14th cap, made a significant contribution to three of the home side's goals.

Chris Holland, 19 and said to be "a new Gazza" at Newcastle, shone for England, as did Bolton's Alan Thompson who was also making his debut at Under-21 level. Now Dave Sexton's team only have to beat closest rivals Portugal in September to clinch a quarter-final place outright.

England: Gerrard, Watson, Gordon, Pearce, Roberts, Nethercott, Holland C., Gallen (Booth), Shipperley, Bart-Williams, Thompson.

Latvia: Digulyov, Isakov, Korablyov, Stepanov (Burlakov), Lisjakovs, Voskans, Lidaks, Nalivaiko, Pakhar, Polyakov, Vucans.
Referee: N. Levnikov (Russia).
Attendance: 7,288.

UMBRO CUP

England 2   Japan 1

3rd June 1995, Wembley

The FA's four-nation summer tournament, the Umbro Cup, began with a Wembley meeting – in distinctly sodden conditions – between the hosts and Japan, the first Asian visitors ever and the would-be hosts of the 2002 World Cup. Terry Venables introduced Neville, Scales, Unsworth (all in the back four) and Collymore as new caps and this experimental line-up found the Oriental combination of high workrate and neat technique more problematic than the home crowd had anticipated.

There was a chance of an early England goal, on seven minutes, which would have settled the nerves as the newcomers attempted to find their international feet. Alan Shearer broke clear of the Japanese defence, but the kind of opportunity he had gobbled up regularly in the Premiership was fired straight at the 'keeper's legs.

Beardsley's clever toe-poked cross from the left after 22 minutes was headed over the top by Collymore in the last English move of quality in the first half. The Japanese were growing in confidence, having kept the score goalless for so long, when a breakthrough came for the home side three minutes into the second period. Shearer played a short pass through a Japanese defender's legs on the edge of the box, leaving Darren Anderton with a clear shot at goal, and his left-footer took a deflection to beat Maekawa's dive.

But it was by no means the end of the Japanese challenge. Miura, who had spent the season in Italy with Genoa, slanted in a near-post corner from the left and Japanese captain Ihara got in front of Unsworth to divert the ball into the far corner of the goal with a flick of the head. Almost immediately Miura was sprinting through to clip the outside of a post with Flowers beaten. Then visions of an embarrassing defeat were dispelled by an England winner with a couple of minutes left. Ihara handled Scales' bouncing volley on the goal-line for a red card and David Platt converted the penalty for his quarter-century of England strikes.

England: Flowers, Neville G, Pearce, Batty (McManaman), Scales, Unsworth, Platt, Beardsley (Gascoigne), Shearer, Collymore (Sheringham), Anderton.

Japan: Maekawa, Narahashi, Ihara, Hashiratani, Soma (Yanagimoto), Yamaguchi, Kitazawa, Tasaka, Miura, Nakayama (Kurosaki), Morishima (Fukuda).
Referee: J. Uilenberg (Holland)
Attendance: 21,142

England 3   Sweden 3

8th June 1995, Leeds

In a heart-stopping finish two goals in the final two minutes saved Terry Venables' nine-match unbeaten record as England Coach. A Swedish team missing eight of their World Cup third-placers were seemingly home and dry at 3–1, when Gascoigne made the most telling contribution of his 27 minutes as substitute by curling in a free-kick for his captain to head England back into contention. Seconds later Darren Anderton crashed home an unlikely equaliser with a left-footer that clipped both posts on the way in. It was England's first "home" fixture away from Wembley since 1966 (v Poland at Goodison Park) and the Elland Road crowd saw a remarkable match – and a great escape by England.

It was new cap Colin Cooper, the Nottingham Forest central defender, who was caught in possession in the tenth minute by the darting Larsson in the build-up to Sweden's opening goal. Gudmundson moved into the space behind Barton to slap in a shot that the advancing Flowers beat away. Mild, following up, knocked a soft shot goalwards and it eluded everyone. Mild, who plays his club football for Servette in Switzerland, was in the right place again on 36 minutes as the unhappy Flowers spilled full-back Sundgrun's optimistic low strike from outside the box.

Ravelli, captaining the visitors in his 126th international – beating Shilton's world record – kept England out with his unorthodox acrobatics until Teddy Sheringham swept in his first international goal three minutes before the break. But Sweden caught their hosts cold just 23 seconds into the second half, Andersson controlling the ball on his chest and lobbing it neatly over the stranded Flowers. 3–1 down, it looked all up for England – until that amazing finale.

England: Flowers, Barton, Le Saux, Barnes (Gascoigne), Cooper, Pallister (Scales), Platt, Beardsley (Barmby), Shearer, Sheringham, Anderton.

Sweden: Ravelli, Sundgrun, Lucic, Bjorklund, Kamark, Alexandersson, Erlingmark (Andersson O.), Mild, Gudmundsson, Larsson, Andersson K. (Lidman).
Referee: L. Mottram (Scotland).
Attendance: 32,008.

England 1 Brazil 3

11th June 1995, Wembley

The World Cup holders got their hands on the Umbro Cup too after another wet afternoon at Wembley. There were times in this last match of a very successful summer tournament when England looked to be more than a match for the talented "Boys from Brazil". Graeme Le Saux, an instant hit on the left side of midfield, volleyed in a superb goal on 39 minutes – his first for England – and the home side began the second half in the lead and looking good.

A clumsy challenge by David Batty on the spring-heeled Edmundo turned the course of the match. Roberto Carlos was expected to blast in a shot from the free-kick twenty yards out in a central position, but up stepped the frail-looking Juninho to curl the ball around the wall and a yard inside the left-hand post. Flowers wasn't even close.

Six minutes on, Juninho split the centre of England's defence as wide as Kamark had done for Sweden's third goal at Elland Road. Ronaldo picked up the pass, moved unchallenged into the box and side-stepped Flowers before knocking the ball in. Brazil clinched the win when Stuart Pearce's attempt at intercepting Carlos's boot upfield succeeded only in diverting the ball into Edmundo's path. The finish was unkind – straight through Flowers' legs. It was England's first home defeat for four years.

England: Flowers, Neville G., Pearce, Batty (Gascoigne), Cooper, Scales (Barton), Platt, Le Saux, Shearer, Sheringham (Collymore), Anderton.

Brazil: Zetti, Jorginho, Aldair (Ronaldao), Marcio Santos, Sampaio, Roberto Carlos, Edmundo, Dunga, Ronaldo (Geovanni), Juninho (Leonardo), Zinho.

Referee: P. Pairetto (Italy).

Attendance: 67,318.

Other Umbro Cup results: Brazil 1 Sweden 0, Brazil 3 Japan 0, Sweden 2 Japan 2.

TOULON UNDER-21 TOURNAMENT

England 0 Brazil 2

6th June 1995, Toulon

England lost out to Brazil as they began their defence of the Toulon trophy at the Stade Mayol. Ray Harford's inexperienced team – only the goalkeeper, Dave Watson, and Julian Joachim, up front, had previously played at Under-21 level – found it hard against a Brazilian outfit revealing the sort of form which had taken them to the final of the recent World Youth Championship in Qatar.

Leonardo scored a brilliant solo goal on the stroke of half-time, running past three defenders before shooting home fiercely from a tight angle. Brazil were constantly on the attack in the second period and Leonardo and Caico combined to leave Leandro with a simple header to seal victory.

England: Watson, Neville P., Richards, Ryder, Croft, Hill, Beckham, Holland P., Joachim, Forster, Myers (Allen).

Brazil: Fabio, Bruno, Adriano, Narciso (Carlinhos), Hermes, Pereira, Alemao, Juninho, Caico, Leandro, Leonardo (Bahinio).

Referee: A. Leduc (France)

England 2 Malaysia 0

8th June 1995, Six-Fours

England gave themselves an excellent chance of reaching the semi-finals and perhaps even going all the way to a fifth trophy in six years after beating a poor Malaysian side in the second group fixture.

Only seven minutes had gone when Andy Marshall's goal-kick was nudged on by Brentford's Nick Forster for Julian Joachim to lift the ball over Azram and open his account for the Under-21s in his sixth appearance. Then Andy Myers drove in from the edge of the box for a vital second goal on 31 minutes.

England: Marshall, Neville P., Richards, Casper, Croft, Hill (Couzens), Beckham, Holland P., Joachim, Forster, Myers.

Malaysia: Azram, Zainal, Effendy, Ridzual, Hasnizam, Ching, Idriss, Chandram, Rusdi, Raj, Azrul (Nasaruddin).

Referee: J. Uilenberg (Holland)

England 1 Angola 0

10th June 1995, La Seyne

England, the trophy holders, clinched the runners-up spot in Group B and booked their place in the semi-finals by beating Angola, something of an unknown quantity at international level, in the Stade Scaglia. Brentford's Nick Forster, winning his third cap, grabbed the all-important goal in the 38th minute to give England a date with the host country. He met a cross from talented Manchester United youngster David Beckham with a firm header into the net.

England had been in danger of going out of the tournament after Beckham had missed from the penalty mark. A draw would have taken the Angolans through instead. Forster, a scoring sensation for Brentford in the Second Division after a move from Gillingham, was one of fourteen players in the England squad who had had no previous experience at Under-21 level but he had blossomed as the group had bonded together. Under the circumstances, which included hot and humid conditions, Ray

Harford's England team had done extremely well to make the last four.

England: Davis, Neville P., Richards, Ryder, Croft, Hill, Beckham, Holland P., Joachim, Forster, Couzens (Myers).

Referee: M. Schelings (Belgium).

France 2   England 0

12th June 1995, Cannes

England Under-21s finally relinquished their grip on the trophy as France beat them in the Cannes semi-final. France would now compete for the title with Brazil, the favourites, who had defeated Scotland 4–0. Two second-half goals were just reward for the hosts' superiority against an under-strength England team that had had its best moments early in the game.

Chelsea's Andy Myers came closest to scoring with a volley that flashed inches wide. Barnsley 'keeper David Watson saved superbly on four occasions and, but for his heroics, England's defeat could have been of embarrassing proportions. Coridon fired France ahead on the hour after a scramble in front of goal and Histillole ended any hopes of a late England revival by tapping into an empty net with two minutes left.

France: Fernandez, Toyes, Moulin, Dindeleux, Rott, Dhorasoo, Dacourt, Brando, Pires, Histillole, Coridon (Mendy).

England: Watson, Neville P., Richards, Ryder (Allen), Croft, Hill, Beckham, Holland P. (Couzens), Joachim, Forster, Myers.

Referee: J. Uilenberg (Holland).

Coach and captain.

19 ● ENGLAND'S FULL INTERNATIONAL TEAMS 1946–1995

(Up to and including 11th June 1995)

* captain   † own goal   Small numerals goals scored   Numbers after sub player replaced

Versus	Venue	Result	1	2	3	4	5
1946–47							
Northern Ireland	A	7–2	Swift	Scott	Hardwick*	W Wright	Franklin
Republic of Ireland	A	1–0	Swift	Scott	Hardwick*	W Wright	Franklin
Wales	H	3–0	Swift	Scott	Hardwick*	W Wright	Franklin
Holland	H	8–2	Swift	Scott	Hardwick*	W Wright	Franklin
Scotland	H	1–1	Swift	Scott	Hardwick*	W Wright	Franklin
France	H	3–0	Swift	Scott	Hardwick*	W Wright	Franklin
Switzerland	A	0–1	Swift	Scott	Hardwick*	W Wright	Franklin
Portugal	A	10–0	Swift	Scott	Hardwick*	W Wright	Franklin
1947–48							
Belgium	A	5–2	Swift	Scott	Hardwick*	Ward	Franklin
Wales	A	3–0	Swift	Scott	Hardwick*	P Taylor	Franklin
Northern Ireland	H	2–2	Swift	Scott	Hardwick*	P Taylor	Franklin
Sweden	H	4–2	Swift	Scott	Hardwick*	P Taylor	Franklin
Scotland	A	2–0	Swift	Scott	Hardwick*	W Wright	Franklin
Italy	A	4–0	Swift*	Scott	J Howe	W Wright	Franklin
1948–49							
Denmark	A	0–0	Swift*	Scott	Aston	W Wright	Franklin
Ireland	A	6–2	Swift	Scott	J Howe	W Wright*	Franklin
Wales	H	1–0	Swift	Scott	Aston	Ward	Franklin
Switzerland	H	6–0	Ditchburn	Ramsey	Aston	W Wright*	Franklin
Scotland	H	1–3	Swift	Aston	J Howe	W Wright*	Franklin
Sweden	A	1–3	Ditchburn	Shimwell	Aston	W Wright*	Franklin
Norway	A	4–1	Swift	Ellerington	Aston	W Wright*	Franklin
France	A	3–1	Williams	Ellerington	Aston	W Wright*	Franklin
1949–50							
Republic of Ireland	H	0–2	Williams	Mozley	Aston	W Wright*	Franklin
Wales	A	4–1	Williams	Mozley	Aston	W Wright*	Franklin
Northern Ireland	H	9–2	Streten	Mozley	Aston	Watson	Franklin
Italy	H	2–0	Williams	Ramsey	Aston	Watson	Franklin
Scotland	A	1–0	Williams	Ramsey	Aston	W Wright*	Franklin
Portugal	A	5–3	Williams	Ramsey	Aston	W Wright*	WH Jones
Belgium	A	4–1	Williams	Ramsey	Aston	W Wright*	WH Jones
Chile	N	2–0	Williams	Ramsey	Aston	W Wright*	L Hughes
USA	N	0–1	Williams	Ramsey	Aston	W Wright*	L Hughes
Spain	N	0–1	Williams	Ramsey	Eckersley	W Wright*	L Hughes
1950–51							
Northern Ireland	A	4–1	Williams	Ramsey	Aston	W Wright*[1]	Chilton
Wales	H	4–2	Williams	Ramsey*	L Smith	Watson	L Compton
Yugoslavia	H	2–2	Williams	Ramsey*	Eckersley	Watson	L Compton
Scotland	H	2–3	Williams	Ramsey	Eckersley	Johnston	J Froggatt

6	7	8	9	10	11	Substitutes
Cockburn	Finney[1]	Carter[1]	Lawton[1]	Mannion[1]	Langton[1]	
Cockburn	Finney[1]	Carter	Lawton	Mannion	Langton	
Cockburn	Finney	Carter	Lawton[1]	Mannion[2]	Langton	
Johnston	Finney[1]	Carter[2]	Lawton[4]	Mannion[1]	Langton	
Johnston	S Matthews	Carter[1]	Lawton	Mannion	Mullen	
Lowe	Finney[1]	Carter[1]	Lawton	Mannion[1]	Langton	
Lowe	S Matthews	Carter	Lawton	Mannion	Langton	
Lowe	S Matthews[1]	Mortensen[4]	Lawton[4]	Mannion	Finney[1]	
W Wright	S Matthews	Mortensen[1]	Lawton[2]	Mannion	Finney[2]	
W Wright	S Matthews	Mortensen[1]	Lawton[1]	Mannion	Finney[1]	
W Wright	S Matthews	Mortensen	Lawton[1]	Mannion[1]	Finney	
W Wright	Finney	Mortensen[3]	Lawton[1]	Mannion	Langton	
Cockburn	S Matthews	Mortensen[1]	Lawton	Pearson	Finney[1]	
Cockburn	S Matthews	Mortensen[1]	Lawton[1]	Mannion	Finney[2]	
Cockburn	S Matthews	Hagan	Lawton	Shackleton	Langton	
Cockburn	S Matthews[1]	Mortensen[3]	Milburn[1]	Pearson[1]	Finney	
W Wright*	S Matthews	Mortensen	Milburn	Shackleton	Finney[1]	
Cockburn	S Matthews	J Rowley[1]	Milburn[1]	Haines[2]	Hancocks[2]	
Cockburn	S Matthews	Mortensen	Milburn[1]	Pearson	Finney	
Cockburn	Finney[1]	Mortensen	Bentley	J Rowley	Langton	
Dickinson	Finney[1]	Morris[1]	Mortensen	Mannion	Mullen[1]	†
Dickinson	Finney	Morris[2]	J Rowley[1]	Mannion	Mullen	
Dickinson	P Harris	Morris	Pye	Mannion	Finney	
Dickinson	Finney	Mortensen[1]	Milburn[3]	Shackleton	Hancocks	
W Wright*	Finney	Mortensen[2]	J Rowley[4]	Pearson[2]	J Froggatt[1]	
W Wright*[1]	Finney	Mortensen	J Rowley[1]	Pearson	J Froggatt	
Dickinson	Finney	Mannion	Mortensen	Bentley[1]	Langton	
Dickinson	Milburn	Mortensen[1]	Bentley	Mannion	Finney[4]	
Dickinson	Milburn	Mortensen[1]	Bentley[1]	Mannion[1]	Finney	Mullen 7[1]
Dickinson	Finney	Mannion[1]	Bentley	Mortensen[1]	Mullen	
Dickinson	Finney	Mannion	Bentley	Mortensen	Mullen	
Dickinson	S Matthews	Mortensen	Milburn	E Baily	Finney	
Dickinson	S Matthews	Mannion	J Lee[1]	E Baily[2]	Langton	
Dickinson	Finney	Mannion[1]	Milburn[1]	E Baily[2]	Medley	
Dickinson	Hancocks	Mannion	Lofthouse[2]	E Baily	Medley	
W Wright*	S Matthews	Mannion	Mortensen	Hassall[1]	Finney[1]	

*captain † own goal Small numerals goals scored Numbers after sub player replaced

Versus	Venue	Result	1	2	3	4	5
Argentina	H	2–1	Williams	Ramsey	Eckersley	W Wright*	J Taylor
Portugal	H	5–2	Williams	Ramsey*	Eckersley	Nicholson[1]	J Taylor

1951–52

Versus	Venue	Result	1	2	3	4	5
France	H	2–2	Williams	Ramsey	Willis	W Wright*	Chilton
Wales	A	1–1	Williams	Ramsey	L Smith	W Wright*	Barrass
Northern Ireland	H	2–0	Merrick	Ramsey	L Smith	W Wright*	Barrass
Austria	H	2–2	Merrick	Ramsey[1]	Eckersley	W Wright*	J Froggatt
Scotland	A	2–1	Merrick	Ramsey	Garrett	W Wright*	J Froggatt
Italy	A	1–1	Merrick	Ramsey	Garrett	W Wright*	J Froggatt
Austria	A	3–2	Merrick	Ramsey	Eckersley	W Wright*	J Froggatt
Switzerland	A	3–0	Merrick	Ramsey	Eckersley	W Wright*	J Froggart

1952–53

Versus	Venue	Result	1	2	3	4	5
Northern Ireland	A	2–2	Merrick	Ramsey	Eckersley	W Wright*	J Froggatt
Wales	H	5–2	Merrick	Ramsey	I. Smith	W Wright*	J Froggatt[1]
Belgium	H	5–0	Merrick	Ramsey	L Smith	W Wright*	J Froggatt
Scotland	H	2–2	Merrick	Ramsey	L Smith	W Wright*	Barrass
Argentina	A	0–0	Merrick	Ramsey	Eckersley	W Wright*	Johnston
Chile	A	2–1	Merrick	Ramsey	Eckersley	W Wright*	Johnston
Uruguay	A	1–2	Merrick	Ramsey	Eckersley	W Wright*	Johnston
USA	A	6–3	Ditchburn	Ramsey	Eckersley	W Wright*	Johnston

1953–54

Versus	Venue	Result	1	2	3	4	5
Wales	A	4–1	Merrick	Garrett	Eckersley	W Wright*	Johnston
FIFA	H	4–4	Merrick	Ramsey[1]	Eckersley	W Wright*	Ufton
Ireland	H	3–1	Merrick	Rickaby	Eckersley	W Wright*	Johnston
Hungary	H	3–6	Merrick	Ramsey[1]	Eckersley	W Wright*	Johnston
Scotland	A	4–2	Merrick	Staniforth	R Byrne	W Wright*	H Clarke
Yugoslavia	A	0–1	Merrick	Staniforth	R Byrne	W Wright*	Owen
Hungary	A	1–7	Merrick	Staniforth	R Byrne	W Wright*	Owen
Belgium	N	4–4	Merrick	Staniforth	R Byrne	W Wright*	Owen
Switzerland	N	2–0	Merrick	Staniforth	R Byrne	McGarry	W Wright*
Uruguay	N	2–4	Merrick	Staniforth	R Byrne	McGarry	W Wright*

1954–55

Versus	Venue	Result	1	2	3	4	5
Northern Ireland	A	2–0	Wood	Foulkes	R Byrne	Wheeler	W Wright*
Wales	H	3–2	Wood	Staniforth	R Byrne	Phillips	W Wright*
West Germany	H	3–1	Williams	Staniforth	R Byrne	Phillips	W Wright*
Scotland	H	7–2	Williams	Meadows	R Byrne	Armstrong	W Wright*
France	A	0–1	Williams	P Sillett	R Byrne	Flowers	W Wright*
Spain	A	1–1	Williams	P Sillett	R Byrne	Dickinson	W Wright*
Portugal	A	1–3	Williams	P Sillett	R Byrne	Dickinson	W Wright*

1955–56

Versus	Venue	Result	1	2	3	4	5
Denmark	A	5–1	Baynham	Hall	R Byrne	McGarry	W Wright*
Wales	A	1–2	Williams	Hall	R Byrne	McGarry	W Wright*
Northern Ireland	H	3–0	Baynham	Hall	R Byrne	Clayton	W Wright*
Spain	H	4–1	Baynham	Hall	R Byrne	Clayton	W Wright*
Scotland	A	1–1	R Matthews	Hall	R Byrne	Dickinson	W Wright*
Brazil	H	4–2	R Matthews	Hall	R Byrne	Clayton	W Wright*
Sweden	A	0–0	R Matthews	Hall	R Byrne	Clayton	W Wright*
Finland	A	5–1	Wood	Hall	R Byrne	Clayton	W Wright*
West Germany	A	3–1	R Matthews	Hall	R Byrne	Clayton	W Wright*

6	7	8	9	10	11	*Substitutes*
Cockburn	Finney	Mortensen[1]	Milburn[1]	Hassall	Metcalfe	
Cockburn	Finney[1]	Pearson	Milburn[2]	Hassall[1]	Metcalfe	
Cockburn	Finney	Mannion	Milburn	Hassall	Medley[1]	†
Dickinson	Finney	T Thompson	Lofthouse	E Baily[1]	Medley	
Dickinson	Finney	Sewell	Lofthouse[2]	Phillips	Medley	
Dickinson	Milton	Broadis	Lofthouse[1]	E Baily	Medley	
Dickinson	Finney	Broadis	Lofthouse	Pearson[2]	J Rowley	
Dickinson	Finney	Broadis[1]	Lofthouse	Pearson	Elliott	
Dickinson	Finney	Sewell[1]	Lofthouse[2]	E Baily	Elliott	
Dickinson	R Allen	Sewell[1]	Lofthouse[2]	E Baily	Finney	
Dickinson	Finney	Sewell	Lofthouse[1]	E Baily	Elliott[1]	
Dickinson	Finney[1]	R Froggatt	Lofthouse[2]	Bentley[1]	Elliott	
Dickinson	Finney	Bentley	Lofthouse[2]	R Froggatt[1]	Elliott[2]	
Dickinson	Finney	Broadis[2]	Lofthouse	R Froggatt	J Froggatt	
Dickinson	Finney	Broadis	Lofthouse	T Taylor	Berry	
Dickinson	Finney	Broadis	Lofthouse[1]	T Taylor[1]	Berry	
Dickinson	Finney	Broadis	Lofthouse	T Taylor[1]	Berry	
Dickinson	Finney[2]	Broadis[1]	Lofthouse[2]	R Froggatt[1]	J Froggatt	
Dickinson	Finney	Quixall	Lofthouse[2]	Wilshaw[2]	Mullen	
Dickinson	S Matthews	Mortensen[1]	Lofthouse	Quixall	Mullen[2]	
Dickinson	S Matthews	Quixall	Lofthouse[1]	Hassall[2]	Mullen	
Dickinson	S Matthews	E Taylor	Mortensen[1]	Sewell[1]	Robb	
Dickinson	Finney	Broadis[1]	R Allen[1]	Nicholls[1]	Mullen[1]	
Dickinson	Finney	Broadis	R Allen	Nicholls	Mullen	
Dickinson	P Harris	Sewell	Jezzard	Broadis[1]	Finney	
Dickinson	S Matthews	Broadis[2]	Lofthouse[2]	T Taylor	Finney	
Dickinson	Finney	Broadis	T Taylor	Wilshaw[1]	Mullen[1]	
Dickinson	S Matthews	Broadis	Lofthouse[1]	Wilshaw	Finney[1]	
Barlow	S Matthews	Revie[1]	Lofthouse	Haynes[1]	Pilkington	
Slater	S Matthews	Bentley[3]	R Allen	Shackleton	Blunstone	
Slater	S Matthews	Bentley[1]	R Allen[1]	Shackleton[1]	Finney	
Edwards	S Matthews	Revie[1]	Lofthouse[2]	Wilshaw[4]	Blunstone	
Edwards	S Matthews	Revie	Lofthouse	Wilshaw	Blunstone	
Edwards	S Matthews	Bentley[1]	Lofthouse	Quixall	Wilshaw	
Edwards	S Matthews	Bentley[1]	Lofthouse	Wilshaw	Blunstone	Quixall 9
Dickinson	Milburn	Revie[2]	Lofthouse[2]	Bradford[1]	Finney	
Dickinson	S Matthews	Revie	Lofthouse	Wilshaw	Finney	†
Dickinson	Finney[1]	Haynes	Jezzard	Wilshaw[2]	Perry	
Dickinson	Finney[1]	Atyeo[1]	Lofthouse	Haynes	Perry[2]	
Edwards	Finney	T Taylor	Lofthouse	Haynes[1]	Perry	
Edwards	S Matthews	Atyeo	T Taylor[2]	Haynes	Grainger[2]	
Edwards	Berry	Atyeo	T Taylor	Haynes	Grainger	
Edwards	Astall[1]	Haynes[1]	T Taylor	Wilshaw[1]	Grainger	Lofthouse 9[2]
Edwards[1]	Astall	Haynes[1]	T Taylor	Wilshaw	Grainger[1]	

● 51

Versus	Venue	Result	1	2	3	4	5
1956–57							
Northern Ireland	A	1–1	R Matthews	Hall	R Byrne	Clayton	W Wright*
Wales	H	3–1	Ditchburn	Hall	R Byrne	Clayton	W Wright*
Yugoslavia	H	3–0	Ditchburn	Hall	R Byrne	Clayton	W Wright*
Denmark	H	5–2	Ditchburn	Hall	R Byrne	Clayton	W Wright*
Scotland	H	2–1	Hodgkinson	Hall	R Byrne	Clayton	W Wright*
Republic of Ireland	H	5–1	Hodgkinson	Hall	R Byrne	Clayton	W Wright*
Denmark	A	4–1	Hodgkinson	Hall	R Byrne	Clayton	W Wright*
Republic of Ireland	A	1–1	Hodgkinson	Hall	R Byrne	Clayton	W Wright*
1957–58							
Wales	A	4–0	Hopkinson	D Howe	R Byrne	Clayton	W Wright*
Northern Ireland	H	2–3	Hopkinson	D Howe	R Byrne	Clayton	W Wright*
France	H	4–0	Hopkinson	D Howe	R Byrne	Clayton	W Wright*
Scotland	A	4–0	Hopkinson	D Howe	Langley	Clayton	W Wright*
Portugal	H	2–1	Hopkinson	D Howe	Langley	Clayton	W Wright*
Yugoslavia	A	0–5	Hopkinson	D Howe	Langley	Clayton	W Wright*
USSR	A	1–1	McDonald	D Howe	T Banks	Clamp	W Wright*
USSR	N	2–2	McDonald	D Howe	T Banks	Clamp	W Wright*
Brazil	N	0–0	McDonald	D Howe	T Banks	Clamp	W Wright*
Austria	N	2–2	McDonald	D Howe	T Banks	Clamp	W Wright*
USSR	N	0–1	McDonald	D Howe	T Banks	Clayton	W Wright*
1958–59							
Northern Ireland	A	3–3	McDonald	D Howe	T Banks	Clayton	W Wright*
USSR	H	5–0	McDonald	D Howe	G Shaw	Clayton	W Wright*
Wales	H	2–2	McDonald	D Howe	G Shaw	Clayton	W Wright*
Scotland	H	1–0	Hopkinson	D Howe	G Shaw	Clayton	W Wright*
Italy	H	2–2	Hopkinson	D Howe	G Shaw	Clayton	W Wright*
Brazil	A	0–2	Hopkinson	D Howe	Armfield	Clayton	W Wright*
Peru	A	1–4	Hopkinson	D Howe	Armfield	Clayton	W Wright*
Mexico	A	1–2	Hopkinson	D Howe	Armfield	Clayton	W Wright*
USA	A	8–1	Hopkinson	D Howe	Armfield	Clayton	W Wright*
1959–60							
Wales	A	1–1	Hopkinson	D Howe	A Allen	Clayton*	T Smith
Sweden	H	2–3	Hopkinson	D Howe	A Allen	Clayton*	T Smith
Northern Ireland	H	2–1	R Springett	D Howe	A Allen	Clayton*	Brown
Scotland	A	1–1	R Springett	Armfield	Wilson	Clayton*	Slater
Yugoslavia	H	3–3	R Springett	Armfield	Wilson	Clayton*	Swan
Spain	A	0–3	R Springett	Armfield	Wilson	R Robson	Swan
Hungary	A	0–2	R Springett	Armfield	Wilson	R Robson	Swan
1960–61							
Northern Ireland	A	5–2	R Springett	Armfield	McNeil	R Robson	Swan
Luxembourg	A	9–0	R Springett	Armfield	McNeil	R Robson	Swan
Spain	H	4–2	R Springett	Armfield	McNeil	R Robson	Swan
Wales	H	5–1	Hodgkinson	Armfield	McNeil	R Robson	Swan
Scotland	H	9–3	R Springett	Armfield	McNeil	R Robson[1]	Swan
Mexico	H	8–0	R Springett	Armfield	McNeil	R Robson[1]	Swan
Portugal	A	1–1	R Springett	Armfield	McNeil	R Robson	Swan
Italy	A	3–2	R Springett	Armfield	McNeil	R Robson	Swan
Austria	A	1–3	R Springett	Armfield	Angus	Miller	Swan
1961–62							
Luxembourg	H	4–1	R Springett	Armfield*	McNeil	R Robson	Swan

6	7	8	9	10	11	*Substitutes*
Edwards	S Matthews[1]	Revie	T Taylor	Wilshaw	Grainger	
Dickinson	S Matthews[1]	Brooks[1]	Finney[1]	Haynes[1]	Grainger	
Dickinson	S Matthews[1]	Brooks[1]	Finney	Haynes	Blunstone	T Taylor 10[2]
Dickinson	S Matthews	Brooks	T Taylor[3]	Edwards[2]	Finney	
Edwards[1]	S Matthews	T Thompson	Finney	Kevan[1]	Grainger	
Edwards	S Matthews	Atyeo[2]	T Taylor[3]	Haynes	Finney	
Edwards	S Matthews	Atyeo[1]	T Taylor[2]	Haynes[1]	Finney	
Edwards	Finney	Atyeo[1]	T Taylor	Haynes	Pegg	
Edwards	Douglas	Kevan	T Taylor	Haynes[2]	Finney[1]	†
Edwards[1]	Douglas	Kevan	T Taylor	Haynes	A'Court[1]	
Edwards	Douglas	R Robson[2]	T Taylor[2]	Haynes	Finney	
Slater	Douglas[1]	R Charlton[1]	Kevan[2]	Haynes	Finney	
Slater	Douglas	R Charlton[2]	Kevan	Haynes	Finney	
Slater	Douglas	R Charlton	Kevan	Haynes	Finney	
Slater	Douglas	R Robson	Kevan[1]	Haynes	Finney	
Slater	Douglas	R Robson	Kevan[1]	Haynes	Finney[1]	
Slater	Douglas	R Robson	Kevan	Haynes	A'Court	
Slater	Douglas	R Robson	Kevan[1]	Haynes[1]	A'Court	
Slater	Brabrook	Broadbent	Kevan	Haynes	A'Court	
McGuinness	Brabrook	Broadbent	R Charlton[2]	Haynes	Finney[1]	
Slater	Douglas	R Charlton[1]	Lofthouse[1]	Haynes[3]	Finney	
Flowers	Clapton	Broadbent[2]	Lofthouse	Haynes	A'Court	
Flowers	Douglas	Broadbent	R Charlton[1]	Haynes	Holden	
Flowers	Bradley[1]	Broadbent	R Charlton[1]	Haynes	Holden	
Flowers	Deeley	Broadbent	R Charlton	Haynes	Holden	
Flowers	Deeley	Greaves[1]	R Charlton	Haynes	Holden	
McGuinness	Holden	Greaves	Kevan[1]	Haynes	R Charlton	Flowers 6, Bradley 7
Flowers[2]	Bradley[1]	Greaves	Kevan[1]	Haynes[1]	R Charlton[3]	
Flowers	Connelly	Greaves[1]	Clough	R Charlton	Holiday	
Flowers	Connelly[1]	Greaves	Clough	R Charlton[1]	Holliday	
Flowers	Connelly	Haynes	Baker[1]	Parry[1]	Holliday	
Flowers	Connelly	Broadbent	Baker	Parry	R Charlton[1]	
Flowers	Douglas[1]	Haynes[1]	Baker	Greaves[1]	R Charlton	
Flowers	Brabrook	Haynes*	Baker	Greaves	R Charlton	
Flowers	Douglas	Haynes*	Baker	Viollet	R Charlton	
Flowers	Douglas[1]	Greaves[2]	R Smith[1]	Haynes*	R Charlton[1]	
Flowers	Douglas	Greaves[3]	R Smith[2]	Haynes*[1]	R Charlton[3]	
Flowers	Douglas[1]	Greaves[1]	R Smith[2]	Haynes*	R Charlton	
Flowers	Douglas	Greaves[2]	R Smith[1]	Haynes*[1]	R Charlton[1]	
Flowers	Douglas[1]	Greaves[3]	R Smith[2]	Haynes*[2]	R Charlton	
Flowers[1]	Douglas[2]	Kevan	Hitchens[1]	Haynes*	R Charlton[3]	
Flowers[1]	Douglas	Greaves	R Smith	Haynes*	R Charlton	
Flowers	Douglas	Greaves[1]	Hitchens[2]	Haynes*	R Charlton	
Flowers	Douglas	Greaves[1]	Hitchens	Haynes*	R Charlton	
Flowers	Douglas	Fantham	Pointer[1]	Viollet[1]	R Charlton[2]	

Versus	Venue	Result	1	2	3	4	5
Wales	A	1–1	R Springett	Armfield	Wilson	R Robson	Swan
Portugal	H	2–0	R Springett	Armfield	Wilson	R Robson	Swan
Northern Ireland	H	1–1	R Springett	Armfield	Wilson	R Robson	Swan
Austria	H	3–1	R Springett	Armfield	Wilson	Anderson	Swan
Scotland	A	0–2	R Springett	Armfield	Wilson	Anderson	Swan
Switzerland	H	3–1	R Springett	Armfield	Wilson	R Robson	Swan
Peru	A	4–0	R Springett	Armfield	Wilson	Moore	Norman
Hungary	N	1–2	R Springett	Armfield	Wilson	Moore	Norman
Argentina	N	3–1	R Springett	Armfield	Wilson	Moore	Norman
Bulgaria	N	0–0	R Springett	Armfield	Wilson	Moore	Norman
Brazil	N	1–3	R Springett	Armfield	Wilson	Moore	Norman
1962–63							
France	H	1–1	R Springett	Armfield*	Wilson	Moore	Norman
Northern Ireland	A	3–1	R Springett	Armfield*	Wilson	Moore	Labone
Wales	H	4–0	R Springett	Armfield*	G Shaw	Moore	Labone
France	A	2–5	R Springett	Armfield*	Henry	Moore	Labone
Scotland	H	1–2	G Banks	Armfield*	G Byrne	Moore	Norman
Brazil	H	1–1	G Banks	Armfield*	Wilson	Milne	Norman
Czechoslovakia	A	4–2	G Banks	Shellito	Wilson	Milne	Norman
East Germany	A	2–1	G Banks	Armfield*	Wilson	Milne	Norman
Switzerland	A	8–1	R Springett	Armfield*	Wilson	Kay[1]	Moore
1963–64							
Wales	A	4–0	G Banks	Armfield*	Wilson	Milne	Norman
Rest of the World	H	2–1	G Banks	Armfield*	Wilson	Milne	Norman
Northern Ireland	H	8–3	G Banks	Armfield*	R Thomson	Milne	Norman
Scotland	A	0–1	G Banks	Armfield*	Wilson	Milne	Norman
Uruguay	H	2–1	G Banks	Cohen	Wilson	Milne	Norman
Portugal	A	4–3	G Banks	Cohen	Wilson	Milne	Norman
Republic of Ireland	A	3–1	Waiters	Cohen	Wilson	Milne	Flowers
USA	A	10–0	G Banks	Cohen	R Thomson	M Bailey	Norman
Brazil	A	1–5	Waiters	Cohen	Wilson	Milne	Norman
Portugal	N	1–1	G Banks	R Thomson	Wilson	Flowers	Norman
Argentina	N	0–1	G Banks	R Thomson	Wilson	Milne	Norman
1964–65							
Northern Ireland	A	4–3	G Banks	Cohen	R Thomson	Milne	Norman
Belgium	H	2–2	Waiters	Cohen	R Thomson	Milne	Norman
Wales	H	2–1	Waiters	Cohen	R Thomson	M Bailey	Flowers*
Holland	A	1–1	Waiters	Cohen	R Thomson	Mullery	Norman
Scotland	H	2–2	G Banks	Cohen	Wilson	Stiles	J Charlton
Hungary	H	1–0	G Banks	Cohen	Wilson	Stiles	J Charlton
Yugoslavia	A	1–1	G Banks	Cohen	Wilson	Stiles	J Charlton
West Germany	A	1–0	G Banks	Cohen	Wilson	Flowers	J Charlton
Sweden	A	2–1	G Banks	Cohen	Wilson	Stiles	J Charlton
1965–66							
Wales	A	0–0	R Springett	Cohen	Wilson	Stiles	J Charlton
Austria	H	2–3	R Springett	Cohen	Wilson	Stiles	J Charlton
Northern Ireland	H	2–1	G Banks	Cohen	Wilson	Stiles	J Charlton
Spain	A	2–0	G Banks	Cohen	Wilson	Stiles	J Charlton
Poland	H	1–1	G Banks	Cohen	Wilson	Stiles	J Charlton
West Germany	H	1–0	G Banks	Cohen	K Newton	Moore*	J Charlton
Scotland	A	4–3	G Banks	Cohen	K Newton	Stiles	J Charlton
Yugoslavia	H	2–0	G Banks	Armfield*	Wilson	Peters	J Charlton

6	7	8	9	10	11	Substitutes
Flowers	Connelly	Douglas[1]	Pointer	Haynes*	R Charlton	
Flowers	Connelly[1]	Douglas	Pointer[1]	Haynes*	R Charlton	
Flowers	Douglas	J Byrne	Crawford	Haynes*	R Charlton[1]	
Flowers[1]	Connelly	Hunt[1]	Crawford[1]	Haynes*	R Charlton	
Flowers	Douglas	Greaves	R Smith	Haynes*	R Charlton	
Flowers[1]	Connelly[1]	Greaves	Hitchens[1]	Haynes*	R Charlton	
Flowers[1]	Douglas	Greaves[3]	Hitchens	Haynes*	R Charlton	
Flowers[1]	Douglas	Greaves	Hitchens	Haynes*	R Charlton	
Flowers[1]	Douglas	Greaves[1]	Peacock	Haynes*	R Charlton[1]	
Flowers	Douglas	Greaves	Peacock	Haynes*	R Charlton	
Flowers	Douglas	Greaves	Hitchens[1]	Haynes*	R Charlton	
Flowers[1]	Hellawell	Crowe	Charnley	Greaves	A Hinton	
Flowers	Hellawell	F Hill	Peacock	Greaves[1]	O'Grady[2]	
Flowers	Connelly[1]	F Hill	Peacock[2]	Greaves[1]	Tambling	
Flowers	Connelly	Tambling[1]	R Smith[1]	Greaves	R Charlton	
Flowers	Douglas[1]	Greaves	R Smith	Melia	R Charlton	
Moore	Douglas[1]	Greaves	R Smith	Eastham	R Charlton	
Moore*	Paine	Greaves[2]	R Smith[1]	Eastham	R Charlton[1]	
Moore	Paine	Hunt[1]	R Smith	Eastham	R Charlton[1]	
Flowers	Douglas[1]	Greaves	J Byrne[2]	Melia[1]	R Charlton[3]	
Moore	Paine	Greaves[1]	R Smith[2]	Eastham	R Charlton[1]	
Moore	Paine[1]	Greaves[1]	R Smith	Eastham	R Charlton	
Moore	Paine[3]	Greaves[4]	R Smith[1]	Eastham	R Charlton	
Moore	Paine	Hunt	J Byrne	Eastham	R Charlton	
Moore*	Paine	Greaves	J Byrne[2]	Eastham	R Charlton	
Moore*	P Thompson	Greaves	J Byrne[3]	Eastham	R Charlton[1]	
Moore*	P Thompson	Greaves[1]	J Byrne[1]	Eastham[1]	R Charlton	
Flowers*	Paine[2]	Hunt[4]	Pickering[3]	Eastham	P Thompson	R Charlton 10[1]
Moore*	P Thompson	Greaves[1]	J Byrne	Eastham	R Charlton	
Moore*	Paine	Greaves	J Byrne	Hunt[1]	P Thompson	
Moore*	P Thompson	Greaves*	J Byrne	Eastham	R Charlton	
Moore*	Paine	Greaves[3]	Pickering[1]	R Charlton	P Thompson	
Moore*	P Thompson	Greaves	Pickering[1]	Venables	A Hinton	†
Young	P Thompson	Hunt	Wignall[2]	J Byrne	A Hinton	
Flowers*	P Thompson	Greaves[1]	Wignall	Venables	R Charlton	
Moore*	P Thompson	Greaves[1]	Bridges	J Byrne	R Charlton[1]	
Moore*	Paine	Greaves[1]	Bridges	Eastham	Connelly	
Moore*	Paine	Greaves	Bridges[1]	Ball	Connelly	
Moore*	Paine[1]	Ball	M Jones	Eastham	Temple	
Moore*	Paine	Ball[1]	M Jones	Eastham	Connelly[1]	
Moore*	Paine	Greaves	Peacock	R Charlton	Connelly	
Moore*	Paine	Greaves	Bridges	R Charlton[1]	Connelly[1]	
Moore*	P Thompson	Baker[1]	Peacock[1]	R Charlton	Connelly	
Moore*	Ball	Hunt[1]	Baker[1]	Eastham	R Charlton	Hunter 9
Moore*[1]	Ball	Hunt	Baker	Eastham	G Harris	
Hunter	Ball	Hunt	Stiles[1]	G Hurst	R Charlton	Wilson 3
Moore*	Ball	Hunt[2]	R Charlton[1]	G Hurst[1]	Connelly	
Hunter	Paine	Greaves[1]	R Charlton[1]	G Hurst	Tambling	

Versus	Venue	Result	1	2	3	4	5
Finland	A	3–0	G Banks	Armfield*	Wilson	Peters[1]	J Charlton[1]
Norway	A	6–1	R Springett	Cohen	G Byrne	Stiles	Flowers
Denmark	A	2–0	Bonetti	Cohen	Wilson	Stiles	J Charlton[1]
Poland	A	1–0	G Banks	Cohen	Wilson	Stiles	J Charlton
Uruguay	H	0–0	G Banks	Cohen	Wilson	Stiles	J Charlton
Mexico	H	2–0	G Banks	Cohen	Wilson	Stiles	J Charlton
France	H	2–0	G Banks	Cohen	Wilson	Stiles	J Charlton
Argentina	H	1–0	G Banks	Cohen	Wilson	Stiles	J Charlton
Portugal	H	2–1	G Banks	Cohen	Wilson	Stiles	J Charlton
West Germany	H	4–2	G Banks	Cohen	Wilson	Stiles	J Charlton

1966–67

Versus	Venue	Result	1	2	3	4	5
Northern Ireland	A	2–0	G Banks	Cohen	Wilson	Stiles	J Charlton
Czechoslovakia	H	0–0	G Banks	Cohen	Wilson	Stiles	J Charlton
Wales	H	5–1	G Banks	Cohen	Wilson	Stiles	J Charlton[1]
Scotland	H	2–3	G Banks	Cohen	Wilson	Stiles	J Charlton[1]
Spain	H	2–0	Bonetti	Cohen	K Newton	Mullery	Labone
Austria	A	1–0	Bonetti	K Newton	Wilson	Mullery	Labone

1967–68

Versus	Venue	Result	1	2	3	4	5
Wales	A	3–0	G Banks	Cohen	K Newton	Mullery	J Charlton
Northern Ireland	H	2–0	G Banks	Cohen	Wilson	Mullery	Sadler
USSR	H	2–2	G Banks	C Knowles	Wilson	Mullery	Sadler
Scotland	A	1–1	G Banks	K Newton	Wilson	Mullery	Labone
Spain	H	1–0	G Banks	C Knowles	Wilson	Mullery	J Charlton
Spain	A	2–1	Bonetti	K Newton	Wilson	Mullery	Labone
Sweden	H	3–1	Stepney	K Newton	C Knowles	Mullery	Labone
West Germany	A	0–1	G Banks	K Newton	C Knowles	Hunter	Labone
Yugoslavia	N	0–1	G Banks	K Newton	Wilson	Mullery	Labone
USSR	N	2–0	G Banks	T Wright	Wilson	Stiles	Labone

1968–69

Versus	Venue	Result	1	2	3	4	5
Romania	A	0–0	G Banks	T Wright	K Newton	Mullery	Labone
Bulgaria	H	1–1	West	K Newton	McNab	Mullery	Labone
Romania	H	1–1	G Banks	T Wright	McNab	Stiles	J Charlton[1]
France	H	5–0	G Banks	K Newton	Cooper	Mullery	J Charlton
Northern Ireland	A	3–1	G Banks	K Newton	McNab	Mullery	Labone
Wales	H	2–1	West	K Newton	Cooper	Moore*	J Charlton
Scotland	H	4–1	G Banks	K Newton	Cooper	Mullery	Labone
Mexico	A	0–0	West	K Newton	Cooper	Mullery	Labone
Uruguay	A	2–1	G Banks	T Wright	K Newton	Mullery	Labone
Brazil	A	1–2	G Banks	T Wright	K Newton	Mullery	Labone

1969–70

Versus	Venue	Result	1	2	3	4	5
Holland	A	1–0	Bonetti	T Wright	E Hughes	Mullery	J Charlton
Portugal	H	1–0	Bonetti	Reaney	E Hughes	Mullery	J Charlton[1]
Holland	H	0–0	G Banks	K Newton	Cooper	Peters	J Charlton
Belgium	A	3–1	G Banks	T Wright	Cooper	Moore*	Labone
Wales	A	1–1	G Banks	T Wright	E Hughes	Mullery	Labone
Northern Ireland	H	3–1	G Banks	K Newton	E Hughes	Mullery	Moore*
Scotland	A	0–0	G Banks	K Newton	E Hughes	Stiles	Labone
Colombia	A	4–0	G Banks	K Newton	Cooper	Mullery	Labone
Ecuador	A	2–0	G Banks	K Newton	Cooper	Mullery	Labone
Romania	N	1–0	G Banks	K Newton	Cooper	Mullery	Labone
Brazil	N	0–1	G Banks	T Wright	Cooper	Mullery	Labone
Czechoslovakia	N	1–0	G Banks	K Newton	Cooper	Mullery	J Charlton

6	7	8	9	10	11	Substitutes
Hunter	Callaghan	Hunt[1]	R Charlton	G Hurst	Ball	
Moore*[1]	Paine	Greaves[4]	R Charlton	Hunt	Connelly[1]	
Moore*	Ball	Greaves	G Hurst	Eastham[1]	Connelly	
Moore*	Ball	Greaves	R Charlton	Hunt[1]	Peters	
Moore*	Ball	Greaves	R Charlton	Hunt	Connelly	
Moore*	Paine	Greaves	R Charlton[1]	Hunt[1]	Peters	
Moore*	Callaghan	Greaves	R Charlton	Hunt[2]	Peters	
Moore*	Ball	G Hurst[1]	R Charlton	Hunt	Peters	
Moore*	Ball	G Hurst	R Charlton[2]	Hunt	Peters	
Moore*	Ball	G Hurst[3]	R Charlton	Hunt	Peters[1]	
Moore*	Ball	G Hurst	R Charlton	Hunt[1]	Peters[1]	
Moore*	Ball	G Hurst	R Charlton	Hunt	Peters	
Moore*	Ball	G Hurst[2]	R Charlton[1]	Hunt	Peters	†
Moore*	Ball	Greaves	R Charlton[1]	G Hurst[1]	Peters	
Moore*	Ball	Greaves[1]	G Hurst	Hunt[1]	Hollins	
Moore*	Ball[1]	Greaves	G Hurst	Hunt	Hunter	
Moore*	Ball[1]	Hunt	R Charlton[1]	G Hurst	Peters[1]	
Moore*	P Thompson	Hunt	R Charlton[1]	G Hurst[1]	Peters	
Moore*	Ball[1]	Hunt	R Charlton	G Hurst	Peters[1]	
Moore*	Ball	G Hurst	Summerbee	R Charlton	Peters[1]	
Moore*	Ball	Hunt	Summerbee	R Charlton[1]	Peters	
Moore*	Ball	Peters[1]	R Charlton	Hunt	Hunter[1]	
Moore*	Bell	Peters[1]	R Charlton[1]	Hunt[1]	Hunter	G Hurst 9
Moore*	Ball	Bell	Summerbee	G Hurst	P Thompson	
Moore*	Ball	Peters	R Charlton	Hunt	Hunter	
Moore*	Hunter	Hunt	R Charlton[1]	G Hurst[1]	Peters	
Moore*	Ball	Hunt	R Charlton	G Hurst	Peters	McNab 2
Moore*	F Lee	Bell	R Charlton	G Hurst[1]	Peters	Reaney 2
Hunter	Radford	Hunt	R Charlton*	G Hurst	Ball	
Moore*	F Lee[1]	Bell	G Hurst[3]	Peters	O'Grady[1]	
Moore*	Ball	F Lee[1]	R Charlton	G Hurst[1]	Peters[1]	
Hunter	F Lee[1]	Bell	Astle	R Charlton[1]	Ball	
Moore*	F Lee	Ball	R Charlton	G Hurst[2]	Peters[2]	
Moore*	F Lee	Ball	R Charlton	G Hurst	Peters	T Wright 2
Moore*	F Lee[1]	Bell	G Hurst[1]	Ball	Peters	
Moore*	Ball	Bell[1]	R Charlton	G Hurst	Peters	
Moore*	F Lee	Bell[1]	R Charlton	G Hurst	Peters	P Thompson 7
Moore*	F Lee	Bell	Astle	R Charlton	Ball	Peters 8
Hunter	F Lee	Bell	M Jones	R Charlton*	Storey-Moore	Mullery 7, G Hurst 9
E Hughes	F Lee	Ball[2]	Osgood	G Hurst[1]	Peters	
Moore*	F Lee[1]	Ball	R Charlton	G Hurst	Peters	
Stiles	Coates	Kidd	R Charlton[1]	G Hurst[1]	Peters[1]	Bell 2
Moore*	P Thompson	Ball	Astle	G Hurst	Peters	Mullery 7
Moore*	F Lee	Ball[1]	R Charlton[1]	G Hurst	Peters[2]	
Moore*	F Lee[1]	Ball	R Charlton	G Hurst	Peters	Kidd 7[1], Sadler 9
Moore*	F Lee	Ball	R Charlton	G Hurst[1]	Peters	T Wright 2, Osgood 7
Moore*	F Lee	Ball	R Charlton	G Hurst	Peters	Astle 7, Bell 9
Moore*	Bell	R Charlton	Astle	A Clarke[1]	Peters	Ball 8, Osgood 10

Versus	Venue	Result	1	2	3	4	5
West Germany	N	2–3	Bonetti	K Newton	Cooper	Mullery[1]	Labone

1970–71

Versus	Venue	Result	1	2	3	4	5
East Germany	H	3–1	Shilton	E Hughes	Cooper	Mullery	Sadler
Malta	A	1–0	G Banks	Reaney	E Hughes	Mullery*	McFarland
Greece	H	3–0	G Banks	Storey	E Hughes	Mullery	McFarland
Malta	H	5–0	G Banks	Lawler[1]	Cooper	Moore*	McFarland
Northern Ireland	A	1–0	G Banks	Madeley	Cooper	Storey	McFarland
Wales	H	0–0	Shilton	Lawler	Cooper	T Smith	Lloyd
Scotland	H	3–1	G Banks	Lawler	Cooper	Storey	McFarland

1971–72

Versus	Venue	Result	1	2	3	4	5
Switzerland	A	3–2	G Banks	Lawler	Cooper	Mullery	McFarland
Switzerland	H	1–1	Shilton	Madeley	Cooper	Storey	Lloyd
Greece	A	2–0	G Banks	Madeley	E Hughes	Bell	McFarland
West Germany	H	1–3	G Banks	Madeley	E Hughes	Bell	Moore*
West Germany	A	0–0	G Banks	Madeley	E Hughes	Storey	McFarland
Wales	A	3–0	G Banks	Madeley	E Hughes[1]	Storey	McFarland
Northern Ireland	H	0–1	Shilton	Todd	E Hughes	Storey	Lloyd
Scotland	A	1–0	G Banks	Madeley	E Hughes	Storey	McFarland

1972–73

Versus	Venue	Result	1	2	3	4	5
Yugoslavia	H	1–1	Shilton	M Mills	Lampard	Storey	Blockley
Wales	A	1–0	Clemence	Storey	E Hughes	Hunter	McFarland
Wales	H	1–1	Clemence	Storey	E Hughes	Hunter[1]	McFarland
Scotland	A	5–0	Shilton	Storey	E Hughes	Bell	Madeley
Northern Ireland	A	2–1	Shilton	Storey	Nish	Bell	McFarland
Wales	H	3–0	Shilton	Storey	E Hughes	Bell	McFarland
Scotland .	H	1–0	Shilton	Storey	E Hughes	Bell	McFarland
Czechoslovakia	A	1–1	Shilton	Madeley	Storey	Bell	McFarland
Poland	A	0–2	Shilton	Madeley	E Hughes	Storey	McFarland
USSR	A	2–1	Shilton	Madeley	E Hughes	Storey	McFarland
Italy	A	0–2	Shilton	Madeley	E Hughes	Storey	McFarland

1973–74

Versus	Venue	Result	1	2	3	4	5
Austria	H	7–0	Shilton	Madeley	E Hughes	Bell[1]	McFarland
Poland	H	1–1	Shilton	Madeley	E Hughes	Bell	McFarland
Italy	H	0–1	Shilton	Madeley	E Hughes	Bell	McFarland
Portugal	A	0–0	Parkes	Nish	Pejic	Dobson	Watson
Wales	A	2–0	Shilton	Nish	Pejic	E Hughes*	McFarland
Northern Ireland	H	1–0	Shilton	Nish	Pejic	E Hughes*	McFarland
Scotland	A	0–2	Shilton	Nish	Pejic	E Hughes*	Hunter
Argentina	H	2–2	Shilton	E Hughes*	Lindsay	Todd	Watson
East Germany	A	1–1	Clemence	E Hughes*	Lindsay	Todd	Watson
Bulgaria	A	1–0	Clemence	E Hughes*	Todd	Watson	Lindsay
Yugoslavia	A	2–2	Clemence	E Hughes*	Lindsay	Todd	Watson

1974–75

Versus	Venue	Result	1	2	3	4	5
Czechoslovakia	H	3–0	Clemence	Madeley	E Hughes*	Dobson	Watson
Portugal	H	0–0	Clemence	Madeley	Watson	E Hughes*	Cooper
West Germany	H	2–0	Clemence	Whitworth	Gillard	Bell[1]	Watson
Cyprus	H	5–0	Shilton	Madeley	Watson	Todd	Beattie
Cyprus	A	1–0	Clemence	Whitworth	Beattie	Watson	Todd
Northern Ireland	A	0–0	Clemence	Whitworth	E Hughes	Bell	Watson
Wales	H	2–2	Clemence	Whitworth	Gillard	G Francis	Watson

6	7	8	9	10	11	*Substitutes*
Moore*	F Lee	Ball	R Charlton	G Hurst	Peters[1]	Bell 9, Hunter 11
Moore*	F Lee[1]	Ball	G Hurst	A Clarke[1]	Peters[1]	
Hunter	Ball	Chivers	Royle	Harvey	Peters[1]	
Moore*	F Lee[1]	Ball	Chivers[1]	G Hurst[1]	Peters	Coates 8
E Hughes	F Lee[1]	Coates	Chivers[2]	A Clarke[1]	Peters	Ball 11
Moore*	F Lee	Ball	Chivers	A Clarke[1]	Peters	
E Hughes	F Lee	Coates	G Hurst	Coates	Peters*	A Clarke 8
Moore*	F Lee	Ball	Chivers[2]	G Hurst	Peters[1]	A Clarke 7
Moore*	F Lee	Madeley	Chivers[1]	G Hurst[1]	Peters	†Radford 10
Moore*	Summerbee[1]	Ball	G Hurst	F Lee	E Hughes	Chivers 7, Marsh 10
Moore*	F Lee	Ball	Chivers[1]	G Hurst[1]	Peters	
Hunter	F Lee[1]	Ball	Chivers	G Hurst	Peters	Marsh 10
Moore*	Ball	Bell	Chivers	Marsh	Hunter	Summerbee 10, Peters 11
Moore*	Summerbee	Bell[1]	MacDonald	Marsh[1]	Hunter	
Hunter	Summerbee	Bell*	MacDonald	Marsh	Currie	Chivers 9, Peters 11
Moore*	Ball[1]	Bell	Chivers	Marsh	Hunter	MacDonald 10
Moore*	Ball	Channon	Royle[1]	Bell	Marsh	
Moore*	Keegan	Chivers	Marsh	Bell[1]	Ball	
Moore*	Keegan	Bell	Chivers	Marsh	Ball	
Moore*	Ball	Channon[1]	Chivers[1]	A Clarke[2]	Peters	†
Moore*	Ball	Channon	Chivers[2]	Richards	Peters	
Moore*	Ball	Channon[1]	Chivers[1]	A Clarke	Peters[1]	
Moore*	Ball	Channon	Chivers	A Clarke	Peters[1]	
Moore*	Ball	Channon	Chivers	A Clarke[1]	Peters	
Moore*	Ball	Bell	Chivers	A Clarke	Peters	
Moore*	Currie	Channon	Chivers[1]	A Clarke	Peters	† MacDonald 10,
Moore*	Currie	Channon	Chivers	A Clarke	Peters	Hunter 11, Summerbee 8
Hunter	Currie[1]	Channon[2]	Chivers[1]	A Clarke[2]	Peters*	
Hunter	Currie	Channon	Chivers	A Clarke[1]	Peters*	Hector 9
Moore*	Currie	Channon	Osgood	A Clarke	Peters	Hector 10
Todd	Bowles	Channon	MacDonald	Brooking	Peters*	Ball 9
Todd	Keegan[1]	Bell	Channon	Weller	Bowles[1]	
Todd	Keegan	Weller[1]	Channon	Bell	Bowles	Hunter 5, Worthington 11
Todd	Channon	Bell	Worthington	Weller	Peters	Watson 5, MacDonald 9
Bell	Keegan	Channon[1]	Worthington[1]	Weller	Brooking	
Dobson	Keegan	Channon[1]	Worthington	Bell	Brooking	
Dobson	Brooking	Bell	Keegan	Channon	Worthington[1]	
Dobson	Keegan[1]	Channon[1]	Worthington	Bell	Brooking	MacDonald 9
Hunter	Bell[2]	G Francis	Worthington	Channon[1]	Keegan	Brooking 4, Thomas 9
Brooking	G Francis	Bell	Thomas	Channon	A Clarke	Todd 5, Worthington 11
Todd	Ball*	MacDonald[1]	Channon	Hudson	Keegan	
Bell	Ball*	Hudson	Channon	MacDonald[5]	Keegan	Thomas 9
Bell	Thomas	Ball*	Channon	MacDonald	Keegan[1]	E Hughes 3, Tueart 11
Todd	Ball*	Viljoen	MacDonald	Keegan	Tueart	Channon 9
Todd	Ball*	Channon	Johnson[2]	Viljoen	Thomas	Little 8

● 59

Versus	Venue	Result	1	2	3	4	5
Scotland	H	5–1	Clemence	Whitworth	Beattie[1]	Bell[1]	Watson
1975–76							
Switzerland	A	2–1	Clemence	Whitworth	Todd	Watson	Beattie
Czechoslovakia	A	1–2	Clemence	Madeley	Gillard	G Francis*	McFarland
Portugal	A	1–1	Clemence	Whitworth	Beattie	G Francis*	Watson
Wales	A	2–1	Clemence	Cherry	M Mills	Neal	P Thompson
Wales	A	1–0	Clemence	Clement	M Mills	Towers	B Greenhoff
Northern Ireland	H	4–0	Clemence	Todd	M Mills	P Thompson	B Greenhoff
Scotland	A	1–2	Clemence	Todd	M Mills	P Thompson	McFarland
Brazil	N	0–1	Clemence	Todd	Doyle	P Thompson	Doyle
Italy	N	3–2	Rimmer	Clement	Neal	P Thompson[1]	Doyle
Finland	A	4–1	Clemence	Todd	M Mills	P Thompson	Madeley
1976–77							
Republic of Ireland	H	1–1	Clemence	Todd	Madeley	Cherry	McFarland
Finland	H	2–1	Clemence	Todd	Beattie	P Thompson	Greenhoff
Italy	A	0–2	Clemence	Clement	M Mills	B Greenhoff	McFarland
Holland	H	0–2	Clemence	Clement	Beattie	Doyle	Watson
Luxembourg	H	5–0	Clemence	Gidman	Cherry	Kennedy[1]	Watson
Northern Ireland	A	2–1	Shilton	Cherry	M Mills	Greenhoff	Watson
Wales	H	0–1	Shilton	Neal	M Mills	Greenhoff	Watson
Scotland	H	1–2	Clemence	Neal	M Mills	Greenhoff	Watson
Brazil	A	0–0	Clemence	Neal	Cherry	B Greenhoff	Watson
Argentina	A	1–1	Clemence	Neal	Cherry	B Greenhoff	Watson
Uruguay	A	0–0	Clemence	Neal	Cherry	B Greenhoff	Watson
1977–78							
Switzerland	H	0–0	Clemence	Neal	Cherry	McDermott	Watson
Luxembourg	A	2–0	Clemence	Cherry	Watson	E Hughes*	R Kennedy[1]
Italy	H	2–0	Clemence	Neal	Cherry	Wilkins	Watson
West Germany	A	1–2	Clemence	Neal	M Mills	Wilkins	Watson
Brazil	H	1–1	Corrigan	M Mills	Cherry	B Greenhoff	Watson
Wales	A	3–1	Shilton	M Mills*	Cherry	B Greenhoff	Watson
Northern Ireland	H	1–0	Clemence	Neal[1]	M Mills	Wilkins	Watson
Scotland	A	1–0	Clemence	Neal	M Mills	Currie	Watson
Hungary	H	4–1	Shilton	Neal[1]	M Mills	Wilkins	Watson
1978–79							
Denmark	A	4–3	Clemence	Neal[1]	M Mills	Wilkins	Watson
Republic of Ireland	A	1–1	Clemence	Neal	M Mills	Wilkins	Watson
Czechoslovakia	H	1–0	Shilton	Anderson	Cherry	P Thompson	Watson
Northern Ireland	H	4–0	Clemence	Neal	M Mills	Currie	Watson[1]
Northern Ireland	A	2–0	Clemence	Neal	M Mills*	P Thompson	Watson[1]
Wales	H	0–0	Corrigan	Cherry	Sansom	Wilkins	Watson
Scotland	H	3–1	Clemence	Neal	M Mills	P Thompson	Watson
Bulgaria	A	3–0	Clemence	Neal	M Mills	P Thompson	Watson[1]
Sweden	A	0–0	Shilton	Anderson	Cherry	McDermott	Watson
Austria	A	3–4	Shilton	Neal	M Mills	P Thompson	Watson
1979–80							
Denmark	H	1–0	Clemence	Neal	M Mills	P Thompson	Watson
Northern Ireland	A	5–1	Shilton	Neal	M Mills	P Thompson	Watson
Bulgaria	H	2–0	Clemence	Anderson	Sansom	P Thompson*	Watson[1]
Republic of Ireland	H	2–0	Clemence	Cherry	Sansom	P Thompson	Watson

6	7	8	9	10	11	*Substitutes*
Todd	Ball*	Channon	Johnson[1]	G Francis[2]	Keegan	Thomas 11
Bell	Currie	G Francis	Channon[1]	Johnson	Keegan[1]	MacDonald 10
Todd	Keegan	Channon[1]	MacDonald	A Clarke	Bell	Watson 5, Thomas 8
Todd	Keegan	Channon[1]	MacDonald	Brooking	Madeley	A Clarke 11, Thomas 9
Doyle	Keegan*	Channon	Boyer	Brooking	Kennedy[1]	Clement 2, P Taylor 8[1]
P Thompson	Keegan	G Francis*	Pearson	Kennedy	P Taylor[1]	
R Kennedy	Keegan	G Francis*[1]	Pearson[1]	Channon[2]	P Taylor	Towers 11, Royle 7
R Kennedy	Keegan	G Francis*	Pearson	Channon[1]	P Taylor	Cherry 9, Doyle 5
G Francis*	Cherry	Brooking	Keegan	Pearson	Channon	
Towers	Wilkins	Brooking	Royle	Channon*[2]	Hill	Corrigan 1, M Mills 3
Cherry	Keegan[2]	Channon[1]	Pearson[1]	Brooking	G Francis*	
Greenhoff	Keegan*	Wilkins	Pearson[1]	Brooking	George	Hill 11
Wilkins	Keegan*	Channon	Royle[1]	Brooking	Tueart[1]	M Mills 10, Hill 11
E Hughes	Keegan*	Channon	Bowles	Cherry	Brooking	Beattie 2
Madeley	Keegan*	Greenhoff	T Francis	Bowles	Brooking	Todd 8, S Pearson 6
E Hughes	Keegan*[1]	Channon[2]	Royle	T Francis[1]	Hill	Mariner 9
Todd	Wilkins	Channon*[1]	Mariner	Brooking	Tueart[1]	Talbot 7
E Hughes	Keegan*	Channon	Pearson	Brooking	R Kennedy	Tueart 10
E Hughes*	T Francis	Channon[1]	Pearson	Talbot	R Kennedy	Cherry 4, Tueart 11
E Hughes	Keegan*	T Francis	Pearson	Wilkins	Talbot	Channon 9, R Kennedy 10
E Hughes	Keegan*	Channon	Pearson[1]	Wilkins	Talbot	R Kennedy 4
E Hughes	Keegan*	Channon	Pearson	Wilkins	Talbot	
E Hughes*	Keegan	Channon	T Francis	R Kennedy	Callaghan	Hill 8, Wilkins 11
Callaghan	McDermott	Wilkins	T Francis	Mariner[1]	G Hill	Whymark 7, Beattie 3
E Hughes*	Keegan[1]	Coppell	R Latchford	Brooking[1]	P Barnes	Pearson 9, T Francis 7
E Hughes*	Keegan	Coppell	S Pearson[1]	Brooking	P Barnes	T Francis 7
Currie	Keegan*[1]	Coppell	R Latchford	T Francis	P Barnes	
Wilkins	Coppell	T Francis	R Latchford[1]	Brooking	P Barnes[1]	Currie 3[1], Mariner 9
E Hughes*	Currie	Coppell	Pearson	Woodcock	B Greenhoff	
E Hughes*	Wilkins	Coppell[1]	Mariner	T Francis	P Barnes	B Greenhoff 6, Brooking 9
E Hughes*	Keegan	Coppell	T Francis[1]	Brooking	P Barnes[1]	B Greenhoff 5, Currie 8[1]
E Hughes*	Keegan[2]	Coppell	Latchford[1]	Brooking	P Barnes	
E Hughes*	Keegan	Coppell	Latchford[1]	Brooking	P Barnes	P Thompson 5, Woodcock 11
Wilkins	Keegan*	Cnppell[1]	Woodcock	Currie	P Barnes	Latchford 9
E Hughes*	Keegan[1]	Coppell	Latchford[2]	Brooking	P Barnes	
Wilkins	Coppell[1]	Wilkins	Latchford	Currie	P Barnes	
E Hughes*	Keegan	Wilkins	Latchford	McDermott	Cunningham	Coppell 7, Brooking 4
Wilkins	Keegan*[1]	Coppell[1]	Latchford	Brooking	P Barnes[1]	
Wilkins	Keegan*[1]	Coppell	Latchford	Brooking	P Barnes[1]	T Francis 9, Woodcock 11
E Hughes*	Keegan	T Francis	T Francis	Woodcock	Cunningham	Wilkins 4, Brooking 8
Wilkins[1]	Keegan*[1]	Coppell[1]	Latchford	Brooking	P Barnes	Clemence 1, T Francis 9 Cunningham 11
Wilkins	Coppell	McDermott	Keegan*[1]	Brooking	P Barnes	
Wilkins	Keegan*	Coppell	T Francis[2]	Brooking	Woodcock[2]	† McDermott 10
Wilkins	Reeves	Hoddle[1]	T Francis	Kennedy	Woodcock	
Robson	Keegan*[2]	McDermott	Johnson	Woodcock	Cunningham	Coppell 9

Versus	Venue	Result	1	2	3	4	5
Spain	A	2–0	Shilton	Neal	M Mills	P Thompson	Watson
Argentina	H	3–1	Clemence	Neal	Sansom	P Thompson	Watson
Wales	A	1–4	Clemence	Neal	Cherry	P Thompson*	Lloyd
Northern Ireland	H	1–1	Corrigan	Cherry	Sansom	E Hughes	Watson
Scotland	A	2–0	Clemence	Cherry	Sansom	P Thompson*	Watson
Australia	A	2–1	Corrigan	Cherry*	Lampard	Talbot	Osman
Belgium	N	1–1	Clemence	Neal	Sansom	P Thompson	Watson
Italy	A	0–1	Shilton	Neal	Sansom	P Thompson	Watson
Spain	N	2–1	Clemence	Anderson	M Mills	P Thompson	Watson

1980–81

Versus	Venue	Result	1	2	3	4	5
Norway	H	4–0	Shilton	Anderson	Sansom	P Thompson*	Watson
Romania	A	1–2	Clemence	Neal	Sansom	P Thompson*	Watson
Switzerland	H	2–1	Shilton	Neal	Sansom	Robson	Watson
Spain	H	1–2	Clemence	Neal	Sansom	Robson	Butcher
Romania	H	0–0	Shilton	Anderson	Sansom	Robson	Watson*
Brazil	H	0–1	Clemence*	Neal	Sansom	Robson	Martin
Wales	H	0–0	Corrigan	Anderson	Sansom	Robson	Watson*
Scotland	H	0–1	Corrigan	Anderson	Sansom	Wilkins	Watson*
Switzerland	A	1–2	Clemence	M Mills	Sansom	Wilkins	Watson
Hungary	A	3–1	Clemence	Neal	M Mills	P Thompson	Watson

1981–82

Versus	Venue	Result	1	2	3	4	5
Norway	A	1–2	Clemence	Neal	M Mills	P Thompson	Osman
Hungary	H	1–0	Shilton	Neal	M Mills	P Thompson	Martin
Northern Ireland	H	4–0	Clemence	Anderson	Sansom	Wilkins[1]	Watson
Wales	A	1–0	Corrigan	Neal	Sansom	P Thompson*	Butcher
Holland	H	2–0	Shilton*	Neal	Sansom	P Thompson	Foster
Scotland	A	1–0	Shilton	M Mills	Sansom	P Thompson	Butcher
Iceland	A	1–1	Corrigan	Anderson	Neal*	Watson	Osman
Finland	A	4–1	Clemence	M Mills	Sansom	P Thompson	Martin
France	N	3–1	Shilton	M Mills*	Sansom	P Thompson	Butcher
Czechoslovakia	N	2–0	Shilton	M Mills*	Sansom	P Thompson	Butcher
Kuwait	N	1–0	Shilton	Neal	M Mills*	P Thompson	Foster
West Germany	N	0–0	Shilton	M Mills*	Sansom	P Thompson	Butcher
Spain	A	0–0	Shilton	M Mills*	Sansom	P Thompson	Butcher

1982–83

Versus	Venue	Result	1	2	3	4	5
Denmark	A	2–2	Shilton	Neal	Sansom	Wilkins*	Osman
West Germany	H	1–2	Shilton	Mabbutt	Sansom	P Thompson	Butcher
Greece	A	3–0	Shilton	Neal	Sansom	P Thompson	Martin
Luxembourg	H	9–0	Clemence	Neal[1]	Sansom	Robson*	Martin
Wales	H	2–1	Shilton*	Neal[1]	Statham	S Lee	Martin
Greece	H	0–0	Shilton*	Neal	Sansom	S Lee	Martin
Hungary	H	2–0	Shilton*	Neal	Sansom	S Lee	Martin
Northern Ireland	A	0–0	Shilton*	Neal	Sansom	Hoddle	Roberts
Scotland	H	2–0	Shilton	Neal	Sansom	S Lee	Roberts
Australia	A	0–0	Shilton*	Thomas	Statham	Williams	Osman
Australia	A	1–0	Shilton*	Neal	Statham	Barham	Osman
Australia	A	1–1	Shilton*	Neal	Pickering	S Lee	Osman

6	7	8	9	10	11	*Substitutes*
Wilkins	Keegan*	Coppell	T Francis[1]	R Kennedy	Woodcock[1]	E Hughes, 2 Cunningham 9
Wilkins	Keegan*[1]	Coppell	Johnson[2]	Woodcock	R Kennedy	Cherry 2 Birtles 9
						Brooking 11
R Kennedy	Coppell	Hoodle	Mariner[1]	Brooking	Barnes	Sansom 2, Wilkins 5
Wilkins	Reeves	Wilkins	Johnson[1]	Brooking	Devonshire	Mariner 7
Wilkins	Coppell[1]	McDermott	Johnson	Mariner	Brooking[1]	E Hughes 10
Butcher	Robson	Sunderland	Mariner[1]	Hoddle[1]	Armstrong	B Greenhoff 7, Ward 10
						Devonshire 11
Wilkins*	Keegan*	Coppell	Johnson	Woodcock	Brooking	McDermott 8, R Kennedy 9
Wilkins	Keegan*	Coppell	Birtles	R Kennedy	Woodcock	Mariner 9
Wilkins	McDermott	Hoddle	Keegan*	Woodcock[1]	Brooking[1]	Cherry 3, Mariner 8
Robson	Gates	McDermott[2]	Mariner[1]	Woodcock[1]	Rix	
Robson	Rix	McDermott	Birtles	Woodcock[1]	Gates	Cunningham 9, Coppell 11
M Mills*	Coppell	McDermott	Mariner[1]	Brooking	Woodcock	† Rix 10
Osman	Keegan*	T Francis	Mariner	Brooking	Hoddle[1]	P Barnes 8, Wilkins 10
Osman	Wilkins	Brooking	Coppell	T Francis	Woodcock	McDermott 11
Wilkins	Coppell	McDermott	Withe	Rix	P Barnes	
Wilkins	Coppell	Hoddle	Withe	Rix	P Barnes	Woodcock 9
Robson	Coppell	Hoddle	Withe	Rix	Woodcock	Martin 5, T Francis 11
Osman	Keegan*	Robson	Coppell	Mariner	T Francis	McDermott 11[1], P Barnes 5
Robson	Keegan*[1]	McDermott	Mariner	Brooking[2]	Coppell	Wilkins 10
Robson[1]	Keegan*	T Francis	Mariner	Hoddle	McDermott	Withe 9, P Barnes 10
Robson	Keegan*	Coppell	Mariner[1]	Brooking	McDermott	Morley 8
Foster	Keegan*[1]	Robson[1]	T Francis	Hoddle[1]	Morley	Regis 9, Woodcock 11
Robson	Wilkins	T Francis[1]	Withe	Hoddle	Morley	McDermott 8, Regis 10
Robson	Wilkins	Devonshire	Mariner[1]	McDermott	Woodcock[1]	Rix 8, Barnes 9
Robson	Keegan*	Coppell	Mariner[1]	Brooking	Wilkins	McDermott 7, T Francis 9
McDermott	Hoddle	Devonshire	Withe	Regis	Morley	Perryman 8, Goddard 10[1]
Robson[2]	Keegan*	Coppell	Mariner[2]	Brooking	Wilkins	Rix 6, T Francis 8
						Woodcock 10
Robson[2]	Coppell	T Francis	Mariner[1]	Rix	Wilkins	Neal 3
Robson	Coppell	T Francis[1]	Mariner	Rix	Wilkins	† Hoddle 6
Hoddle	Coppell	T Francis[1]	Mariner	Rix	Wilkins	
Robson	Coppell	T Francis	Mariner	Rix	Wilkins	Woodcock 8
Robson	Rix	T Francis	Mariner	Woodcock	Wilkins	Brooking 7, Keegan 10
Butcher	Morley	Robson	Mariner	T Francis[2]	Rix	Hill 7
Wilkins*	R Hill	Regis	Mariner	Armstrong	Devonshire	Woodcock 8[1], Blissett 9
						Rix 10
Robson*	S Lee[1]	Mabbutt	Mariner	Woodcock[2]	Morley	
Butcher	Coppell[1]	S Lee	Woodcock[1]	Blissett[3]	Mabbutt	† Chamberlain 7[1], Hoddle 11[1]
Butcher[1]	Mabbutt	Blissett	Mariner	Cowans	Devonshire	
Butcher	Coppell	Mabbutt	T Francis	Woodcock	Devonshire	Blissett 10, Rix 11
Butcher	Mabbutt	T Francis[1]	Withe[1]	Blissett	Cowans	
Butcher	Mabbutt	T Francis	Withe	Blissett	Cowans	J Barnes 10
Butcher	Robson*[1]	T Francis	Withe	Hoddle	Cowans[1]	Mabbutt 7, Blissett 9
Butcher	Barham	Gregory	Blissett	T Francis	Cowans	J Barnes 3, Walsh 9
Butcher	Gregory	T Francis	Walsh[1]	Cowans	J Barnes	Williams 3
Butcher	Gregory	T Francis[1]	Walsh	Cowans	J Barnes	Spink 1, Thomas 2, Blissett 9

● 63

Versus	Venue	Result	1	2	3	4	5
1983–84							
Denmark	H	0–1	Shilton	Neal	Sansom	S Lee	Osman
Hungary	A	3–0	Shilton	Gregory	Sansom	S Lee[1]	Martin
Luxembourg	A	4–0	Clemence	Duxbury	Sansom	S Lee	Martin
France	A	0–2	Shilton	Duxbury	Sansom	S Lee	Roberts
Northern Ireland	H	1–0	Shilton	Anderson	A Kennedy	S Lee	Roberts
Wales	A	0–1	Shilton	Duxbury	A Kennedy	S Lee	Martin
Scotland	A	1–1	Shilton	Duxbury	Sansom	Wilkins	Roberts
USSR	H	0–2	Shilton	Duxbury	Sansom	Wilkins	Roberts
Brazil	A	2–0	Shilton	Duxbury	Sansom	Wilkins	Watson
Uruguay	A	0–2	Shilton	Duxbury	Sansom	Wilkins	Watson
Chile	A	0–0	Shilton	Duxbury	Sansom	Wilkins	Watson
1984–85							
East Germany	H	1–0	Shilton	Duxbury	Sansom	Williams	Wright
Finland	H	5–0	Shilton	Duxbury	Sansom[1]	Williams	Wright
Turkey	A	8–0	Shilton	Anderson[1]	Sansom	Williams	Wright
Northern Ireland	A	1–0	Shilton	Anderson	Sansom	Steven	Martin
Republic of Ireland	H	2–1	Bailey	Anderson	Sansom	Steven[1]	Wright
Romania	A	0–0	Shilton	Anderson	Sansom	Steven	Wright
Finland	A	1–1	Shilton	Anderson	Sansom	Steven	Fenwick
Scotland	A	0–1	Shilton	Anderson	Sansom	Hoddle	Fenwick
Italy	N	1–2	Shilton	Stevens	Sansom	Steven	Wright
Mexico	A	0–1	Bailey	Anderson	Sansom	Hoddle	Fenwick
West Germany	N	3–0	Shilton	Stevens	Sansom	Hoddle	Wright
USA	A	5–0	Woods	Anderson	Sansom	Hoddle	Fenwick
1985–86							
Romania	H	1–1	Shilton	Stevens	Sansom	Reid	Wright
Turkey	H	5–0	Shilton	Stevens	Sansom	Hoddle	Wright
Northern Ireland	H	0–0	Shilton	GA Stevens	Sansom	Hoddle	Wright
Egypt	A	4–0	Shilton	Stevens	Sansom	Cowans[1]	Wright
Israel	A	2–1	Shilton	Stevens	Sansom	Hoddle	Martin
USSR	A	1–0	Shilton	Anderson	Sansom	Hoddle	Wright
Scotland	H	2–1	Shilton	Stevens	Sansom	Hoddle[1]	Watson
Mexico	N	3–0	Shilton	Anderson	Sansom	Hoddle	Fenwick
Canada	A	1–0	Shilton	Stevens	Sansom	Hoddle	Martin
Portugal	N	0–1	Shilton	Stevens	Sansom	Hoddle	Fenwick
Morocco	N	0–0	Shilton	Stevens	Sansom	Hoddle	Fenwick
Poland	N	3–0	Shilton*	Stevens	Sansom	Hoddle	Fenwick
Paraguay	N	3–0	Shilton*	Stevens	Sansom	Hoddle	Martin
Argentina	N	1–2	Shilton*	Stevens	Sansom	Hoddle	Fenwick
1986–87							
Sweden	A	0–1	Shilton*	Anderson	Sansom	Hoddle	Martin
Northern Ireland	H	3–0	Shilton	Anderson	Sansom	Hoddle	Watson
Yugoslavia	H	2–0	Woods	Anderson[1]	Sansom	Hoddle	Wright
Spain	A	4–2	Shilton	Anderson	Sansom	Hoddle	Adams
Northern Ireland	A	2–0	Shilton	Anderson	Sansom	Mabbutt	Wright
Turkey	A	0–0	Woods	Anderson	Sansom	Hoddle	Adams

6	7	8	9	10	11	*Substitutes*
Butcher	Wilkins*	Gregory	Mariner	T Francis	J Barnes	Blissett 4, Chamberlain 11
Butcher	Robson*	Hoddle[1]	Mariner[1]	Blissett	Mabbutt	Withe 10
Butcher[1]	Robson*[2]	Hoddle	Mariner[1]	Woodcock	Devonshire	J Barnes 10
Butcher	Robson*	Stein	Walsh	Hoddle	Williams	J Barnes 4, Woodcock 8
Butcher	Robson*	Wilkins	Woodcock[1]	T Francis	Rix	
Wright	Wilkins*	Gregory	Walsh	Woodcock	Armstrong	Fenwick 5, Blissett 11
Fenwick	Chamberlain	Robson*	Woodcock[1]	Blissett	J Barnes	Hunt 7, Lineker 9
Fenwick	Chamberlain	Robson*	T Francis	Blissett	J Barnes	Hateley 9, Hunt 11
Fenwick	Robson*	Chamberlain	Hateley[1]	Woodcock	J Barnes[1]	Allen 10
Fenwick	Robson*	Chamberlain	Hateley	Allen	J Barnes	Woodcock 10
Fenwick	Robson*	Chamberlain	Hateley	Allen	J Barnes	S Lee 8
Butcher	Robson*[1]	Wilkins	Mariner	Woodcock	J Barnes	Hateley 9, T Francis 10
Butcher	Robson*[1]	Wilkins	Hateley[2]	Woodcock[1]	J Barnes	GA Stevens 2, Chamberlain 7
Butcher	Robson*[3]	Wilkins	Withe	Woodcock[2]	J Barnes[2]	GA Stevens 4, Francis 10
Butcher	Steven	Wilkins*	Hateley[1]	Woodcock	J Barnes	T Francis 10
Butcher	Robson*	Wilkins	Hateley	Lineker[1]	Waddle	Hoddle 7, Davenport 9
Butcher	Robson*	Wilkins	Mariner	T Francis	J Barnes	Lineker 9, Waddle 11
Butcher	Robson*	Wilkins	Hateley[1]	T Francis	J Barnes	Waddle 4
Butcher	Robson*	Wilkins	Hateley	T Francis	J Barnes	Lineker 4, Waddle 11
Butcher	Robson*	Wilkins	Hateley[1]	T Francis	Waddle	Hoddle 4, Lineker 10 J Barnes 11
Watson	Robson*	Wilkins	Hateley	T Francis	J Barnes	K Dixon 4, Reid 8, Waddle 11
Butcher	Robson*[1]	Reid	K Dixon[2]	Lineker	Waddle	Bracewell 7, J Barnes 10
Butcher	Robson*	Bracewell	K Dixon[2]	Lineker[2]	Waddle	Watson 3, Steven 4[1] Reid 7, J Barnes 11
Fenwick	Robson*	Hoddle[1]	Hateley	Lineker	Waddle	Woodcock 10, J Barnes 11
Fenwick	Robson*[1]	Wilkins	Hateley	Lineker[3]	Waddle[1]	Steven 7, Woodcock 9
Fenwick	Bracewell	Wilkins*	K Dixon	Lineker	Waddle	
Fenwick	Steven[1]	Wilkins*	Hateley	Lineker	Wallace[1]	† Woods 1, Hill 7 Beardsley 10
Butcher	Robson*[2]	Wilkins	Dixon	Beardsley	Waddle	Woods 1, Woodcock 9 J Barnes 10
Butcher	Cowans	Wilkins*	Beardsley	Lineker	Waddle[1]	Hodge 7, Steven 11
Butcher[1]	Wilkins*	T Francis	Hateley	Hodge	Waddle	Reid 7, GA Stevens 10
Butcher	Robson*	Wilkins	Hateley[2]	Beardsley[1]	Waddle	GA Stevens 7, Steven 8 K Dixon 9, J Barnes 11
Butcher	Hodge	Wilkins*	Hateley[1]	Lineker	Waddle	Woods 1, Reid 8 Beardsley 10, J Barnes 11
Butcher	Robson*	Wilkins	Hateley	Lineker	Waddle	Hodge 7, Beardsley 11
Butcher	Robson*	Wilkins	Hateley	Lineker	Waddle	Hodge 7, GA Stevens 9
Butcher	Hodge	Reid	Beardsley	Lineker[3]	Steven	Waddle 9, K Dixon 10
Butcher	Hodge	Reid	Beardsley[1]	Lineker[2]	Steven	GA Stevens 8, Hateley 9
Butcher	Hodge	Reid	Beardsley	Lineker[1]	Steven	Waddle 8, J Barnes 11
Butcher	Steven	Wilkins	K Dixon	Hodge	J Barnes	Cottee 7, Waddle 11
Butcher	Robson*	Hodge	Beardsley	Lineker[2]	Waddle[1]	Cottee 9
Butcher*	Mabbutt[1]	Hodge	Beardsley	Lineker	Waddle	Wilkins 8, Steven 11
Butcher	Robson*	Hodge	Beardsley	Lineker[4]	Waddle	Woods 1, Steven 11
Butcher	Robson*[1]	Hodge	Beardsley	Lineker	Waddle[1]	Woods 1
Mabbutt	Robson*	Hodge	Allen	Lineker	Waddle	J Barnes 8, Hateley 9

Versus	Venue	Result	1	2	3	4	5
Brazil	H	1–1	Shilton	Stevens	Pearce	Reid	Adams
Scotland	A	0–0	Woods	Stevens	Pearce	Hoddle	Wright
1987–88							
West Germany	A	1–3	Shilton*	Anderson	Sansom	Hoddle	Adams
Turkey	H	8–0	Shilton	Stevens	Sansom	Steven	Adams
Yugoslavia	A	4–1	Shilton	Stevens	Sansom	Steven	Adams[1]
Israel	A	0–0	Woods	Stevens	Pearce	Webb	Watson
Holland	H	2–2	Shilton	Stevens	Sansom	Steven	Adams[1]
Hungary	A	0–0	Woods	Anderson	Pearce	Steven	Adams
Scotland	H	1–0	Shilton	Stevens	Sansom	Webb	Watson
Colombia	H	1–1	Shilton	Anderson	Sansom	McMahon	Wright
Switzerland	A	1–0	Shilton	Stevens	Sansom	Webb	Wright
Republic of Ireland	N	0–1	Shilton	Stevens	Sansom	Webb	Wright
Holland	N	1–3	Shilton	Stevens	Sansom	Hoddle	Wright
USSR	N	1–3	Woods	Stevens	Sansom	Hoddle	Watson
1988–89							
Denmark	H	1–0	Shilton	Stevens	Pearce	Rocastle	Adams
Sweden	H	0–0	Shilton	Stevens	Pearce	Webb	Adams
Saudi Arabia	A	1–1	Seaman	Sterland	Pearce	M Thomas	Adams[1]
Greece	A	2–1	Shilton	Stevens	Pearce	Webb	Walker
Albania	A	2–0	Shilton	Stevens	Pearce	Webb	Walker
Albania	H	5–0	Shilton	Stevens	Pearce	Webb	Walker
Chile	H	0–0	Shilton	Parker	Pearce	Webb	Walker
Scotland	A	2–0	Shilton	Stevens	Pearce	Webb	Walker
Poland	H	3–0	Shilton	Stevens	Pearce	Webb[1]	Walker
Denmark	A	1–1	Shilton	Parker	Pearce	Webb	Walker
1989–90							
Sweden	A	0–0	Shilton	Stevens	Pearce	Webb	Walker
Poland	A	0–0	Shilton	Stevens	Pearce	McMahon	Walker
Italy	H	0–0	Shilton	Stevens	Pearce	McMahon	Walker
Yugoslavia	H	2–1	Shilton	Parker	Pearce	M Thomas	Walker
Brazil	H	1–0	Shilton	Stevens	Pearce	McMahon	Walker
Czechoslovakia	H	4–2	Shilton	Dixon	Pearce[1]	Steven	Walker
Denmark	H	1–0	Shilton	Stevens	Pearce	McMahon	Walker
Uruguay	H	1–2	Shilton	Parker	Pearce	Hodge	Walker
Tunisia	A	1–1	Shilton	Stevens	Pearce	Hodge	Walker
Republic of Ireland	N	1–1	Shilton	Stevens	Pearce	Gascoigne	Walker
Holland	N	0–0	Shilton	Parker	Pearce	Wright	Walker
Egypt	N	1–0	Shilton*	Parker	Pearce	Gascoigne	Walker
Belgium	N	1–0	Shilton	Parker	Pearce	Wright	Walker
Cameroon	N	3–2	Shilton	Parker	Pearce	Wright	Walker
West Germany	N	1–1	Shilton	Parker	Pearce	Wright	Walker

6	7	8	9	10	11	*Substitutes*
Butcher	Robson*	J Barnes	Beardsley	Lineker[1]	Waddle	Hateley 10
Butcher	Robson*	Hodge	Beardsley	Hateley	Waddle	
Mabbutt	Reid	J Barnes	Beardsley	Lineker[1]	Waddle	Pearce 3, Webb 4, Hateley 11
Butcher	Robson*[1]	Webb[1]	Beardsley[1]	Lineker[3]	J Barnes[2]	Hoddle 4, Regis 9
Butcher	Robson*[1]	Webb	Beardsley[1]	Lineker	J Barnes[1]	Reid 7, Hoddle 8
Wright	Allen	McMahon	Beardsley*	J Barnes	Waddle	Fenwick 6, Harford 7
Watson	Robson*	Webb	Beardsley	Lineker*[1]	J Barnes	Wright 6, Hoddle 8
						Hateley 9
Pallister	Robson*	McMahon	Beardsley	Lineker	Waddle	Stevens 3, Hateley 9
						Cottee 10, Hoddle 11
Adams	Robson*	Steven	Beardsley[1]	Lineker	J Barnes	Waddle 8
Adams	Robson*	Waddle	Beardsley	Lineker[1]	J Barnes	Hoddle 8, Hateley 9
Adams	Robson*	Steven	Beardsley	Lineker*	J Barnes	Woods 1, Watson 6
						Reid 7, Waddle 8
Adams	Robson*	Waddle	Beardsley	Lineker	J Barnes	Hoddle 4, Hateley 9
Adams	Robson*[1]	Steven	Beardsley	Lineker	J Barnes	Waddle 8, Hateley 9
Adams[1]	Robson*	Steven	McMahon	Lineker	J Barnes	Webb 9, Hateley 10
Butcher	Robson*	Webb[1]	Harford	Beardsley	Hodge	Woods 1, Walker 5
						Cottee 9, Gascoigne 10
Butcher	Robson*	Beardsley	Waddle	Lineker	J Barnes	Walker 5, Cottee 11
Pallister	Robson*	Rocastle	Beardsley	Lineker	Waddle	Gascoigne 4, A Smith 9
						Marwood 11
Butcher	Robson*[1]	Rocastle	A Smith	Lineker	J Barnes[1]	Beardsley 9
Butcher	Robson*[1]	Rocastle	Waddle	Lineker	J Barnes[1]	Beardsley 9, A Smith 10
Butcher	Robson*	Rocastle	Beardsley[2]	Lineker[1]	Waddle[1]	Parker 2, Gascoigne 8[1]
Butcher	Robson*	Gascoigne	Clough	Fashanu	Waddle	Cottee 10
Butcher	Robson*	Steven	Fashanu	Cotttee	Waddle[1]	Bull 9[1], Gascoigne 10
Butcher	Robson*	Waddle	Beardsley	Lineker[1]	J Barnes[1]	Rocastle 8, A Smith 9
Butcher	Robson*	Rocastle	Beardsley	Lineker[1]	J Barnes	Seaman 1, McMahon 4
						Bull 9, Waddle 11
Butcher*	Beardsley	McMahon	Waddle	Lineker	J Barnes	Gascoigne 4, Rocastle 11
Butcher	Robson*	Rocastle	Beardsley	Lineker	Waddle	
Butcher	Robson*	Waddle	Beardsley	Lineker	J Barnes	Beasant 1, Winterburn 3
						Hodge 4 Phelan 7, Platt 9
Butcher	Robson*[2]	Rocastle	Bull	Lineker	Waddle	Beasant 1, Dorigo 3, Platt 4
						McMahon 7, Hodge 8
Butcher*	Platt	Waddle	Beardsley	Lineker[1]	J Barnes	Woods 1, Gascoigne 9
Butcher	Robson*	Gascoigne[1]	Bull[2]	Lineker	Hodge	Seaman 1, Dorigo 3
						Wright 5, McMahon 7
Butcher*	Hodge	Gascoigne	Waddle	Lineker[1]	J Barnes	Woods 1, Dorigo 3
						Platt 4 Rocastle 9, Bull 10
Butcher	Robson*	Gascoigne	Waddle	Lineker	J Barnes[1]	Beardsley 4, Bull 10
Butcher	Robson*	Waddle	Gascoigne	Lineker	J Barnes	Beardsley 4, Wright 6
						Platt 8, Bull 10[1]
Butcher	Waddle	Robson*	Beardsley	Lineker[1]	J Barnes	McMahon 9, Bull 10
Butcher	Robson*	Waddle	Gascoigne	Lineker	J Barnes	Platt 7, Bull 8
Wright[1]	McMahon	Waddle	Bull	Lineker	J Barnes	Platt 8, Beardsley 9
Butcher*	McMahon	Waddle	Gascoigne	Lineker	J Barnes	Platt 7[1], Bull 11
Butcher*	Platt[1]	Waddle	Gascoigne	Lineker[2]	J Barnes	Steven 6, Beardsley 11
Butcher*	Platt	Waddle	Gascoigne	Lineker[1]	Beardsley	Steven 6

● 67

Versus	Venue	Result	1	2	3	4	5
Italy	A	1–2	Shilton*	Stevens	Dorigo	Parker	Walker
1990–91							
Hungary	H	1–0	Woods	Dixon	Pearce	Parker	Walker
Poland	H	2–0	Woods	Dixon	Pearce	Parker	Walker
Republic of Ireland	A	1–1	Woods	Dixon	Pearce	Adams	Walker
Cameroon	H	2–0	Seaman	Dixon	Pearce	Steven	Walker
Republic of Ireland	H	1–1	Seaman	Dixon[1]	Pearce	Adams	Walker
Turkey	A	1–0	Seaman	Dixon	Pearce	Wise[1]	Walker
USSR	H	3–1	Woods	Stevens	Dorigo	Wise	Parker
Argentina	H	2–2	Seaman	Dixon	Pearce	Batty	Walker
Australia	A	1–0	Woods	Parker	Pearce	Batty	Walker
New Zealand	A	1–0	Woods	Parker	Pearce	Batty	Walker
New Zealand	A	2–0	Woods	Charles	Pearce*[1]	Wise	Walker
Malaysia	A	4–2	Woods	Charles	Pearce	Batty	Walker
1991–92							
Germany	H	0–1	Woods	Dixon	Dorigo	Batty	Pallister
Turkey	H	1–0	Woods	Dixon	Pearce	Batty	Walker
Poland	A	1–1	Woods	Dixon	Pearce	Gray	Walker
France	H	2–0	Woods	R Jones	Pearce*	Keown	Walker
Czechoslovakia	A	2–2	Seaman	Keown[1]	Pearce*	Rocastle	Walker
CIS	A	2–2	Woods	Stevens	Sinton	Palmer	Walker
Hungary	A	1–0	Martyn	Stevens	Dorigo	Curle	Walker
Brazil	H	1–1	Woods	Stevens	Dorigo	Palmer	Walker
Finland	A	2–1	Woods	Stevens	Pearce	Keown	Walker
Denmark	N	0–0	Woods	Curle	Pearce	Palmer	Walker
France	N	0–0	Woods	Batty	Pearce	Palmer	Walker
Sweden	A	1–2	Woods	Batty	Pearce	Keown	Walker
1992–93							
Spain	A	0–1	Woods	Dixon	Pearce*	Ince	Walker
Norway	H	1–1	Woods	Dixon	Pearce*	Batty	Walker
Turkey	H	4–0	Woods	Dixon	Pearce*[1]	Palmer	Walker
San Marino	H	6–0	Woods	Dixon	Dorigo	Palmer[1]	Walker
Turkey	A	2–0	Woods	Dixon	Sinton	Palmer	Walker
Holland	H	2–2	Woods	Dixon	Keown	Palmer	Walker
Poland	A	1–1	Woods	Bardsley	Dorigo	Palmer	Walker
Norway	A	0–2	Woods	Dixon	Pallister	Palmer	Walker
United States	A	0–2	Woods	Dixon	Dorigo	Palmer	Pallister
Brazil	N	1–1	Flowers	Barrett	Dorigo	Walker	Pallister
Germany	N	1–2	Martyn	Barrett	Sinton	Walker	Pallister
1993–94							
Poland	H	3–0	Seaman	Jones	Pearce*[1]	Ince	Pallister
Holland	A	0–2	Seaman	Parker	Dorigo	Ince	Pallister
San Marino	A	7–1	Seaman	Dixon	Pearce*	Ince[2]	Pallister
Denmark	H	1–0	Seaman	Parker	Le Saux	Ince	Adams
Greece	H	5–0	Flowers	Jones	Le Saux	Richardson	Bould

6	7	8	9	10	11	*Substitutes*
Wright	Platt[1]	Steven	McMahon	Lineker	Beardsley	Waddle 6, Webb 9
Wright	Platt	Gascoigne	Bull	Lineker*[1]	J Barnes	Dorigo 3, Waddle 9
Wright	Platt	Gascoigne	Bull	Lineker*[1]	J Barnes	Beardsley 9[1], Waddle 10
Wright	Platt[1]	Cowans	Beardsley	Lineker*	McMahon	
Wright	Robson	Gascoigne	I Wright	Lineker*[2]	J Barnes	Pallister 7, Hodge 8
Wright	Robson	Platt	Beardsley	Lineker*	J Barnes	Sharpe 4, I Wright 10
Pallister	Platt	G Thomas	A Smith	Lineker*	J Barnes	Hodge 8
Wright*	Platt[2]	G Thomas	A Smith[1]	I Wright	J Barnes	Batty 4, Beardsley 10
Wright	Platt[1]	G Thomas	A Smith	Lineker*[1]	J Barnes	Clough 11
Wright	Platt	G Thomas	Clough	Lineker*	Hirst	† Wise 10, Salako 11
Barrett	Platt	G Thomas	Wise	Lineker*[1]	Walters	Deane 4, Salako 11
Wright	Platt	G Thomas	Deane	I Wright	Salako	Hirst 9[1]
Wright	Platt	G Thomas	Clough	Lineker*[4]	Salako	
Parker	Platt	Steven	A Smith	Lineker*	Salako	Stewart 8, Merson 11
Mabbutt	Robson	Platt	A Smith[1]	Lineker*	Waddle	
Mabbutt	Platt	G Thomas	Rocastle	Lineker*[1]	Sinton	A Smith 4, Daley 11
Wright	Webb	G Thomas	Clough	Shearer[1]	Hirst	Lineker 11[1]
Mabbutt	Platt	Merson[1]	Clough	Hateley	J Barnes	Dixon 4, Lineker 6 Stewart 9, Dorigo 11
Keown	Platt	Steven[1]	Shearer	Lineker*[1]	Daley	Martyn 1, Curle 3 Stewart 8, Clough 9
Keown	Webb[1]	Palmer	Merson	Lineker*	Daley	Seaman 1, Sinton 4, Batty 7 A Smith 9, I Wright 10
Keown	Daley	Steven	Platt[1]	Lineker*	Sinton	Pearce 3, Merson 7, Webb 8 Rocastle 11
Wright	Platt[2]	Steven	Webb	Lineker*	J Barnes	Palmer 2, Daley 8, Merson 11
Keown	Platt	Steven	A Smith	Lineker*	Merson	Daley 2, Webb 11
Keown	Platt	Steven	Shearer	Lineker*	Palmer	
Palmer	Platt[1]	Webb	Sinton	Lineker*	Daley	Merson 9, A Smith 10
Wright	White	Platt	Clough	Shearer	Sinton	Bardsley 2, Palmer 2 Merson 7, Deane 11
Adams	Platt[1]	Gascoigne	Shearer	I Wright	Ince	Palmer 2, Merson 10
Adams	Platt	Gascoigne[2]	Shearer[1]	I Wright	Ince	
Adams	Platt*[4]	Gascoigne	Ferdinand[1]	J Barnes	Batty	
Adams	Platt*[1]	Gascoigne[1]	J Barnes	I Wright	Ince	Clough 2, Sharpe 10
Adams	Platt*[1]	Gascoigne	Ferdinand	J Barnes*[1]	Ince	Merson 8
Adams	Platt*	Gascoigne	Sheringham	J Barnes	Ince	I Wright 4[1], Clough 8
Adams	Platt*	Gascoigne	Ferdinand	Sheringham	Sharpe	Clough 5, I Wright 10
Batty	Ince*	Clough	Sharpe	Ferdinand	J Barnes	Walker 4, I Wright 10
Batty	Ince*	Clough	I Wright	Sinton	Sharpe	Platt 6[1], Palmer 7, Merson 8
Ince	Platt*[1]	Clough	Sharpe	J Barnes	Merson	Keown 5, I Wright 8 Winterburn 9
Adams	Platt	Gascoigne[1]	Ferdinand[1]	Wright	Sharpe	
Adams	Platt*	Palmer	Shearer	Merson	Sharpe	Sinton 8, I Wright 10
Walker	Platt	Ripley	Ferdinand[1]	I Wright[4]	Sinton	
Pallister	Platt*[1]	Gascoigne	Shearer	Beardsley	Anderton	Batty 4, Le Tissier 8
Adams	Platt*[2]	Merson	Shearer[1]	Beardsley[1]	Anderton[1]	Pearce 2, I Wright 10 Le Tissier 11

Versus	Venue	Result	1	2	3	4	5
Norway	H	0–0	Seaman	Jones	Le Saux	Ince	Bould
1994–95							
United States	H	2–0	Seaman	Jones	Le Saux	Venison	Adams
Romania	H	1–1	Seaman	Jones	Le Saux	Ince	Adams*
Nigeria	H	1–0	Flowers	Jones	Le Saux	Lee	Howey
Rep. of Ireland	A	0–1§	Seaman	Barton	Le Saux	Ince	Adams
Uruguay	H	0–0	Flowers	Jones	Le Saux	Venison	Adams
Japan	H	2–1	Flowers	Neville	Pearce	Batty	Scales
Sweden	H	3–3	Flowers	Barton	Le Saux	Barnes	Cooper
Brazil	H	1–3	Flowers	Neville	Pearce	Batty	Cooper

‡ *West Germany won 4–3 on penalties*
§ *Match abandoned after 27 minutes*

6	7	8	9	10	11	Substitutes
Adams	Platt*	Wise	Shearer	Beardsley	Anderton	Le Tissier 4, Wright 11
Pallister	Platt*[1]	Barnes	Shearer[2]	Sheringham	Anderton	Ferdinand 9, Wright 10
Pallister	Lee[1]	Wright	Shearer	Barnes	Le Tissier	Pearce 2, Wise 7, Sheringham 8
Ruddock	Platt*[1]	Beardsley	Shearer	Barnes	Wise	McManaman 4, Le Tissier 8, Sheringham 9
Pallister	Platt*	Beardsley	Shearer	Le Tissier	Anderton	
Pallister	Platt*	Beardsley	Sheringham	Barnes	Anderton	McManaman 3, Barmby 8, Cole 9
Unsworth	Platt*[1]	Beardsley	Shearer	Collymore	Anderton[1]	McManaman 4, Gascoigne 8, Sheringham 10
Pallister	Platt*[1]	Beardsley	Shearer	Sheringham[1]	Anderton[1]	Gascoigne 4, Scales 6, Barmby 8
Scales	Platt*	Le Saux[1]	Shearer	Sheringham	Anderton	Gascoigne 4, Barton 6, Collymore 10

● 71

20 ● ENGLAND'S INTERNATIONAL MATCHES 1872–1995

WCQ	World Cup Qualifier
WCF	World Cup Finals
ECQ	European Championship Qualifier
ECF	European Championship Finals
RC	Rous Cup
BJT	Brazilian Jubilee Tournament
USBT	US Bicentennial Tournament
USC	US Cup

v Albania

| 1989 | 8/3 | Tirana | W | 2–0 | WCQ |
| 1989 | 26/4 | Wembley | W | 5–0 | WCQ |

P 2, W 2, D 0, L 0, F 7, A 0

v Argentina

1951	9/5	Wembley	W	2–1	
1953	17/5	Buenos Aires	D	0–0	*
1962	2/6	Rancagua	W	3–1	WCF
1964	6/6	Rio de Janeiro	L	0–1	BJT
1966	23/7	Wembley	W	1–0	WCF
1974	22/5	Wembley	D	2–2	
1977	12/6	Buenos Aires	D	1–1	
1980	13/5	Wembley	W	3–1	
1986	22/6	Mexico City	L	1–2	WCF
1991	25/5	Wembley	D	2–2	

* Abandoned after 21 minutes

P 10, W 4, D 4, L 2, F 15, A 11

v Australia

1980	31/5	Sydney	W	2–1
1983	12/6	Sydney	D	0–0
1983	15/6	Brisbane	W	1–0
1983	19/6	Melbourne	D	1–1
1991	1/6	Sydney	W	1–0

P 5, W 3, D 2, L 0, F 5, A 2

v Austria

1908	6/6	Vienna	W	6–1	
1908	8/6	Vienna	W	11–1	
1909	1/6	Vienna	W	8–1	
1930	14/5	Vienna	D	0–0	
1932	7/12	Chelsea	W	4–3	
1936	6/5	Vienna	L	1–2	
1951	28/11	Wembley	D	2–2	
1952	25/5	Vienna	W	3–2	
1958	15/6	Boras	D	2–2	WCF
1961	27/5	Vienna	L	1–3	
1962	4/4	Wembley	W	3–1	
1965	20/10	Wembley	L	2–3	
1967	27/5	Vienna	W	1–0	

| 1973 | 26/9 | Wembley | W | 7–0 |
| 1979 | 13/6 | Vienna | L | 3–4 |

P 15, W 8, D 3, L 4, F 54, A 25

v Belgium

1921	21/5	Brussels	W	2–0	
1923	19/3	Arsenal	W	6–1	
1923	1/11	Antwerp	D	2–2	
1924	8/12	West Bromwich	W	4–0	
1926	24/5	Antwerp	W	5–3	
1927	11/5	Brussels	W	9–1	
1928	19/5	Antwerp	W	3–1	
1929	11/5	Brussels	W	5–1	
1931	16/5	Brussels	W	4–1	
1936	9/5	Brussels	L	2–3	
1947	21/9	Brussels	W	5–2	
1950	18/5	Brussels	W	4–1	
1952	26/11	Wembley	W	5–0	
1954	17/6	Basle	D	4–4	WCE
1964	21/10	Wembley	D	2–2	
1970	25/2	Brussels	W	3–1	
1980	12/6	Turin	D	1–1	ECF
1990	26/6	Bologna	W	1–0	WCF

P 18, W 13, D 4, L 1, F 67, A 24

v Bohemia

| 1908 | 13/6 | Prague | W | 4–0 |

P 1, W 1, D 0, L 0, F 4, A 0

v Brazil

1956	9/5	Wembley	W	4–2	
1958	11/6	Gothenburg	D	0–0	WCF
1959	13/5	Rio de Janeiro	L	0–2	
1962	10/6	Vina del Mar	L	1–3	WCF
1963	8/5	Wembley	D	1–1	
1964	30/5	Rio de Janeiro	L	1–5	BJT
1969	12/6	Rio de Janeiro	L	1–2	
1970	7/6	Guadalajara	L	0–1	WCF
1976	23/5	Los Angeles	L	0–1	USBT
1977	8/6	Rio de Janeiro	D	0–0	
1978	19/4	Wembley	D	1–1	
1981	12/5	Wembley	L	0–1	
1984	10/6	Rio de Janeiro	W	2–0	
1987	19/5	Wembley	D	1–1	RC
1990	28/3	Wembley	W	1–0	
1992	17/5	Wembley	D	1–1	
1993	13/6	Washington	D	1–1	USC
1995	11/6	Wembley	L	1–3	

P 18, W 3, D 7, L 8, F 16, A 25

v Bulgaria

1962	7/6	Rancagua	D	0–0	WCF
1968	11/12	Wembley	D	1–1	
1974	1/6	Sofia	W	1–0	
1979	6/6	Sofia	W	3–0	ECQ
1979	22/11	Wembley	W	2–0	ECQ

P 5, W 3, D 2, L 0, F 7, A 1

v Cameroon

| 1990 | 1/7 | Naples | W | 3–2 | WCF |
| 1991 | 6/2 | Wembley | W | 2–0 | |

P 2, W 2, D 0, L 0, F 5, A 2

v Canada

| 1986 | 24/5 | Vancouver | W | 1–0 | |

P 1, W 1, D 0, L 0, F 1, A 0

v Chile

1950	25/6	Rio de Janeiro	W	2–0	WCF
1953	24/5	Santiago	W	2–1	
1984	17/6	Santiago	D	0–0	
1989	23/5	Wembley	D	0–0	RC

P 4, W 2, D 2, L 0, F 4, A 1

v CIS

| 1992 | 29/4 | Moscow | W | 2–2 | |

P 1, W 0, D 1, L 0, F 2, A 2

v Colombia

| 1970 | 20/5 | Bogota | W | 4–0 | |
| 1988 | 24/5 | Wembley | D | 1–1 | RC |

P 2, W 1, D 1, L 0, F 5, A 1

v Cyprus

| 1975 | 16/4 | Wembley | W | 5–0 | ECQ |
| 1975 | 11/5 | Limassol | W | 1–0 | ECQ |

P 2, W 2, D 0, L 0, F 6, A 0

v Czechoslovakia

1934	16/5	Prague	L	1–2	
1937	1/12	Tottenham	W	5–4	
1963	29/5	Bratislava	W	4–2	
1966	2/11	Wembley	D	0–0	
1970	11/6	Guadalajara	W	1–0	WCF
1973	27/5	Prague	D	1–1	
1974	30/10	Wembley	W	3–0	ECQ
1975	30/10	Bratislava	L	1–2	ECQ
1978	29/11	Wembley	W	1–0	
1982	20/6	Bilbao	W	2–0	WCF
1990	25/4	Wembley	W	4–2	
1992	25/3	Prague	D	2–2	

P 12, W 7, D 3, L 2, F 25, A 15

v Denmark

1948	26/9	Copenhagen	D	0–0	
1955	2/10	Copenhagen	W	5–1	
1956	5/12	Wolverhampton	W	5–2	WCQ
1957	15/5	Copenhagen	W	4–1	WCQ
1966	3/7	Copenhagen	W	2–0	
1978	20/9	Copenhagen	W	4–3	ECQ
1979	12/9	Wembley	W	1–0	ECQ
1982	22/9	Copenhagen	D	2–2	ECQ
1983	21/9	Wembley	L	0–1	ECQ
1988	14/9	Wembley	W	1–0	
1989	7/6	Copenhagen	D	1–1	
1990	15/5	Wembley	W	1–0	
1992	11/6	Malmö	D	0–0	ECF
1994	9/3	Wembley	W	1–0	

P 14, W 9, D 4, L 1, F 27, A 11

v Ecuador

| 1970 | 24/5 | Quito | W | 2–0 | |

P 1, W 1, D 0, L 0, F 2, A 0

v Egypt

| 1986 | 29/1 | Cairo | W | 4–0 | |
| 1990 | 21/6 | Cagliari | W | 1–0 | WCF |

P 2, W 2, D 0, L 0, F 5, A 0

v FIFA

| 1953 | 21/10 | Wembley | D | 4–4 | |

P 1, W 0, D 1, L 0, F 4, A 4

v Finland

1937	20/5	Helsinki	W	8–0	
1956	20/5	Helsinki	W	5–1	
1966	26/6	Helsinki	W	3–0	
1976	13/6	Helsinki	W	4–1	WCQ
1976	13/10	Wembley	W	2–1	WCQ
1982	3/6	Helsinki	W	4–1	
1984	17/10	Wembley	W	5–0	WCQ
1985	22/5	Helsinki	D	1–1	WCQ
1992	3/6	Helsinki	W	2–1	

P 9, W 8, D 1, L 0, F 34, A 6

v France

1923	10/5	Paris	W	4–1	
1924	17/5	Paris	W	3–1	
1925	21/5	Paris	W	3–2	
1927	26/5	Paris	W	6–0	
1928	17/5	Paris	W	5–1	
1929	9/5	Paris	W	4–1	
1931	14/5	Paris	L	2–5	
1933	6/12	Tottenham	W	4–1	
1938	26/5	Paris	W	4–2	
1947	3/5	Arsenal	W	3–0	
1949	22/5	Paris	W	3–1	

1951	3/10	Arsenal	D	2-2	
1955	15/5	Paris	L	0-1	
1957	27/11	Wembley	W	4-0	
1962	3/10	Sheffield	D	1-1	ECQ
1963	27/2	Paris	L	2-5	ECQ
1966	20/7	Wembley	W	2-0	WCF
1969	12/3	Wembley	W	5-0	
1982	16/6	Bilbao	W	3-1	WCF
1984	29/2	Paris	L	0-2	
1992	19/2	Wembley	W	2-0	
1992	14/6	Malmö	D	0-0	ECF

P 22, W 15, D 3, L 4, F 62, A 27

v East Germany

1963	2/6	Leipzig	W	2-1
1970	25/11	Wembley	W	3-1
1974	29/5	Leipzig	D	1-1
1984	12/9	Wembley	W	1-0

P 4, W 3, D 1, L 0, F 7, A 3

v West Germany

1930	10/5	Berlin	D	3-3	†
1935	4/12	Tottenham	W	3-0	†
1938	14/5	Berlin	W	6-3	†
1954	1/12	Wembley	W	3-1	
1956	26/5	Berlin	W	3-1	
1965	12/5	Nuremberg	W	1-0	
1966	23/2	Wembley	W	1-0	
1966	30/7	Wembley	W	4-2	WCF
1968	1/6	Hanover	L	0-1	
1970	14/6	Leon	L	2-3	WCF
1972	29/4	Wembley	L	1-3	ECQ
1972	13/5	Berlin	D	0-0	ECQ
1975	12/3	Wembley	W	2-0	
1978	22/2	Munich	L	1-2	
1982	29/6	Madrid	D	0-0	WCF
1982	13/10	Wembley	L	1-2	
1985	12/6	Mexico City	W	3-0	
1987	9/9	Düsseldorf	L	1-3	
1990	4/7	Turin	D	1-1	*WCF

P 19, W 9, D 3, L 7, F 36, A 25

* After extra time (England lost 3-4 on penalties)
† as Germany

v Germany

| 1991 | 11/9 | Wembley | L | 0-1 | |
| 1993 | 19/6 | Detroit | L | 1-2 | USC |

P 2, W 0, D 0, L 2, F 1, A 3

v Greece

1971	21/4	Wembley	W	3-0	ECQ
1971	1/12	Athens	W	2-0	ECQ
1982	17/11	Salonika	W	3-0	ECQ
1983	30/3	Wembley	D	0-0	ECQ
1989	8/2	Athens	W	2-1	
1994	17/5	Wembley	W	5-0	

P 6, W 5, D 1, L 0, F 15, A 1

v Holland

1935	18/5	Amsterdam	W	1-0	
1946	27/11	Huddersfield	W	8-2	
1964	9/12	Amsterdam	D	1-1	
1969	5/11	Amsterdam	W	1-0	
1970	14/1	Wembley	D	0-0	
1977	9/2	Wembley	L	0-2	
1982	25/5	Wembley	W	2-0	
1988	23/3	Wembley	D	2-2	
1988	15/6	Düsseldorf	L	1-3	ECF
1990	16/6	Cagliari	D	0-0	WCF
1993	28/4	Wembley	D	2-2	WCQ
1993	13/10	Rotterdam	L	0-2	WCQ

P 12, W 4, D 5, L 3, F 18, A 14

v Hungary

1908	10/6	Budapest	W	7-0	
1909	29/5	Budapest	W	4-2	
1909	31/5	Budapest	W	8-2	
1934	10/5	Budapest	L	1-2	
1936	2/12	Arsenal	W	6-2	
1953	25/11	Wembley	L	3-6	
1954	23/5	Budapest	L	1-7	
1960	22/5	Budapest	L	0-2	
1962	31/5	Rancagua	L	1-2	WCF
1965	5/5	Wembley	W	1-0	
1978	24/5	Wembley	W	4-1	
1981	6/6	Budapest	W	3-1	WCQ
1981	18/11	Wembley	W	1-0	WCQ
1983	27/4	Wembley	W	2-0	ECQ
1983	12/10	Budapest	W	3-0	ECQ
1988	27/4	Budapest	D	0-0	
1990	12/9	Wembley	W	1-0	
1992	12/5	Budapest	W	1-0	

P 18, W 12, D 1, L 5, F 47, A 27

v Iceland

| 1982 | 2/6 | Reykjavik | D | 1-1 |

P 1, W 0, D 1, L 0, F 1, A 1

v Ireland

1882	18/2	Belfast	W	13-0
1883	24/2	Liverpool	W	7-0
1884	23/2	Belfast	W	8-1
1885	28/2	Manchester	W	4-0
1886	13/3	Belfast	W	6-1
1887	5/2	Sheffield	W	7-0
1888	31/3	Belfast	W	5-1
1889	2/3	Everton	W	6-1
1890	15/3	Belfast	W	9-1
1891	7/3	Wolverhampton	W	6-1
1892	5/3	Belfast	W	2-0

1893	25/2	Birmingham	W	6-1	
1894	3/3	Belfast	D	2-2	
1895	9/3	Derby	W	9-0	
1896	7/3	Belfast	W	2-0	
1897	20/2	Nottingham	W	6-0	
1898	5/3	Belfast	W	3-2	
1899	18/2	Sunderland	W	13-2	
1900	17/3	Dublin	W	2-0	
1901	9/3	Southampton	W	3-0	
1902	22/3	Belfast	W	1-0	
1903	14/2	Wolverhampton	W	4-0	
1904	12/3	Belfast	W	3-1	
1905	25/2	Middlesbrough	D	1-1	
1906	17/2	Belfast	W	5-0	
1907	16/2	Everton	W	1-0	
1908	15/2	Belfast	W	3-1	
1909	13/2	Bradford	W	4-0	
1910	12/2	Belfast	D	1-1	
1911	11/2	Derby	W	2-1	
1912	10/2	Dublin	W	6-1	
1913	15/2	Belfast	L	1-2	
1914	14/2	Middlesbrough	L	0-3	
1919	25/10	Belfast	D	1-1	
1920	23/10	Sunderland	W	2-0	
1921	22/10	Belfast	D	1-1	
1922	21/10	West Bromwich	W	2-0	
1923	20/10	Belfast	L	1-2	
1924	22/10	Everton	W	3-1	
1925	24/10	Belfast	D	0-0	
1926	20/10	Liverpool	D	3-3	
1927	22/10	Belfast	L	0-2	
1928	22/10	Everton	W	2-1	
1929	19/10	Belfast	W	3-0	
1930	20/10	Sheffield	W	5-1	
1931	17/10	Belfast	W	6-2	
1932	17/10	Blackpool	W	1-0	
1933	14/10	Belfast	W	3-0	
1935	6/2	Everton	W	2-1	
1935	19/10	Belfast	W	3-1	
1936	18/11	Stoke	W	3-1	
1937	23/10	Belfast	W	5-1	
1938	16/11	Manchester	W	7-0	
1946	28/9	Belfast	W	7-2	
1947	5/11	Everton	D	2-2	
1948	9/10	Belfast	W	6-2	
1949	16/11	Manchester	W	9-2	WCQ
1950	7/10	Belfast	W	4-1	
1951	14/11	Aston Villa	W	2-0	
1952	4/10	Belfast	D	2-2	
1953	11/11	Everton	W	3-1	WCQ
1954	2/10	Belfast	W	2-0	
1955	2/11	Wembley	W	3-0	
1956	6/10	Belfast	D	1-1	
1957	6/11	Wembley	L	2-3	
1958	4/10	Belfast	D	3-3	
1959	18/11	Wembley	W	2-1	
1960	8/10	Belfast	W	5-2	
1961	22/11	Wembley	D	1-1	
1962	20/10	Belfast	W	3-1	
1963	20/11	Wembley	W	8-3	
1964	3/10	Belfast	W	4-3	
1965	10/11	Wembley	W	2-1	
1966	20/10	Belfast	W	2-0	ECQ
1967	22/11	Wembley	W	2-0	ECQ
1969	3/5	Belfast	W	3-1	
1970	21/4	Wembley	W	3-1	
1971	15/5	Belfast	W	1-0	
1972	23/5	Wembley	L	0-1	
1973	12/5	Everton	W	2-1	
1974	15/5	Wembley	W	1-0	
1975	17/5	Belfast	D	0-0	
1976	11/5	Wembley	W	4-0	
1977	28/5	Belfast	W	2-1	
1978	16/5	Wembley	W	1-0	
1979	7/2	Wembley	W	4-0	ECQ
1979	19/5	Belfast	W	2-0	
1979	17/10	Belfast	W	5-1	ECQ
1980	20/5	Wembley	D	1-1	
1982	23/2	Wembley	W	4-0	
1983	28/5	Belfast	D	0-0	
1984	4/4	Wembley	W	1-0	
1985	27/2	Belfast	W	1-0	WCQ
1985	13/11	Wembley	D	0-0	WCQ
1986	15/10	Wembley	W	3-0	ECQ
1987	1/4	Belfast	W	2-0	ECQ

P 96, W 74, D 16, L 6, F 319, A 80

v Israel

1986	26/2	Tel Aviv	W	2-1	
1988	17/2	Tel Aviv	D	0-0	

P 2, W 1, D 1, L 0, F 2, A 1

v Italy

1933	13/5	Rome	D	1-1	
1934	14/11	Arsenal	W	3-2	
1939	13/5	Milan	D	2-2	
1948	16/5	Turin	W	4-0	
1949	30/11	Tottenham	W	2-0	
1952	18/5	Florence	D	1-1	
1959	6/5	Wembley	D	2-2	
1961	24/5	Rome	W	3-2	
1973	14/6	Turin	L	0-2	
1973	14/11	Wembley	L	0-1	
1976	28/5	New York	W	3-2	USBT
1976	17/11	Rome	L	0-2	WCQ
1977	16/11	Wembley	W	2-0	WCQ
1980	15/6	Turin	L	0-1	ECF
1985	6/6	Mexico City	L	1-2	
1989	15/11	Wembley	D	0-0	
1990	7/7	Bari	L	1-2	WCF

P 17, W 6, D 5, L 6, F 25, A 22

v Japan

1995	3/6	Wembley	W	2-1	

P 1, W 1, D 0, L 0, F 2, A 1

v Kuwait

1982	25/6	Bilbao	W	1–0	WCF

P 1, W 1, D 0, L 0, F 1, A 0

v Luxembourg

1927	21/5	Luxembourg	W	5–2	
1960	19/10	Luxembourg	W	9–0	WCQ
1961	28/9	Arsenal	W	4–1	WCQ
1977	30/3	Wembley	W	5–0	WCQ
1977	12/10	Luxembourg	W	2–0	WCQ
1982	15/12	Wembley	W	9–0	ECQ
1983	16/11	Luxembourg	W	4–0	ECQ

P 7, W 7, D 0, L 0, F 38, A 3

v Malaysia

1991	12/6	Kuala Lumpur	W	4–2	

P 1, W 1, D 0, L 0, F 4, A 2

v Malta

1971	3/2	Valletta	W	1–0	ECQ
1971	12/5	Wembley	W	5–0	ECQ

P 2, W 2, D 0, L 0, F 6, A 0

v Mexico

1959	24/5	Mexico City	L	1–2	
1961	10/5	Wembley	W	8–0	
1966	16/7	Wembley	W	2–0	WCF
1969	1/6	Mexico City	D	0–0	
1985	9/6	Mexico City	L	0–1	
1986	17/5	Los Angeles	W	3–0	

P 6, W 3, D 1, L 2, F 14, A 3

v Morocco

1986	6/6	Monterrey	D	0–0	WCF

P 1, W 0, D 1, L 0, F 0, A 0

v New Zealand

1991	3/6	Auckland	W	1–0	
1991	8/6	Wellington	W	2–0	

P 2, W 2, D 0, L 0, F 3, A 0

v Nigeria

1994	16/11	Wembley	W	1–0	

P 1, W 1, D 0, L 0, F 1, A 0

v Northern Ireland (see Ireland)

v Norway

1937	14/5	Oslo	W	6–0	
1938	9/11	Newcastle	W	4–0	
1949	18/5	Oslo	W	4–1	
1966	29/6	Oslo	W	6–1	
1980	10/9	Wembley	W	4–0	WCQ
1981	9/9	Oslo	L	1–2	WCQ
1992	14/10	Wembley	D	1–1	WCQ
1993	2/6	Oslo	L	0–2	WCQ
1994	22/5	Wembley	D	0–0	

P 9, W 5, D 2, L 2, F 26, A 7

v Paraguay

1986	18/6	Mexico City	W	3–0	WCF

P 1, W 1, D 0, L 0, F 3, A 0

v Peru

1959	17/5	Lima	L	1–4	
1962	20/5	Lima	W	4–0	

P 2, W 1, D 0, L 1, F 5, A 4

v Poland

1966	5/1	Everton	D	1–1	
1966	5/7	Chorzow	W	1–0	
1973	6/6	Chorzow	L	0–2	WCQ
1973	17/10	Wembley	D	1–1	WCQ
1986	11/6	Monterrey	W	3–0	WCF
1989	3/6	Wembley	W	3–0	WCQ
1989	11/10	Katowice	D	0–0	WCQ
1990	17/10	Wembley	W	2–0	ECQ
1991	13/11	Poznan	D	1–1	ECQ
1993	29/5	Katowice	D	1–1	WCQ
1993	8/9	Wembley	W	3–0	WCQ

P 11, W 5, D 5, L 1, F 16, A 6

v Portugal

1947	25/5	Lisbon	W	10–0	
1950	14/5	Lisbon	W	5–3	
1951	19/5	Everton	W	5–2	
1955	22/5	Oporto	L	1–3	
1958	7/5	Wembley	W	2–1	
1961	21/5	Lisbon	D	1–1	WCQ
1961	25/10	Wembley	W	2–0	WCQ
1964	17/5	Lisbon	W	4–3	
1964	4/6	São Paolo	D	1–1	BJT
1966	26/7	Wembley	W	2–1	WCF
1969	10/12	Wembley	W	1–0	
1974	3/4	Lisbon	D	0–0	
1974	20/11	Wembley	D	0–0	ECQ
1975	19/11	Lisbon	D	1–1	ECQ
1986	3/6	Monterrey	L	0–1	WCF

P 15, W 8, D 5, L 2, F 35, A 17

v Republic of Ireland

1946	30/9	Dublin	W	1–0	
1949	21/9	Everton	L	0–2	
1957	8/5	Wembley	W	5–1	WCQ
1957	19/5	Dublin	D	1–1	WCQ
1964	24/5	Dublin	W	3–1	

1976	8/9	Wembley	D	1–1	
1978	25/10	Dublin	D	1–1	ECQ
1980	6/2	Wembley	W	2–0	ECQ
1985	26/3	Wembley	W	2–1	
1988	12/6	Stuttgart	L	0–1	ECF
1990	11/6	Cagliari	D	1–1	WCF
1990	14/11	Dublin	D	1–1	ECQ
1991	27/3	Wembley	D	1–1	ECQ

P 13, W 5, D 6, L 2, F 19, A 12

v Rest of Europe

1938	26/10	Arsenal	W	3–0

P 1, W 1, D 0, L 0, F 3, A 0

v Rest of the World

1963	23/10	Wembley	W	2–1

P 1, W 1, D 0, L 0, F 2, A 1

v Romania

1939	24/5	Bucharest	W	2–0	
1968	6/11	Bucharest	D	0–0	
1969	15/1	Wembley	D	1–1	
1970	2/6	Guadalajara	W	1–0	WCF
1980	15/10	Bucharest	L	1–2	WCQ
1981	29/4	Wembley	D	0–0	WCQ
1985	1/5	Bucharest	D	0–0	WCQ
1985	11/9	Wembley	D	1–1	WCQ
1994	12/10	Wembley	D	1–1	

P 9, W 2, D 6, L 1, F 7, A 5

v San Marino

1993	17/2	Wembley	W	6–0	WCQ
1993	17/11	Bologna	W	7–1	WCQ

P 2, W 2, D 0, L 0, F 13, A 1

v Saudi Arabia

1988	16/11	Riyadh	D	1–1

P 1, W 0, D 1, L 0, F 1, A 1

v Scotland

1872	30/11	Glasgow	D	0–0	
1873	8/3	Kennington	W	4–2	
1874	7/3	Glasgow	L	1–2	
1875	6/3	Kennington	D	2–2	
1876	4/3	Glasgow	L	0–3	
1877	3/3	Kennington	L	1–3	
1878	2/3	Glasgow	L	2–7	
1879	5/4	Kennington	W	5–4	
1880	13/3	Glasgow	L	4–5	
1881	12/3	Kennington	L	1–6	
1882	11/3	Glasgow	L	1–5	
1883	10/3	Sheffield	L	2–3	
1884	15/3	Glasgow	L	0–1	
1885	21/3	Kennington	D	1–1	
1886	31/3	Glasgow	D	1–1	
1887	19/3	Blackburn	L	2–3	
1888	17/3	Glasgow	W	5–0	
1889	13/4	Kennington	L	2–3	
1890	5/4	Glasgow	D	1–1	
1891	6/4	Blackburn	W	2–1	
1892	2/4	Glasgow	W	4–1	
1893	1/4	Richmond	W	5–2	
1894	7/4	Glasgow	D	2–2	
1895	6/4	Everton	W	3–0	
1896	4/4	Glasgow	L	1–2	
1897	3/4	Crystal Palace	L	1–2	
1898	2/4	Glasgow	W	3–1	
1899	8/4	Birmingham	W	2–1	
1900	7/4	Glasgow	L	1–4	
1901	30/3	Crystal Palace	D	2–2	
1902	3/3	Birmingham	D	2–2	
1903	4/4	Sheffield	L	1–2	
1904	9/4	Glasgow	W	1–0	
1905	1/4	Crystal Palace	W	1–0	
1906	7/4	Glasgow	L	1–2	
1907	6/4	Newcastle	D	1–1	
1908	4/4	Glasgow	D	1–1	
1909	3/4	Crystal Palace	W	2–0	
1910	2/4	Glasgow	L	0–2	
1911	1/4	Everton	D	1–1	
1912	23/3	Glasgow	D	1–1	
1913	5/4	Chelsea	W	1–0	
1914	14/4	Glasgow	L	1–3	
1920	10/4	Sheffield	W	5–4	
1921	9/4	Glasgow	L	0–3	
1922	8/4	Aston Villa	L	0–1	
1923	14/4	Glasgow	D	2–2	
1924	12/4	Wembley	D	1–1	
1925	4/4	Glasgow	L	0–2	
1926	17/4	Manchester	L	0–1	
1927	2/4	Glasgow	W	2–1	
1928	31/3	Wembley	L	1–5	
1929	13/4	Glasgow	L	0–1	
1930	5/4	Wembley	W	5–2	
1931	28/3	Glasgow	L	0–2	
1932	9/4	Wembley	W	3–0	
1933	1/4	Glasgow	L	1–2	
1934	14/4	Wembley	W	3–0	
1935	6/4	Glasgow	L	0–2	
1936	4/4	Wembley	D	1–1	
1937	17/4	Glasgow	L	1–3	
1938	9/4	Wembley	L	0–1	
1939	15/4	Glasgow	W	2–1	
1947	12/4	Wembley	D	1–1	
1948	10/4	Glasgow	W	2–0	
1949	9/4	Wembley	L	1–3	
1950	15/4	Glasgow	W	1–0	WCQ
1951	14/4	Wembley	L	2–3	
1952	5/4	Glasgow	W	2–1	
1953	18/4	Wembley	D	2–2	
1954	3/4	Glasgow	W	4–2	WCQ
1955	2/4	Wembley	W	7–2	
1956	14/4	Glasgow	D	1–1	
1957	6/4	Wembley	W	2–1	

1958	19/4	Glasgow	W	4-0	
1959	11/4	Wembley	W	1-0	
1960	19/4	Glasgow	D	1-1	
1961	15/4	Wembley	W	9-3	
1962	14/4	Glasgow	L	0-2	
1963	6/4	Wembley	L	1-2	
1964	11/4	Glasgow	L	0-1	
1965	10/4	Wembley	D	2-2	
1966	2/4	Glasgow	W	4-3	
1967	15/4	Wembley	L	2-3	ECQ
1968	24/2	Glasgow	D	1-1	ECQ
1969	10/5	Wembley	W	4-1	
1970	25/4	Glasgow	D	0-0	
1971	22/5	Wembley	W	3-1	
1972	27/5	Glasgow	W	1-0	
1973	14/2	Glasgow	W	5-0	
1973	19/5	Wembley	W	1-0	
1974	18/5	Glasgow	L	0-2	
1975	24/5	Wembley	W	5-1	
1976	15/5	Glasgow	L	1-2	
1977	4/6	Wembley	L	1-2	
1978	20/5	Glasgow	W	1-0	
1979	26/5	Wembley	W	3-1	
1980	24/5	Glasgow	W	2-0	
1981	23/5	Wembley	L	0-1	
1982	29/5	Glasgow	W	1-0	
1983	1/6	Wembley	W	2-0	
1984	26/5	Glasgow	D	1-1	
1985	25/5	Glasgow	L	0-1	RC
1986	23/4	Wembley	W	2-1	RC
1987	23/5	Glasgow	D	0-0	RC
1988	21/5	Wembley	W	1-0	RC
1989	27/5	Glasgow	W	2-0	RC

P 107, W 43, D 24, L 40, F 188, A 168

v Spain

1929	15/5	Madrid	L	3-4	
1931	9/12	Arsenal	W	7-1	
1950	2/7	Rio de Janeiro	L	0-1	WCF
1955	18/5	Madrid	D	1-1	
1955	30/11	Wembley	W	4-1	
1960	15/5	Madrid	L	0-3	
1960	26/10	Wembley	W	4-2	
1965	8/12	Madrid	W	2-0	
1967	24/5	Wembley	W	2-0	
1968	3/4	Wembley	W	1-0	ECQ
1968	8/5	Madrid	W	2-1	ECQ
1980	26/3	Barcelona	W	2-0	
1980	18/6	Naples	W	2-1	ECF
1981	25/3	Wembley	L	1-2	
1982	5/7	Madrid	D	0-0	WCF
1987	18/2	Madrid	W	4-2	
1992	9/9	Santander	L	0-1	

P 17, W 10, D 2, L 5, F 35, A 20

v Sweden

1923	21/5	Stockholm	W	4-2	
1923	24/5	Stockholm	W	3-1	
1937	17/5	Stockholm	W	4-0	
1947	19/11	Arsenal	W	4-2	
1949	13/5	Stockholm	L	1-3	
1956	16/5	Stockholm	D	0-0	
1959	28/10	Wembley	L	2-3	
1965	16/5	Gothenburg	W	2-1	
1968	22/5	Wembley	W	3-1	
1979	10/6	Stockholm	D	0-0	
1986	10/9	Stockholm	L	0-1	
1988	19/10	Wembley	D	0-0	WCQ
1989	6/9	Stockholm	D	0-0	WCQ
1992	17/6	Stockholm	L	1-2	ECF
1995	8/6	Leeds	D	3-3	

P 15, W 6, D 5, L 4, F 27, A 19

v Switzerland

1933	29/5	Berne	W	4-0	
1938	21/5	Zurich	L	1-2	
1947	18/5	Zurich	L	0-1	
1948	2/12	Arsenal	W	6-0	
1952	28/5	Zurich	W	3-0	
1954	20/6	Berne	W	2-0	WCF
1962	9/5	Wembley	W	3-1	
1963	5/6	Basle	W	8-1	
1971	13/10	Basle	W	3-2	ECQ
1971	10/11	Wembley	D	1-1	ECQ
1975	3/9	Basle	W	2-1	
1977	7/9	Wembley	D	0-0	
1980	19/11	Wembley	W	2-1	WCQ
1981	30/5	Basle	L	1-2	WCQ
1988	28/5	Lausanne	W	1-0	

P 15, W 10, D 2, L 3, F 37, A 12

v Tunisia

1990	2/6	Tunis	D	1-1

P 1, W 0, D 1, L 0, F 1, A 1

v Turkey

1984	14/11	Istanbul	W	8-0	WCQ
1985	16/10	Wembley	W	5-0	WCQ
1987	29/4	Izmir	D	0-0	ECQ
1987	14/10	Wembley	W	8-0	ECQ
1991	1/5	Izmir	W	1-0	ECQ
1991	16/10	Wembley	W	1-0	ECQ
1992	18/11	Wembley	W	4-0	WCQ
1993	31/3	Izmir	W	2-0	WCQ

P 8, W 7, D 1, L 0, F 29, A 0

v USA

1950	29/6	Belo Horizonte	L	0-1	WCF
1953	8/6	New York	W	6-3	
1959	28/5	Los Angeles	W	8-1	
1964	27/5	New York	W	10-0	
1985	16/6	Los Angeles	W	5-0	
1993	9/6	Boston	L	0-2	
1994	7/9	Wembley	W	2-0	

P 7, W 5, D 0, L 2, F 31, A 7

v USSR (see also CIS)

1958	18/5	Moscow	D	1-1	
1958	8/6	Gothenburg	D	2-2	WCF
1958	17/6	Gothenburg	L	0-1	WCF
1958	22/10	Wembley	W	5-0	
1967	6/12	Wembley	D	2-2	
1968	8/6	Rome	W	2-0	ECF
1973	10/6	Moscow	W	2-1	
1984	2/6	Wembley	L	0-2	
1986	26/3	Tbilisi	W	1-0	
1988	18/6	Frankfurt	L	1-3	ECF
1991	21/5	Wembley	W	3-1	

P 11, W 5, D 3, L 3, F 19, A 13

v Uruguay

1953	31/5	Montevideo	L	1-2	
1954	26/6	Basle	L	2-4	WCF
1964	6/5	Wembley	W	2-1	
1966	11/7	Wembley	D	0-0	WCF
1969	8/6	Montevideo	W	2-1	
1977	15/6	Montevideo	D	0-0	
1984	13/6	Montevideo	L	0-2	
1990	22/5	Wembley	L	1-2	
1995	29/3	Wembley	D	0-0	

P 9, W 2, D 3, L 4, F 8, A 12

v Wales

1879	18/1	Kennington	W	2-1	
1880	15/3	Wrexham	W	3-2	
1881	26/2	Blackburn	L	0-1	
1882	13/3	Wrexham	L	3-5	
1883	3/2	Kennington	W	5-0	
1884	17/3	Wrexham	W	4-0	
1885	14/3	Blackburn	D	1-1	
1886	29/3	Wrexham	W	3-1	
1887	26/2	Kennington	W	4-0	
1888	4/2	Crewe	W	5-1	
1889	23/2	Stoke	W	4-1	
1890	15/3	Wrexham	W	3-1	
1891	7/5	Sunderland	W	4-1	
1892	5/3	Wrexham	W	2-0	
1893	13/3	Stoke	W	6-0	
1894	12/3	Wrexham	W	5-1	
1895	18/3	Kennington	D	1-1	
1896	16/3	Cardiff	W	9-1	
1897	29/3	Sheffield	W	4-0	
1898	28/3	Wrexham	W	3-0	
1899	20/3	Bristol	W	4-0	
1900	26/3	Cardiff	D	1-1	
1901	18/3	Newcastle	W	6-0	
1902	3/3	Wrexham	D	0-0	
1903	2/3	Portsmouth	W	2-0	
1904	29/2	Wrexham	D	2-2	
1905	27/3	Liverpool	W	3-1	
1906	19/3	Cardiff	W	1-0	
1907	18/3	Fulham	D	1-1	
1908	16/3	Wrexham	W	7-1	

1909	15/3	Nottingham	W	2-0	
1910	14/3	Cardiff	W	1-0	
1911	13/3	Millwall	W	3-0	
1912	11/3	Wrexham	W	2-0	
1913	17/3	Bristol	W	4-3	
1914	16/3	Cardiff	W	2-0	
1920	15/3	Arsenal	L	1-2	
1921	14/3	Cardiff	D	0-0	
1922	13/3	Liverpool	W	1-0	
1923	5/3	Cardiff	D	2-2	
1924	3/3	Blackburn	L	1-2	
1925	28/2	Swansea	W	2-1	
1926	1/3	Crystal Palace	L	1-3	
1927	12/2	Wrexham	D	3-3	
1927	28/11	Burnley	L	1-2	
1928	17/11	Swansea	W	3-2	
1929	20/11	Chelsea	W	6-0	
1930	22/11	Wrexham	W	4-0	
1931	18/11	Liverpool	W	3-1	
1932	16/11	Wrexham	D	0-0	
1933	15/11	Newcastle	L	1-2	
1934	29/9	Cardiff	W	4-0	
1936	5/2	Wolverhampton	L	1-2	
1936	17/10	Cardiff	L	1-2	
1937	17/11	Middlesbrough	W	2-1	
1938	22/10	Cardiff	L	2-4	
1946	13/11	Manchester	W	3-0	
1947	18/10	Cardiff	W	3-0	
1948	10/11	Aston Villa	W	1-0	
1949	15/10	Cardiff	W	4-1	WCQ
1950	15/11	Sunderland	W	4-2	
1951	20/10	Cardiff	D	1-1	
1952	12/11	Wembley	W	5-2	
1953	10/10	Cardiff	W	4-1	WCQ
1954	10/11	Wembley	W	3-2	
1955	22/10	Cardiff	L	1-2	
1956	14/11	Wembley	W	3-1	
1957	19/10	Cardiff	W	4-0	
1958	26/11	Aston Villa	D	2-2	
1959	17/10	Cardiff	D	1-1	
1960	23/11	Wembley	W	5-1	
1961	14/10	Cardiff	D	1-1	
1962	21/11	Wembley	W	4-0	
1963	12/10	Cardiff	W	4-0	
1964	18/11	Wembley	W	2-1	
1965	2/10	Cardiff	D	0-0	
1966	16/11	Wembley	W	5-1	ECQ
1967	21/10	Cardiff	W	3-0	ECQ
1969	7/5	Wembley	W	2-1	
1970	18/4	Cardiff	D	1-1	
1971	19/5	Wembley	D	0-0	
1972	20/5	Cardiff	W	3-0	
1972	15/11	Cardiff	W	1-0	WCQ
1973	24/1	Wembley	D	1-1	WCQ
1973	15/5	Wembley	W	3-0	
1974	11/5	Cardiff	W	2-0	
1975	21/5	Wembley	D	2-2	
1976	24/3	Wrexham	W	2-1	
1976	8/5	Cardiff	W	1-0	
1977	31/5	Wembley	L	0-1	

● 79

1978	3/5	Cardiff	W	3-1
1979	23/5	Wembley	D	0-0
1980	17/5	Wrexham	L	1-4
1981	20/5	Wembley	D	0-0
1982	27/4	Cardiff	W	1-0
1983	23/2	Wembley	W	2-1
1984	2/5	Wrexham	L	0-1

P 97 W 62, D 21, L 14, F 239, A 90

v Yugoslavia

1939	18/5	Belgrade	L	1-2
1950	22/11	Highbury	D	2-2

1954	16/5	Belgrade	L	0-1	
1956	28/11	Wembley	W	3-0	
1958	11/5	Belgrade	L	0-5	
1960	11/5	Wembley	D	3-3	
1965	9/5	Belgrade	D	1-1	
1966	4/5	Wembley	W	2-0	
1968	5/6	Florence	L	0-1	ECF
1972	11/10	Wembley	D	1-1	
1974	5/6	Belgrade	D	2-2	
1986	12/11	Wembley	W	2-0	ECQ
1987	11/11	Belgrade	W	4-1	ECQ
1989	13/12	Wembley	W	2-1	

P 14, W 5, D 5, L 4, F 23, A 20

21 ● SEMI-PROFESSIONAL INTERNATIONAL/FA REPRESENTATIVE MATCHES 1994–1995

FA XI 1   Huntingdonshire FA 1

18th October 1994, Warboys Town FC

FA XI: Ladley (Holbeach United), Mountain (Spalding United), Fuff (Rushden & Diamonds), Quow (Sudbury Town), Gray (Holbeach United), Rhule (Stamford), Crunkhorn (Holbeach United), Carr (Raunds Town), Keeble (Raunds Town), Boon (Stotfold), Fortune (Holbeach United).
Subs.: Crane (Rushden & Diamonds) for Ladley, Genovese (Holbeach United) for Quow.
Scorer: Genovese
Team Manager: Domenic Genovese

FA XI 2   Northern Premier League 2

15th November 1994, Emley FC

FA XI: Farrelly (Macclesfield Town), Cross (Altrincham), Bimson (Macclesfield Town), France (Altrincham), Reid (Altrincham), Connor (Runcorn), Thomas (Runcorn), McDonald (Macclesfield Town), Green (Altrincham), Carmody (Altrincham), Sharratt (Altrincham).
Subs.: Anderson (Stalybridge Celtic) for Connor, Terry (Altrincham) for Thomas, Sorvel (Macclesfield Town) for McDonald.
Scorers: Connor, Green
Team Manager: John King

FA XI 1   Isthmian League 0

7th December 1994, Metropolitan Police FC

FA XI: Williams (Dover Athletic), Tucker (Woking), Wye L. (Woking), Brown W. (Welling United), Brown K. (Woking), Wye S. (Woking), Brown D. (Woking), Browne (Dover Athletic), Leworthy (Dover Athletic), Robbins (Welling United), Broom (Dagenham & Redbridge).
Subs.: Batty (Woking) for Williams, Rattray (Woking) for Robbins, Booth (Farnborough Town) for Browne.
Scorer: Rattray
Team Manager: Geoff Chapple

FA XI 4   British Students 0

10th January 1995, Halesowen Town FC

FA XI: Goodwin (Telford United), Bignot (Telford United), Bancroft (Kidderminster Harriers), Yates (Kidderminster Harriers), Foster (Telford United), Forsyth (Kidderminster Harriers), Snape (Halesowen Town), Stott (Bromsgrove Rovers), May (Stafford Rangers), Carter (Bromsgrove Rovers), Coogan (Solihull Borough).
Subs.: Skelding (Bromsgrove Rovers) for Bignot, Steadman (Kidderminster Harriers) for Goodwin, Weir (Kidderminster Harriers) for Foster, Burton (Westfields) for May, O'Connor (Hednesford Town) for Carter.
Scorers: Carter, Stott, May, Forsyth
Team Manager: Graham Allner

FA XI 2   Combined Services 0

17th January 1995, Nantwich Town FC

FA XI: Morris (Runcorn), Norman (Macclesfield Town), Robertson (Runcorn), Ruffer (Runcorn), Howarth (Macclesfield Town), Bimson (Macclesfield Town), Terry (Altrincham), Dove (Southport), Burke (Stalybridge Celtic), Power (Macclesfield Town), Sorvel (Macclesfield Town).
Subs.: Payne (Macclesfield Town) for Howarth.
Scorers: Terry, Dove
Team Manager: Sammy McIlroy

England 1   Wales 0

28th February 1995, Yeovil Town FC

England: Batty (Woking), Webb (Kidderminster Harriers), Hogarth (Guiseley), Reid (Altrincham), Brown K. (Woking), Stott (Bromsgrove Rovers), Terry (Altrincham), Forsyth (Kidderminster Harriers), Ross (Marine), Humphreys (Kidderminster Harriers), Watson (Marine).
Subs.: Hine (Gateshead) for Forsyth, Arnold (Kettering Town) for Watson.
Scorer: Hine
Team Manager: Tony Jennings

Holland 0   England 0

11th April 1995, Aalsmeer

England: Batty (Woking), Webb (Kidderminster Harriers), Hogarth (Guiseley), Brown K. (Woking), Holden (Kettering Town), Forsyth (Kidderminster Harriers), Venables (Stevenage Borough), Hine (Gateshead), Ross (Marine), Arnold (Kettering Town), Humphreys (Kidderminster Harriers).

Subs.: Farrelly (Macclesfield Town) for Batty, Stott (Bromsgrove Rovers) for Hine, Browne (Dover Athletic) for Arnold, Howarth (Macclesfield Town) for Holden, Watson (Marine) for Humphreys.

Team Manager: Tony Jennings

FA XI 3   Highland League 4

19th May 1995, St. Albans City FC

FA XI: Williams (Dover Athletic), Webb (Kidderminster Harriers), Ashby (Kettering Town), Brown K. (Woking), Reid (Altrincham), Richardson (Dagenham & Redbridge), Venables (Stevenage Borough), Forsyth (Kidderminster Harriers), Stott (Bromsgrove Rovers), Bolton (Kingstonian), May (Stafford Rangers).

Subs.: Mogg (Bath City) for Williams, Richardson (Bromsgrove Rovers) for Reid, Pye (Enfield) for Venables, Hayles (Stevenage Borough) for Bolton, Taylor (Bromsgrove Rovers) for May.

Scorers: Richardson, May, Hayles

Team Manager: Tony Jennings

Gibraltar 2   England 3

31st May 1995, Gibraltar

England: Batty (Woking), Webb (Kidderminster Harriers), Ashby (Kettering Town), Brown K. (Woking), Holden (Kettering Town), Stott (Bromsgrove Rovers), Venables (Stevenage Borough), Forsyth (Kidderminster Harriers), Bolton (Kingstonian), Taylor (Bromsgrove Rovers), Richardson (Dagenham & Redbridge).

Subs.: Farrelly (Macclesfield Town) for Batty, McDonald (Macclesfield Town) for Stott, May (Stafford Rangers) for Richardson.

Scorers: Taylor, Bolton, Venables

Team Manager: Tony Jennings

22 ● FA CUP WINNERS 1872–1995

Final venues:

1872 & 1874–92	Kennington Oval	1895–1914	Crystal Palace
1873	Lillie Bridge, London	1915	Old Trafford, Manchester
1893	Fallowfield, Manchester	1920–22	Stamford Bridge, London
1894	Goodison Park, Liverpool	1923 to date	Wembley Stadium

Year	Winners		Runners-up	Result	
1872	Wanderers	v	Royal Engineers	1–0	
1873	Wanderers	v	Oxford University	2–0	
1874	Oxford University	v	Royal Engineers	2–0	
1875	Royal Engineers	v	Old Etonians	2–0	after 1–1 draw
1876	Wanderers	v	Old Etonians	3–0	after 0–0 draw
1877	Wanderers	v	Oxford University	2–0	after extra time
1878	Wanderers*	v	Royal Engineers	3–1	
1879	Old Etonians	v	Clapham Rovers	1–0	
1880	Clapham Rovers	v	Oxford University	1–0	
1881	Old Carthusians	v	Old Etonians	3–0	
1882	Old Etonians	v	Blackburn Rovers	1–0	
1883	Blackburn Olympic	v	Old Etonians	2–1	after extra time
1884	Blackburn Rovers	v	Queen's Park, Glasgow	2–1	
1885	Blackburn Rovers	v	Queen's Park, Glasgow	2–0	
1886	Blackburn Rovers†	v	West Bromwich Albion	2–0	after 0–0 draw
1887	Aston Villa	v	West Bromwich Albion	2–0	
1888	West Bromwich Albion	v	Preston North End	2–1	
1889	Preston North End	v	Wolverhampton Wanderers	3–0	
1890	Blackburn Rovers	v	Sheffield Wednesday	6–1	
1891	Blackburn Rovers	v	Notts County	3–1	
1892	West Bromwich Albion	v	Aston Villa	3–0	
1893	Wolverhampton Wanderers	v	Everton	1–0	
1894	Notts County	v	Bolton Wanderers	4–1	
1895	Aston Villa	v	West Bromwich Albion	1–0	
1896	Sheffield Wednesday	v	Wolverhampton Wanderers	2–1	
1897	Aston Villa	v	Everton	3–2	
1898	Nottingham Forest	v	Derby County	3–1	
1899	Sheffield United	v	Derby County	4–1	
1900	Bury	v	Southampton	4–0	
1901	Tottenham Hotspur	v	Sheffield United	3–1	after 2–2 draw
1902	Sheffield United	v	Southampton	2–1	after 1–1 draw
1903	Bury	v	Derby County	6–0	
1904	Manchester City	v	Bolton Wanderers	1–0	
1905	Aston Villa	v	Newcastle United	2–0	
1906	Everton	v	Newcastle United	1–0	
1907	Sheffield Wednesday	v	Everton	2–1	
1908	Wolverhampton Wanderers	v	Newcastle United	3–1	
1909	Manchester United	v	Bristol City	1–0	
1910	Newcastle United	v	Barnsley	2–0	after 1–1 draw
1911	Bradford City	v	Newcastle United	1–0	after 0–0 draw
1912	Barnsley	v	West Bromwich Albion	1–0	after 0–0 draw

* Won outright but restored to The Association
† A special trophy was awarded for third consecutive win

Year	Winners		Runners-up	Result	
1913	Aston Villa	v	Sunderland	1–0	
1914	Burnley	v	Liverpool	1–0	
1915	Sheffield United	v	Chelsea	3–0	
1920	Aston Villa	v	Huddersfield Town	1–0	after extra time
1921	Tottenham Hotspur	v	Wolverhampton Wanderers	1–0	
1922	Huddersfield Town	v	Preston North End	1–0	
1923	Bolton Wanderers	v	West Ham United	2–0	
1924	Newcastle United	v	Aston Villa	2–0	
1925	Sheffield United	v	Cardiff City	1–0	
1926	Bolton Wanderers	v	Manchester City	1–0	
1927	Cardiff City	v	Arsenal	1–0	
1928	Blackburn Rovers	v	Huddersfield Town	3–1	
1929	Bolton Wanderers	v	Portsmouth	2–0	
1930	Arsenal	v	Huddersfield Town	2–0	
1931	West Bromwich Albion	v	Birmingham City	2–1	
1932	Newcastle United	v	Arsenal	2–1	
1933	Everton	v	Manchester City	3–0	
1934	Manchester City	v	Portsmouth	2–1	
1935	Sheffield Wednesday	v	West Bromwich Albion	4–2	
1936	Arsenal	v	Sheffield United	1–0	
1937	Sunderland	v	Preston North End	3–1	
1938	Preston North End	v	Huddersfield Town	1–0	after extra time
1939	Portsmouth	v	Wolverhampton Wanderers	4–1	
1946	Derby County	v	Charlton Athletic	4–1	after extra time
1947	Charlton Athletic	v	Burnley	1–0	after extra time
1948	Manchester United	v	Blackpool	4–2	
1949	Wolverhampton Wanderers	v	Leicester City	3–1	
1950	Arsenal	v	Liverpool	2–0	
1951	Newcastle United	v	Blackpool	2–0	
1952	Newcastle United	v	Arsenal	1–0	
1953	Blackpool	v	Bolton Wanderers	4–3	
1954	West Bromwich Albion	v	Preston North End	3–2	
1955	Newcastle United	v	Manchester City	3–1	
1956	Manchester City	v	Birmingham City	3–1	
1957	Aston Villa	v	Manchester United	2–1	
1958	Bolton Wanderers	v	Manchester United	2–0	
1959	Nottingham Forest	v	Luton Town	2–1	
1960	Wolverhampton Wanderers	v	Blackburn Rovers	3–0	
1961	Tottenham Hotspur	v	Leicester City	2–0	
1962	Tottenham Hotspur	v	Burnley	3–1	
1963	Manchester United	v	Leicester City	3–1	
1964	West Ham United	v	Preston North End	3–2	
1965	Liverpool	v	Leeds United	2–1	after extra time
1966	Everton	v	Sheffield Wednesday	3–2	
1967	Tottenham Hotspur	v	Chelsea	2–1	
1968	West Bromwich Albion	v	Everton	1–0	after extra time
1969	Manchester City	v	Leicester City	1–0	
1970	Chelsea	v	Leeds United	2–1	after 2–2 draw both games extra time
1971	Arsenal	v	Liverpool	2–1	after extra time
1972	Leeds United	v	Arsenal	1–0	
1973	Sunderland	v	Leeds United	1–0	
1974	Liverpool	v	Newcastle United	3–0	
1975	West Ham United	v	Fulham	2–0	
1976	Southampton	v	Manchester United	1–0	
1977	Manchester United	v	Liverpool	2–1	
1978	Ipswich Town	v	Arsenal	1–0	

Year	Winners		Runners-up	Result	
1979	Arsenal	v	Manchester United	3–2	
1980	West Ham United	v	Arsenal	1–0	
1981	Tottenham Hotspur	v	Manchester City	3–2	after 1–1 draw after extra time
1982	Tottenham Hotspur	v	Queens Park Rangers	1–0	after 1–1 draw after extra time
1983	Manchester United	v	Brighton & Hove Albion	4–0	after 2–2 draw after extra time
1984	Everton	v	Watford	2–0	
1985	Manchester United	v	Everton	1–0	after extra time
1986	Liverpool	v	Everton	3–1	
1987	Coventry City	v	Tottenham Hotspur	3–2	after extra time
1988	Wimbledon	v	Liverpool	1–0	
1989	Liverpool	v	Everton	3–2	after extra time
1990	Manchester United	v	Crystal Palace	1–0	after 3–3 draw after extra time
1991	Tottenham Hotspur	v	Nottingham Forest	2–1	after extra time
1992	Liverpool	v	Sunderland	2–0	
1993	Arsenal	v	Sheffield Wednesday	2–1	after 1–1 draw both games extra time
1994	Manchester United	v	Chelsea	4–0	
1995	Everton	v	Manchester United	1–0	

Everton – winners of the FA Cup sponsored by Littlewoods Pools.

23 ● FA CUP – FINAL TIE 1995
Sponsored by Littlewoods Pools

Everton 1   Manchester United 0

On the final day of FA Carling Premiership fixtures (14 May), just six days before the Cup Final, Manchester United had a realistic chance of achieving a "double double" – winning League and Cup in two consecutive seasons. Their valiant efforts to retain the title at West Ham, bombarding Miklosko's goal for a winning strike that would have edged Blackburn by a point and secured the crown for a third successive year, in the end came to nothing. Now their Cup ambitions were frustrated by another highly experienced goalkeeper – Welsh international Neville Southall, making his 650th appearance for Everton. Southall kept United at bay with some inspired stops in the second half at Wembley, including one fantastic double save from substitute Paul Scholes, and Everton won the 114th Final with Paul Rideout's headed goal in the 30th minute.

Joe Royle, an Everton legend as a player who had represented them in attack in the 1968 Final, took over as their manager from Mike Walker in November when they were threatened with relegation. He got the players working harder than ever to pull the team out of the bottom positions – they eventually finished 15th – and as a bonus he brought a trophy back to Goodison for the first time in eight years. United's game plan for the Final had been to combat Everton's tenacious "Dogs of War" by using Mark Hughes as a lone striker, packing the midfield and trying to swarm forward at every opportunity. For their part, Everton relied on the deft skills of the Swede, Anders Limpar, to orchestrate their counter attacks.

Limpar limped off before the end, but his contribution had been highly significant. The turning point arrived on the half-hour when, with most United players stranded upfield, Ince lost possession and suddenly Limpar was tearing down the field unchecked in the inside–right channel. He cleverly slid the ball out wide to full-back Matt Jackson, in acres of space on the right, and as his low cross arrowed in, Graham Stuart shot firmly against the underside of the crossbar as he fell backwards. Rideout beat Irwin to the rebound and headed cleanly and decisively past Schmeichel and Bruce, side by side on the goal-line. The goal was timed at 29 minutes 51 seconds.

United emerged from the dressing room for the second half without Bruce, their battle-scarred captain, but with the occasionally magical Ryan Giggs. He would often weave his way down the left with Everton defenders twisting this way and that to block his path to goal. After one burst to the touchline, Giggs saw his deflected centre headed onto the top of the bar by Brian McClair. United upped the tempo as they desperately sought an equaliser, but Southall and a backs-to-the-wall rearguard kept them out. A late Gary Pallister header was grasped tightly by the Welshman. He – and Everton – were not about to let their chance of Cup glory go.

Everton: Southall, Jackson, Hinchcliffe, Watson, Ablett, Parkinson, Horne, Stuart, Rideout (Ferguson), Limpar (Amokachi), Unsworth.

Manchester United: Schmeichel, Irwin, Bruce (Giggs), Pallister, Neville, Sharpe (Scholes), Ince, Keane, Butt, McClair, Hughes.

Referee: G. Ashby (Worcestershire FA)
Attendance: 79,592
Guest of Honour: HRH The Duke of Kent
Presenting the Cup: HRH Prince Charles

24 ● FA CUP 1994–1995
Sponsored by Littlewoods Pools

Preliminary round – 27 August 1994

(*Replays in italics*)			*Results*	*Att*
Dunston Fed Brewery	v	Darlington Cleveland Soc	1–0	65
Seaham Red Star	v	Easington Colliery	3–1	60
Brandon United	v	Alnwick Town	5–2	53
Crook Town	v	Billingham Town	1–1	74
Billingham Town	*v*	*Crook Town*	*1–2*	*180*
Murton	v	Hebburn	3–2	34
Stockton	v	RTM Newcastle	2–2	27
RTM Newcastle	*v*	*Stockton*	*6–1*	*87*
Guisborough Town	v	Eppleton CW	2–0	82
Harrogate Town	v	Esh Winning	7–0	231
Penrith	v	Tow Law Town	2–3	139
Evenwood Town	v	Consett	0–3	31
Ryhope CA	v	Pickering Town	1–5	38
South Shields	v	Prudhoe Town	7–1	144
Clitheroe	v	Bamber Bridge	1–0	320
Farsley Celtic	v	Great Harwood Town	3–1	111
Whickham	v	Willington	1–2	29
(*at Willington FC*)				
West Auckland Town	v	Workington	1–1	85
Workington	*v*	*West Auckland Town*	*1–2*	*249*
Yorkshire Amateur	v	Atherton LR	0–1	90
Atherton Collieries	v	Blidworth MW	1–1	101
Blidworth MW	*v*	*Atherton Collieries*	*1–3*	*38*
Belper Town	v	Blackpool(wren)Rovers	2–1	165
Alfreton Town	v	Ashton United	3–1	130
Chadderton	v	Armthorpe Welfare	3–2	73
Arnold Town	v	Castleton Gabriels	3–2	175
Caernarfon Town	v	Darwen	3–1	383
Congleton Town	v	Curzon Ashton	4–2	135
Bradford (Park Avenue)	v	Burscough	0–3	130
Hatfield Main	v	Brigg Town	1–2	73
Goole Town	v	Glossop North End	0–2	145
Denaby United	v	Hallam	1–1	81
Hallam	*v*	*Denaby United*	*1–0*	*129*
Fleetwood	v	Eastwood Town	0–3	135
Glasshoughton Welfare	v	Eccleshill United	1–0	70
Maine Road	v	Louth United	3–1	38
Bootle	v	Maltby MW	0–0	54
Maltby MW	*v*	*Bootle*	*1–0*	*100*
Immingham Town	v	Heanor Town	1–2	38
(*at Goole Town FC*)				
Liversedge	v	Ilkeston Town	2–2	101
Ilkeston Town	*v*	*Liversedge*	*4–1*	*416*
Prescot AFC	v	Pontefract Collieries	2–0	110
Thackley	v	Radcliffe Borough	0–2	99
Nantwich Town	v	Newcastle Town	2–1	160
Ossett Town	v	Mossley	0–0	126
Mossley	*v*	*Ossett Town*	*3–0*	*147*

Winterton Rangers	v	Stocksbridge Park Steels	3–0	40
Ossett Albion	v	Rossendale United	1–4	51
Sheffield	v	Rossington Main	3–1	40
St Helens Town	v	Salford City	7–1	47
Armitage	v	Brierley Hill Town	1–1	55
Brierley Hill Town	*v*	*Armitage*	*1–3*	*60*
Long Buckby	v	Northampton Spencer	3–3	73
Northampton Spencer	*v*	*Long Buckby*	*2–1*	*101*
Blakenall	v	Banbury United	3–2	79
Bolehall Swifts	v	Barwell	3–1	72
Stratford Town	v	Halesowen Harriers	0–2	82
Grantham Town	v	Leicester United	2–0	258
Hinckley Athletic	v	Hinckley Town	2–1	445
Cogenhoe United	v	Eastwood Hanley	1–1	89
Eastwood Hanley	*v*	*Cogenhoe United*	*0–0*	*102*
Cogenhoe United	*v*	*Eastwood Hanley*	*2–4*	*198*
Wednesfield	v	Desborough Town	1–1	53
Desborough Town	*v*	*Wednesfield*	*2–1*	*97*
Lye Town	v	Racing Club Warwick	2–0	86
(at Halesowen Harriers FC)				
Bridgnorth Town	v	Bilston Town	3–1	132
Oldbury United	v	Moor Green	1–3	116
Pelsall Villa	v	Newport Pagnell Town	2–0	92
Sutton Coldfield Town	v	Stourport Swifts	2–3	118
Dudley Town	v	Rothwell Town	2–1	144
Stapenhill	v	Rushall Olympic	2–1	87
Stourbridge	v	Sandwell Borough	1–1	175
(at Sandwell Borough FC)				
Sandwell Borough	*v*	*Stourbridge*	*2–0*	*87*
Redditch United	v	Bedworth United	7–0	147
Evesham United	v	Tamworth	1–3	304
Westfields	v	Wellingborough Town	1–1	133
Wellingborough Town	*v*	*Westfields*	*1–3*	*65*
Hucknall Town	v	West Midlands Police	0–0	174
West Midlands Police	*v*	*Hucknall Town*	*1–1*	*87*
Hucknall Town	*v*	*West Midlands Police*	*0–1*	*292*
Cornard United	v	Chatteris Town	2–0	60
Lowestoft Town	v	Diss Town	2–2	272
Diss Town	*v*	*Lowestoft Town*	*3–3*	*410*
Diss Town	*v*	*Lowestoft Town*	*1–0*	*598*
Bourne Town	v	Billericay Town	1–4	120
Bury Town	v	Boston Town	0–4	145
Holbeach United	v	Heybridge Swifts	1–2	85
Burnham Ramblers	v	Kings Lynn	2–3	138
Eynesbury Rovers	v	Gorleston	2–3	81
Haverhill Rovers	v	Great Yarmouth Town	2–1	85
Mirrlees Blackstone	v	Stamford	2–2	110
Stamford	*v*	*Mirrlees Blackstone*	*4–1*	*278*
Spalding United	v	March Town United	1–0	130
Stowmarket Town	v	Tiptree United	2–2	76
Tiptree United	*v*	*Stowmarket Town*	*3–1*	*61*
Newmarket Town	v	Soham Town Rangers	4–2	215
Hertford Town	v	Saffron Walden Town	2–5	116
Kingsbury Town	v	Kempston Rovers	1–4	
Witham Town	v	Watton United	1–0	66
Wisbech Town	v	Fakenham Town	3–0	312
Brimsdown Rovers	v	Sudbury Wanderers	1–1	80
Sudbury Wanderers	*v*	*Brimsdown Rovers*	*1–0*	*98*

(Replays in italics)			Results	Att
Arlesey Town	v	Brook House	1–2	90
Aveley	v	Wootton Blue Cross	1–1	34
Wootton Blue Cross	*v*	*Aveley*	*1–3*	*80*
Berkhamsted Town	v	Baldock Town	1–3	128
Bowers United	v	Barking	1–4	123
Chalfont St Peter	v	Dunstable		
(*walkover for Chalfont St Peter – Dunstable removed from the Competition*)				
Biggleswade Town	v	Feltham & Hounslow Borough	0–1	92
(*at Feltham & Hounslow Borough FC*)				
Collier Row	v	Cheshunt	2–1	122
Burnham	v	Clapton	4–0	84
(*at Flackwell Heath FC*)				
Ruislip Manor	v	Flackwell Heath	5–0	122
Thamesmead Town	v	Bedfont	0–3	43
Haringey Borough	v	Ford United	1–2	14
(*at Ford United FC*)				
Hoddesdon Town	v	Harefield United	1–1	46
(*at Ware FC*)				
Harefield United	*v*	*Hoddesdon Town*	*1–0*	*47*
Hillingdon Borough	v	Royston Town	2–2	55
Royston Town	*v*	*Hillingdon Borough*	*1–2*	*58*
Romford	v	Wingate & Finchley	2–0	254
Southall	v	Langford	2–1	92
(*at Langford FC*)				
Leighton Town	v	Leyton	2–2	205
Leyton	*v*	*Leighton Town*	*1–0*	*92*
Leatherhead	v	Letchworth Garden City	8–0	82
Welwyn Garden City	v	Viking Sports	1–1	50
Viking Sports	*v*	*Welwyn Garden City*	*0–1*	*70*
Tring Town	v	Wealdstone	0–1	124
Walthamstow Pennant	v	Ware	2–2	37
Ware	*v*	*Walthamstow Pennant*	*4–0*	*76*
Stotfold	v	Tower Hamlets	2–1	52
Slade Green	v	Tilbury	0–3	76
Arundel	v	Burgess Hill Town	1–3	73
Hampton	v	Pagham	1–0	121
Banstead Athletic	v	Ash United		
(*walkover for Banstead Athletic – Ash United withdrawn*)				
Bracknell Town	v	Ashford Town	1–3	161
Tonbridge	v	Chipstead	1–1	447
Chipstead	*v*	*Tonbridge*	*0–3*	*142*
Croydon	v	Three Bridges	7–0	85
Eastbourne Town	v	Egham Town	1–7	146
(*at Langney Sports FC*)				
Corinthian	v	Crowborough Athletic	9–0	33
Uxbridge	v	Corinthian-Casuals	1–0	90
Worthing	v	Horsham	1–0	411
Herne Bay	v	Langney Sports	3–0	223
Horsham YMCA	v	Lancing	2–1	89
Folkestone Invicta	v	Hailsham Town	2–0	190
Northwood	v	Godalming & Guildford	2–1	109
Canterbury City	v	Newhaven	6–0	53
Lewes	v	Fisher	0–1	67
Oakwood	v	Peacehaven & Telscombe	0–3	56
Littlehampton Town	v	Merstham	2–7	51
(*at Portfield FC*)				
Croydon Athletic	v	Malden Vale	5–2	68
Ramsgate	v	Redhill	4–0	91

Hanwell Town	v	Whyteleafe	1–2	53
Shoreham	v	Ringmer	1–0	133
Steyning Town	v	Sheppey United	0–2	40
Epsom & Ewell	v	Wembley	1–3	53
Selsey	v	Portfield	1–4	115
Whitstable Town	v	Tunbridge Wells	2–3	146
Windsor & Eton	v	Whitehawk	1–0	129
Buckingham Town	v	Brockenhurst	1–0	119
Abingdon Town	v	Cove	0–0	141
Cove	*v*	*Abingdon Town*	*1–0*	*90*
Bemerton Heath Harl	v	Aldershot Town	0–4	1035
Bournemouth	v	Basingstoke Town	0–0	200
Basingstoke Town	*v*	*Bournemouth*	*3–1*	*204*
Fareham Town	v	Eastleigh	3–1	125
Fleet Town	v	Oxford City	3–1	198
Hungerford Town	v	Gosport Borough	3–2	102
Maidenhead United	v	Havant Town	0–1	63
Poole Town	v	Witney Town	3–0	202
Thame United	v	Devizes Town	2–0	88
Ryde	v	Thatcham Town	3–2	55
Salisbury City	v	Totton AFC	5–0	249
Bridport	v	Backwell United	1–2	201
Yate Town	v	Swanage Town & Herston	2–1	127
Elmore	v	Chippenham Town	4–0	50
Forest Green Rovers	v	Cinderford Town	0–0	271
Cinderford Town	*v*	*Forest Green Rovers*	*3–2*	*373*
(*at Gloucester City FC*)				
Odd Down	v	Newport AFC	0–6	272
Ilfracombe Town	v	Paulton Rovers	0–2	91
Melksham Town	v	Keynsham Town	4–1	85
Glastonbury	v	Frome Town	4–1	90
Bideford	v	Falmouth Town	2–1	215
Taunton Town	v	Clevedon Town	3–2	467
Welton Rovers	v	Saltash United	1–1	58
Saltash United	*v*	*Welton Rovers*	*4–0*	*105*
Calne Town	v	Torrington	1–3	60

First round qualifying – 10 September 1994

Barrow	v	Chester-Le-Street Town	4–1	848
Seaham Red Star	v	Billingham Synthonia	2–2	63
Billingham Synthonia	*v*	*Seaham Red Star*	*2–0*	*58*
Dunston Fed Brewery	v	Brandon United	2–0	94
Crook Town	v	Blyth Spartans	0–2	210
Bishop Auckland	v	Harrogate Railway	2–0	233
RTM Newcastle	v	Gateshead	0–3	330
Murton	v	Guisborough Town	1–1	32
Guisborough Town	*v*	*Murton*	*3–4*	*73*
Harrogate Town	v	Gretna	4–1	252
Spennymoor United	v	Shildon	4–1	372
Consett	v	Northallerton	1–1	48
Northallerton	*v*	*Consett*	*1–3*	*68*
Tow Law Town	v	Pickering Town	4–0	147
South Shields	v	Netherfield	0–0	250
Netherfield	*v*	*South Shields*	*0–1*	*120*
Durham City	v	Peterlee Newtown	5–0	50
Farsley Celtic	v	Whitley Bay	3–0	221

Clitheroe	v	Willington	1–2	185
West Auckland Town	v	Whitby Town	0–2	125
Chadderton	v	Winsford United	1–1	170
Winsford United	*v*	*Chadderton*	*5–6*	*120*
Atherton Collieries	v	Buxton	2–0	119
Atherton LR	v	Belper Town	1–1	142
Belper Town	*v*	*Atherton LR*	*0–2*	*176*
Alfreton Town	v	Guiseley	2–2	291
Guiseley	*v*	*Alfreton Town*	*4–2*	*458*
Brigg Town	v	Morecambe	0–4	146
Caernarfon Town	v	Chorley	2–2	322
Chorley	*v*	*Caernarfon Town*	*2–1*	*152*
Arnold Town	v	Congleton Town	1–2	217
Burscough	v	Horwich RMI	1–0	256
Colwyn Bay	v	Flixton	4–0	607
Hallam	v	Hyde United	0–3	225
Glossop North End	v	Eastwood Town	2–2	203
Eastwood Town	*v*	*Glossop North End*	*1–1*	*144*
Glossop North End	*v*	*Eastwood Town*	*3–5*	*330*
Glasshoughton Welfare	v	Worksop Town	0–5	145
Droylsden	v	Lincoln United	0–3	146
Maltby MW	v	Knowsley United	0–4	60
Maine Road	v	Heanor Town	1–0	43
Ilkeston Town	v	Lancaster City	2–2	455
Lancaster City	*v*	*Ilkeston Town*	*3–1*	*169*
Emley	v	Oldham Town	4–1	242
Radcliffe Borough	v	North Ferriby United	1–0	124
Prescot AFC	v	Nantwich Town	1–3	150
Mossley	v	Northwich Victoria	2–4	446
Frickley Athletic	v	Skelmersdale United	1–1	139
Skelmersdale United	*v*	*Frickley Athletic*	*1–4*	*107*
Rossendale United	v	Matlock Town	1–2	171
Winterton Rangers	v	Sheffield	0–1	32
St Helens Town	v	Warrington Town	0–4	185
Atherstone United	v	Boldmere St Michaels	1–1	341
Boldmere St Michaels	*v*	*Atherstone United*	*0–1*	*213*
Northampton Spencer	v	Hednesford Town	1–4	104
Armitage	v	Blakenall	2–2	68
Blakenall	*v*	*Armitage*	*2–0*	*91*
Bolehall Swifts	v	Solihull Borough	2–3	76
Desborough Town	v	Chasetown	1–0	79
Grantham Town	v	Burton Albion	2–4	404
Halesowen Harriers	v	Hinckley Athletic	3–3	127
Hinckley Athletic	*v*	*Halesowen Harriers*	*2–1*	*263*
Eastwood Hanley	v	Rushden & Diamonds	1–0	165
Corby Town	v	Paget Rangers	0–5	157
Bridgnorth Town	v	Pershore Town	1–1	131
Pershore Town	*v*	*Bridgnorth Town*	*0–2*	*230*
Lye Town	v	Moor Green	1–5	136
Pelsall Villa	v	Raunds Town	0–1	172
Rocester	v	Stewarts & Lloyds	1–0	102
Dudley Town	v	Leek Town	0–1	201
Stourport Swifts	v	Stapenhill	2–1	83
Sandwell Borough	v	Gresley Rovers	1–2	105
Halesowen Town	v	Willenhall Town	2–1	551
Tamworth	v	Telford United	1–1	1057
Telford United	*v*	*Tamworth*	*4–1*	*650*
Redditch United	v	Westfields	1–1	182

● 91

Westfields	v	Redditch United	2–3	*137*
West Midlands Police	v	Gainsborough Trinity	0–0	58
Gainsborough Trinity	v	*West Midlands Police*	6–0	*385*
Bishop's Stortford	v	Braintree Town	1–1	514
Braintree Town	v	*Bishop's Stortford*	3–0	*345*
Diss Town	v	Sudbury Town	1–0	398
Cornard United	v	Billericay Town	0–4	102
Boston Town	v	Basildon United	1–0	61
Boston United	v	Harwich & Parkeston	2–0	1057
Kings Lynn	v	Halstead Town	0–1	523
Heybridge Swifts	v	Gorleston	0–0	137
Gorleston	v	*Heybridge Swifts*	0–2	*173*
Haverhill Rovers	v	Felixstowe Town	1–1	76
Felixstowe Town	v	*Haverhill Rovers*	2–0	*80*
Saffron Walden Town	v	Stevenage Borough	1–4	483
Spalding United	v	Cambridge City	0–3	175
Stamford AFC	v	Tiptree United	2–3	109
Newmarket Town	v	Hitchin Town	1–2	198
Chelmsford City	v	Barton Rovers	1–0	751
Witham Town	v	Wivenhoe Town	2–0	133
Kempston Rovers	v	Wisbech Town	2–4	158
Sudbury Wanderers	v	Hendon	0–1	184
Aylesbury United	v	Boreham Wood	3–1	541
Aveley	v	Edgware Town	1–2	31
Brook House	v	Baldock Town	0–7	120
Barking	v	Canvey Island	3–1	160
Chesham United	v	Concord Rangers	4–2	397
Feltham & Hounslow Boro	v	Dagenham & Redbridge	1–3	572
(at Dagenham & Redbridge FC)				
Chalfont St Peter	v	Collier Row	2–2	52
Collier Row	v	*Chalfont St Peter*	2–1	*120*
Burnham	v	East Thurrock United	2–0	120
(at East Thurrock United FC)				
Enfield	v	Hemel Hempstead	5–2	550
Bedfont	v	Purfleet	0–3	60
Ruislip Manor	v	Ford United	2–1	121
Harefield United	v	Hornchurch	0–3	29
Leatherhead	v	Hayes	1–1	222
Hayes	v	*Leatherhead*	4–0	*252*
Romford	v	Grays Athletic	4–3	387
Hillingdon Borough	v	Southall	2–1	92
Leyton	v	St Albans City	1–2	246
Tilbury	v	Staines Town	0–1	83
Wealdstone	v	Harrow Borough	0–1	401
Welwyn Garden City	v	Ware	1–2	168
Stotfold	v	Yeading	1–3	121
Bromley	v	Bognor Regis Town	3–2	372
Hampton	v	Gravesend & Northfleet	1–1	303
Gravesend & Northfleet	v	*Hampton*	1–0	*444*
Burgess Hill Town	v	Banstead Athletic	4–3	198
Ashford Town	v	Chatham Town	5–0	350
Uxbridge	v	Dorking	1–1	113
Dorking	v	*Uxbridge*	3–1	*81*
Croydon	v	Carshalton Athletic	0–0	235
Carshalton Athletic	v	*Croydon*	5–0	*326*
Tonbridge	v	Egham Town	3–1	451
Corinthian	v	Hastings Town	1–2	147
Northwood	v	Erith & Belvedere	3–0	94

			Results	Att
Herne Bay	v	Dulwich Hamlet	1–3	392
Worthing	v	Horsham YMCA	5–3	311
Folkestone Invicta	v	Sittingbourne	1–0	551
Croydon Athletic	v	Metropolitan Police	2–2	48
Metropolitan Police	*v*	*Croydon Athletic*	*0–1*	*73*
Fisher 93	v	Kingstonian	2–4	257
Canterbury City	v	Peacehaven & Telscombe	1–2	60
Merstham	v	Margate	0–2	246
(at Margate FC)				
Molesey	v	Southwick	1–1	103
Southwick	*v*	*Molesey*	*0–1*	*91*
Whyteleafe	v	Dover Athletic	0–0	392
Dover Athletic	*v*	*Whyteleafe*	*3–0*	*829*
Ramsgate	v	Shoreham	0–0	94
Shoreham	*v*	*Ramsgate*	*2–0*	*116*
Sheppey United	v	Chertsey Town	0–1	149
Walton & Hersham	v	Wick	3–0	240
Portfield	v	Tooting & Mitcham United	0–3	85
Wembley	v	Tunbridge Wells	4–1	65
Windsor & Eton	v	Welling United	0–1	224
Wokingham Town	v	Bicester Town	5–0	230
Cove	v	Andover	0–2	41
Buckingham Town	v	Aldershot Town	2–1	780
Basingstoke Town	v	Newport(IW)	2–4	246
Dorchester Town	v	Lymington AFC	3–1	505
Fleet Town	v	Newbury Town	0–1	200
Fareham Town	v	Hungerford Town	1–2	200
Havant Town	v	Bashley	1–1	111
Bashley	*v*	*Havant Town*	*3–1*	*185*
Waterlooville	v	Westbury United	1–0	108
Thame United	v	Wimborne Town	0–0	123
Wimborne Town	*v*	*Thame United*	*3–3*	*173*
Thame United	*v*	*Wimborne Town*	*3–1*	*169*
Poole Town	v	Ryde	5–1	164
Salisbury City	v	Worcester City	2–0	433
Gloucester City	v	Exmouth Town	3–0	557
Yate Town	v	Merthyr Tydfil	0–3	335
Backwell United	v	Elmore	0–6	74
Cinderford Town	v	Mangotsfield United	3–2	255
(at Gloucester City FC)				
Trowbridge Town	v	Minehead	7–0	312
Paulton Rovers	v	Moreton Town	2–0	156
Newport AFC	v	Melksham Town	4–1	980
Glastonbury	v	Barnstaple Town	0–3	95
Tiverton Town	v	St Blazey	7–1	461
Taunton Town	v	Weston–Super–Mare	2–2	531
Weston–Super–Mare	*v*	*Taunton Town*	*3–2*	*490*
Bideford	v	Saltash United	4–0	152
Torrington	v	Weymouth	2–0	205

Second round qualifying – 24 September 1994

Blyth Spartans	v	Dunston Federation Brewery	3–2	467
Barrow	v	Billingham Synthonia	5–2	779
Harrogate Town	v	Murton	1–0	304
Bishop Auckland	v	Gateshead	3–1	388
South Shields	v	Tow Law Town	2–2	316

Tow Law Town	v	*South Shields*	2–1	240
Spennymoor United	v	Consett	3–2	287
Whitby Town	v	Willington	6–1	192
Durham City	v	Farsley Celtic	1–0	110
Guiseley	v	Atherton LR	3–1	588
Chadderton	v	Atherton Collieries	1–2	192
Burscough	v	Congleton Town	0–0	256
Congleton Town	v	*Burscough*	3–3	142
Burscough	v	*Congleton Town*	2–2	335
Congleton Town	v	*Burscough*	5–2	178
Morecambe	v	Chorley	4–2	585
Worksop Town	v	Eastwood Town	0–2	448
Colwyn Bay	v	Hyde United	2–2	619
Hyde United	v	*Colwyn Bay*	8–0	318
Lancaster City	v	Maine Road	3–2	146
Lincoln City	v	Knowsley United	3–2	165
Northwich Victoria	v	Nantwich Town	10–0	860
Emley	v	Radcliffe Borough	2–0	269
Warrington Town	v	Sheffield	2–1	170
Frickley Athletic	v	Matlock Town	3–1	217
Solihull Borough	v	Blakenall	4–0	180
Atherstone Utd	v	Hednesford Town	3–4	513
Eastwood Hanley	v	Hinckley Athletic	2–2	137
Hinckley Athletic	v	*Eastwood Hanley*	0–1	272
Desborough Town	v	Burton Albion	0–2	261
Raunds Town	v	Moor Green	1–2	203
Paget Rangers	v	Bridgnorth Town	2–1	104
Gresley Rovers	v	Stourport Swifts	4–0	462
Rocester	v	Leek Town	0–4	553
Gainsborough Trinity	v	Redditch United	3–1	404
Halesowen Town	v	Telford United	1–1	773
Telford United	v	*Halesowen Town*	3–1	701
Boston Town	v	Billericay Town	1–2	82
Braintree Town	v	Diss Town	2–1	358
Felixstowe Town	v	Heybridge Swifts	1–5	110
Boston United	v	Halstead Town	3–0	1085
Hitchin Town	v	Tiptree United	3–3	304
Tiptree United	v	*Hitchin Town*	3–1	187
Stevenage Borough	v	Cambridge City	0–2	1124
Hendon	v	Wisbech Town	2–1	267
Chelmsford City	v	Witham Town	1–0	1107
Barking	v	Baldock Town	2–2	125
Baldock Town	v	*Barking*	3–2	215
Aylesbury United	v	Edgware Town	2–0	586
Burnham	v	Collier Row	0–1	90
Chesham United	v	Dagenham & Redbridge	2–0	657
Hornchurch	v	Ruislip Manor	0–1	140
Enfield	v	Purfleet	3–1	544
St Albans City	v	Hillingdon Borough	11–1	425
Hayes	v	Romford	1–2	421
Yeading	v	Ware	8–0	89
Staines Town	v	Harrow Borough	5–3	284
Ashford Town	v	Burgess Hill Town	3–2	429
Bromley	v	Gravesend & Northfleet	2–2	605
Gravesend & Northfleet	v	*Bromley*	1–1	729
Gravesend & Northfleet	v	*Bromley*	1–0	824
Hastings Town	v	Tonbridge	1–1	569
Tonbridge	v	*Hastings Town*	0–1	649

94 ●

Dorking	v	Carshalton Athletic	0–8	366
Folkestone Invicta	v	Worthing	1–2	562
Northwood	v	Dulwich Hamlet	1–4	224
Margate	v	Peacehaven & Telscombe	1–1	299
Peacehaven & Telscombe	*v*	*Margate*	*3–5*	*268*
Croydon Athletic	v	Kingstonian	1–2	255
Chertsey Town	v	Shoreham	1–0	247
Molesey	v	Dover Athletic	1–4	350
Welling United	v	Wembley	1–4	604
Walton & Hersham	v	Tooting & Mitcham United	3–0	273
Newport(IW)	v	Buckingham Town	1–0	363
Wokingham Town	v	Andover	3–0	255
Bashley	v	Hungerford Town	3–0	211
Dorchester Town	v	Newbury Town	4–2	586
Salisbury City	v	Poole Town	3–2	481
Waterlooville	v	Thame United	4–0	146
Cinderford Town	v	Elmore	5–4	67
(*at Elmore FC*)				
Gloucester City	v	Merthyr Tydfil	7–1	746
Barnstaple Town	v	Newport AFC	1–2	392
Trowbridge Town	v	Paulton Rovers	4–1	403
Torrington	v	Bideford	1–5	310
Tiverton Town	v	Weston-Super-Mare	4–2	805

Third round qualifying – 8 October 1994

Blyth Spartans	v	Barrow	3–1	899
Harrogate Town	v	Bishop Auckland	0–3	644
Tow Law Town	v	Spennymoor United	0–0	622
Spennymoor United	*v*	*Tow Law Town*	*2–1*	*781*
Whitby Town	v	Durham City	1–1	280
Durham City	*v*	*Whitby Town*	*3–1*	*400*
Guiseley	v	Atherton Collieries	3–1	559
Congleton Town	v	Morecambe	0–3	305
Eastwood Town	v	Hyde United	1–1	355
Hyde United	*v*	*Eastwood Town*	*3–0*	*414*
Lancaster City	v	Lincoln United	5–1	259
Northwich Victoria	v	Emley	2–1	1002
Warrington Town	v	Frickley Athletic	2–0	252
Solihull Borough	v	Hednesford Town	3–0	391
Eastwood Hanley	v	Burton Albion	0–1	385
Moor Green	v	Paget Rangers	4–1	289
Gresley Rovers	v	Leek Town	3–1	808
Gainsborough Trinity	v	Telford United	0–3	732
Billericay Town	v	Braintree Town	1–1	506
Braintree Town	*v*	*Billericay Town*	*3–3*	*603*
Billericay Town	*v*	*Braintree Town*	*2–3*	*846*
Heybridge Swifts	v	Boston United	3–0	447
Hitchin Town	v	Cambridge City	3–3	653
Cambridge City	*v*	*Hitchin Town*	*2–3*	*439*
Hendon	v	Chelmsford City	0–1	572
Baldock Town	v	Aylesbury United	0–2	464
Collier Row	v	Chesham United	0–1	329
Ruislip Manor	v	Enfield	0–3	443
St Albans City	v	Romford	1–0	924
Yeading	v	Staines Town	4–1	264
Ashford Town	v	Gravesend & Northfleet	2–1	890

Hastings Town	v	Carshalton Athletic	2–2	657
Carshalton Athletic	*v*	*Hastings Town*	*1–2*	*712*
Worthing	v	Dulwich Hamlet	2–1	594
Margate	v	Kingstonian	0–1	588
Chertsey Town	v	Dover Athletic	0–0	676
Dover Athletic	*v*	*Chertsey Town*	*1–0*	*1037*
Wembley	v	Walton & Hersham	0–1	140
Newport(IW)	v	Wokingham Town	3–0	489
Bashley	v	Dorchester Town	1–1	389
Dorchester Town	*v*	*Bashley*	*0–2*	*799*
Salisbury City	v	Waterlooville	3–3	539
Waterlooville	*v*	*Salisbury City*	*0–1*	*519*
Cinderford Town	v	Gloucester City	0–2	1002
(*at Gloucester City FC*)				
Newport AFC	v	Trowbridge Town	2–2	1125
Trowbridge Town	*v*	*Newport AFC*	*1–1*	*641*
Trowbridge Town	*v*	*Newport AFC*	*3–1*	*834*
Bideford	v	Tiverton Town	1–8	527

Fourth round qualifying – 22 October 1994

Accrington Stanley	v	Spennymoor United	0–1	751
Southport	v	Stalybridge Celtic	2–1	1207
Altrincham	v	Marine	2–1	1221
Guiseley	v	Durham City	6–0	978
Bishop Auckland	v	Macclesfield Town	2–2	745
Macclesfield Town	*v*	*Bishop Auckland*	*0–1*	*1086*
Morecambe	v	Witton Albion	0–1	1092
Northwich Victoria	v	Blyth Spartans	2–0	1179
Hyde United	v	Warrington Town	1–1	658
Warrington Town	*v*	*Hyde United*	*0–2*	*1061*
Halifax Town	v	Lancaster City	3–1	779
Stafford Rangers	v	Slough Town	0–4	660
St Albans City	v	Enfield	0–0	1585
Enfield	*v*	*St Albans City*	*4–2*	*1342*
Chesham United	v	Bromsgrove Rovers	1–1	838
Bromsgrove Rovers	*v*	*Chesham United*	*0–1*	*1468*
Braintree Town	v	Gresley Rovers	0–2	691
Burton Albion	v	Hitchin Town	0–1	937
Nuneaton Borough	v	Heybridge Swifts	2–2	1131
Heybridge Swifts	*v*	*Nuneaton Borough*	*3–2*	*915*
VS Rugby	v	Chelmsford City	0–0	765
Chelmsford City	*v*	*VS Rugby*	*2–1*	*2376*
Yeading	v	Telford United	1–0	325
Moor Green	v	Aylesbury United	1–1	399
Aylesbury United	*v*	*Moor Green*	*3–1*	*1186*
Solihull Borough	v	Kettering Town	2–4	1052
Gloucester City	v	Worthing	1–1	1013
Worthing	*v*	*Gloucester City*	*2–1*	*1187*
Marlow	v	Sutton United	1–0	680
Tiverton Town	v	Farnborough Town	4–4	1144
Farnborough Town	*v*	*Tiverton Town*	*1–5*	*1229*
Dover Athletic	v	Kingstonian	1–2	1258
Hastings Town	v	Crawley Town	1–1	1142
Crawley Town	*v*	*Hastings Town*	*3–2*	*1407*
Walton & Hersham	v	Yeovil Town	3–2	963
Salisbury City	v	Ashford Town	2–3	701

			Results	Att
Newport(IW)	v	Trowbridge Town	1–0	861
Cheltenham Town	v	Bashley	1–1	876
Bashley	*v*	*Cheltenham Town*	*2–1*	*577*

First round proper – 12 November 1994

York City	v	Rotherham United	3–3	4020
Rotherham United	*v*	*York City*	*3–0*	*4391*
Chesterfield	v	Scarborough	0–0	2902
Scarborough	*v*	*Chesterfield*	*2–0*	*1564*
Hyde United	v	Darlington	1–3	2315
Wrexham	v	Stockport County	1–0	4740
Walsall	v	Rochdale	3–0	3619
Wigan Athletic	v	Spennymoor United	4–0	2183
Crewe Alexandra	v	Gresley Rovers	7–1	4539
Chester City	v	Witton Albion	2–0	2666
Burnley	v	Shrewsbury Town	2–1	9269
Bishop Auckland	v	Bury	0–0	3135
Bury	*v*	*Bishop Auckland*	*1–1*	*3517*
(*Bury won on kicks from the penalty mark, 4–2*)				
Guiseley	v	Carlisle United	1–4	6548
(*at Bradford City FC*)				
Halifax Town	v	Runcorn	1–1	1286
Runcorn	*v*	*Halifax Town*	*1–3*	*728*
(*at Witton Albion FC*)				
Preston North End	v	Blackpool	1–0	14036
Altrincham	v	Southport	3–2	2523
Hull City	v	Lincoln City	0–1	5758
Mansfield Town	v	Northwich Victoria	3–1	2999
Doncaster Rovers	v	Huddersfield Town	1–4	6626
Port Vale	v	Hartlepool United	6 0	6199
Bradford City	v	Scunthorpe United	1–1	5481
Scunthorpe United	*v*	*Bradford City*	*3–2*	*4514*
Exeter City	v	Crawley Town	1–0	3214
Marlow	v	Oxford United	2–0	3000
Kingstonian	v	Brighton & Hove Albion	2–1	3815
Walton & Hersham	v	Swansea City	0–2	2230
Slough Town	v	Birmingham City	0–4	13394
(*at Birmingham City FC*)				
Newport(IW)	v	Aylesbury United	2–3	2217
Kettering Town	v	Plymouth Argyle	0–1	4602
Peterborough United	v	Northampton Town	4–0	8739
Yeading	v	Colchester United	2–2	1715
Colchester United	*v*	*Yeading*	*7–1*	*4016*
Bournemouth AFC	v	Worthing	3–1	3922
Hereford United	v	Hitchin Town	2–2	3078
Hitchin Town	*v*	*Hereford United*	*4–2*	*3098*
Bath City	v	Bristol Rovers	0–5	6751
Heybridge Swifts	v	Gillingham	0–2	4614
(*at Colchester United FC*)				
Kidderminster Harriers	v	Torquay United	1–1	4114
Torquay United	*v*	*Kidderminster Harriers*	*1–0*	*3809*
Barnet	v	Woking	4–4	3114
Woking	*v*	*Barnet*	*1–0*	*4859*
Cambridge United	v	Brentford	2–2	3353
Brentford	*v*	*Cambridge United*	*1–2*	*4096*
Ashford Town	v	Fulham	2–2	3363

(Replays in italics)			Results	Att
Fulham	v	*Ashford Town*	5–3	*6539*
Enfield	v	Cardiff City	1–0	2345
Chesham United	v	Bashley	0–1	1302
Tiverton Town	v	Leyton Orient	1–3	3000
Wycombe Wanderers	v	Chelmsford City	4–0	5654

Second round proper – 3 December 1994

Scarborough	v	Port Vale	1–0	2382
Wrexham	v	Rotherham United	5–2	4521
Lincoln City	v	Huddersfield Town	1–0	4143
Altrincham	v	Wigan Athletic	1–0	3020
Crewe Alexandra	v	Bury	1–2	4835
Carlisle United	v	Darlington	2–0	8365
Chester City	v	Burnley	1–2	4231
Birmingham City	v	Scunthorpe United	0–0	13832
Scunthorpe United	v	*Birmingham City*	*1–2*	*6280*
Halifax Town	v	Mansfield Town	0–0	2396
Mansfield Town	v	*Halifax Town*	*2–1*	*2648*
Preston North End	v	Walsall	1–1	9767
Walsall	v	*Preston North End*	*4–0*	*6468*
Gillingham	v	Fulham	1–1	6253
Fulham	v	*Gillingham*	*0–1*	*6536*
Bashley	v	Swansea City	0–1	2047
Plymouth Argyle	v	Bournemouth AFC	2–1	6739
Hitchin Town	v	Wycombe Wanderers	0–5	2765
Marlow	v	Woking	2–1	2845
Leyton Orient	v	Bristol Rovers	0–2	5071
Enfield	v	Torquay United	1–1	2326
Torquay United	v	*Enfield*	*0–1*	*3174*
Exeter City	v	Colchester United	1–2	3528
Kingstonian	v	Aylesbury United	1–4	1891
Peterborough United	v	Cambridge United	0–2	9576

Third round proper – 7 January 1995

Leicester City	v	Enfield	2–0	17351
Scarborough	v	Watford	0–0	3544
Watford	v	*Scarborough*	*2–0*	*7047*
Coventry City	v	West Bromwich Albion	1–1	16555
West Bromwich Albion	v	*Coventry City*	*1–2*	*23230*
Mansfield Town	v	Wolverhampton Wanderers	2–3	6701
Sheffield United	v	Manchester United	0–2	22322
Wimbledon	v	Colchester United	1–0	6903
Swindon Town	v	Marlow	2–0	7007
Millwall	v	Arsenal	0–0	17715
Arsenal	v	*Millwall*	*0–2*	*32319*
Gillingham	v	Sheffield Wednesday	1–2	10425
Birmingham City	v	Liverpool	0–0	25326
Liverpool	v	*Birmingham City*	*1–1*	*36275*
(Liverpool won on kicks from the penalty mark, 2–0)				
Newcastle United	v	Blackburn Rovers	1–1	31574
Blackburn Rovers	v	*Newcastle United*	*1–2*	*22658*
Notts County	v	Manchester City	2–2	12376
Manchester City	v	*Notts County*	*5–2*	*14261*

(Replays in italics)

Aylesbury United	v	Queens Park Rangers	0–4	15417
(at QPR)				
Grimsby Town	v	Norwich City	0–1	11198
Swansea City	v	Middlesbrough	1–1	8407
Middlesbrough	*v*	*Swansea City*	*1–2*	*14274*
Southampton	v	Southend United	2–0	13003
Sunderland	v	Carlisle United	1–1	15523
Carlisle United	*v*	*Sunderland*	*1–3*	*12201*
Tottenham Hotspur	v	Altrincham	3–0	25057
Wrexham	v	Ipswich Town	2–1	8324
Nottingham Forest	v	Plymouth Argyle	2–0	19821
Reading	v	Oldham Athletic	1–3	8886
Portsmouth	v	Bolton Wanderers	3–1	9721
Walsall	v	Leeds United	1–1	8619
Leeds United	*v*	*Walsall*	*5–2*	*18083*
Bury	v	Tranmere Rovers	2–2	5755
Tranmere Rovers	*v*	*Bury*	*3–0*	*7921*
Everton	v	Derby County	1–0	29300
Wycombe Wanderers	v	West Ham United	0–2	9007
Bristol City	v	Stoke City	0–0	9683
Stoke City	*v*	*Bristol City*	*1–3*	*11572*
Luton Town	v	Bristol Rovers	1–1	7571
Bristol Rovers	*v*	*Luton Town*	*0–1*	*8213*
Barnsley	v	Aston Villa	0–2	11479
Chelsea	v	Charlton Athletic	3–0	24485
Crystal Palace	v	Lincoln City	5–1	6631
Cambridge United	v	Burnley	2–4	6277

Fourth round proper – 28 January 1995

Manchester United	v	Wrexham	5–2	43222
Millwall	v	Chelsea	0–0	18573
Chelsea	*v*	*Millwall*	*1–1*	*25515*
(Millwall won on kicks from the penalty mark 5–4)				
Tranmere Rovers	v	Wimbledon	0–2	11637
Manchester City	v	Aston Villa	1–0	21177
Nottingham Forest	v	Crystal Palace	1–2	16970
Portsmouth	v	Leicester City	0–1	14928
Coventry City	v	Norwich City	0–0	15101
Norwich City	*v*	*Coventry City*	*3–1*	*14673*
Queens Park Rangers	v	West Ham United	1–0	17694
Luton Town	v	Southampton	1–1	9938
Southampton	*v*	*Luton Town*	*6–0*	*15075*
Newcastle United	v	Swansea City	3–0	34372
Sheffield Wednesday	v	Wolverhampton Wanderers	0–0	21757
Wolverhampton Wanderers	*v*	*Sheffield Wednesday*	*1–1*	*28136*
(Wolverhampton Wanderers won on kicks from the penalty mark, 4–3)				
Leeds United	v	Oldham Athletic	3–2	25010
Sunderland	v	Tottenham Hotspur	1–4	21135
Watford	v	Swindon Town	1–0	11207
Burnley	v	Liverpool	0–0	20551
Liverpool	*v*	*Burnley*	*1–0*	*32109*
Bristol City	v	Everton	0–1	19816

Fifth round proper – 8 February 1995

			Results	Att
Newcastle United	v	Manchester City	3–1	33214
Manchester United	v	Leeds United	3–1	42744
Wolverhampton Wanderers	v	Leicester City	1–0	28544
Queens Park Rangers	v	Millwall	1–0	16457
Liverpool	v	Wimbledon	1–1	25124
Wimbledon	*v*	*Liverpool*	*0–2*	*12553*
Watford	v	Crystal Palace	0–0	13814
Crystal Palace	*v*	*Watford*	*1–0*	*10321*
Tottenham Hotspur	v	Southampton	1–1	28091
Southampton	*v*	*Tottenham Hotspur*	*2–6*	*15172*
Everton	v	Norwich City	5–0	31616

Sixth round proper – 11 March 1995

Liverpool	v	Tottenham Hotspur	1–2	39592
Everton	v	Newcastle United	1–0	35213
Crystal Palace	v	Wolverhampton Wanderers	1–1	14604
Wolverhampton Wanderers	*v*	*Crystal Palace*	*1–4*	*27548*
Manchester United	v	Queens Park Rangers	2–0	42830

Semi-finals – 9 April 1995

Manchester United (*at Aston Villa FC*)	v	Crystal Palace	2–2	38256
Crystal Palace (*at Aston Villa FC*)	*v*	*Manchester United*	*0–2*	*17987*
Tottenham Hotspur (*at Leeds United FC*)	v	Everton	1–4	38226

Paul Rideout (second from right) scores in the Final.

25 ● FA CUP 1995–1996 EXEMPTIONS
Sponsored by Littlewoods Pools

44 Clubs exempt to the Third Round Proper

Arsenal	Leeds United	Reading
Aston Villa	Leicester City	Sheffield United
Barnsley	Liverpool	Sheffield Wednesday
Birmingham City	Luton Town	Southampton
Blackburn Rovers	Manchester City	Southend United
Bolton Wanderers	Manchester United	Stoke City
Charlton Athletic	Middlesbrough	Sunderland
Chelsea	Millwall	Tottenham Hotspur
Coventry City	Newcastle United	Tranmere Rovers
Crystal Palace	Norwich City	Watford
Derby County	Nottingham Forest	West Bromwich Albion
Everton	Oldham Athletic	West Ham United
Grimsby Town	Portsmouth	Wimbledon
Huddersfield Town	Port Vale	Wolverhampton Wanderers
Ipswich Town	Queens Park Rangers	

52 Clubs exempt to the First Round Proper

Altrincham*	Darlington	Preston North Fnd
Barnet	Doncaster Rovers	Rochdale
Blackpool	Enfield*	Rotherham United
Bournemouth AFC	Exeter City	Scarborough
Bradford City	Fulham	Scunthorpe United
Brentford	Gillingham	Shrewsbury Town
Brighton & Hove Albion	Hartlepool United	Stockport County
Bristol City	Hereford United	Swansea City
Bristol Rovers	Hull City	Swindon Town
Burnley	Kidderminster Harriers†	Torquay United
Bury	Leyton Orient	Walsall
Cambridge United	Lincoln City	Wigan Athletic
Cardiff City	Mansfield Town	Woking†
Carlisle United	Northampton Town	Wrexham
Chester City	Notts County	Wycombe Wanderers
Chesterfield	Oxford United	York City
Colchester United	Peterborough United	
Crewe Alexandra	Plymouth Argyle	

† *Trophy Finalists*   * *Clubs outside The Football League considered most appropriate*

20 Clubs to the Fourth Round Qualifying

Aylesbury United	Kettering Town	Southport
Bashley	Kingstonian	Stalybridge Celtic
Bath City	Macclesfield Town	Sutton United
Bromsgrove Rovers	Marlow	Witton Albion
Crawley Town	Nuneaton Borough	Yeading
Halifax Town	Runcorn	Yeovil Town
Hitchin Town	Slough Town	

26 ● FA UMBRO TROPHY – FINAL TIE 1995

Woking 2   Kidderminster Harriers 1   (after extra time)

In eight years Woking had come from the Isthmian League Division Two South to the brink of the Football League. They had graced Wembley for the first time in winning the FA Amateur Cup Final against Ilford in 1958 and the finest achievement in the club's 106-year history had been to beat Runcorn and take home the FA Trophy in 1994. With most of the team back at Wembley twelve months later, their experience helped them to a repeat performance against Kidderminster Harriers, the Surrey club thereby becoming only the second in the history of the competition to retain the Trophy. (Scarborough were the first in 1977.) In a very successful season Geoff Chapple's team also finished runners-up to Macclesfield in the GM Vauxhall Conference.

Woking enjoyed a sensational start to the 26th Final of what is now known as the "FA Umbro Trophy" to reflect its sponsor. In the first few seconds Kidderminster skipper Simeon Hodson headed nervously behind for a corner-kick under pressure from the lurking Darran Hay, the scorer of one of Woking's goals in the previous year's Final. And, before a minute of the match had elapsed, Scott Steele chipped Kevin Rose from 25 yards and the 'keeper didn't even get close. 1–0 to Woking.

But Kidderminster, with a sprinkling of England sem-pro' internationals in their line-up, hardly broke stride and moved purposefully down the flanks throughout the first half. The crosses rained in – and so did the headers as the Woking defence showed a frightening lack of mobility at times. Two efforts from centre-back Chris Brindley – voted "Man of the Match" – and one from Paul Davies looked destined for the back of the net. The breakthrough came two minutes into the second half: John Deakin volleyed into the goalmouth from the left side of the box and, after a spot of pinball as several players struggled to get a clean touch, Davies had just enough presence of mind to guide the ball slowly inside Laurence Batty's right-hand post for the equaliser.

There were few clear-cut chances for the rest of the ninety minutes, though Rose did supremely well to tip over a menacing 30-yard free-kick from Colin Fielder which looked to be curling into the top corner. There were three substitutions in extra time as the pace slackened and the old emeny cramp became a factor. With two minutes on the clock and a Wednesday night replay at West Bromwich looming – a ground with happy memories for both clubs – Woking fashioned a Trophy-winning goal. Mark Tucker launched himself into a huge header at the far post from veteran Clive Walker's flag-kick, leaping at least a foot higher than two Kidderminster defenders, and Fielder met the ball with his forehead as it flashed across the face of the goal. There were bodies on the goal-line – but he wasn't going to miss.

Woking: Batty, Tucker, Wye L., Fielder, Brown K., Crumplin (Rattray), Wye S., Ellis, Steele, Hay (Newbery), Walker.

Kidderminster Harriers: Rose, Hodson, Bancroft, Webb, Brindley (Cartwright), Forsyth, Deakin, Yates, Humphreys (Hughes), Davies, Purdie.

Referee: D. J. Gallagher (Oxfordshire)

Attendance: 17,815

Chief Guest: Mr. A. Hadfield, Managing Director, Umbro UK Limited

27 ● FA UMBRO TROPHY 1994–1995

Preliminary round – 3 September 1994

(*Replays in italics*)			*Results*	*Att*
Chester-le-Street Town	v	Tow Law Town	2–4	133
Fisher 93	v	Whyteleafe	1–1	82
Whyteleafe	*v*	*Fisher 93*	*1–0*	*51*
Poole Town	v	Havant Town	1–2	160
(*at Havant Town FC*)				

First round qualifying – 17 September 1994

Whitley Bay	v	Bamber Bridge	0–4	197
Bedlington Terriers	v	Peterlee Newtown	2–1	
West Auckland Town	v	Shildon	5–0	58
Harrogate Town	v	Eppleton CW	4–0	177
Tow Law Town	v	Lancaster City	2–3	146
Consett	v	RTM Newcastle	0–0	54
RTM Newcastle	*v*	*Consett*	*2–0*	*101*
Guisborough Town	v	Murton	2–0	
Hebburn	v	Prudhoe Town	2–1	
Accrington Stanley	v	Emley	1–0	473
Workington	v	Great Harwood Town	2–2	224
Great Harwood Town	*v*	*Workington*	*4–2*	*103*
Dunston Fed Brewery	v	Netherfield	2–0	102
Bridgnorth Town	v	Sutton Coldfield Town	2–0	105
Leicester United	v	Caernarfon Town	2–2	84
Caernarfon Town	*v*	*Leicester United*	*1–2*	*307*
Goole Town	v	Knowsley United	1–1	
Knowsley United	*v*	*Goole Town*	*6–2*	
Gresley Rovers	v	Congleton Town	3–1	422
Chorley	v	Bilston Town	2–0	159
Redditch United	v	Eastwood Town	0–1	141
Mossley	v	Dudley Town	2–2	177
Dudley Town	*v*	*Mossley*	*4–5*	*103*
Farsley Celtic	v	Droylsden	1–1	
Droylsden	*v*	*Farsley Celtic*	*6–3*	*79*
Fleetwood	v	Radcliffe Borough	3–0	
Horwich RMI	v	Nuneaton Borough	0–3	185
Hinckley Town	v	Ilkeston Town	3–3	103
Ilkeston Town	*v*	*Hinckley Town*	*1–0*	*361*
Matlock Town	v	Buxton	2–1	
Armitage	v	Curzon Ashton	1–4	33
Stourbridge	v	Gainsborough Trinity	3–6	160
Solihull Borough	v	Atherton LR	1–0	128
Burton Albion	v	Ashton United	1–1	
Ashton United	*v*	*Burton Albion*	*3–0*	*157*
Moor Green	v	Worksop Town	8–4	265
Alfreton Town	v	Bedworth United	2–4	156
Kings Lynn	v	Burnham	3–3	311
Burnham	v	Kings Lynn	2–0	107
Leyton	v	Purfleet	0–1	103
Berkhamsted Town	v	Boreham Wood	0–2	92

Wivenhoe Town	v	Rothwell Town	1–2	111
Hayes	v	Tamworth	1–0	284
Racing Club Warwick	v	Harrow Borough	1–3	120
(tie ordered to be replayed)				
Racing Club Warwick	v	Harrow Borough	2–5	109
Heybridge Swifts	v	Billericay Town	2–0	277
Rushden & Diamonds	v	Hendon	0–0	1174
Hendon	*v*	*Rushden & Diamonds*	*1–4*	*141*
Wembley	v	Bury Town	5–2	67
Aylesbury United	v	Barking	5–0	471
Cambridge City	v	Bishop's Stortford	6–1	318
Ruislip Manor	v	Baldock Town	0–3	
Sudbury Town	v	Corby Town	5–0	339
VS Rugby	v	Braintree Town	4–3	399
Hastings Town	v	Gravesend & Northfleet	0–2	446
Chertsey Town	v	Tonbridge	3–1	334
Whyteleafe	v	Uxbridge	1–2	73
Dulwich Hamlet	v	Dorking	3–1	198
Ashford Town	v	Bognor Regis Town	3–4	359
Molesey	v	Sittingbourne	1–0	120
Wealdstone	v	Bromley	3–0	203
Tooting & Mitcham Utd	v	Walton & Hersham	0–2	219
Margate	v	Yeading	0–2	247
Erith & Belvedere	v	Staines Town	0–1	70
Gloucester City	v	Weymouth	1–0	558
Newbury Town	v	Buckingham Town	0–0	
(at Thatcham Town FC)				
Buckingham Town	*v*	*Newbury Town*	*1–1*	*86*
Buckingham Town	*v*	*Newbury Town*	*0–2*	*117*
Maidenhead United	v	Fareham Town	0–1	
Yate Town	v	Forest Green Rovers	0–2	160
Havant Town	v	Waterlooville	3–0	481
Evesham United	v	Basingstoke Town	0–1	105
Newport AFC	v	Aldershot Town	1–3	2144
Abingdon Town	v	Witney Town	1–1	337
Witney Town	*v*	*Abingdon Town*	*1–0*	
Dorchester Town	v	Wokingham Town	2–0	436
Newport(IW)	v	Salisbury City	2–4	230
Clevedon Town	v	Bashley	1–1	223
Bashley	*v*	*Clevedon Town*	*1–0*	*111*

Second round qualifying – 15 October 1994

Droylsden	v	Hebburn	2–2	170
Hebburn	*v*	*Droylsden*	*0–4*	*85*
RTM Newcastle	v	Dunston Federation Brewery	0–2	98
Curzon Ashton	v	Harrogate Town	4–2	64
Guisborough Town	v	Bedlington Terriers	2–1	135
Chorley	v	Bamber Bridge	1–2	688
Lancaster City	v	Knowsley United	1–1	174
Knowsley United	*v*	*Lancaster City*	*2–1*	*63*
Great Harwood Town	v	Fleetwood	1–2	85
Accrington Stanley	v	West Auckland Town	2–2	349
West Auckland Town	*v*	*Accrington Stanley*	*3–1*	*60*
Baldock Town	v	Matlock Town	2–0	244
Nuneaton Borough	v	Ashton United	1–2	973
Rothwell Town	v	Eastwood Town	5–4	146

			Results	Att
Ilkeston Town	v	Leicester United	6–1	481
Bedworth United	v	Bridgnorth Town	2–0	156
Mossley	v	Moor Green	1–3	181
Solihull Borough	v	VS Rugby	0–1	289
Gainsborough Trinity	v	Gresley Rovers	1–1	477
Gresley Rovers	*v*	*Gainsborough Trinity*	*1–0*	*457*
Yeading	v	Burnham	0–0	153
Burnham	*v*	*Yeading*	*0–4*	*142*
Heybridge Swifts	v	Chertsey Town	1–1	223
Chertsey Town	*v*	*Heybridge Swifts*	*3–1*	*235*
Sudbury Town	v	Hayes	2–0	358
Dulwich Hamlet	v	Aylesbury United	1–2	238
Walton & Hersham	v	Cambridge City	2–1	244
Wealdstone	v	Purfleet	0–3	239
Boreham Wood	v	Uxbridge	1–1	92
Uxbridge	*v*	*Boreham Wood*	*1–2*	*98*
Rushden & Diamonds	v	Wembley	2–1	1173
Molesey	v	Staines Town	4–2	205
Gravesend & Northfleet	v	Harrow Borough	1–1	502
Harrow Borough	*v*	*Gravesend & Northfleet*	*5–1*	*212*
Basingstoke Town	v	Aldershot Town	0–1	1554
Havant Town	v	Dorchester Town	1–3	188
Salisbury City	v	Bognor Regis Town	0–0	438
Bognor Regis Town	*v*	*Salisbury City*	*4–2*	*140*
Forest Green Rovers	v	Newbury Town	1–1	161
Newbury Town	*v*	*Forest Green Rovers*	*2–1*	*103*
(at Wokingham Town FC)				
Witney Town	v	Bashley	1–2	117
Gloucester City	v	Fareham Town	3–0	531

Third round qualifying – 26 November 1994

Northallerton	v	Blyth Spartans	0–2	178
Warrington Town	v	Colwyn Bay	1–1	208
Colwyn Bay	*v*	*Warrington Town*	*3–0*	*434*
Knowsley United	v	Ashton United	1–4	72
Fleetwood	v	Spennymoor United	1–1	230
Spennymoor United	*v*	*Fleetwood*	*3–0*	*309*
Curzon Ashton	v	Gresley Rovers	0–1	160
Barrow	v	Winsford United	1–1	867
Winsford United	*v*	*Barrow*	*4–2*	*216*
Frickley Athletic	v	Whitby Town	1–2	
Guisborough Town	v	West Auckland Town	1–2	175
Hyde United	v	Boston United	1–0	354
Dunston FB	v	Ilkeston Town	2–3	163
Bamber Bridge	v	Grantham Town	3–1	452
Droylsden	v	Leek Town	0–1	226
Gretna	v	Seaham Red Star	2–1	
Rushden & Diamonds	v	Crawley Town	2–1	1369
Cheltenham Town	v	Worthing	4–0	664
Aldershot Town	v	Rothwell Town	1–1	2003
(tie awarded to Rothwell Town – Aldershot played an ineligible player)				
Sudbury Town	v	Carshalton Athletic	6–1	413
Gloucester City	v	Chelmsford City	0–2	
Grays Athletic	v	Chertsey Town	0–0	281
Chertsey Town	*v*	*Grays Athletic*	*1–1*	*250*
Grays Athletic	*v*	*Chertsey Town*	*3–1*	*191*

Hednesford Town	v	Trowbridge Town	2-1	668
Bedworth United	v	Boreham Wood	0-1	277
Worcester City	v	Molesey	2-2	704
Molesey	*v*	*Worcester City*	*2-0*	*220*
Moor Green	v	Marlow	0-0	327
Marlow	*v*	*Moor Green*	*1-0*	*275*
Bashley	v	Yeading	1-1	327
Yeading	*v*	*Bashley*	*1-0*	*171*
St Albans City	v	Purfleet	4-3	357
Baldock Town	v	Walton & Hersham	1-1	233
Walton & Hersham	*v*	*Baldock Town*	*2-1*	*240*
Halesowen Town	v	Hitchin Town	4-0	676
Aylesbury United	v	Dorchester Town	2-1	636
Weston-Super-Mare	v	Chesham United	1-3	435
Kingstonian	v	Harrow Borough	3-1	
VS Rugby	v	Bognor Regis Town	2-1	439
Atherstone United	v	Newbury Town	1-2	254

First round proper – 21 January 1995

Runcorn	v	Northwich Victoria	2-1	954
Leek Town	v	Durham City	2-1	251
Gretna	v	Halesowen Town	1-1	171
Halesowen Town	*v*	*Gretna*	*4-1*	*724*
Telford United	v	Southport	2-0	804
Witton Albion	v	Guiseley	0-0	412
Guiseley	*v*	*Witton Albion*	*2-2*	*547*
Witton Albion	*v*	*Guiseley*	*1-2*	*570*
Gresley Rovers	v	Stafford Rangers	2-0	1032
Bamber Bridge	v	Halifax Town	1-0	1052
Hednesford Town	v	Altrincham	1-2	715
Stalybridge Celtic	v	Hyde United	3-3	1061
Hyde United	*v*	*Stalybridge Celtic*	*3-1*	*970*
Billingham Synthonia	v	Ashton United	1-2	194
Bishop Auckland	v	Gateshead	0-1	341
West Auckland Town	v	Macclesfield Town	1-2	581
(*at Macclesfield Town FC*)				
Colwyn Bay	v	Blyth Spartans	1-1	448
Blyth Spartans	*v*	*Colwyn Bay*	*2-2*	*452*
Colwyn Bay	*v*	*Blyth Spartans*	*2-1*	*573*
Marine	v	Whitby Town	3-1	374
Spennymoor United	v	Morecambe	0-3	472
Ilkeston Town	v	Winsford United	4-2	427
Newbury Town	v	Rothwell Town	1-2	318
Boreham Wood	v	Grays Athletic	1-0	211
VS Rugby	v	Aylesbury United	2-1	517
Woking	v	Chesham United	3-0	1488
Molesey	v	Cheltenham Town	0-2	303
Chelmsford City	v	Yeovil Town	2-4	1331
Merthyr Tydfil	v	Slough Town	3-2	413
Rushden & Diamonds	v	Sudbury Town	3-1	1301
Stevenage Borough	v	Dagenham & Redbridge	2-1	1004
St Albans City	v	Kidderminster Harriers	2-3	721
Kingstonian	v	Yeading	3-2	261
Welling United	v	Marlow	2-2	449
Marlow	*v*	*Welling*	*1-5*	*380*
Farnborough Town	v	Dover Athletic	1-0	609

Sutton United	v	Bath City	1–1	534
Bath City	*v*	*Sutton United*	*1–0*	*643*
Bromsgrove Rovers	v	Enfield	1–3	1439
Walton & Hersham	v	Kettering Town	2–2	398
Kettering Town	*v*	*Walton & Hersham*	*1–0*	

Second round proper – 11 February 1995

Farnborough Town	v	Rushden & Diamonds	0–1	602
Halesowen Town	v	Guiseley	2–1	731
Bath City	v	Marine	1–2	858
Runcorn	v	Leek Town	4–2	859
Ashton United	v	Macclesfield Town	0–5	
Altrincham	v	VS Rugby	1–1	1087
VS Rugby	*v*	*Altrincham*	*1–2*	*781*
Colwyn Bay	v	Enfield	1–2	756
Gresley Rovers	v	Morecambe	2–3	1113
Merthyr Tydfil	v	Bamber Bridge	2–1	
Gateshead	v	Rothwell Town	6–1	422
Hyde United	v	Telford United	2–0	879
Woking	v	Cheltenham Town	3–1	1128
Welling United	v	Ilkeston Town	1–1	727
Ilkeston Town	*v*	*Welling United*	*3–0*	*1280*
Yeovil Town	v	Stevenage Borough	1–1	1815
Stevenage Borough	*v*	*Yeovil Town*	*2–0*	*1713*
Kingstonian	v	Kidderminster Harriers	0–0	851
Kidderminster Harriers	*v*	*Kingstonian*	*1–0*	*1452*
Boreham Wood	v	Kettering Town	2–1	800

Third round proper – 4 March 1995

Marine	v	Boreham Wood	2–0	542
Runcorn	v	Hyde United	0–0	1059
Hyde United	*v*	*Runcorn*	*4–0*	*931*
Gateshead	v	Macclesfield Town	0–1	2585
Rushden & Diamonds	v	Halesowen Town	6–1	2547
Ilkeston Town	v	Kidderminster Harriers	2–2	2349
Kidderminster Harriers	*v*	*Ilkeston Town*	*2–1*	*1634*
Stevenage Borough	v	Woking	0–3	2631
Morecambe	v	Altrincham	2–3	1657
Enfield	v	Merthyr Tydfil	1–1	1208
Merthyr Tydfil	*v*	*Enfield*	*0–1*	

Fourth round proper – 25 March 1995

Marine	v	Hyde United	1–3	1130
Enfield	v	Rushden & Diamonds	1–1	1792
Rushden & Diamonds	*v*	*Enfield*	*4–3*	*3007*
Kidderminster Harriers	v	Altrincham	5–0	2660
Macclesfield Town	v	Woking	0–1	3019

Semi-finals

1st Leg – 8 April 1995

			Results	Att
Kidderminster Harriers	v	Hyde United	2–0	3059
Rushden & Diamonds	v	Woking	1–0	4375

2nd Leg – 15 April 1995

			Results	Att
Hyde United	v	Kidderminster Harriers	1–0	2103
Woking	v	Rushden & Diamonds	2–0	4643

Kidderminster Harriers won on aggregate 2–1
Woking won on aggregate 2–1

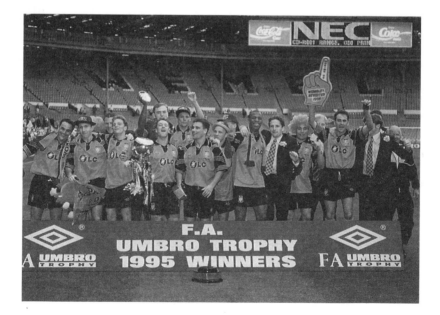

Woking – winners of the FA Umbro Trophy.

28 ● FA TROPHY WINNERS 1970–1995

Year	Venue	Winners		Runners-up	Result
1970	Wembley	Macclesfield Town	v	Telford United	2–0
1971	Wembley	Telford United	v	Hillingdon Borough	3–2
1972	Wembley	Stafford Rangers	v	Barnet	3–0
1973	Wembley	Scarborough	v	Wigan Athletic	2–1*
1974	Wembley	Morecambe	v	Dartford	2–1
1975	Wembley	Matlock Town	v	Scarborough	4–0
1976	Wembley	Scarborough	v	Stafford Rangers	3–2*
1977	Wembley	Scarborough	v	Dagenham	2–1
1978	Wembley	Altrincham	v	Leatherhead	3–1
1979	Wembley	Stafford Rangers	v	Kettering Town	2–0
1980	Wembley	Dagenham	v	Mossley	2–1
1981	Wembley	Bishop's Stortford	v	Sutton United	1–0
1982	Wembley	Enfield	v	Altrincham	1–0*
1983	Wembley	Telford United	v	Northwich Victoria	2–1
1984	Wembley	Northwich Victoria	v	Bangor City	1–1
	Stoke	Northwich Victoria	v	Bangor City	2–1
1985	Wembley	Wealdstone	v	Boston United	2–1
1986	Wembley	Altrincham	v	Runcorn	1–0
1987	Wembley	Kidderminster Harriers	v	Burton Albion	0–0
	West Bromwich	Kidderminster Harriers	v	Burton Albion	2–1
1988	Wembley	Enfield	v	Telford United	0–0
	West Bromwich	Enfield	v	Telford United	3–2
1989	Wembley	Telford United	v	Macclesfield Town	1–0*
1990	Wembley	Barrow	v	Leek Town	3–0
1991	Wembley	Wycombe Wanderers	v	Kidderminster Harriers	2–1
1992	Wembley	Colchester United	v	Witton Albion	3–1
1993	Wembley	Wycombe Wanderers	v	Runcorn	4–1
1994	Wembley	Woking	v	Runcorn	2–1
1995	Wembley	Woking	v	Kidderminster Harriers	2–1*

* After extra time

29 ● FA UMBRO TROPHY 1995–96 EXEMPTIONS

32 Clubs Exempt to the First Round Proper

Altrincham
Bath City
Bromsgrove Rovers
Cheltenham Town
Colwyn Bay
Dagenham & Redbridge
Dover Athletic
Enfield
Farnborough Town
Gateshead
Guiseley

Halifax Town
Hednesford Town
Hyde United
Kettering Town
Kidderminster Harriers
Kingstonian
Macclesfield Town
Marine
Merthyr Tydfil
Morecambe
Northwich Victoria

Runcorn
Rushden & Diamonds
Slough Town
Southport
Stalybridge Celtic
Stevenage Borough
Telford United
Welling United
Woking
Yeovil Town

32 Clubs Exempt to the Third Round Qualifying

Ashton United
Aylesbury United
Bamber Bridge
Bishop Auckland
Blyth Spartans
Boreham Wood
Boston United
Bromley
Burton Albion
Buxton
Cambridge City

Chelmsford City
Dorchester Town
Gainsborough Trinity
Gloucester City
Grays Athletic
Gresley Rovers
Gretna
Halesowen Town
Hayes
Hitchin Town
Ilkeston Town

Leek Town
Molesey
Rothwell Town
Spennymoor United
St Albans City
Stafford Rangers
Sutton United
VS Rugby
Witton Albion
Yeading

30 ● FA CARLSBERG VASE – FINAL TIE 1995

Arlesey Town 2   Oxford City 1

Arlesey Town of the South Midlands League won the 21st Final of the competition now known as the "FA Carlsberg Vase" and a 13,000 crowd witnessed a hard-fought match in the Wembley sunshine. Arlesey had finished in the top six in both seasons since returning to the South Midlands from the United Counties League in 1992 and had been Vase quarter-finalists in 1994. Now rookie managers Robbie O'Keefe and Phil Cavener had guided a club with a 104-year history all the way to Wembley and it seemed like the whole town was there to support them.

Paul Palma, wearing the No. 4 shirt for Arlesey, was a constant threat to Diadora League Oxford City's rearguard in the first half. A carpenter by trade, and possessing great touch on the pitch for a big man, he gave his team a priceless lead on 26 minutes. Oxford's Martin Brown was deceived by the bounce in a one-on-one situation with Palma and suddenly a goal was very much on the cards. The Arlesey striker veered to the left as he entered the box, then flipped a shot with the outside of his right foot well wide of Colin Fleet and into the net via the top of his left-hand post.

But the Bedfordshire club's scoring hero failed to finish the match. Launching himself into a sprint down the right with the last Oxford defender two minutes from the break, he pulled up suddenly and clearly pulled a muscle. Oxford City had never been to Wembley, though they had appeared in three FA Amateur Cup Finals before the First World War. They had actually lost their ground in 1988 and been forced to miss a complete season before reforming as a

youth side. Now they were pushing hard to equalise in the Vase Final, perhaps feeling that Arlesey had become a less potent striking force without Palma.

The goal came on 56 minutes after Chris Fontaine had pulled a short cross back from the by-line. Sherwood's shot from close range was beaten away, but the other Fontaine – brother Steve – had enough time to set himself for a powerful shot into the net. But Arlesey's key player in the second period was substitute Tony Ward, a quantity surveyor who had overcome the disability of having only one arm to play at the highest non-League level. He replaced Palma in attack and rushed all over the place, constantly putting Oxford's defence under pressure.

Ward, 29 and a former player for Stevenage, Hitchin, Barton and Letchworth, clipped the top of the Oxford bar with a 30-yarder on 78 minutes, but Arlesey secured a Vase-winning goal a minute later. Even in a crowded box Sandor Gyalog, the son of a Hungarian immigrant, single-mindedly sent in an unstoppable volley from near the penalty mark. The last memory, with Arlesey's huge support jumping for joy, was of Ward taking off his boots and lobbing them into the crowd.

Arlesey Town: Young, Cardines, Bambrick, Palma (Ward), Hull, Gonsalves, Gyalog, Cox, Kane, O'Keefe, Marshall (Nicholls).

Oxford City: Fleet, Brown M. (Fisher), Hume, Shepherd, Muttock, Hamilton (Kemp), Thomas, Spittle, Sherwood, Fontaine S., Fontaine C.

Referee: Mr. G.S. Willard (Sussex)

Attendance: 13,670

Chief Guest: Mr. E. Dinesen, Chief Executive Carlsberg-Tetley

31 ● FA CARLSBERG VASE 1994–1995

Extra Preliminary round – 3 September 1994

			Results	Att
(Replays in italics)				
Cleator Moor Celtic	v	Norton & Stockton Ancients	1–2	56
Morpeth Town	v	Horden CW	4–3	95
Langley Park	v	Shotton Comrades	3–1	31
Marske United	v	Seaton Delaval Amateurs	4–3	
Ponteland United	v	North Shields	8–1	80
Sunderland Kennek Roker	v	Annfield Plain	4–1	42
Waterloo Dock	v	Kimberley Town	3–0	48
Maghull	v	Merseyside Police	1–2	39
South Normanton Ath	v	Long Eaton United	3–0	88
Staveley MW	v	Daisy Hill	3–1	150
Rainworth MW	v	Wythenshawe Amateur	3–1	250
Heswall	v	Cheadle Town	2–1	34
Borrowash Victoria	v	Nuthall	2–2	42
Nuthall	*v*	*Borrowash Victoria*	*1–1*	*39*
Borrowash Victoria	*v*	*Nuthall*	*2–2*	*47*
(Abandoned due to a waterlogged pitch)				
Borrowash Victoria	*v*	*Nuthall*	*1–0*	*103*
Shirebrook Town	v	Grove United	1–2	50
Vauxhall	v	Lucas Sports	6–3	22
Nettleham	v	Glapwell	0–2	
Garforth Town	v	Oakham United	0–1	70
Harworth CI	v	Castleton Gabriels	4–3	35
Ashville	v	Hall Road Rangers	0–1	60
Clipstone Welfare	v	Poulton Victoria	1–3	70
Holwell Sports	v	Birstall United	4–3	90
Friar Lane OB	v	St Andrews	1–2	149
Cradley Town	v	Westfields	1–1	
Westfields	*v*	*Cradley Town*	*5–1*	*36*
Knowle	v	Pegasus Juniors	4–0	20
Northfield Town	v	Darlaston	4–1	
Kings Heath	v	Meir KA	0–1	18
Lutterworth Town	v	Bloxwich Town	0–0	24
Bloxwich Town	*v*	*Lutterworth Town*	*0–0*	*24*
Bloxwich Town	*v*	*Lutterworth Town*	*2–0*	*20*
Gedling Town	v	Coleshill Town	4–2	41
Brantham Athletic	v	Mildenhall Town	4–1	46
Great Wakering Rovers	v	Clacton Town	2–0	105
Swaffham Town	v	Somersham Town	1–1	80
Somersham Town	*v*	*Swaffham Town*	*1–2*	*54*
Downham Town	v	Stanway Rovers	4–1	24
(at Long Sutton Athletic FC)				
Warboys Town	v	Hullbridge Sports	5–1	92
Southend Manor	v	Maldon Town	1–2	35
Milton Keynes	v	Shillington	0–5	35
Stansted	v	Potters Bar Town	0–1	
East Ham United	v	Leverstock Green	0–3	36
Rayners Lane	v	Eton Wick	0–3	32

(Replays in italics)			Results	Att
St Margaretsbury	v	Cockfosters	1-2	
(at Hertford Town FC)				
Harpenden Town	v	Brentwood	1-0	30
Beaconsfield SYCOB	v	Eton Manor	4-1	11
London Colney	v	Waltham Abbey	4-0	
Tower Hamlets	v	Totternhoe	9-1	72
West Wickham	v	Cobham	0-4	60
Worthing United	v	East Grinstead	2-1	48
Stamco	v	Furness	2-1	119
Thamesmead Town	v	Eastbourne United	2-1	58
Cranleigh	v	Broadbridge Heath	0-2	75
Greenwich Borough	v	Mile Oak	3-4	45
Sherborne Town	v	North Leigh	0-3	
Flight Refuelling	v	Peppard	2-1	36
Petersfield Town	v	Hamworthy United	6-0	40
Sandhurst Town	v	Carterton Town	1-2	37
Bridgwater Town	v	Dawlish Town	4-1	250
Chard Town	v	Bishop Sutton	1-2	67
Cadbury Heath	v	Brislington	1-5	105
Cirencester Town	v	DRG AFC	3-2	45
Bristol Manor Farm	v	Almondsbury Town	1-3	41
(at Almondsbury Town FC)				
Crediton United	v	Clyst Rovers	0-1	89
Wotton Rovers	v	Old Georgians	2-2	20
Old Georgians	*v*	*Wotton Rovers*	*0-2*	*21*

Preliminary round – 1 October 1994

Alnwick Town	v	Esh Winning	3-0	38
Ponteland United	v	West Allotment Celtic	2-2	75
West Allotment Celtic	*v*	*Ponteland United*	*0 1*	*125*
Penrith	v	Billingham Town	7-0	75
Walker	v	Washington	3-4	25
Morpeth Town	v	Ryhope CA	1-0	61
Crook Town	v	Langley Park	9-0	87
Pickering Town	v	Harrogate Railway	4-0	71
Darlington Cleveland Soc	v	Wolviston	3-5	25
Marske United	v	Willington	3-4	80
Easington Colliery	v	Evenwood Town	1-2	11
Norton & Stockton Ancients	v	Sunderland Kennek Roker	4-2	30
Armthorpe Welfare	v	North Ferriby United	2-3	69
Salford City	v	Skelmersdale United	1-1	25
Skelmersdale United	*v*	*Salford City*	*1-1*	*82*
Salford City	*v*	*Skelmersdale United*	*2-0*	*35*
Hucknall Town	v	Formby	5-1	116
Chadderton	v	Sheffield	4-1	98
Maltby MW	v	Blackpool(Wren)Rovers	1-4	40
Borrowash Victoria	v	Blidworth MW	3-1	47
Heanor Town	v	Kidsgrove Athletic	2-1	125
Rossendale United	v	St Helens Town	1-2	115
Tadcaster Albion	v	Glapwell	3-1	63
Ashfield United	v	Harworth CI	3-0	64
Heswall	v	Darwen	1-0	59
Ossett Town	v	Grove United	1-1	94
Grove United	*v*	*Ossett Town*	*1-0*	*40*
Oakham United	v	Merseyside Police	2-1	65
Worsbro Bridge MW	v	Prescot AFC	3-2	100

Priory (Eastwood)	v	Trafford	0–7	26
Louth United	v	Hallam	2–1	60
Bradford (Park Avenue)	v	South Normanton Ath	6–4	165
Clitheroe	v	Waterloo Dock	3–4	111
Winterton Rangers	v	Newcastle Town	0–1	28
Lincoln United	v	Poulton Victoria	4–5	97
Res Parkgate	v	Denaby United	2–0	65
Staveley MW	v	Bootle	0–2	85
Maine Road	v	Immingham Town	1–0	37
Bacup Borough	v	Glasshoughton Welfare	2–4	70
Yorkshire Amateur	v	Rainworth MW	0–2	44
Atherton Collieries	v	Hatfield Main	0–1	45
Liversedge	v	Hall Road Rangers	2–4	51
Pontefract Collieries	v	Ossett Albion	1–5	50
Oldham Town	v	Rossington Main	1–1	50
Rossington Main	*v*	*Oldham Town*	*0–4*	*47*
Vauxhall	v	Eccleshill United	3–2	17
Knowle	v	Willenhall Town	0–2	71
Stourport Swifts	v	Bolehall Swifts	3–2	50
Highgate United	v	St Andrews	1–5	20
Brierley Hill Town	v	Barwell	0–1	20
Meir KA	v	Chasetown	4–2	50
Shepshed Dynamo	v	Holwell Sports	2–3	171
Halesowen Harriers	v	Stewarts & Lloyds	1–2	68
Stapenhill	v	Gedling Town	2–3	50
Oldbury United	v	Shifnal Town	4–2	67
Knypersley Victoria	v	Westfields	4–1	99
Blakenall	v	Rocester	2–1	75
Lye Town	v	Stratford Town	3–1	56
Paget Rangers	v	Boldmere St Michaels	2–1	168
Long Buckby	v	Wellingborough Town	3–0	35
Sandwell Borough	v	Northampton Spencer	0–1	22
Northfield Town	v	Bloxwich Town	0–1	88
Rushall Olympic	v	Newport Pagnell Town	1–2	54
Desborough Town	v	Wednesfield	1–5	74
Brantham Athletic	v	Cornard United	2–0	53
Harwich & Parkeston	v	Stowmarket Town	0–2	173
Holbeach United	v	Eynesbury Rovers	0–4	81
Sudbury Wanderers	v	Haverhill Rovers	2–2	42
Haverhill Rovers	*v*	*Sudbury Wanderers*	*2–2*	*78*
Haverhill Rovers	*v*	*Sudbury Wanderers*	*1–0*	*85*
Swaffham Town	v	Long Sutton Athletic	4–1	90
Burnham Ramblers	v	Gorleston	1–1	79
Gorleston	*v*	*Burnham Ramblers*	*5–0*	*131*
Watton United	v	Wroxham	0–4	75
Warboys Town	v	Downham Town	1–0	92
Ipswich Wanderers	v	Felixstowe Town	0–2	80
Norwich United	v	Newmarket Town	0–3	35
Stamford AFC	v	Sawbridgeworth Town	1–0	72
Bowers United	v	Great Yarmouth Town	1–0	53
Woodbridge Town	v	Maldon Town	0–1	149
Hadleigh United	v	March Town United	4–3	122
Chatteris Town	v	Witham Town	1–6	41
Great Wakering Rovers	v	Fakenham Town	2–2	192
Fakenham Town	*v*	*Great Wakering Rovers*	*2–4*	*325*
Ely City	v	Tiptree United	1–4	43
Histon	v	Spalding United	2–3	59
Bourne Town	v	Mirrlees Blackstone	2–1	105

(Replays in italics)			Results	Att
Ashford Town (Middx)	v	Stotfold	1−2	100
Harlow Town	v	Hanwell Town	0−0	79
Hanwell Town	*v*	*Harlow Town*	*0−2*	*70*
Haringey Borough	v	Wootton Blue Cross	1−1	33
Wootton Blue Cross	*v*	*Haringey Borough*	*1−3*	*80*
Hampton	v	Viking Sports	0−1	100
Northwood	v	Ford United	2−0	91
East Thurrock United	v	Leverstock Green	5−2	120
London Colney	v	Harpenden Town	1−0	65
Harefield United	v	Langford	6−1	35
Kingsbury Town	v	Royston Town	0−2	65
Cockfosters	v	Edgware Town	3−0	122
Southall	v	Eton Wick	3−4	38
Brook House	v	Biggleswade Town	7−5	55
Potton United	v	Hemel Hempstead	1−3	95
Kempston Rovers	v	Concord Rangers	1−2	39
Beaconsfield SYCOB	v	Tower Hamlets	1−2	13
Tilbury	v	Shillington	3−1	58
Welwyn Garden City	v	Wingate & Finchley	3−5	43
Leighton Town	v	Bedford Town	2−1	386
Letchworth Garden City	v	Dunstable		
(*walkover for Letchworth Garden City – Dunstable removed from the Competition*)				
Ware	v	Hertford Town	1−2	
Hornchurch	v	Flackwell Heath	5−0	73
Clapton	v	Hillingdon Borough	0−1	27
Cheshunt	v	Romford	0−3	116
Potters Bar Town	v	Feltham & Hounslow Borough	2−1	67
Croydon Athletic	v	Whitstable Town	2−7	54
Southwick	v	Chichester City	8−0	134
Sheppey United	v	Stamco	2−4	127
Burgess Hill Town	v	Chipstead	1−0	107
Corinthian	v	Canterbury City	4−3	35
Camberley Town	v	Ramsgate	3−2	45
Cobham	v	Epsom & Ewell	0−0	79
Epsom & Ewell	*v*	*Cobham*	*0−1*	*51*
Newhaven	v	Chatham Town	1−4	95
Three Bridges	v	Slade Green	2−1	89
Wick	v	Eastbourne Town	3−0	124
Deal Town	v	Arundel	5−2	179
Selsey	v	Broadbridge Heath	2−0	44
Redhill	v	Leatherhead	3−4	150
Mile Oak	v	Thamesmead Town	1−4	92
Corinthian-Casuals	v	Bracknell Town	1−4	35
Steyning Town	v	Dartford	1−3	255
Worthing United	v	Horsham	0−4	121
Langney Sports	v	Ash United	3−0	158
Ringmer	v	Shoreham	0−3	144
Bedfont	v	Beckenham Town	1−3	36
Folkestone Invicta	v	Horsham YMCA	5−1	203
Cray Wanderers	v	Merstham	1−1	54
Merstham	*v*	*Cray Wanderers*	*2−1*	*49*
Crowborough Athletic	v	Pagham	2−1	90
Portfield	v	Oakwood	2−0	63
Lancing	v	Egham Town	0−3	64
Godalming & Guildford	v	Littlehampton Town	3−4	88
Bemerton Heath Harlequins	v	Eastleigh	2−2	71
Eastleigh	*v*	*Bemerton Heath Harlequins*	*3−0*	*112*
Gosport Borough	v	Hungerford Town	2−3	106

● **115**

			Results	Att
Thatcham Town	v	First Tower United	2–5	127
Totton AFC	v	Abingdon United	1–3	74
Swanage Town & Herston	v	Westbury United	0–4	69
Cove	v	Carterton Town	4–3	34
Flight Refuelling	v	Lymington AFC	1–2	76
Swindon Supermarine	v	Brockenhurst	1–2	55
Wantage Town	v	Fleet Town	2–1	70
Kintbury Rangers	v	Bournemouth	2–3	49
Bicester Town	v	Milton United	1–2	125
Christchurch	v	Petersfield Town	2–3	36
North Leigh	v	Calne Town	3–3	94
Calne Town	*v*	*North Leigh*	*0–3*	*45*
Banbury United	v	Ryde	3–0	175
Cirencester Town	v	Tuffley Rovers	1–3	77
Porthleven	v	Fairford Town	6–1	125
Cinderford Town	v	Bishop Sutton	3–1	89
(*at Bishop Sutton FC*)				
Frome Town	v	Devizes Town	2–2	123
Devizes Town	*v*	*Frome Town*	*2–1*	*82*
Clyst Rovers	v	Glastonbury	3–2	35
Torrington	v	Bridgwater Town	3–1	125
Ilfracombe Town	v	Odd Down	3–2	95
Bridport	v	Backwell United	2–1	171
Melksham Town	v	Barnstaple Town	1–2	87
Chippenham Town	v	Brislington	3–1	124
Elmore	v	Warminster Town	5–1	19
Larkhall Athletic	v	Saltash United	1–3	48
Minehead	v	Exmouth Town	0–4	45
Keynsham Town	v	St Blazey	5–3	70
Newquay	v	Mangotsfield United	1–3	103
Almondsbury Town	v	Wotton Rovers	1–2	52
Wellington Town	v	Liskeard Athletic	1–3	75
Hallen	v	Shortwood United	1–2	56

First round – 29 October 1994

Ponteland United	v	Washington	1–2	45
Crook Town	v	Willington	0–1	92
Ossett Albion	v	Wolviston	8–0	71
Whickham	v	Norton & Stockton Ancients	3–1	40
Pickering Town	v	Evenwood Town	1–0	78
Thackley	v	Morpeth Town	4–0	97
Blackpool(Wren)Rovers	v	Waterloo Dock	0–2	
Alnwick Town	v	South Shields	1–4	100
North Ferriby United	v	Penrith	2–1	
Oldham Town	v	Tadcaster Albion	3–0	62
Bootle	v	Newcastle Town	7–6	33
Hall Road Rangers	v	Trafford	0–1	31
Grove United	v	Hatfield Main	1–1	
Hatfield Main	*v*	*Grove United*	*4–2*	*70*
Borrowash Victoria	v	Chadderton	3–1	39
Poulton Victoria	v	Parkgate	4–1	92
Bradford (Park Avenue)	v	St Helens Town	3–0	251
Ashfield United	v	Stocksbridge Park Steels	1–2	73
Rainworth MW	v	Vauxhall	1–0	
Hucknall Town	v	Nantwich Town	2–1	138
Oakham United	v	Louth United	2–0	50

Worsbro Bridge MW	v	Glossop North End	2–4	300
Heanor Town	v	Salford City	2–1	
Maine Road	v	Glasshoughton Welfare	5–2	40
Flixton	v	Heswall	8–1	80
St Andrews	v	Bloxwich Town	2–0	25
Paget Rangers	v	Barwell	2–3	
Lye Town	v	Wednesfield	1–3	59
Meir KA	v	Gedling Town	1–1	79
Gedling Town	*v*	*Meir KA*	*2–4*	
Arnold Town	v	Long Buckby	2–0	232
Knypersley Victoria	v	Oldbury United	0–1	102
Stewarts & Lloyds	v	Raunds Town	1–5	
Cogenhoe United	v	Bourne Town	4–1	45
Holwell Sports	v	West Midlands Police	1–1	65
West Midlands Police	*v*	*Holwell Sports*	*2–0*	*35*
Pershore Town	v	Willenhall Town	0–2	116
Northampton Spencer	v	Blakenall	1–2	59
Spalding United	v	Stamford	2–1	193
Stourport Swifts	v	Newport Pagnell Town	0–2	
Northwood	v	Tiptree United	6–3	
Potters Bar Town	v	Hadleigh United	3–4	110
Harefield United	v	Tring Town	0–2	37
Hertford Town	v	Swaffham Town	2–0	
Newmarket Town	v	Brimsdown Rovers	2–0	90
Maldon Town	v	Haringey Borough	5–1	70
Letchworth Garden City	v	Aveley	1–2	30
(*tie awarded to Letchworth Garden City – Aveley played an ineligible player*)				
Barton Rovers	v	Felixstowe Town	2–1	
Collier Row	v	Concord Rangers	3–1	75
Cockfosters	v	Halstead Town	0–1	160
Stotfold	v	Witham Town	0–0	83
Witham Town	*v*	*Stotfold*	*0–2*	*80*
Viking Sports	v	Tower Hamlets	3–4	55
Gorleston	v	Harlow Town	5–1	143
Hornchurch	v	East Thurrock United	1–2	93
Great Wakering Rovers	v	Tilbury	4–2	144
Wroxham	v	Brantham Athletic	2–2	
Brantham Athletic	*v*	*Wroxham*	*0–1*	*45*
Royston Town	v	Brook House	1–1	57
Brook House	*v*	*Royston Town*	*2–2*	
Brook House	*v*	*Royston Town*	*0–2*	*57*
Eynesbury Rovers	v	Hemel Hempstead	1–0	122
Hillingdon Borough	v	Stowmarket Town	4–2	61
Basildon United	v	Haverhill Rovers	3–0	97
Bowers United	v	Wingate & Finchley	2–5	65
Leighton Town	v	Soham Town Rangers	2–0	205
Warboys Town	v	London Colney	3–2	157
Lowestoft Town	v	Romford	5–0	313
Littlehampton Town	v	Camberley Town	2–2	250
Camberley Town	*v*	*Littlehampton Town*	*4–0*	
Cobham	v	Horsham	2–3	120
North Leigh	v	Lewes	3–2	88
Shoreham	v	Bracknell Town	2–1	78
Wantage Town	v	Hailsham Town	1–4	120
Crowborough Athletic	v	Cove	1–5	132
Milton United	v	Langney Sports	6–2	65
Eton Wick	v	Andover	6–4	84
Hungerford Town	v	Portfield	4–1	93

Bournemouth	v	Beckenham Town	5–0	150
Stamco	v	Whitstable Town	4–2	400
Burgess Hill Town	v	Wick	0–3	136
Oxford City	v	Herne Bay	4–1	155
Abingdon United	v	Selsey	0–2	23
Thame United	v	Leatherhead	1–2	88
Deal Town	v	Dartford	3–2	357
Three Bridges	v	Thamesmead Town	1–3	98
Eastleigh	v	Banbury United	2–1	
Egham Town	v	Brockenhurst	6–2	53
Chatham Town	v	Merstham	4–0	125
Southwick	v	Petersfield Town	1–2	
Folkestone Invicta	v	Corinthian	1–2	183
First Tower United	v	Lymington AFC	3–4	
Mangotsfield United	v	Moreton Town	2–0	112
Torrington	v	Welton Rovers	3–0	105
Elmore	v	Clyst Rovers	4–0	140
Ilfracombe Town	v	Falmouth Town	1–9	153
Tuffley Rovers	v	Wotton Rovers	2–1	52
Bridport	v	Shortwood United	6–0	162
Chippenham Town	v	Cinderford Town	3–4	127
Westbury United	v	Devizes Town	0–0	105
Devizes Town	*v*	*Westbury United*	*1–2*	*92*
Barnstaple Town	v	Keynsham Town	3–1	145
Liskeard Athletic	v	Bideford	2–1	110
Torpoint Athletic	v	Exmouth Town	4–1	69
Saltash United	v	Porthleven	6–3	110

Second round – 19 November 1994

Heanor Town	v	Hatfield Main	2–4	230
South Shields	v	Flixton	3–2	288
Cammell Laird	v	Meir KA	2–2	100
Meir KA	*v*	*Cammell Laird*	*0–2*	*134*
Whickham	v	Pickering Town	0–0	100
Pickering Town	*v*	*Whickham*	*3–2*	*121*
Brandon United	v	Dunkirk	2–1	34
Arnold Town	v	Trafford	2–1	294
North Ferriby United	v	Thackley	0–3	144
Waterloo Dock	v	Hucknall Town	1–2	
Burscough	v	Brigg Town	2–0	212
Rainworth MW	v	Poulton Victoria	0–4	
Stocksbridge Park Steels	v	Oakham United	2–1	131
Glossop North End	v	Bootle	2–0	242
Eastwood Hanley	v	Bradford (Park Avenue)	3–1	184
Ossett Albion	v	Stockton	2–0	83
Maine Road	v	Borrowash Victoria	2–1	79
Belper Town	v	Washington	5–0	161
Oldham Town	v	Willington	1–2	57
Great Wakering Rovers	v	Raunds Town	1–2	195
Diss Town	v	Cogenhoe United	3–2	429
Hoddesdon Town	v	Arlesey Town	0–2	76
Boston Town	v	Walthamstow Pennant	1–0	203
Tower Hamlets	v	West Midlands Police	2–2	65
West Midlands Police	*v*	*Tower Hamlets*	*1–0*	*95*
Letchworth Garden City	v	Hadleigh United	0–3	65
Stotfold	v	Warboys Town	3–1	131

St Andrews	v Willenhall Town	3-1	
Oadby Town	v Wednesfield	5-4	200
Collier Row	v Newport Pagnell Town	7-0	137
Wisbech Town	v Blakenall	3-1	609
Halstead Town	v Saffron Walden Town	4-2	285
East Thurrock United	v Canvey Island	0-2	373
Wroxham	v Pelsall Villa	0-1	253
Royston Town	v Basildon United	0-1	
Eynesbury Rovers	v Spalding United	2-0	178
Newmarket Town	v Tring Town	2-1	133
Lowestoft Town	v Maldon Town	3-1	227
Gorleston	v Barton Rovers	0-4	151
Leighton Town	v Wingate & Finchley	0-3	210
Barwell	v Hertford Town	2-1	
Oldbury United	v Hinckley Athletic	1-2	134
Wick	v Chalfont St Peter	2-1	165
Horsham	v Malden Vale	1-1	178
Malden Vale	*v Horsham*	*1-3*	
Cove	v Hailsham Town	2-3	
Hillingdon Borough	v Northwood	0-1	170
Stamco	v Leatherhead	4-0	306
Corinthian	v Egham Town	4-3	40
Windsor & Eton	v Shoreham	2-3	
Metropolitan Police	v Eton Wick	3-1	87
Camberley Town	v Banstead Athletic	0-2	
Thamesmead Town	v Croydon	1-6	72
Peacehaven & Telscombe	v Deal Town	3-0	171
Whitehawk	v Chatham Town	1-0	95
Selsey	v Tunbridge Wells	0-1	115
Eastleigh	v Lymington AFC	6-3	145
Milton United	v Oxford City	1-4	191
Bridport	v Falmouth Town	1-3	238
Liskeard Athletic	v Cinderford Town	3-1	160
Petersfield Town	v Taunton Town	0-7	155
Bournemouth	v Torpoint Athletic	4-3	
North Leigh	v Elmore	0-4	112
Tiverton Town	v Saltash United	9-0	560
Westbury United	v Tuffley Rovers	4-1	70
Wimborne Town	v Torrington	4-2	
Barnstaple Town	v Hungerford Town	3-1	255
Mangotsfield United	v Paulton Rovers	3-2	192

Third round – 10 December 1994

Oadby Town	v Ossett Albion	0-6	256
Hatfield Main	v Maine Road	0-1	138
Barwell	v Brandon United	0-1	
Thackley	v Cammell Laird	1-1	
Cammell Laird	*v Thackley*	*1-1*	
Thackley	*v Cammell Laird*	*1-2*	*126*
Eastwood Hanley	v Pickering Town	3-1	78
Poulton Victoria	v St Andrews	2-3	133
Arnold Town	v Burscough	2-3	293
Glossop North End	v Stocksbridge Pk Steels	0-5	312
South Shields	v Hucknall Town	3-1	232
Belper Town	v Willington	6-4	238
Wisbech Town	v Stotfold	3-4	708

Hadleigh United	v	Corinthian	3–1 193
Newmarket Town	v	Canvey Island	0–5 198
Wingate and Finchley	v	Basildon United	1–2 200
Diss Town	v	Barton Rovers	3–1 384
Lowestoft Town	v	Raunds Town	1–3 305
Metropolitan Police	v	Collier Row	2–1 70
Eynesbury Rovers	v	Halstead Town	2–3 279
Hinckley Athletic	v	Pelsall Villa	1–2 190
Boston Town	v	Arlesey Town	1–2 161
West Midlands Police	v	Northwood	3–2 47
Bournemouth	v	Croydon	1–2 130
Hailsham Town	v	Eastleigh	0–4 250
Taunton Town	v	Westbury United	4–2 334
Wick	v	Elmore	4–4 204
Elmore	*v*	*Wick*	*4–1*
Tiverton Town	v	Horsham	4–1 687
Banstead Athletic	v	Falmouth Town	3–5
Mangotsfield United	v	Whitehawk	4–0 183
Stamco	v	Shoreham	5–3 426
Oxford City	v	Peacehaven & Telscombe	1–0 143
Wimborne Town	v	Barnstaple Town	1–4 237
Tunbridge Wells	v	Liskeard Athletic	1–1 240
Liskeard Athletic	*v*	*Tunbridge Wells*	*2–0* *240*

Fourth round – 14 January 1995

Burscough	v	Brandon United	3–0 355
Stocksbridge Park Steels	v	Eastwood Hanley	1–1 239
Eastwood Hanley	*v*	*Stocksbridge Park Steels*	*3–1* *175*
Pelsall Villa	v	Cammell Laird	1–2 400
Halstead Town	v	Hadleigh United	5–5 521
Hadleigh United	*v*	*Halstead Town*	*3–2* *518*
West Midlands Police	v	Raunds Town	0–2 120
Ossett Albion	v	Diss Town	1–1 467
Diss Town	*v*	*Ossett Albion*	*1–1* *1197*
Ossett Albion	*v*	*Diss Town*	*0–3* *308*
St Andrews	v	Maine Road	2–1 205
Belper Town	v	South Shields	4–0
Liskeard Athletic	v	Falmouth Town	0–2 550
Stotfold	v	Basildon United	0–4 325
Mangotsfield United	v	Canvey Island	1–5 404
Barnstaple Town	v	Arlesey Town	0–2 333
Croydon	v	Oxford City	1–2 112
Taunton Town	v	Elmore	2–1 946
Eastleigh	v	Metropolitan Police	1–3 200
Stamco	v	Tiverton Town	4–3 1798

Fifth round – 4 February 1995

Raunds Town	v	St Andrews	3–0 435
Arlesey Town	v	Diss Town	1–0 909
Falmouth Town	v	Belper Town	1–5 906
Taunton Town	v	Oxford City	0–3 847
Canvey Island	v	Stamco	3–0 1211
Cammell Laird	v	Burscough	4–2 400
Metropolitan Police	v	Hadleigh United	4–1 245
Eastwood Hanley	v	Basildon United	2–3 265

Sixth round – 25 February 1995

			Results	Att
Arlesey Town	v	Cammell Laird	3–0	1180
Oxford City	v	Canvey Island	2–0	1444
Metropolitan Police	v	Belper Town	0–1	667
Basildon United	v	Raunds Town	0–2	699

Semi-finals

First Leg – 18 March 1995

			Results	Att
Raunds Town	v	Arlesey Town	3–0	1218
Belper Town	v	Oxford City	1–0	1953

Second Leg – 25 March 1995

			Results	Att
Arlesey Town	v	Raunds Town	5–0	830
(Arlesey Town won on aggregate 5–3)				
Oxford City	v	Belper Town	3–1	1760
(Oxford City won on aggregate 3–2)				

Arlesey Town – winners of the FA Carlsberg Vase.

32 ● FA VASE WINNERS 1975–1995

Year	Venue	Winners		Runners-up	Result
1975	Wembley	Hoddesdon Town	v	Epsom & Ewell	2–1
1976	Wembley	Billericay Town	v	Stamford	1–0*
1977	Wembley	Billericay Town	v	Sheffield	1–1*
	Nottingham	Billericay Town	v	Sheffield	2–1
1978	Wembley	Blue Star	v	Barton Rovers	2–1
1979	Wembley	Billericay Town	v	Almondsbury Greenway	4–1
1980	Wembley	Stamford	v	Guisborough Town	2–0
1981	Wembley	Whickham	v	Willenhall Town	3–2*
1982	Wembley	Forest Green Rovers	v	Rainworth Miners' Welfare	3–0
1983	Wembley	VS Rugby	v	Halesowen Town	1–0
1984	Wembley	Stansted	v	Stamford	3–2
1985	Wembley	Halesowen Town	v	Fleetwood Town	3–1
1986	Wembley	Halesowen Town	v	Southall	3–0
1987	Wembley	St Helens Town	v	Warrington Town	3–2
1988	Wembley	Colne Dynamoes	v	Emley	1–0*
1989	Wembley	Tamworth	v	Sudbury Town	1–1*
	Peterborough	Tamworth	v	Sudbury Town	3–0
1990	Wembley	Yeading	v	Bridlington Town	0–0*
	Leeds	Yeading	v	Bridlington Town	1–0
1991	Wembley	Guiseley	v	Gresley Rovers	4–4*
	Sheffield	Guiseley	v	Gresley Rovers	3–1
1992	Wembley	Wimborne Town	v	Guiseley	5–3
1993	Wembley	Bridlington Town	v	Tiverton Town	1–0
1994	Wembley	Diss Town	v	Taunton Town	2–1*
1995	Wembley	Arlesey Town	v	Oxford City	2–1

* *After extra time*

33 ● FA CARLSBERG VASE 1995–96 EXEMPTIONS

32 Clubs to the Second Round Proper

Arlesey Town
Armitage
Belper Town
Billingham Synthonia
Burnham
Cammell Laird
Canvey Island
Chester le Street Town
Consett
Diss Town
Dorking
Dunston FB
Durham City
Goole Town
Guisborough Town
Hebburn

Metropolitan Police
Mossley
Murton
Newbury Town
Northallerton
Peterlee Newtown
Prudhoe Town
Raunds Town
RTM Newcastle
Seaham Red Star
Shildon
Taunton Town
Tow Law Town
West Auckland Town
Whitby Town
Wivenhoe Town

32 Clubs to the First Round Proper

Banstead Athletic
Barnstaple Town
Basildon United
Boston Town
Brandon United
Burscough
Collier Row
Croydon
Dunkirk
Eastleigh
Eastwood Hanley
Elmore
Falmouth Town
Glossop North End
Hadleigh United
Halstead Town

Hinckley Athletic
Mangotsfield United
Oadby Town
Pelsall Villa
Peacehaven & Telscombe
Paulton Rovers
South Shields
St Andrews
Stamco
Stocksbridge Park Steels
Thackley
Tiverton Town
Tunbridge Wells
Whitehawk
Wimborne Town
Wisbech Town

34 ● FA YOUTH CUP WINNERS 1953–1995

The FA Youth Cup Final is played on a two-leg basis but the 1978 final between Crystal Palace and Aston Villa was a single match. The only final which needed a replay was the 1983 contest between Norwich and Everton.

Year	Winners		Runners-up	Result
1953	Manchester United	v	Wolverhampton Wanderers	9–3
1954	Manchester United	v	Wolverhampton Wanderers	5–4
1955	Manchester United	v	West Bromwich Albion	7–1
1956	Manchester United	v	Chesterfield	4–3
1957	Manchester United	v	West Ham United	8–2
1958	Wolverhampton Wanderers	v	Chelsea	7–6
1959	Blackburn Rovers	v	West Ham United	2–1
1960	Chelsea	v	Preston North End	5–2
1961	Chelsea	v	Everton	5–3
1962	Newcastle United	v	Wolverhampton Wanderers	2–1
1963	West Ham United	v	Liverpool	6–5
1964	Manchester United	v	Swindon Town	5–2
1965	Everton	v	Arsenal	3–2
1966	Arsenal	v	Sunderland	5–3
1967	Sunderland	v	Birmingham City	2–0
1968	Burnley	v	Coventry City	3–2
1969	Sunderland	v	West Bromwich Albion	6–3
1970	Tottenham Hotspur	v	Coventry City	4–3
1971	Arsenal	v	Cardiff City	2–0
1972	Aston Villa	v	Liverpool	5–2
1973	Ipswich Town	v	Bristol City	4–1
1974	Tottenham Hotspur	v	Huddersfield Town	2–1
1975	Ipswich Town	v	West Ham United	5–1
1976	West Bromwich Albion	v	Wolverhampton Wanderers	5–0
1977	Crystal Palace	v	Everton	1–0
1978	Crystal Palace	v	Aston Villa	1–0
1979	Millwall	v	Manchester City	2–0
1980	Aston Villa	v	Manchester City	3–2
1981	West Ham United	v	Tottenham Hotspur	2–1
1982	Watford	v	Manchester United	7–6
1983	Norwich City	v	Everton	6–5*
1984	Everton	v	Stoke City	4–2
1985	Newcastle United	v	Watford	4–1
1986	Manchester City	v	Manchester United	3–1
1987	Coventry City	v	Charlton Athletic	2–1
1988	Arsenal	v	Doncaster Rovers	6–1
1989	Watford	v	Manchester City	2–1
1990	Tottenham Hotspur	v	Middlesbrough	3–2
1991	Millwall	v	Sheffield Wednesday	3–0
1992	Manchester United	v	Crystal Palace	6–3
1993	Leeds United	v	Manchester United	4–1
1994	Arsenal	v	Millwall	5–3
1995	Manchester United	v	Tottenham Hotspur	2–2†

* aggregate score after replay
† won on penalty-kicks

35 ● FA COUNTY YOUTH CUP WINNERS 1953–1995

From 1945 to 1969 the FA County Youth Cup final was played over two legs. Since 1970 it has been a one-match final and only twice (in 1988 and 1990) has a reply been required.

Year	Winners		Runners-up	Result
1945	Staffordshire	v	Wiltshire	3 – 2
1946	Berks & Bucks	v	Durham	4 – 3
1947	Durham	v	Essex	4 – 2
1948	Essex	v	Liverpool	5 – 3
1949	Liverpool	v	Middlesex	4 – 3
1950	Essex	v	Middlesex	4 – 3
1951	Middlesex	v	Leicestershire & Rutland	3 – 1
1952	Sussex	v	Liverpool	3 – 1
1953	Sheffield & Hallam	v	Hampshire	5 – 3
1954	Liverpool	v	Gloucestershire	4 – 1
1955	Bedfordshire	v	Sheffield & Hallam	2 – 0
1956	Middlesex	v	Staffordshire	3 – 2
1957	Hampshire	v	Cheshire	4 – 3
1958	Staffordshire	v	London	8 – 0
1959	Birmingham	v	London	7 – 5
1960	London	v	Birmingham	6 – 4
1961	Lancashire	v	Nottinghamshire	6 – 3
1962	Middlesex	v	Nottinghamshire	3 – 2
1963	Durham	v	Essex	3 – 2
1964	Sheffield & Hallam	v	Birmingham	1 – 0
1965	Northumberland	v	Middlesex	7 – 4
1966	Leics & Rutland	v	London	6 – 5
1967	Northamptonshire	v	Hertfordshire	5 – 4
1968	North Riding	v	Devon	7 – 4
1969	Northumberland	v	Sussex	1 – 0
1970	Hertfordshire	v	Cheshire	2 – 1
1971	Lancashire	v	Gloucestershire	2 – 0
1972	Middlesex	v	Liverpool	2 – 0
1973	Hertfordshire	v	Northumberland	3 – 0
1974	Nottinghamshire	v	London	2 – 0
1975	Durham	v	Bedfordshire	2 – 1
1976	Northamptonshire	v	Surrey	7 – 1
1977	Liverpool	v	Surrey	3 – 0
1978	Liverpool	v	Kent	3 – 1
1979	Hertfordshire	v	Liverpool	4 – 1
1980	Liverpool	v	Lancashire	2 – 0
1981	Lancashire	v	East Riding	3 – 1
1982	Devon	v	Kent	3 – 2*
1983	London	v	Gloucestershire	3 – 0
1984	Cheshire	v	Manchester	2 – 1
1985	East Riding	v	Middlesex	2 – 1
1986	Hertfordshire	v	Manchester	4 – 0
1987	North Riding	v	Gloucestershire	3 – 1
1988	East Riding	v	Middlesex	1 – 1
	East Riding	*v*	*Middlesex*	*5 – 3*
1989	Liverpool	v	Hertfordshire	2 – 1

Year	Winners		Runners-up	Result
1990	Staffordshire	v	Hampshire	1–1
	Staffordshire	*v*	*Hampshire*	*2–1*
1991	Lancashire	v	Surrey	6–0
1992	Nottinghamshire	v	Surrey	1–0
1993	Durham	v	Liverpool	4–0
1994	West Riding	v	Sussex	3–1
1995	Liverpool	v	Essex	3–2

* after extra time

36 ● FA YOUTH CUP 1994–1995

Extra Preliminary round

Atherton LR	v	Warrington Town		
(walkover for Warrington Town – Atherton LR withdrawn)				
Mansfield Town	v	Wrexham	1–4	114
Worksop Town	v	Redditch United	1–2	
Bedworth United	v	Stourport Swifts	3–1	55
Corby Town	v	Wednesfield	2–1	20
Barkingside	v	Stevenage Borough	0–4	54
Eton Manor	v	Hemel Hempstead	1–2	40
(at Hemel Hempstead FC)				
Ruislip Manor	v	Wingate & Finchley	2–4	44
Bromley	v	Sittingbourne	1–2	74
Bracknell Town	v	Kingstonian	0–2	17
Farnborough Town	v	Windsor & Eton	3–2	
Newhaven	v	Basingstoke Town		
(walkover for Basingstoke Town – Newhaven withdrawn)				

Preliminary round

Harrogate Town	v	Darlington	4–2	91
Hartlepool United	v	Lancaster City	1–0	47
Chorley	v	Carlisle United	0–7	47
Morecambe	v	Guisborough Town	2–0	126
Chadderton	v	Bolton Wanderers	1–1	103
Bolton Wanderers	*v*	*Chadderton*	*4–2*	*199*
Chesterfield	v	Huddersfield Town	0–2	85
Lincoln City	v	Warrington Town	7–5	95
Wigan Athletic	v	Bury	0–1	82
Port Vale	v	Marine	3–1	58
Rochdale	v	Southport	2–1	88
Stalybridge Celtic	v	Wrexham	1–10	128
Stockport County	v	Oldham Town	3–1	206
Hinckley Athletic	v	Burton Albion	1–2	40
Hinckley Town	v	Lutterworth Town	2–1	33
Hednesford Town	v	Redditch United	2–0	63
Pelsall Villa	v	Birstall United	2–3	34
Bridgnorth Town	v	Bilston Town	1–4	65
Brierley Hill Town	v	Chasetown	0–1	39
Nuneaton Borough	v	Bedworth United	1–1	75
Bedworth United	*v*	*Nuneaton Borough*	*0–1*	*134*
Oldbury United	v	Boldmere St Michaels	2–4	48
Lye Town	v	Daventry Town	2–2	24
Daventry Town	*v*	*Lye Town*	*0–4*	*22*
Northampton Spencer	v	Rushden & Diamonds	0–6	49
Stratford Town	v	Corby Town	1–0	49
VS Rugby	v	Kettering Town	3–3	74
Kettering Town	*v*	*VS Rugby*	*7–1*	*105*
Halstead Town	v	Braintree Town	1–5	105
March Town United	v	Saffron Walden Town	1–2	30
Wivenhoe Town	v	Bishop's Stortford	0–0	65
Bishop's Stortford	*v*	*Wivenhoe Town*	*2–0*	*42*

(Replays in italics)   *Results*   *Att*

Concord Rangers	v	Chatteris Town	4 – 4	25
Chatteris Town	*v*	*Concord Rangers*	*2 – 5*	*35*
Enfield	v	Baldock Town	6 – 1	65
Barnet	v	Royston Town	12 – 1	79
St Albans City	v	Canvey Island	0 – 1	
Letchworth GC	v	East Thurrock United	1 – 8	40
Edgware Town	v	Brook House	4 – 4	52
Brook House	*v*	*Edgware Town*	*6 – 1*	*37*
Hillingdon Borough	v	Kempston Rovers	4 – 0	27
Kingsbury Town	v	Stevenage Borough	3 – 3	49
Stevenage Borough	*v*	*Kingsbury Town*	*5 – 2*	*89*
Leighton Town	v	Clapton	1 – 0	40
Hampton	v	Feltham & Hounslow Borough	1 – 4	54
Hanwell Town	v	Harefield United		

(walkover for Harefield United, Hanwell Town withdrawn)

Harlow Town	v	Hemel Hempstead	2 – 6	46
Hayes	v	Flackwell Heath	1 – 1	50
Flackwell Heath	*v*	*Hayes*	*1 – 2*	*36*
Viking Sports	v	Staines Town		

(walkover for Staines Town – Viking Sports not entered)

Waltham Abbey	v	Welwyn Garden City	1 – 3	45
Wembley	v	Wingate & Finchley	1 – 2	90
Bedfont	v	Uxbridge	1 – 0	37
Corinthian	v	Ashford Town	4 – 1	11

(after abandoned match 50 mins due to floodlight failure, 0 – 2)

Dover Athletic	v	Gillingham	0 – 3	53
Herne Bay	v	Sittingbourne	0 – 4	31
Dartford	v	Chatham Town	6 – 1	78
Crawley Town	v	Chertsey Town	4 – 2	73
Marlow	v	Croydon Athletic	1 – 2	40
Dorking	v	Kingstonian	1 – 3	100
Egham Town	v	Chipstead		

(walkover for Chipstead – Egham Town withdrawn)

Thamesmead Town	v	Welling United	1 – 1	78
Welling United	*v*	*Thamesmead Town*	*3 – 1*	*86*
Tonbridge	v	Malden Vale	0 – 1	40
Redhill	v	Farnborough Town	0 – 3	68
Whyteleafe	v	Whitstable Town	3 – 6	62
Three Bridges	v	Ringmer	6 – 1	43
Whitehawk	v	Woking	2 – 2	64
Woking	*v*	*Whitehawk*	*3 – 1*	*78*
Aldershot Town	v	Basingstoke Town	3 – 0	117
Fleet Town	v	Southwick	4 – 0	62
Wokingham Town	v	Newbury Town	1 – 1	48
Newbury Town	*v*	*Wokingham Town*	*2 – 0*	*42*

(at Wokingham Town FC)

Oxford City	v	Maidenhead United	4 – 4	40
Maidenhead United	*v*	*Oxford City*	*0 – 6*	*24*
Thatcham Town	v	Banbury United	1 – 2	15
Chippenham Town	v	Abingdon Town	1 – 4	38
Dorchester Town	v	Bashley	2 – 2	37
Bashley	*v*	*Dorchester Town*	*1 – 0*	*52*
Weymouth	v	Weston-Super-Mare	1 – 2	37
Yeovil Town	v	Romsey Town	7 – 0	202
Clevedon Town	v	Eastleigh		

(walkover for Eastleigh – Clevedon Town withdrawn)

Cheltenham Town	v	Yate Town	4 – 0	40
Forest Green Rovers	v	Gloucester City	3 – 3	82

Gloucester City	*v*	*Forest Green Rovers*	5–4	*80*
Hereford United	v	Worcester City	6–0	90
Mangotsfield United	v	Bristol Rovers	0–3	68

First round qualifying

Morecambe	v	Harrogate Town	6–0	101
Carlisle United	v	Hartlepool United	7–2	51
Bury	v	Bolton Wanderers	4–0	299
Lincoln City	v	Huddersfield Town	1–10	73
Stockport County	v	Port Vale	0–1	235
Wrexham	v	Rochdale	2–1	68
Birstall United	v	Burton Albion	2–2	50
Burton Albion	*v*	*Birstall United*	*1–0*	*53*
Hednesford Town	v	Hinckley Town	0–4	47
Boldmere St Michaels	v	Bilston Town	3–0	29
Nuneaton Borough	v	Chasetown	3–1	60
Kettering Town	v	Lye Town	1–1	70
Lye Town	*v*	*Kettering Town*	*1–1*	*93*
(Kettering Town won on kicks from the penalty mark, 5–4)				
Stratford Town	v	Rushden & Diamonds	1–1	81
Rushden & Diamonds	*v*	*Stratford Town*	*3–2*	*42*
Concord Rangers	v	Braintree Town	0–7	30
Bishop's Stortford	v	Saffron Walden Town	3–2	49
East Thurrock United	v	Enfield	2–2	63
Enfield	*v*	*East Thurrock United*	*1–0*	*46*
Canvey Island	v	Barnet	0–3	90
Leighton Town	v	Brook House	8–0	60
Stevenage Borough	v	Hillingdon Borough	2–3	89
Hayes	v	Feltham & Hounslow Borough	1–5	
Hemel Hempstead	v	Harefield United	1–2	20
Bedfont	v	Staines Town	3–4	85
Wingate & Finchley	v	Welwyn Garden City	2–4	70
Dartford	v	Corinthian	3–1	100
Sittingbourne	v	Gillingham	2–2	126
Gillingham	*v*	*Sittingbourne*	*2–1*	*190*
Chipstead	v	Crawley Town	1–3	42
Kingstonian	v	Croydon Athletic	0–0	82
Croydon Athletic	*v*	*Kingstonian*	*4–1*	*37*
Whitstable Town	v	Welling United	1–3	76
Farnborough Town	v	Malden Vale	2–0	46
Fleet Town	v	Three Bridges	1–2	24
Aldershot Town	v	Woking	2–3	150
Abingdon Town	v	Newbury Town	2–5	62
Banbury United	v	Oxford City	2–3	53
Eastleigh	v	Bashley	0–1	63
Yeovil Town	v	Weston-Super-Mare	8–2	197
Bristol Rovers	v	Cheltenham Town	3–0	56
Hereford United	v	Gloucester City	2–0	45

Second round qualifying

Morecambe	v	Carlisle United	1–8	166
Bury	v	Huddersfield Town	2–0	265
Port Vale	v	Wrexham	0–5	81
Burton Albion	v	Hinckley Town	1–0	48

(Replays in italics)			Results	Att
Boldmere St Michaels	v	Nuneaton Borough	2–1	41
Kettering Town	v	Rushden & Diamonds	3–4	202
Braintree Town	v	Bishop's Stortford	2–4	69
Enfield	v	Barnet	0–3	98
(tie awarded to Enfield – Barnet played an ineligible player)				
Leighton Town	v	Hillingdon Borough	1–0	102
Feltham & Hounslow Boro	v	Harefield United	4–1	37
Staines Town	v	Welwyn Garden City	2–1	45
Dartford	v	Gillingham	0–3	149
Crawley Town	v	Croydon Athletic	2–2	117
Croydon Athletic	v	Crawley Town	2–2	56
(Croydon Athletic won on kicks from the penalty mark, 4–3)				
Welling United	v	Farnborough Town	3–0	81
Three Bridges	v	Woking	1–2	91
Newbury Town	v	Oxford City	1–2	38
(at Oxford City FC)				
Bashley	v	Yeovil Town	2–3	71
Bristol Rovers	v	Hereford United	2–2	50
Hereford United	v	Bristol Rovers	1–3	40

First round proper

Doncaster Rovers	v	Scunthorpe United	2–0	261
Hull City	v	Blackburn Rovers	0–3	120
Carlisle United	v	Sunderland	0–2	247
Preston North End	v	Rotherham United	4–1	258
Newcastle United	v	Everton	0–2	261
Oldham Athletic	v	Bury	3–0	264
Grimsby Town	v	Sheffield Wednesday	1–3	102
Tranmere Rovers	v	Burnley	5–0	401
Barnsley	v	Blackpool	1–3	121
Leicester City	v	Kidderminster Harriers	4–1	162
Northampton Town	v	Walsall	1–2	180
(at Walsall FC)				
Peterborough United	v	Rushden & Diamonds	7–1	126
Shrewsbury Town	v	Birmingham City	1–2	148
Aston Villa	v	Derby County	1–1	116
Derby County	v	Aston Villa	0–3	236
Boldmere St Michaels	v	Cambridge City	2–1	54
Wrexham	v	Burton Albion	8–0	161
Wolverhampton Wanderers	v	Cambridge United	1–1	204
Cambridge United	v	Wolverhampton Wanderers	2–6	148
Woking	v	Charlton Athletic	0–8	214
Bishop's Stortford	v	Ipswich Town	0–2	125
Wycombe Wanderers	v	Gillingham	2–1	133
Luton Town	v	Staines Town	5–0	129
Lewes	v	Croydon Athletic	0–2	33
Enfield	v	Fulham	1–2	52
Leighton Town	v	Sutton United	4–2	120
Watford	v	Welling United	0–0	177
Welling United	v	Watford	2–1	262
Witney Town	v	Boreham Wood	1–3	60
Dulwich Hamlet	v	Feltham & Hounslow Boro	4–1	50
Cardiff City	v	Torquay United	3–1	61
Exeter City	v	Plymouth Argyle	0–2	175
Bournemouth AFC	v	Swansea City	5–0	120
Bristol Rovers	v	Oxford United	0–2	58

Oxford City	v	Yeovil Town	0–2	88
Southampton	v	Reading	1–0	225
bye: Colchester United				

Second round proper

Peterborough United	v	Everton	0–1	818
Liverpool	v	Tranmere Rovers	1–2	679
Stoke City	v	Notts County	1–0	231
Crewe Alexandra	v	Blackburn Rovers	3–0	1050
Nottingham Forest	v	Leicester City	2–1	102
Aston Villa	v	Leeds United	1–0	161
Manchester United	v	Wrexham	4–1	1240
Sunderland	v	Sheffield Wednesday	1–1	284
Sheffield Wednesday	*v*	*Sunderland*	*0–1*	*164*
York City	v	Birmingham City	0–0	128
Birmingham City	*v*	*York City*	*0–2*	*205*
Middlesbrough	v	Oldham Athletic	4–3	147
Manchester City	v	Walsall	1–1	317
Walsall	*v*	*Manchester City*	*1–1*	*266*
(*Manchester City won on kicks from the penalty mark, 4–1*)				
West Bromwich Albion	v	Doncaster Rovers	0–1	233
Preston North End	v	Blackpool	1–2	307
Bradford City	v	Sheffield United	1–1	230
Sheffield United	*v*	*Bradford City*	*3–0*	*168*
Arsenal	v	Brighton & Hove Albion	5–0	175
West Ham United	v	Wimbledon	2–2	538
Wimbledon	*v*	*West Ham United*	*4–2*	*252*
Wycombe Wanderers	v	Luton Town	1–0	140
Leyton Orient	v	Chelsea	0–0	168
Chelsea	*v*	*Leyton Orient*	*0–2*	*109*
Tottenham Hotspur	v	Boldmere St Michaels	10–0	253
Norwich City	v	Millwall	2–1	237
Ipswich Town	v	Croydon Athletic	3–0	140
Wolverhampton Wanderers	v	Brentford	2–0	296
Bournemouth AFC	v	Bristol City	0–0	66
Bristol City	*v*	*Bournemouth AFC*	*3–1*	*189*
Colchester United	v	Yeovil Town	3–0	170
Dulwich Hamlet	v	Welling United	1–1	120
Welling United	*v*	*Dulwich Hamlet*	*1–3*	*201*
Oxford United	v	Leighton Town	6–0	169
Fulham	v	Boreham Wood	5–0	254
Portsmouth	v	Swindon Town	0–0	129
Swindon Town	*v*	*Portsmouth*	*1–1*	*181*
(*Portsmouth won on kicks from the penalty mark, 11–10*)				
Charlton Athletic	v	Cardiff City	2–1	488
Southend United	v	Crystal Palace	2–1	103
Queens Park Rangers	v	Plymouth Argyle	3–1	
Southampton	v	Coventry City	0–5	251

Third round proper

Bristol City	v	Nottingham Forest	0–0	301
Nottingham Forest	*v*	*Bristol City*	*0–1*	*155*
Crewe Alexandra	v	Oxford United	1–0	933
Sheffield United	v	York City	1–0	153

● **131**

			Results	Att
Wycombe Wanderers	v	Colchester United	0–5	127
Sunderland	v	Doncaster Rovers	0–0	350
Doncaster Rovers	*v*	*Sunderland*	*0–2*	*114*
Stoke City	v	Norwich City	0–0	266
Norwich City	*v*	*Stoke City*	*0–1*	*248*
Dulwich Hamlet	v	Fulham	0–2	160

(tie awarded to Dulwich Hamlet – Fulham played an inelgible player)

Manchester City	v	Portsmouth	2–2	559
Portsmouth	*v*	*Manchester City*	*0–1*	*281*
Aston Villa	v	Leyton Orient	1–0	595
Tottenham Hotspur	v	Wolverhampton Wanderers	4–2	78
Southend United	v	Tranmere Rovers	4–3	149
Queens Park Rangers	v	Arsenal	0–2	365
Wimbledon	v	Ipswich Town	4–0	204
Everton	v	Blackpool	6–5	728
Manchester United	v	Charlton Athletic	1–1	1430
Charlton Athletic	*v*	*Manchester United*	*2–5*	*3515*
Coventry City	v	Middlesbrough	2–2	389
Middlesbrough	*v*	*Coventry City*	*2–6*	*314*

Fourth round proper

Aston Villa	v	Colchester United	4–0	446
Tottenham Hotspur	v	Southend United	1–1	349
Southend United	*v*	*Tottenham Hotspur*	*1–2*	
Dulwich Hamlet	v	Bristol City	2–3	
Manchester United	v	Arsenal	2–1	2701
Sunderland	v	Crewe Alexandra	3–1	
Everton	v	Sheffield United	1–3	
Coventry City	v	Manchester City	2–3	
Stoke City	v	Wimbledon	1–2	545

Fifth round proper

Sunderland	v	Manchester City	2–2	
Manchester City	*v*	*Sunderland*	*3–1*	*633*
Bristol City	v	Tottenham Hotspur	1–2	
Aston Villa	v	Manchester United	2–3	4377
Wimbledon	v	Sheffield United	3–3	207
Sheffield United	*v*	*Wimbledon*	*2–3*	*1245*

Semi-finals

1st Leg

Manchester City	v	Tottenham Hotspur	0–5	2587
Manchester United	v	Wimbledon	2–1	6167

2nd Leg

Tottenham Hotspur	v	Manchester City	2–1	648

(Tottenham Hotspur won 7–1 on aggregate)

Wimbledon	v	Manchester United	0–3	4441

(Manchester United won 5–1 on aggregate)

Final

1st Leg
Tottenham Hotspur   v   Manchester United   2 – 1   3503

2nd Leg
Manchester United   v   Tottenham Hotspur   1 – 0   20190

(Manchester United won on kicks from the penalty mark, 4 – 3)

37 ● FA COUNTY YOUTH CUP 1994–1995

First round

(*Replays in italics*)

Results

Lancashire	v	East Riding	0–3
Westmorland	v	Sheffield & Hallamshire	1–2
Liverpool	v	Nottinghamshire	3–2
North Riding	v	Lincolnshire	0–3
Herefordshire	v	Northamptonshire	0–2
Leicestershire & Rutland	v	Worcestershire	3–3
Worcestershire	*v*	*Leicestershire & Rutland*	*1–3*
Hertfordshire	v	Cambridgeshire	4–1
Bedfordshire	v	London	2–1
Berks & Bucks	v	Surrey	0–1
Dorset	v	Devon	2–3
Wiltshire	v	Somerset & Avon	3–3
Somerset & Avon	*v*	*Wiltshire*	*3–1*
Hampshire	v	Army	3–1

Counties receiving byes to the Second Round

Birmingham	Derbyshire	Huntingdonshire	Norfolk	Shropshire
Cheshire	Durham	Kent	Northumberland	Suffolk
Cornwall	Essex	Manchester	Oxfordshire	Sussex
Cumberland	Gloucestershire	Middlesex	Staffordshire	West Riding

Second round

Shropshire	v	West Riding	1–3
Cumberland	v	East Riding	1–1
East Riding	*v*	*Cumberland*	*0–1*
Northumberland	v	Sheffield & Hallamshire	3–1
Durham	v	Liverpool	0–1
Manchester	v	Lincolnshire	4–1
Derbyshire	v	Northamptonshire	6–0
Cheshire	v	Leicestershire & Rutland	2–1
Birmingham	v	Hertfordshire	1–4
Huntingdonshire	v	Staffordshire	3–2
Norfolk	v	Bedfordshire	3–2
Suffolk	v	Surrey	1–2
Gloucestershire	v	Sussex	3–1
Kent	v	Essex	3–4
Oxfordshire	v	Devon	4–2
Middlesex	v	Somerset & Avon (South)	1–3
Cornwall	v	Hampshire	5–0

Third round

Derbyshire	v	Liverpool	2–4
West Riding	v	Cheshire	4–2
Hertfordshire	v	Northumberland	1–1

Northumberland	*v*	*Hertfordshire*	*2–1*
Manchester	v	Cumberland	2–1
Oxfordshire	v	Essex	1–2
Huntingdonshire	v	Somerset & Avon (South)	2–4
Cornwall	v	Surrey	3–2
Gloucestershire	v	Norfolk	2–3

Fourth Round

Liverpool	v	Norfolk	2–2
Norfolk	*v*	*Liverpool*	*0–1*
Somerset & Avon (South)	v	Essex	1–3
Manchester	v	Northumberland	0–1
West Riding	v	Cornwall	1–2

Semi-finals

Liverpool	v	Cornwall	2–2
Cornwall	*v*	*Liverpool*	*0–3*
Northumberland	v	Essex	0–2

Final – 29 April 1995

Liverpool	v	Essex	3–2

38 ● YOUTH INTERNATIONAL MATCHES 1994–1995

Date	Venue				Result	

Under-18

Date	Venue				Result	
24.7.94	Larvik	Norway	v	England	3–3	*
26.7.94	Vikersund	Norway	v	England	2–3	
6.9.94	Reading	England	v	France	2–3	
13.11.94	High Wycombe	England	v	Slovenia	3–0	*
17.11.94	Reading	England	v	Latvia	0–0	*
22.2.95	Walsall	England	v	Denmark	5–6	
29.3.95	Budapest	Hungary	v	England	0–1	*
25.4.95	Walsall	England	v	Hungary	0–2	*

* UEFA Championship – Qualifying Competition

Under-16

Date	Venue				Result	
3.8.94	Vejle	Denmark	v	England	0–1	
4.8.94	Vildbjerg	Iceland	v	England	4–3	
6.8.94	Aby	Norway	v	England	0–3	
7.8.94	Vejle	Austria	v	England	0–3	
17.9.94	Rotterdam	Holland	v	England	1–1	
16.11.94	Sakarya	Turkey	v	England	3–2	
21.1.95	Lisbon	Portugal	v	England	0–0	
24.2.95	Athens	Greece	v	England	0–4	*
26.2.95	Athens	Romania	v	England	2–3	*
24.4.95	Eupen	Scotland	v	England	1–1	†
26.4.95	Verviers	Slovakia	v	England	1–2	†
28.4.95	Waremmien	Portugal	v	England	1–3	†
1.5.95	Eupen	France	v	England	1–0	†

* UEFA Championship – Qualifying Competition
† UEFA Championship – Finals

England Under-18 Caps

	Norway	Norway	France	Slovenia	Latvia	Denmark	Hungary	Hungary
N. Cutler (West Bromwich Albion)	1		1	1	1	1		
P. Neville (Manchester United)	2	2	2				2	2
G. Power (Queens Park Rangers)	3	3	3*					
J. Howell (Arsenal)	4	7*						
J. O'Connor (Everton)	5	5	6*	6	6	6	4	4
D. Mills (Norwich City)	6	3*				5		
L. Bowyer (Charlton Athletic)	7	4	7	8	8	8		
D. Beresford (Oldham Athletic)	8		4*	7		10*	6	7
K. Davies (Chesterfield)	9	9	10	9	9	10	10	
S. Hughes (Arsenal)	10	10	8		11*			
T. Cooke (Manchester United)	11	9*	11	11	7	9	9	11
D. Murphy (Crewe Alexandra)	4*	7	9	10	10		7	10
S. Spencer (Tottenham Hotspur)	8*	8						
M. Tyler (Peterborough United)		1						
G. Allen (Everton)		6	6	2*	2	2		
M. Walley (Nottingham Forest)		11						
R. Taylor (Arsenal)			3	3	3			
D. Thompson (Liverpool)			4	4	4	7		
C. Plummer (Queens Park Rangers)			5					
A. Furnell (Peterborough United)			10*					
P. Murray (Carlisle United)				2				
D. Hodges (Wimbledon)				5	5			
L. Hendrie (Aston Villa)				8*	11	4*		
J. Woodsford (Luton Town)					9*			
H. Aljofrey (Bolton Wanderers)						3		
I. Ashbee (Derby County)						4		
I. Moore (Tranmere Rovers)						11	11	9
M. Millett (Wigan Athletic)						3*		
K. Davis (Luton Town)							1	1
J. Stuart (Charlton Athletic)							3	5
A. Westwood (Manchester United)							5	3
S. Clemence (Tottenham Hotspur)							8	8
A. Ducros (Coventry City)							6*	7*
L. Piper (Wimbledon)								6
M. Broomes (Blackburn Rovers)								6*

* *substitute*

England Under-16 Caps

	Holland	Turkey	Portugal	Greece	Romania	Scotland	Slovakia	Portugal	France
L. Weaver (Leyton Orient)	1	1*							
E. Dickman (Manchester United)	2	2	2	2	2	2	2	2	2
N. Clement (Chelsea)	3	3			11*	3*	5*	5	5
J. Curtis (Manchester United)	4	4	4	4	4	4	4	4	4
M. Perry (Queens Park Rangers)	5	5							
J. Morris (Chelsea)	6	8	8	10	10	6	6	6	6
S. Brightwell (Manchester Utd.)	7	7	7*	7*	7	7			7*
M. Gower (Tottenham Hotspur)	8	6	6	6	6	8		8	8
J. Bunn (Tottenham Hotspur)	9						8	11	11*
M. Wilson (Manchester United)	10	10*							
M. Platts (Sheffield Wednesday)	11	10	11*						
P. Heritage (Sheffield United)	1*	1	1	1	1	1			1
M. Wicks (Arsenal and Manchester United)	4*	3*	5	5	5	5	5		
P. Smith (Crewe Alexandra)	9*	11*						11*	
A. Ormerod (Middlesbrough)	10*	7*	10*	8*		8*	7	7	7
A. Wright (Leeds United)	11*	11	11	11	11	11	11	7*	11
M. Branch (Everton)		9	9	9	9	9	9	9	9
J. Crowe (Arsenal)			3	3	3	3	3	3	3
R. O'Connor (Wimbledon)			7	7	7*				
L. Staton (Blackburn Rovers)			10	8	8	10	10	10	10
R. Burgess (Aston Villa)			9*						
J. O'Toole (Everton)							1	1	

substitute

Squad for Nordic Championship – August 1994

M. Branch (Everton), S. Brightwell (Manchester United), N. Clement (Chelsea), T. Culshaw (Liverpool), J. Curtis (Manchester United), E. Dickman (Manchester United), M. Gower (Tottenham Hotspur), P. Heritage (Sheffield United), J. Morris (Chelsea), J. O'Toole (Everton), M. Perry (Queens Park Rangers), P. Smith (Crewe Alexandra), L. Staton (Blackburn Rovers), M. Wicks (Arsenal), M. Wilson (Manchester United), A. Wright (Leeds United).

40 ● EUROPEAN UNDER-16 CHAMPIONSHIP FINALS

BELGIUM – 24th April to 6th May 1995

First Stage

Date	Venue					Result

Group A

24.4.95	Meulebeke	Poland	v	Czech Republic	1 – 2
24.4.95	Meulebeke	Sweden	v	Italy	0 – 0
26.4.95	Handzame	Poland	v	Sweden	0 – 1
26.4.95	Handzame	Czech Republic	v	Italy	1 – 0
28.4.95	Eernegem	Italy	v	Poland	0 – 0
28.4.95	Maldegem	Czech Republic	v	Sweden	4 – 1

Czech Republic and Sweden qualified for quarter-finals

Group B

24.4.95	Elsden	Belgium	v	France	4 – 1
24.4.95	Elsden	Norway	v	Austraia	0 – 1
26.4.95	Hasselt	Belgium	v	Norway	3 – 0
26.4.95	Hasselt	France	v	Austria	1 – 0
28.4.95	Tongeren	Austria	v	Belgium	0 – 0
28.4.95	Waremmien	France	v	Norway	4 – 0

Belgium and France qualified for quarter-finals

Group C

24.4.95	Aalter	Slovenia	v	Turkey	0 – 2
24.4.95	Aalter	Germany	v	Spain	0 – 3
26.4.95	Deinze	Slovenia	v	Germany	0 – 3
26.4.95	Deinze	Turkey	v	Spain	0 – 2
28.4.95	Eernegem	Spain	v	Slovenia	3 – 1
28.4.95	Maldegem	Turkey	v	Germany	1 – 4

Spain and Germany qualified for quarter-finals

Group D

24.4.95	Eupen	Scotland	v	England	1 – 1
24.4.95	Eupen	Portugal	v	Slovakia	4 – 0
26.4.95	Verviers	Scotland	v	Portugal	1 – 3
26.4.95	Verviers	England	v	Slovakia	2 – 1
28.4.95	Tongeren	Slovakia	v	Scotland	2 – 1
28.4.95	Waremmien	England	v	Portugal	3 – 1

England and Portugal qualified for quarter-finals

Quarter-Finals

1.5.95	Roeselare	Czech Republic	v	Germany	0 – 2
1.5.95	Roeselare	Spain	v	Sweden	1 – 0
1.5.95	Eupen	Belgium	v	Portugal	0 – 1
1.5.95	Eupen	England	v	France	0 – 1

Semi-Finals

3.5.95	Geel	Germany	v	Portugal	1 – 3
3.5.95	Sereslen	Spain	v	France	2 – 0

Third/Fourth Place

6.5.95	Anderlecht	Germany	v	France	2 – 1

Final

6.5.95	Anderlecht	Portugal	v	Spain	2 – 0

The England Under-16 squad.

41 ● YOUTH INTERNATIONAL MATCHES 1947–1995

WYC = World Youth Championship
IYT = International Youth Tournament
* Qualifying Competition
† Professionals
§ Abandoned

v Algeria

†1984	22/4	Cannes	W	3–0	

v Argentina

†1981	5/10	Sydney	D	1–1	WYC

v Australia

†1981	8/10	Sydney	D	1–1	WYC
†1993	20/3	Sydney	W	2–1	WYC

v Austria

1949	19/4	Zeist	W	4–2	IYT
1952	17/4	Barcelona	D	5–5	IYT
1957	16/4	Barcelona	L	0–3	IYT
1958	4/3	Highbury	W	3–2	
1958	1/6	Graz	W	4–3	
1960	20/4	Vienna	L	0–1	IYT
†1964	1/4	Rotterdam	W	2–1	IYT
†1980	6/9	Pazin	L	0–1	
†1981	29/5	Bonn	W	7–0	IYT
†1981	3/9	Umag	W	3–0	
†1984	6/9	Izola	D	2–2	

v Belgium

1948	16/4	West Ham	W	3–1	IYT
1951	22/3	Cannes	D	1–1	IYT
1953	31/3	Brussels	W	2–0	IYT
§1956	7/11	Brussels	W	3–2	
1957	13/11	Sheffield	W	2–0	
†1965	15/4	Ludwigshafen	W	3–0	IYT
1969	11/3	West Ham	W	1–0	IYT*
†1969	26/3	Waregem	W	2–0	IYT
1972	13/5	Palma	D	0–0	IYT*
†1973	4/6	Viareggio	D	0–0	IYT
†1977	19/5	Lokeren	W	1–0	IYT
†1979	17/1	Brussels	W	4–0	
†1980	8/9	Labia	W	6–1	
†1983	13/4	Birmingham	D	1–1	
†1988	20/5	Chatel	D	0–0	
†1990	24/7	Nyiregyhaza	D	1–1	IYT
†1990	16/10	Sunderland	D	0–0	IYT*
†1991	16/10	Eernegem	L	0–1	IYT*

v Brazil

†1986	29/3	Cannes	D	0–0	
†1986	13/5	Peking	L	1–2	
†1987	2/6	Niteroi	L	0–2	

v Bulgaria

1956	28/3	Salgotarjan	L	1–2	IYT
1960	16/4	Graz	L	0–1	IYT
1962	24/4	Ploesti	D	0–0	IYT
†1968	7/4	Nimes	D	0–0	IYT
†1969	26/3	Waregem	W	2–0	IYT
†1972	13/5	Palma	D	0–0	IYT
†1979	31/5	Vienna	L	0–1	IYT

v Cameroon

†1981	3/10	Sydney	W	2–0	WYC
†1985	1/6	Toulon	W	1–0	

v China

†1983	31/3	Cannes	W	5–1	
†1985	26/8	Baku	L	0–2	WYC
†1986	5/5	Peking	W	1–0	

v Czechoslovakia

1955	7/4	Lucca	L	0–1	IYT
†1966	21/5	Rijeka	L	2–3	IYT
†1969	20/5	Leipzig	W	3–1	IYT
1979	24/5	Bischofshofen	W	3–0	IYT
†1979	8/9	Pula	L	1–2	
†1982	11/4	Cannes	L	0–1	
†1983	20/5	Highbury	D	1–1	IYT
†1989	26/4	Bystrica	L	0–1	IYT*
†1989	14/11	Portsmouth	W	1–0	IYT*
†1990	25/4	Wembley	D	1–1	

v Denmark

†1955	1/10	Plymouth	W	9–2	
1956	20/5	Esbjerg	W	2–1	
†1979	31/10	Esbjerg	W	3–1	IYT*
1980	26/3	Coventry	W	4–0	IYT*
†1982	15/7	Stjordal	W	5–2	
†1983	16/7	Holbeck	L	0–1	
†1987	16/2	Manchester	W	2–1	
†1990	28/3	Wembley	D	0–0	
†1991	6/2	Oxford	L	1–5	
†1993	30/3	Stoke	W	4–2	
†1993	7/7	Nykobing	W	5–0	
†1995	22/2	Walsall	L	5–6	

v Egypt

†1981	11/10	Sydney	W	4–2	WYC
†1992	13/10	Bournemouth	W	2–1	

v Finland

†1975	19/5	Berne	D	1–1	IYT

v France

1957	24/3	Fontainebleau	W	1–0	
1958	22/3	Eastbourne	L	0–1	
†1966	23/5	Rijeka	L	1–2	IYT
†1967	11/5	Istanbul	W	2–0	IYT
†1968	25/1	Paris	L	0–1	
1978	8/2	C Palace	W	3–1	IYT*
1978	1/3	Paris	D	0–0	IYT*
†1979	2/6	Vienna	D	0–0	IYT
†1982	12/4	Cannes	L	0–1	
†1983	2/4	Cannes	L	0–2	
1984	1/3	Watford	W	4–0	
†1984	23/4	Cannes	L	1–2	
†1985	7/6	Toulon	L	1–3	
†1986	31/3	Cannes	L	1–2	
†1986	11/5	Peking	D	1–1	
†1988	22/5	Monthey	L	1–2	
†1988	15/11	Bradford	D	1–1	IYT*
†1989	11/10	Martigues	D	0–0	IYT*
†1990	22/5	Wembley	L	1–3	
†1992	7/10	Boulogne	L	0–2	
1993	18/7	Stoke	W	2–0	IYT
†1993	27/10	Besançon	L	0–2	IYT*
†1993	16/11	Yeovil	D	3–3	IYT*
†1994	6/9	Reading	L	2–3	

v East Germany

1958	7/4	Neunkirchen	W	1–0	IYT
1959	8/3	Zwickau	L	3–4	
1960	2/4	Portsmouth	D	1–1	
†1965	25/4	Essen	L	2–3	IYT
†1969	22/5	Magdeburg	L	0–4	IYT
†1973	10/6	Florence	W	3–2	IYT
†1984	25/5	Moscow	D	1–1	IYT
†1988	21/5	Monthey	W	1–0	

v West Germany

1953	4/4	Boom	W	3–1	IYT
1954	15/4	Gelsenkirchen	D	2–2	IYT
1956	1/4	Sztalinvaros	W	2–1	IYT
1957	31/3	Oberhausen	W	4–1	
1958	12/3	Bolton	L	1–2	
1961	12/3	Flensberg	L	0–2	
†1962	31/3	Northampton	W	1–0	
†1967	14/2	Mönchengladbach	W	1–0	
†1972	22/5	Barcelona	W	2–0	IYT
†1975	25/1	Las Palmas	W	4–2	
†1976	14/11	Monte Carlo	D	1–1	
†1979	28/5	Salzburg	W	2–0	IYT
†1979	1/9	Pula	D	1–1	
†1983	5/9	Pazin	W	2–0	

v Ghana

1993	17/3	Sydney	L	1–2	WYC

v Greece

1957	18/4	Barcelona	L	2–3	IYT
1959	2/4	Dimitrovo	W	4–0	IYT
†1977	23/5	Beveren	D	1–1	IYT
†1983	28/6	Puspokladany	W	1–0	
†1988	26/10	Tranmere	W	5–0	IYT*
†1989	8/3	Xanthi	W	5–0	IYT*

v Holland

1948	17/4	Tottenham	W	3–2	IYT
1951	26/3	Cannes	W	2–1	IYT
†1954	21/11	Arnhem	L	2–3	
†1955	5/11	Norwich	W	3–1	
1957	2/3	Brentford	D	5–5	
1957	14/4	Barcelona	L	1–2	IYT
1957	2/10	Amsterdam	W	3–2	
1961	9/3	Utrecht	L	0–1	
†1962	31/1	Brighton	W	4–0	
†1962	22/4	Ploesti	L	0–3	IYT
†1963	13/4	Wimbledon	W	5–0	IYT
1968	9/4	Nîmes	W	1–0	IYT
†1974	13/2	West Brom	D	1–1	IYT*
†1974	27/2	The Hague	W	1–0	IYT*
†1980	23/5	Halle	W	1–0	IYT*
†1982	9/4	Cannes	W	1–0	
†1985	7/4	Cannes	L	1–3	
†1987	1/8	Wembley	W	3–1	
†1993	20/7	Walsall	W	4–1	IYT

v Hungary

1954	11/4	Düsseldorf	L	1–3	IYT
1956	31/3	Tatabanya	L	2–4	IYT
1956	23/10	Tottenham	W	2–1	
†1956	25/10	Sunderland	W	2–1	
†1965	21/4	Wuppertal	W	5–0	IYT
†1975	16/5	Olten	W	3–1	IYT
†1977	16/10	Las Palmas	W	3–0	IYT
†1979	5/9	Pula	W	2–0	
†1980	11/9	Pula	L	1–2	
†1981	7/9	Porec	W	4–0	
†1983	29/7	Debrecen	L	1–2	
†1983	3/9	Umag	W	3–2	
†1986	30/3	Cannes	W	2–0	
†1995	29/3	Budapest	W	1–0	IYT*
†1995	25/4	Walsall	L	0–2	IYT*

v Iceland

†1973	31/5	Viareggio	W	2–0	IYT
†1977	21/5	Turnhout	D	0–0	IYT
†1983	7/9	Reykjavik	W	3–0	IYT*
1983	19/9	Blackburn	W	4–0	IYT*
1983	12/10	Reykjavik	W	3–0	
†1983	1/11	Crystal Palace	W	3–0	

†1984	16/10	Manchester	W	5−3	IYT*
†1985	11/9	Reykjavik	W	5−0	IYT*
†1990	12/9	Reykjavik	W	3−2	IYT*
†1991	12/9	Crystal Palace	W	2−1	IYT*

v Israel

| †1962 | 20/5 | Tel Aviv | W | 3−1 | |
| †1962 | 22/5 | Haifa | L | 1−2 | |

v Italy

1958	13/4	Luxembourg	L	0−1	IYT
1959	25/3	Sofia	L	1−3	IYT
1961	4/4	Braga	L	2−3	IYT
†1965	23/4	Marl-Huels	W	3−1	IYT
†1966	25/5	Rijeka	D	1−1	IYT
†1967	5/5	Izmir	W	1−0	IYT
†1973	14/2	Cava Dei Tirreni	L	0−1	
†1973	14/3	Highbury	W	1−0	
†1973	7/6	Viareggio	W	1−0	IYT
†1978	19/11	Monte Carlo	L	1−2	
†1979	28/2	Rome	W	1−0	IYT*
†1979	4/4	Birmingham	W	2−0	IYT*
†1983	22/5	Watford	D	1−1	IYT
†1984	20/4	Cannes	W	1−0	
†1985	5/4	Cannes	D	2−2	

v Latvia

| †1994 | 17/11 | Reading | D | 0−0 | IYT* |

v Luxembourg

1950	25/5	Vienna	L	1−2	IYT
1954	17/4	Bad Neuenahr	L	0−2	IYT
1957	2/2	West Ham	W	7−1	
1957	17/11	Luxembourg	W	3−0	
1958	9/4	Esch sur Alzette	W	5−0	IYT
†1984	29/5	Moscow	W	2−0	IYT

v Malta

| †1969 | 18/5 | Wolfen | W | 6−0 | IYT |
| †1979 | 26/5 | Salzburg | W | 3−0 | IYT |

v Mexico

†1984	18/4	Cannes	W	4−0	
†1985	5/6	Toulon	W	2−0	
†1985	29/8	Baku	L	0−1	WYC
†1991	27/3	Port of Spain	L	1−3	
†1993	14/3	Melbourne	D	0−0	WYC

v Northern Ireland

1948	15/5	Belfast	D	2−2	
1949	18/4	Haarlem	D	3−3	IYT
1949	14/5	Hull	W	4−2	
1950	6/5	Belfast	L	0−1	
1951	5/5	Liverpool	W	5−2	
1952	19/4	Belfast	L	0−2	
1953	11/4	Wolverhampton	D	0−0	

1954	10/4	Bruehl	W	5−0	IYT
1954	8/5	Newtownards	D	2−2	
1955	14/5	Watford	W	3−0	
1956	12/5	Belfast	D	0−1	
1957	11/5	Leyton	W	6−2	
1958	10/5	Bangor	L	2−4	
1959	9/5	Liverpool	W	5−0	
1960	14/5	Belfast	W	5−2	
1961	13/5	Manchester	W	2−0	
1962	12/5	Londonderry	L	1−2	
†1963	23/4	Wembley	W	4−0	IYT
1963	11/5	Oldham	D	1−1	
1964	25/1	Belfast	W	3−1	
1965	22/1	Birkenhead	L	2−3	
1966	26/2	Belfast	W	4−0	
1967	25/2	Stockport	W	3−0	
1968	23/2	Belfast	L	0−2	
1969	28/2	Birkenhead	L	0−2	
1970	28/2	Lurgan	L	1−3	
1971	6/3	Blackpool	D	1−1	IYT
1972	11/3	Chester	D	1−1	
1972	17/5	Sabadell	W	4−0	IYT
1973	24/3	Wellington	W	3−0	
1974	19/4	Birkenhead	L	1−2	
†1975	13/5	Kriens	W	3−0	IYT
†1980	16/5	Arnstadt	W	1−0	IYT
†1981	11/2	Walsall	W	1−0	IYT*
†1981	11/3	Belfast	W	3−0	IYT*

v Norway

†1982	13/7	Levanger	L	1−4	
†1983	14/7	Korsor	W	1−0	
1992	24/7	Amberg	D	1−1	
†1994	24/7	Larvik	D	3−3	
†1994	26/7	Vikersund	W	3−2	

v Paraguay

| †1985 | 24/8 | Baku | D | 2−2 | WYC |

v Poland

1960	18/4	Graz	W	4−2	IYT
†1964	26/3	Breda	D	1−1	IYT
†1971	26/5	Presov	D	0 0	IYT
†1972	20/5	Valencia	W	1−0	IYT
†1975	21/1	Las Palmas	D	1−1	
1978	9/5	Chorzow	L	0−2	IYT
†1979	3/9	Porec	L	0−1	
†1980	25/5	Leipzig	W	2−1	IYT
†1982	17/7	Steinkver	W	3−2	
†1983	12/7	Stagelse	W	1−0	
†1990	15/5	Wembley	W	3−0	
†1992	20/7	Regensburg	W	6−1	IYT

v Portugal

1954	18/4	Bonn	L	0−2	IYT
1961	2/4	Lisbon	L	0−4	IYT
†1964	3/4	The Hague	W	4−0	IYT
†1971	30/5	Prague	W	3−0	IYT

†1978	13/11	Monte Carlo	W	2–0	
†1980	18/5	Rosslau	D	1–1	IYT
†1982	7/4	Cannes	W	3–0	
†1992	22/7	Schweinfurt	D	1–1	IYT

v Qatar

†1981	14/10	Sydney	L	1–2	WYC
†1983	4/4	Cannes	D	1–1	

v Republic of Ireland

1953	5/4	Leuven	W	2–0	IYT
†1964	30/3	Middleburg	W	6–0	IYT
†1968	7/2	Dublin	D	0–0	IYT*
†1968	28/2	Portsmouth	W	4–1	IYT*
†1970	14/1	Dublin	W	4–1	IYT*
†1970	4/2	Luton	W	10–0	IYT*
†1975	9/5	Brunnen	W	1–0	IYT
†1985	26/2	Dublin	L	0–1	IYT*
†1986	25/2	Leeds	W	2–0	IYT*
†1988	17/2	Stoke	W	2–0	
†1988	20/9	Dublin	W	2–0	
†1993	24/8	Port Vale	D	2–2	

v Romania

1957	15/10	Tottenham	W	4–2	
1958	11/4	Luxembourg	W	1–0	IYT
1959	31/3	Pazardijc	L	1–2	IYT
†1963	15/4	Highbury	W	3–0	IYT
†1981	17/10	Adelaide	L	0–1	WYC
†1993	7/9	Port Vale	D	1–1	IYT*
†1993	13/10	Bucharest	D	1–1	IYT*

v Saar

1954	13/4	Dortmund	D	1–0	IYT
1955	9/4	Prato	W	3–1	IYT

v Scotland

1947	25/10	Doncaster	W	4–2	
1948	30/10	Aberdeen	L	1–3	
1949	21/4	Utrecht	L	0–1	IYT
1950	4/2	Carlisle	W	7–1	
1951	3/2	Kilmarnock	W	6–1	
1952	15/3	Sunderland	W	3–1	
1953	7/2	Glasgow	W	4–3	
1954	6/2	Middlesbrough	W	2–1	
1955	5/3	Kilmarnock	L	3–4	
1956	3/3	Preston	D	2–2	
1957	9/3	Aberdeen	W	3–1	
1958	1/3	Hull	W	2–0	
1959	28/2	Aberdeen	D	1–1	
1960	27/2	Newcastle	D	1–1	
1961	25/2	Elgin	W	3–2	
1962	24/2	Peterborough	W	4–2	
†1963	19/4	White City	W	1–0	IYT
1963	18/5	Dumfries	W	3–1	

1964	22/2	Middlesbrough	D	1–1	
1965	27/2	Inverness	L	1–2	
1966	5/2	Hereford	W	5–3	
1967	4/2	Aberdeen	L	0–1	
†1967	1/3	Southampton	W	1–0	IYT*
†1967	15/3	Dundee	D	0–0	IYT*
1968	3/2	Walsall	L	0–5	
1969	1/2	Stranraer	D	1–1	
1970	31/1	Derby	L	1–2	
1971	30/1	Greenock	L	1–2	
1972	29/1	Bournemouth	W	2–0	
1973	20/1	Kilmarnock	W	3–2	
1974	26/1	Brighton	D	2–2	
†1981	27/5	Aachen	L	0–1	IYT
†1982	23/2	Glasgow	L	0–1	IYT*
†1982	23/3	Coventry	D	2–2	IYT*
†1983	15/5	Birmingham	W	4–2	IYT
1983	5/10	Middlesbrough	W	3–1	IYT
1983	19/10	Motherwell	W	4–0	
†1984	27/11	Fulham	L	0–1	IYT*
1985	8/4	Cannes	W	1–0	IYT*
†1986	25/3	Aberdeen	L	1–4	IYT*

v Slovenia

†1994	13/11	High Wycombe	W	3–0	IYT*

v South Korea

†1993	7/3	Melbourne	D	1–1	WYC

v Spain

1952	15/4	Barcelona	L	1–4	IYT
1957	26/9	Birmingham	D	4–4	
1958	5/4	Saarbrücken	D	2–2	IYT
†1958	8/10	Madrid	W	4–2	
1961	30/3	Lisbon	D	0–0	IYT
†1964	27/2	Murcia	W	2–1	
†1964	5/4	Amsterdam	W	4–0	IYT
†1965	17/4	Heilbronn	D	0–0	IYT
†1966	30/3	Swindon	W	3–0	
†1967	7/5	Manisa	W	2–1	IYT
†1971	31/3	Pamplona	L	2–3	
†1971	20/4	Luton	D	1–1	
†1972	9/2	Alicante	D	0–0	
†1972	15/3	Sheffield	W	4–1	IYT*
†1975	25/2	Bristol	D	1–1	IYT*
†1975	18/3	Madrid	W	1–0	IYT*
†1976	12/11	Monte Carlo	W	3–0	
†1978	7/5	Bukowas	W	1–0	IYT
†1978	17/11	Monte Carlo	D	1–1	
†1981	25/5	Siegen	L	1–2	IYT
†1983	13/5	Stoke	W	1–0	IYT
†1990	29/7	Gyula	L	0–1	IYT
†1991	25/5	Wembley	D	1–1	
†1991	15/6	Faro	L	0–1	WYC
†1993	17/2	Alicante	D	1–1	
†1993	22/7	Walsall	W	5–1	IYT

v Sweden

†1971	24/5	Poprad	W	1–0	IYT
†1981	5/9	Pazin	W	3–2	
†1984	10/9	Rovinj	D	1–1	
†1986	10/11	West Brom	D	3–3	

v Switzerland

1950	26/5	Stockerau	W	2–1	IYT
1951	27/3	Nice	W	3–1	IYT
1952	13/4	Barcelona	W	4–0	IYT
1955	11/4	Florence	D	0–0	IYT
1956	11/3	Schaffhausen	W	2–0	
1956	13/10	Brighton	D	2–2	
1958	26/5	Zurich	W	3–0	
†1960	8/10	Leyton	W	4–3	
1962	22/11	Coventry	W	1–0	
†1963	21/3	Bienne	W	7–1	
†1973	2/6	Forte Dei Marmi	W	2–0	IYT
†1975	11/5	Buochs	W	4–0	IYT
†1980	4/9	Rovinj	W	3–0	
†1982	6/9	Porec	W	2–0	
†1983	26/7	Hajduboszormeny	W	4–0	
†1983	1/9	Porec	W	4–2	
†1988	19/5	Sion	W	2–0	
†1992	17/11	Port Vale	W	7–2	

v Syria

†1991	18/6	Faro	D	3–3	WYC

v Thailand

†1986	7/5	Peking	L	1–2	

v Trinidad & Tobago

†1991	25/3	Port of Spain	W	4–0	

v Turkey

1959	29/3	Dimitrovo	D	1–1	IYT
†1978	5/5	Wodzislaw	D	1–1	IYT
†1992	17/11	High Wycombe	W	2–1	
†1993	11/3	Melbourne	W	1–0	WYC
†1993	25/7	Nottingham	W	1–0	IYT

v Uruguay

†1977	9/10	Las Palmas	D	1–1	
†1987	10/6	Montevideo	D	2–2	
†1991	20/6	Faro	D	0–0	WYC

v USA

†1993	9/3	Melbourne	W	1–0	WYC

v USSR

†1963	17/4	Tottenham	W	2–0	IYT
†1967	13/5	Istanbul	L	0–1	IYT
†1968	11/4	Nîmes	D	1–1	IYT
†1971	28/5	Prague	D	1–1	IYT

†1978	10/10	Las Palmas	W	1–0	
†1982	4/9	Umag	W	1–0	
†1983	29/3	Cannes	D	0–0	
†1983	17/5	Aston Villa	L	0–2	IYT
1984	3/5	Ludwigsburg	L	0–2	
†1984	27/5	Moscow	D	1–1	IYT
†1984	8/9	Porec	W	1–0	
†1985	3/4	Cannes	W	2–1	
†1985	3/6	Toulon	L	0–2	
†1990	26/7	Debrecen	L	1–3	IYT

v Wales

1948	28/2	High Wycombe	W	4–3	
1948	15/4	London	W	4–0	
1949	26/2	Swansea	D	0–0	
1950	25/2	Worcester	W	1–0	
1951	17/2	Wrexham	D	1–1	
1952	23/2	Plymouth	W	6–0	
1953	21/2	Swansea	W	4–2	
1954	20/2	Derby	W	2–1	
1955	19/2	Milford Haven	W	7–2	
1956	18/2	Shrewsbury	W	5–1	
1957	9/2	Cardiff	W	7–1	
1958	15/2	Reading	W	8–2	
1959	14/2	Portmadoc	W	3–0	
1960	19/3	Canterbury	D	1–1	
1961	18/3	Newtown	W	4–0	
1962	17/3	Swindon	W	4–0	
1963	16/3	Haverfordwest	W	1–0	
1964	14/3	Leeds	W	2–1	
1965	20/3	Newport	D	2–2	
1966	19/3	Northampton	W	4–1	
1967	18/3	Cwmbran	D	3–3	
1968	16/3	Watford	L	2–3	
1969	15/3	Haverfordwest	W	3–1	
†1970	25/2	Newport	D	0–0	IYT*
†1970	18/3	Leyton	L	1–2	
1970	20/4	Reading	D	0–0	
1971	20/2	Aberystwyth	L	1–2	
1972	19/2	Swindon	W	4–0	
1973	24/2	Portmadoc	W	4–1	
†1974	9/1	West Brom	W	1–0	IYT*
1974	2/3	Shrewsbury	W	2–1	
†1974	13/3	Cardiff	L	0–1	IYT*
†1976	11/2	Cardiff	W	1–0	IYT*
†1976	3/3	Manchester	L	2–3	IYT*
†1977	9/3	West Brom	W	1–0	IYT*
†1977	23/3	Cardiff	D	1–1	IYT*
†1991	30/4	Wrexham	W	1–0	IYT*
†1991	22/5	Yeovil	W	3–0	IYT*

v Yugoslavia

1953	2/4	Liège	D	1–1	IYT
1958	4/2	Chelsea	D	2–2	
1962	20/4	Ploesti	L	0–5	IYT
†1967	9/5	Izmir	D	1–1	IYT
†1971	22/5	Bardejor	W	1–0	IYT
†1972	17/5	Barcelona	W	1–0	IYT
†1976	16/11	Monte Carlo	L	0–3	

1978	15/11	Monte Carlo	D	1–1		†1983	25/7	Debrecen	D	4–4
†1980	20/5	Altenberg	W	2–0	IYT	†1983	8/9	Pula	D	2–2
†1981	10/9	Pula	W	5–0		1984	5/5	Boblingen	W	1–0
†1982	9/9	Pula	W	1–0		†1984	12/9	Buje	L	1–4

42 ● FA PREMIER LEAGUE AND FOOTBALL LEAGUE CHAMPIONS 1888–1995

FA Premier League Champions 1992–95

Season	Winners	Pts	Max	Season	Winners	Pts	Max
1992–93	Manchester United	84	126	1994–95	Blackburn Rovers	89	126
1993–94	Manchester United	92	126				

Football League Champions 1888–1992

First Division 1888–1992

Season	Winners	Pts	Max	Season	Winners	Pts	Max
1888–89	Preston North End	40	44	1926–27	Newcastle United	56	84
1889–90	Preston North End	33	44	1927–28	Everton	53	84
1890–91	Everton	29	44	1928–29	Sheffield Wednesday	52	84
1891–92	Sunderland	42	52	1929–30	Sheffield Wednesday	60	84
1892–93	Sunderland	48	60	1930–31	Arsenal	66	84
1893–94	Aston Villa	44	60	1931–32	Everton	56	84
1894–95	Sunderland	47	60	1932–33	Arsenal	58	84
1895–96	Aston Villa	45	60	1933–34	Arsenal	59	84
1896–97	Aston Villa	47	60	1934–35	Arsenal	58	84
1897–98	Sheffield United	42	60	1935–36	Sunderland	56	84
1898–99	Aston Villa	45	68	1936–37	Manchester City	57	84
1899–1900	Aston Villa	50	68	1937–38	Arsenal	52	84
1900–01	Liverpool	45	68	1938–39	Everton	59	84
1901–02	Sunderland	44	68	1946–47	Liverpool	57	84
1902–03	Sheffield Wednesday	42	68	1947–48	Arsenal	59	84
1903–04	Sheffield Wednesday	47	68	1948–49	Portsmouth	58	84
1904–05	Newcastle United	48	68	1949–50*	Portsmouth	53	84
1905–06	Liverpool	51	76	1950–51	Tottenham Hotspur	60	84
1906–07	Newcastle United	51	76	1951–52	Manchester United	57	84
1907–08	Manchester United	52	76	1952–53*	Arsenal	54	84
1908–09	Newcastle United	53	76	1953–54	Wolverhampton Wanderers	57	84
1909–10	Aston Villa	53	76	1954–55	Chelsea	52	84
1910–11	Manchester United	52	76	1955–56	Manchester United	60	84
1911–12	Blackburn Rovers	49	76	1956–57	Manchester United	64	84
1912–13	Sunderland	54	76	1957–58	Wolverhampton Wanderers	64	84
1913–14	Blackburn Rovers	51	76	1958–59	Wolverhampton Wanderers	61	84
1914–15	Everton	46	76	1959–60	Burnley	55	84
1919–20	West Bromwich Albion	60	84	1960–61	Tottenham Hotspur	66	84
1920–21	Burnley	59	84	1961–62	Ipswich Town	56	84
1921–22	Liverpool	57	84	1962–63	Everton	61	84
1922–23	Liverpool	60	84	1963–64	Liverpool	57	84
1923–24*	Huddersfield Town	57	84	1964–65*	Manchester United	61	84
1924–25	Huddersfield Town	58	84	1965–66	Liverpool	61	84
1925–26	Huddersfield Town	57	84	1966–67	Manchester United	60	84

* Won on goal average/difference   No competition 1915–19 and 1939–46

Season	Winners	Pts	Max	Season	Winners	Pts	Max
1967–68	Manchester City	58	84	1980–81	Aston Villa	60	84
1968–69	Leeds United	67	84	1981–82	Liverpool	87	126
1969–70	Everton	66	84	1982–83	Liverpool	82	126
1970–71	Arsenal	65	84	1983–84	Liverpool	80	126
1971–72	Derby County	53	84	1984–85	Everton	90	126
1972–73	Liverpool	60	84	1985–86	Liverpool	88	126
1973–74	Leeds United	62	84	1986–87	Everton	86	126
1974–75	Derby County	58	84	1987–88	Liverpool	90	120
1975–76	Liverpool	60	84	1988–89*	Arsenal	76	114
1976–77	Liverpool	57	84	1989–90	Liverpool	79	114
1977–78	Nottingham Forest	64	84	1990–91	Arsenal	83	114
1978–79	Liverpool	68	84	1991–92	Leeds United	82	126
1979–80	Liverpool	60	84				

Football League Champions 1892–1995

First Division 1992–1995 (Second Division 1892–1992)

Season	Winners	Pts	Max	Season	Winners	Pts	Max
1892–93	Small Heath	36	44	1933–34	Grimsby Town	59	76
1893–94	Liverpool	50	56	1934–35	Brentford	61	76
1894–95	Bury	48	60	1935–36	Manchester United	56	76
1895–96*	Liverpool	46	60	1936–37	Leicester City	56	76
1896–97	Notts County	42	60	1937–38	Aston Villa	57	76
1897–98	Burnley	48	60	1938–39	Blackburn Rovers	55	84
1898–99	Manchester City	52	68	1946–47	Manchester City	62	84
1899–1900	Sheffield Wednesday	54	68	1947–48	Birmingham City	59	84
1900–01	Grimsby Town	49	68	1948–49	Fulham	57	84
1901–02	West Bromwich Albion	55	68	1949–50	Tottenham Hotspur	61	84
1902–03	Manchester City	54	68	1950–51	Preston North End	57	84
1903–04	Preston North End	50	68	1951–52	Sheffield Wednesday	53	84
1904–05	Liverpool	58	68	1952–53	Sheffield United	60	84
1905–06	Bristol City	66	76	1953–54*	Leicester City	56	84
1906–07	Nottingham Forest	60	76	1954–55*	Birmingham City	54	84
1907–08	Bradford City	54	76	1955–56	Sheffield Wednesday	55	84
1908–09	Bolton Wanderers	52	76	1956–57	Leicester City	61	84
1909–10	Manchester City	54	76	1957–58	West Ham United	57	84
1910–11	West Bromwich Albion	53	76	1958–59	Sheffield Wednesday	62	84
1911–12	Derby County	54	76	1959–60	Aston Villa	59	84
1912–13	Preston North End	53	76	1960–61	Ipswich Town	59	84
1913–14	Notts County	53	76	1961–62	Liverpool	62	84
1914–15	Derby County	53	76	1962–63	Stoke City	53	84
1919–20	Tottenham Hotspur	70	76	1963–64	Leeds United	63	84
1920–21	Birmingham	58	76	1964–65	Newcastle United	57	84
1921–22	Nottingham Forest	56	76	1965–66	Manchester City	59	84
1922–23	Notts County	53	76	1966–67	Coventry City	59	84
1923–24	Leeds United	54	76	1967–68	Ipswich Town	59	84
1924–25	Leicester City	59	76	1968–69	Derby County	63	84
1925–26	Sheffield Wednesday	60	76	1969–70	Huddersfield Town	60	84
1926–27	Middlesbrough	62	76	1970–71	Leicester City	59	84
1927–28	Manchester City	59	76	1971–72	Norwich City	57	84
1928–29	Middlesbrough	55	76	1972–73	Burnley	62	84
1929–30	Blackpool	58	76	1973–74	Middlesbrough	65	84
1930–31	Everton	61	76	1974–75	Manchester United	61	84
1931–32	Wolverhampton Wanderers	56	76	1975–76	Sunderland	56	84
1932–33	Stoke City	56	76	1976–77	Wolverhampton Wanderers	57	84

* *Won on goal average/difference   No competition 1915–19 and 1939–46*

Season	Winners	Pts	Max	Season	Winners	Pts	Max
1977–78	Bolton Wanderers	58	84	1986–87	Derby County	84	126
1978–79	Crystal Palace	57	84	1987–88	Millwall	82	132
1979–80	Leicester City	55	84	1988–89	Chelsea	99	138
1980–81	West Ham United	66	84	1989–90	Leeds United	85	138
1981–82	Luton Town	88	126	1990–91	Oldham Athletic	88	138
1982–83	Queens Park Rangers	85	126	1991–92	Ipswich Town	84	138
1983–84*	Chelsea	88	126	1992–93	Newcastle United	96	138
1984–85	Oxford United	84	126	1993–94	Crystal Palace	90	138
1985–86	Norwich City	84	126	1994–95	Middlesborough	82	138

Third Division (S) 1920–1958

Season	Winners	Pts	Max	Season	Winners	Pts	Max
1920–21	Crystal Palace	59	84	1936–37	Luton Town	58	84
1921–22*	Southampton	61	84	1937–38	Millwall	56	84
1922–23	Bristol City	59	84	1938–39	Newport County	55	84
1923–24	Portsmouth	59	84	1946–47	Cardiff City	66	84
1924–25	Swansea Town	57	84	1947–48	Queens Park Rangers	61	84
1925–26	Reading	57	84	1948–49	Swansea Town	62	84
1926–27	Bristol City	62	84	1949–50	Notts County	58	84
1927–28	Millwall	65	84	1950–51	Nottingham Forest	70	92
1928–29*	Charlton Athletic	54	84	1951–52	Plymouth Argyle	66	92
1929–30	Plymouth Argyle	68	84	1952–53	Bristol Rovers	64	92
1930–31	Notts County	59	84	1953–54	Ipswich Town	64	92
1931–32	Fulham	57	84	1954–55	Bristol City	70	92
1932–33	Brentford	62	84	1955–56	Leyton Orient	66	92
1933–34	Norwich City	61	84	1956–57*	Ipswich Town	59	92
1934–35	Charlton Athletic	61	84	1957–58	Brighton and Hove Albion	60	92
1935–36	Coventry City	57	84				

Third Division (N) 1921–1958

Season	Winners	Pts	Max	Season	Winners	Pts	Max
1921–22	Stockport County	56	76	1936–37	Stockport County	60	84
1922–23	Nelson	51	76	1937–38	Tranmere Rovers	56	84
1923–24	Wolverhampton Wanderers	63	84	1938–39	Barnsley	67	84
1924–25	Darlington	58	84	1946–47	Doncaster Rovers	72	84
1925–26	Grimsby Town	61	84	1947–48	Lincoln City	60	84
1926–27	Stoke City	63	84	1948–49	Hull City	65	84
1927–28	Bradford	63	84	1949–50	Doncaster Rovers	55	84
1928–29	Bradford City	63	84	1950–51	Rotherham United	71	92
1929–30	Port Vale	67	84	1951–52	Lincoln City	69	92
1930–31	Chesterfield	58	84	1952–53	Oldham Athletic	59	92
1931–32*	Lincoln City	57	80	1953–54	Port Vale	69	92
1932–33	Hull City	59	84	1954–55	Barnsley	65	92
1933–34	Barnsley	62	84	1955–56	Grimsby Town	68	92
1934–35	Doncaster Rovers	57	84	1956–57	Derby County	63	92
1935–36	Chesterfield	60	84	1957–58	Scunthorpe United	66	92

Second Division 1992–1995 (Third Division 1958–1992)

Season	Winners	Pts	Max	Season	Winners	Pts	Max
1958–59	Plymouth Argyle	62	92	1966–67	Queens Park Rangers	67	92
1959–60	Southampton	61	92	1967–68	Oxford United	57	92
1960–61	Bury	68	92	1968–69*	Watford	64	92
1961–62	Portsmouth	65	92	1969–70	Orient	62	92
1962–63	Northampton Town	62	92	1970–71	Preston North End	61	92
1963–64*	Coventry City	60	92	1971–72	Aston Villa	70	92
1964–65	Carlisle United	60	92	1972–73	Bolton Wanderers	61	92
1965–66	Hull City	69	92				

* *Won on goal average/difference*   *No competition 1915–19 and 1939–46*

Season	Winners	Pts	Max	Season	Winners	Pts	Max
1973–74	Oldham Athletic	62	92	1984–85	Bradford City	94	138
1974–75	Blackburn Rovers	60	92	1985–86	Reading	94	138
1975–76	Hereford United	63	92	1986–87	AFC Bournemouth	97	138
1976–77	Mansfield Town	64	92	1987–88	Sunderland	93	138
1977–78	Wrexham	61	92	1988–89	Wolverhampton Wanderers	92	138
1978–79	Shrewsbury Town	61	92	1989–90	Bristol Rovers	93	138
1979–80	Grimsby Town	62	92	1990–91	Cambridge United	86	138
1980–81	Rotherham United	61	92	1991–92	Brentford	82	138
1981–82*	Burnley	80	138	1992–93	Stoke City	93	138
1982–83	Portsmouth	91	138	1993–94	Reading	89	138
1983–84	Oxford United	95	138	1994–95	Birmingham City	89	138

Third Division 1992–1995 (Fourth Division 1958–1992)

Season	Winners	Pts	Max	Season	Winners	Pts	Max
1958–59	Port Vale	64	92	1977–78	Watford	71	92
1959–60	Walsall	65	92	1978–79	Reading	65	92
1960–61	Peterborough United	66	92	1979–80	Huddersfield Town	66	92
1961–62	Millwall	56	88	1980–81	Southend United	67	92
1962–63	Brentford	62	92	1981–82	Sheffield United	96	138
1963–64*	Gillingham	60	92	1982–83	Wimbledon	98	138
1964–65	Brighton and Hove Albion	63	92	1983–84	York City	101	138
1965–66	Doncaster Rovers	59	92	1984–85	Chesterfield	91	138
1966–67	Stockport County	64	92	1985–86	Swindon Town	102	138
1967–68	Luton Town	66	92	1986–87	Northampton Town	99	138
1968–69	Doncaster Rovers	59	92	1987–88	Wolverhampton Wanderers	90	138
1969–70	Chesterfield	64	92	1988–89	Rotherham United	82	138
1970–71	Notts County	69	92	1989–90	Exeter City	89	138
1971–72	Grimsby Town	63	92	1990–91	Darlington	83	138
1972–73	Southport	62	92	1991–92	Burnley	83	126
1973–74	Peterborough United	65	92	1992–93	Cardiff City	83	126
1974–75	Mansfield Town	68	92	1993–94	Shrewsbury Town	79	126
1975–76	Lincoln City	74	92	1994–95	Carlisle United	91	126
1976–77	Cambridge United	65	92				

Won on goal average/difference   No competition 1939–46

Blackburn Rovers – winners of the FA Carling Premiership.

43 ● REVIEW OF THE LEAGUE SEASON 1994-1995

In the most exciting football finale for years two clubs – Blackburn Rovers and Manchester United – each went into its last match on 14 May with a chance of winning the FA Carling Premiership title. Rovers hadn't been champions of the top division for 81 years, whereas United were on course for the elusive "double double". Rovers faced a difficult last fixture at Anfield: Roy Evans promised that his Liverpool players, with professional pride at stake, would do their utmost to deny former Kop favourite Kenny Dalglish the title. He was true to his word as Jamie Redknapp's last-minute goal from a free-kick won the match for Liverpool (2–1) and deprived the visitors of all three points. United, two points behind at kick-off, would have captured their third successive Premiership crown with a victory at Upton Park. Brian McClair's headed goal cancelled out Michael Hughes' earlier effort for West Ham but they couldn't manage one more priceless goal. So Blackburn's long wait is over – now they take on Real Madrid, Juventus and the rest in the European Champions' League.

At the opposite end of the table there was a frantic scrap to avoid the drop into the Endsleigh Insurance League. With four clubs to go down and positions shifting so quickly because of the three points for a win system, even clubs in mid-table with a couple of weeks to go were anxiously looking over their shoulders. Leicester and Ipswich finished well clear at the bottom and Norwich, after an encouraging first half of the season, also went down after losing to a late goal at Leeds (2–1) on 30 April. The other relegated club was Crystal Palace, for whom appearances in the semi-finals of both the FA Cup and Coca-Cola Cup were scant consolation. A 3–2 defeat at Newcastle on the last day confirmed the worst; Aston Villa and Sheffield Wednesday breathed a sigh of relief.

Middlesbrough, with ex-Manchester United and England captain Bryan Robson as player-manager, won the Endsleigh League First Division by just three points and with it the only automatic promotion spot for the Premiership. A 2–1 home victory against Luton on 30 April, the club's last match ever at Ayresome Park, proved decisive. Bolton, despite the distraction of a Wembley visit in the Coca-Cola Cup, and Wolves, with attendances at Molineux regularly around the 25,000 mark, joined Reading and Tranmere in the play-offs. Never had there been so much at stake.

Birmingham City, still with bubbly character Barry Fry in charge, bounced back a year after being relegated to top the Second Division and clinch a

place back in the First. They won 2–1 at Huddersfield on the final day (6 May) and the only club that could have caught them, Brentford, managed one point from their match at Bristol Rovers when three were essential. "The Bees" were joined by Crewe, Bristol Rovers and Huddersfield with their new ground in the play-offs. At the other end, with a massive five to go down, Bournemouth couldn't have fancied their chances after seven straight defeats at the start of the season and a bottom place at the turn of the year. But a crowd three times the average Dean Court gate saw them overcome Shrewsbury 3–0 in their last match (2 May) and beat the drop by two points.

Carlisle United were convincing winners of the Third Division – by eight points. Walsall, who had held Leeds to a draw in the FA Cup, also achieved automatic promotion as runners-up. Chesterfield, Bury, Preston and Mansfield would contest the play-offs.

Endsleigh League Play-Offs

Division 1

Semi-Finals
Tranmere Rovers v Reading 1–3, 0–0

Wolverhampton Wanderers v Bolton Wanderers 2–1, 0–2

Final
Bolton Wanderers v Reading 4–3 (*at Wembley*)

Division 2

Semi-Finals
Bristol Rovers v Crewe Alexandra 0–0, 1–1
(*Bristol Rovers won on away goal*)

Huddersfield Town v Brentford 1–1, 1–1
(*Huddersfield Town won on penalty-kicks*)

Final
Bristol Rovers v Huddersfield Town 1–2

Division 3

Semi-Finals
Mansfield Town v Chesterfield 1–1, 2–5

Preston North End v Bury 0–1, 0–1

Final
Chesterfield v Bury 2–0

44 ● FINAL LEAGUE TABLES 1994–1995

FA Carling Premiership

		P		HOME					AWAY					
			W	D	L	F	A	W	D	L	F	A	Pts	GD
1	Blackburn Rovers	42	17	2	2	54	21	10	6	5	26	18	89	+41
2	Manchester United	42	16	4	1	42	4	10	6	5	35	24	88	+49
3	Nottingham Forest	42	12	6	3	36	18	10	5	6	36	25	77	+29
4	Liverpool	42	13	5	3	38	13	8	6	7	27	24	74	+28
5	Leeds United	42	13	5	3	35	15	7	8	6	24	23	73	+21
6	Newcastle United	42	14	6	1	46	20	6	6	9	21	27	72	+20
7	Tottenham Hotspur	42	10	5	6	32	25	6	9	6	34	33	62	+8
8	Queens Park Rangers	42	11	3	7	36	26	6	6	9	25	33	60	+2
9	Wimbledon	42	9	5	7	26	26	6	6	9	22	39	56	−17
10	Southampton	42	8	9	4	33	27	4	9	8	28	36	54	−2
11	Chelsea	42	7	7	7	25	22	6	8	7	25	33	54	−5
12	Arsenal	42	6	9	6	27	21	7	3	11	25	28	51	+3
13	Sheffield Wednesday	42	7	7	7	26	26	6	5	10	23	31	51	−8
14	West Ham United	42	9	6	6	28	19	4	5	12	16	29	50	−4
15	Everton	42	8	9	4	31	23	3	8	10	13	28	50	−7
16	Coventry City	42	7	7	7	23	25	5	7	9	21	37	50	−18
17	Manchester City	42	8	7	6	37	28	4	6	11	16	36	49	−11
18	Aston Villa	42	6	9	6	27	24	5	6	10	24	32	48	−5
19	Crystal Palace	42	6	6	9	16	23	5	6	10	18	26	45	−15
20	Norwich City	42	8	8	5	27	21	2	5	14	10	33	43	−17
21	Leicester City	42	5	6	10	28	37	1	5	15	17	43	29	−35
22	Ipswich Town	42	5	3	13	24	34	2	3	16	12	59	27	−57

Endsleigh Insurance League First Division

		P	W	D	L	F	A	W	D	L	F	A	Pts	Gls
				HOME						AWAY				
1	Middlesbrough	46	15	4	4	41	19	8	9	6	26	21	82	67
2	Reading	46	12	7	4	34	21	11	3	9	24	23	79	58
3	Bolton Wanderers	46	16	6	1	43	13	5	8	10	24	32	77	67*
4	Wolverhampton Wanderers	46	15	5	3	39	18	6	8	9	38	43	76	77
5	Tranmere Rovers	46	17	4	2	51	23	5	6	12	16	35	76	67
6	Barnsley	46	15	6	2	42	19	5	6	12	21	33	72	63
7	Watford	46	14	6	3	33	17	5	7	11	19	29	70	52
8	Sheffield United	46	12	9	2	41	21	5	8	10	33	34	68	74
9	Derby County	46	12	6	5	44	23	6	6	11	22	28	66	66
10	Grimsby Town	46	12	7	4	36	19	5	7	11	26	37	65	62
11	Stoke City	46	10	7	6	31	21	6	8	9	19	32	63	50
12	Millwall	46	11	8	4	36	22	5	6	12	24	38	62	60
13	Southend United	46	13	2	8	33	25	5	6	12	21	48	62	54
14	Oldham Athletic	46	12	7	4	34	21	4	6	13	26	39	61	60
15	Charlton Athletic	46	11	6	6	33	25	5	5	13	25	41	59	58
16	Luton Town	46	8	6	9	35	30	7	7	9	26	34	58	61
17	Port Vale	46	11	5	7	30	24	4	8	11	28	40	58	58
18	Portsmouth	46	9	8	6	31	28	6	5	12	22	35	58	53
19	West Bromwich Albion	46	13	3	7	33	24	3	7	13	18	33	58	51
20	Sunderland	46	5	12	6	22	22	7	6	10	19	23	54	41
21	Swindon Town	46	9	6	8	28	27	3	6	14	26	46	48	54
22	Burnley	46	8	7	8	36	33	3	6	14	13	41	46	49
23	Bristol City	46	8	8	7	26	28	3	4	16	16	35	45	42
24	Notts County	46	7	8	8	26	28	2	5	16	19	38	40	45

* promoted via the play-offs.

Endsleigh Insurance League Second Division

			HOME					AWAY						
		P	W	D	L	F	A	W	D	L	F	A	Pts	Gls
1	Birmingham City	46	15	6	2	53	18	10	8	5	31	19	89	84
2	Brentford	46	14	4	5	44	15	11	6	6	37	24	85	81
3	Crewe Alexandra	46	14	3	6	46	33	11	5	7	34	35	83	80
4	Bristol Rovers	46	15	7	1	48	20	7	9	7	22	20	82	70
5	Huddersfield Town	46	14	5	4	45	21	8	10	5	34	28	81	79*
6	Wycombe Wanderers	46	13	7	3	36	19	8	8	7	24	27	78	60
7	Oxford United	46	13	6	4	30	18	8	6	9	36	34	75	66
8	Hull City	46	13	6	4	40	18	8	5	10	30	39	74	70
9	York City	46	13	4	6	37	21	8	5	10	30	30	72	67
10	Swansea City	46	10	8	5	23	13	9	6	8	34	32	71	57
11	Stockport County	46	12	3	8	40	29	7	5	11	23	31	65	63
12	Blackpool	46	11	4	8	40	36	7	6	10	24	34	64	64
13	Wrexham	46	10	7	6	38	27	6	8	9	27	37	63	65
14	Bradford City	46	8	6	9	29	32	8	6	9	28	32	60	57
15	Peterborough United	46	7	11	5	26	29	7	7	9	28	40	60	54
16	Brighton & Hove Albion	46	9	10	4	25	15	5	7	11	29	38	59	54
17	Rotherham United	46	12	6	5	36	26	2	8	13	21	35	56	57
18	Shrewsbury Town	46	9	9	5	34	27	4	5	14	20	35	53	54
19	Bournemouth	46	9	4	10	30	34	4	7	12	19	35	50	49
20	Cambridge United	46	8	9	6	33	28	3	6	14	19	41	48	52
21	Plymouth Argyle	46	7	6	10	22	36	5	4	14	23	47	46	45
22	Cardiff City	46	5	6	12	25	31	4	5	14	21	43	38	46
23	Chester City	46	5	6	12	23	42	1	5	17	14	42	29	37
24	Leyton Orient	46	6	6	11	21	29	0	2	21	9	46	26	30

* *promoted via the play-offs.*

Endsleigh Insurance League Third Division

				HOME				AWAY						
		P	W	D	L	F	A	W	D	L	F	A	Pts	Gls
1	Carlisle United	42	14	5	2	34	14	13	5	3	33	17	91	67
2	Walsall	42	15	3	3	42	18	9	8	4	33	22	83	75
3	Chesterfield	42	11	7	3	26	10	12	5	4	36	27	81	62*
4	Bury	42	13	7	1	39	13	10	4	7	34	23	80	73
5	Preston North End	42	13	3	5	37	17	6	7	8	21	24	67	58
6	Mansfield Town	42	10	5	6	45	27	8	6	7	39	32	65	84
7	Scunthorpe United	42	12	2	7	40	30	6	6	9	28	33	62	68
8	Fulham	42	11	5	5	39	22	5	9	7	21	32	62	60
9	Doncaster Rovers	42	9	5	7	28	20	8	5	8	30	23	61	58
10	Colchester United	42	8	5	8	29	30	8	5	8	27	34	58	56
11	Barnet	42	8	7	6	37	27	7	4	10	19	36	56	56
12	Lincoln City	42	10	7	4	34	22	5	4	12	20	33	56	54
13	Torquay United	42	10	8	3	35	25	4	5	12	19	32	55	54
14	Wigan Athletic	42	7	6	8	28	30	7	4	10	25	30	52	53
15	Rochdale	42	8	6	7	25	23	4	8	9	19	44	50	44
16	Hereford United	42	9	6	6	22	19	3	7	11	23	43	49	45
17	Northampton Town	42	8	5	8	25	29	2	9	10	20	38	.44	45
18	Hartlepool United	42	9	5	7	33	32	2	5	14	10	37	43	43
19	Gillingham	42	8	7	6	31	25	2	4	15	15	39	41	46
20	Darlington	42	7	5	9	25	24	4	3	14	18	33	41	43
21	Scarborough	42	4	7	10	26	31	4	3	14	23	39	34	49
22	Exeter City	42	5	5	11	25	36	3	5	13	11	34	34	36

promoted via the play-offs.

FA CARLING PREMIERSHIP

	Arsenal	Aston Villa	Blackburn Rovers	Chelsea	Coventry City	Crystal Palace	Everton	Ipswich Town	Leeds United	Leicester City	Liverpool	Manchester City	Manchester United	Newcastle United	Norwich City	Nottingham Forest	Queens Park Rangers	Sheffield Wednesday	Southampton	Tottenham Hotspur	West Ham United	Wimbledon
Arsenal	•	0-0	0-0	3-1	2-1	1-2	1-1	4-1	1-3	1-1	0-1	3-0	0-0	2-3	5-1	1-0	1-3	0-0	1-1	1-1	0-1	0-0
Aston Villa	0-4	•	0-1	3-0	0-0	1-1	0-0	2-0	0-0	4-4	2-0	1-1	1-2	1-0	0-0	0-2	2-1	1-1	1-1	1-0	0-2	7-1
Blackburn Rovers	3-1	3-1	•	2-1	4-0	2-1	3-0	4-1	1-1	3-0	3-2	2-3	2-4	1-0	0-0	3-0	4-0	3-1	3-2	2-0	4-2	2-1
Chelsea	2-1	1-0	1-2	•	2-2	0-0	0-1	2-0	0-3	4-0	0-0	3-0	2-3	1-1	2-0	0-2	1-0	1-1	0-2	1-1	1-2	1-1
Coventry City	0-1	0-1	1-1	2-2	•	1-4	0-0	2-0	2-1	4-2	1-1	1-0	2-3	0-0	1-0	0-0	0-1	2-0	1-3	0-4	2-0	1-1
Crystal Palace	0-3	0-1	1-2	0-1	0-2	•	1-0	3-0	1-2	2-0	1-6	2-1	1-1	0-1	0-1	1-2	0-0	1-4	0-0	1-1	1-0	0-0
Everton	1-1	2-2	1-2	3-3	0-2	3-1	•	4-1	3-0	1-1	2-0	1-1	1-0	2-0	2-1	1-2	2-2	1-1	0-0	0-0	1-0	0-0
Ipswich Town	0-2	0-1	1-3	2-2	2-0	0-2	0-1	•	2-0	4-1	1-3	1-2	2-3	0-2	1-2	0-1	0-1	1-2	2-1	1-3	1-1	2-2
Leeds United	1-0	1-0	1-1	2-3	3-0	3-1	1-0	4-0	•	2-1	0-2	2-0	2-1	0-0	1-2	0-1	4-0	0-1	0-0	1-1	2-2	3-1
Leicester City	2-1	1-1	0-0	1-1	2-2	0-1	2-2	2-0	1-3	•	1-2	0-1	0-4	1-3	1-0	2-4	1-1	0-1	4-3	3-1	1-2	3-4
Liverpool	3-0	3-2	1-1	3-1	2-3	0-0	0-0	0-1	0-1	2-0	•	2-0	0-0	1-3	4-0	2-4	1-1	4-1	3-1	1-1	0-0	3-0
Manchester City	1-2	2-2	1-3	1-2	0-0	1-1	4-0	2-0	0-0	0-0	2-1	•	0-3	0-0	2-0	3-3	2-3	3-2	3-3	5-2	3-0	2-0
Manchester United	3-0	1-0	1-0	0-0	2-0	3-0	2-0	9-0	0-0	1-1	2-0	5-0	•	2-0	1-0	1-2	2-0	1-0	2-1	0-0	3-0	3-0
Newcastle United	1-0	3-1	1-1	4-2	4-0	3-2	2-0	1-1	1-2	3-1	1-1	0-0	1-1	•	3-0	2-1	2-1	2-1	5-1	3-3	2-0	2-1
Norwich City	0-0	1-1	2-1	3-0	2-2	0-0	0-0	3-0	2-1	2-1	1-2	1-1	0-2	2-1	•	0-1	4-2	0-0	2-2	0-2	1-0	1-2
Nottingham Forest	2-2	1-2	0-2	3-0	2-2	1-0	2-3	4-1	3-0	1-0	1-1	1-1	1-1	0-0	1-0	•	3-2	4-1	3-0	2-2	1-1	3-1
Queens Park Rangers	3-1	2-0	0-1	1-0	2-2	0-1	2-3	1-2	3-2	2-0	2-1	1-2	2-3	3-0	2-0	1-1	•	3-2	2-2	2-1	2-1	3-1
Sheffield Wednesday	3-1	1-2	1-1	1-1	5-1	1-0	0-0	4-1	1-1	1-0	1-2	1-1	1-0	0-0	0-0	1-7	0-2	•	1-1	3-4	0-1	3-1
Southampton	1-0	2-1	1-1	0-1	0-0	3-1	2-0	3-1	1-3	2-2	0-2	2-2	2-2	3-1	1-1	1-1	2-1	0-0	•	4-3	1-1	2-3
Tottenham Hotspur	1-0	3-4	3-1	0-0	1-3	0-0	2-1	3-0	1-1	1-0	0-0	2-1	0-1	4-2	1-0	1-4	1-1	3-1	1-2	•	3-1	1-2
West Ham United	0-2	1-0	2-0	1-2	0-1	1-0	2-2	1-1	0-0	1-0	3-0	3-0	1-1	1-3	2-2	3-1	0-0	0-2	2-0	1-2	•	3-0
Wimbledon	1-3	4-3	0-3	1-1	2-0	2-0	2-1	1-1	0-0	2-1	2-1	0-1	0-1	3-2	1-0	2-2	1-3	0-1	0-2	1-2	1-0	•

ENDSLEIGH INSURANCE LEAGUE FIRST DIVISION

	Barnsley	Bolton Wanderers	Bristol City	Burnley	Charlton Athletic	Derby County	Grimsby Town	Luton Town	Middlesbrough	Millwall	Notts County	Oldham Athletic	Port Vale	Portsmouth	Reading	Sheffield United	Southend United	Stoke City	Sunderland	Swindon Town	Tranmere Rovers	Watford	West Bromwich Albion	Wolverhampton Wanderers
Barnsley	•	3-0	2-1	0-1	2-1	2-1	4-1	3-1	1-1	4-1	1-1	1-1	3-1	1-0	0-2	2-1	0-0	2-0	2-0	2-1	2-2	0-0	2-0	1-3
Bolton Wanderers	2-1	•	0-1	1-1	5-1	1-1	3-3	3-0	1-0	1-0	3-1	2-2	3-1	1-1	1-1	3-1	2-1	3-1	3-1	3-0	1-0	3-0	1-0	5-1
Bristol City	3-2	0-1	•	1-1	2-1	1-0	3-1	0-0	3-0	0-1	2-0	2-2	2-1	1-1	1-0	2-1	3-0	1-0	1-1	3-2	0-1	3-0	1-0	1-1
Burnley	0-1	2-2	1-1	•	2-0	3-2	1-2	2-2	0-3	0-1	2-1	2-2	4-3	1-2	2-1	2-1	5-1	3-1	1-1	1-0	0-1	1-1	1-1	0-1
Charlton Athletic	2-2	1-2	3-2	2-0	•	3-4	4-0	1-0	2-1	1-2	2-0	2-1	1-1	1-2	1-2	1-1	4-2	0-1	0-1	1-0	0-1	1-1	1-1	3-2
Derby County	1-0	3-1	1-0	2-2	2-2	•	2-2	0-0	0-1	3-2	1-3	1-1	1-1	1-0	1-0	2-3	4-1	3-0	3-1	1-0	5-0	3-0	1-1	3-3
Grimsby Town	1-0	3-3	1-0	4-0	0-1	0-1	•	5-0	2-1	3-0	1-3	1-1	2-0	2-0	0-1	0-0	2-0	0-1	3-1	3-0	2-0	1-1	0-2	0-0
Luton Town	0-1	0-3	3-0	2-0	0-1	0-1	5-0	•	2-1	1-1	2-1	1-1	3-0	2-0	0-1	0-6	1-2	2-3	3-0	3-1	2-0	0-0	1-1	1-0
Middlesbrough	1-1	0-3	3-0	2-0	0-1	0-2	2-1	2-1	•	3-0	0-0	1-1	3-0	4-0	0-1	3-6	1-2	2-3	2-2	3-1	2-0	0-0	1-1	3-0
Millwall	0-1	0-1	0-1	2-3	3-1	2-4	1-1	2-1	0-0	•	0-0	1-3	1-3	2-2	2-0	2-1	3-1	1-1	0-0	2-3	1-1	2-0	2-2	1-0
Notts County	1-3	1-1	1-1	3-0	3-3	0-0	0-2	0-0	1-1	0-1	•	1-3	2-2	2-2	1-0	2-1	1-2	2-0	0-0	0-1	0-1	2-1	2-0	4-1
Oldham Athletic	1-0	3-1	2-0	1-0	0-2	2-1	1-1	0-0	1-0	2-1	1-1	•	3-1	1-1	3-1	2-1	1-0	0-0	1-1	1-1	0-1	2-1	1-0	2-4
Port Vale	2-1	1-1	1-1	2-1	0-2	1-0	1-2	0-0	2-1	2-1	0-2	1-3	•	3-2	0-2	2-1	2-2	0-1	1-0	1-1	3-2	2-1	2-1	1-2
Portsmouth	3-0	1-1	0-0	1-1	1-1	1-0	1-1	0-1	1-1	0-1	2-1	3-1	3-3	•	1-1	1-0	5-0	4-0	2-0	0-0	0-0	2-1	1-0	4-1
Reading	0-3	2-1	0-0	2-1	2-1	1-0	2-1	2-1	2-1	1-1	2-0	3-1	0-2	0-0	•	1-0	2-0	1-1	1-1	3-0	1-0	4-1	2-0	2-4
Sheffield United	0-0	3-1	3-0	2-0	2-1	2-1	3-1	1-3	1-1	1-1	3-0	3-1	1-2	3-1	1-1	•	2-2	1-1	0-0	2-2	2-0	3-0	2-1	3-3
Southend United	3-1	2-1	2-1	0-1	2-1	1-1	0-0	3-0	0-2	4-3	1-1	0-1	0-1	1-2	4-1	1-3	•	1-1	0-0	2-0	0-0	0-4	1-0	0-1
Stoke City	0-0	1-1	2-1	2-0	3-2	0-0	3-0	2-1	1-1	0-1	2-1	0-1	0-0	0-2	2-0	1-1	4-1	•	0-1	2-0	1-0	1-0	4-1	1-0
Sunderland	2-0	2-1	1-2	0-0	1-1	1-1	3-1	1-2	1-1	0-1	3-0	1-1	1-0	1-2	1-1	1-0	2-2	0-1	•	1-0	1-0	1-0	0-0	3-0
Swindon Town	0-0	0-1	1-1	1-1	0-1	1-1	3-1	1-2	2-1	3-1	3-0	3-1	2-0	0-0	2-1	1-3	2-2	0-1	1-0	•	3-2	1-0	0-0	3-2
Tranmere Rovers	6-1	1-0	2-0	4-1	0-1	3-1	2-0	4-2	1-1	0-1	3-2	1-2	1-1	4-2	1-0	2-1	2-2	0-1	1-0	3-2	•	2-1	3-1	2-1
Watford	3-2	2-0	1-0	2-0	2-0	3-0	0-0	1-0	1-3	0-2	0-1	3-1	3-2	0-2	0-1	2-1	3-0	1-0	1-3	1-0	2-1	•	1-0	1-1
West Bromwich Albion	2-1	1-0	1-0	2-0	0-1	2-1	1-1	1-1	3-1	2-1	0-0	3-1	0-0	0-2	2-1	0-1	2-5	0-1	4-1	2-2	5-1	0-1	•	2-0
Wolverhampton Wanderers	0-0	3-1	2-0	2-0	2-0	0-2	3-1	2-1	0-2	1-0	2-1	2-1	2-1	1-0	1-1	2-2	5-0	2-0	1-3	1-1	2-0	1-1	2-0	•

	Birmingham City	Blackpool	Bournemouth	Bradford City	Brentford	Brighton & Hove Albion	Bristol Rovers	Cambridge United	Cardiff City	Chester City	Crewe Alexandra	Huddersfield Town	Hull City	Leyton Orient	Oxford United	Peterborough United	Plymouth Argyle	Rotherham United	Shrewsbury Town	Stockport County	Swansea City	Wrexham	Wycombe Wanderers	York City
Birmingham City	•	7-1	0-0	0-0	2-0	3-3	2-0	1-1	2-1	1-0	5-0	1-1	2-2	2-0	3-0	4-0	4-2	2-1	2-0	1-0	0-1	5-2	0-1	4-2
Blackpool	1-1	•	3-1	2-0	1-2	2-2	0-2	2-3	2-1	3-1	0-0	1-4	1-2	2-1	2-1	4-0	5-2	2-2	2-1	1-1	2-1	2-1	0-1	0-1
Bournemouth	2-1	1-2	•	2-3	0-1	2-2	0-0	1-0	3-2	1-1	1-1	0-2	2-3	2-0	2-1	0-3	0-0	2-2	3-0	2-0	3-2	1-3	0-1	0-5
Bradford City	1-1	0-1	2-3	•	0-1	0-3	2-0	1-0	3-2	1-1	1-1	3-4	2-3	2-0	0-2	4-2	0-0	0-1	1-1	1-2	1-3	1-3	2-0	1-4
Brentford	1-2	3-2	1-2	4-3	•	2-1	3-0	6-0	2-3	1-1	0-2	3-4	0-1	3-0	2-0	4-2	7-0	0-3	1-1	1-2	1-3	0-2	2-1	0-0
Brighton & Hove Albion	0-1	2-2	1-1	1-0	1-1	•	1-2	2-0	0-0	1-0	0-1	3-3	0-1	0-0	1-1	1-1	1-2	1-1	1-1	2-0	1-1	4-0	0-1	0-0
Bristol Rovers	1-1	0-0	1-1	4-0	2-2	3-0	•	2-1	2-2	2-1	2-2	1-1	0-2	1-0	3-2	2-0	1-2	2-0	0-4	2-0	1-1	4-2	1-1	3-0
Cambridge United	1-0	2-1	1-1	2-4	2-3	0-2	1-1	•	3-1	1-2	1-2	1-1	2-2	2-1	1-2	2-0	1-2	2-1	4-1	2-2	1-3	0-2	1-1	1-1
Cardiff City	0-1	0-0	1-1	0-0	1-0	0-2	0-0	3-1	•	2-1	1-2	0-0	0-2	2-1	2-0	1-1	1-2	2-1	1-3	2-1	2-2	0-0	0-2	1-0
Chester City	0-4	0-0	1-1	1-2	2-1	1-2	0-0	1-3	0-2	•	0-1	0-0	1-2	2-0	1-3	1-1	0-1	0-0	0-1	1-0	2-0	1-0	0-2	3-1
Crewe Alexandra	2-1	4-3	2-0	0-1	0-2	4-0	2-1	4-2	0-0	2-1	•	3-3	3-2	2-0	3-2	1-1	2-2	3-1	0-4	2-1	0-2	1-3	1-2	0-1
Huddersfield Town	1-2	1-1	3-1	0-1	0-2	3-0	0-2	3-1	5-1	5-1	0-1	•	1-1	2-0	3-1	4-1	0-1	2-0	2-2	0-1	1-1	1-1	1-3	1-2
Hull City	0-0	0-1	0-1	2-0	0-2	2-2	0-0	1-0	4-2	5-1	1-2	3-3	•	2-0	3-1	1-1	1-1	0-2	2-2	4-0	1-0	1-1	0-2	0-4
Leyton Orient	2-1	0-1	3-1	1-0	0-2	2-1	0-0	1-1	2-0	2-0	7-1	2-1	0-1	•	3-1	0-2	1-0	2-1	3-0	2-0	2-0	1-0	0-2	0-0
Oxford United	2-1	0-1	3-2	0-1	0-0	0-0	0-0	1-0	2-0	2-0	1-4	3-1	4-0	3-2	•	1-0	1-0	2-1	1-1	4-0	1-2	0-0	0-2	0-1
Peterborough United	1-1	3-2	0-3	1-0	0-2	2-1	0-0	2-2	2-1	2-0	2-1	2-1	2-1	0-0	1-4	•	1-1	2-1	2-2	0-1	1-0	0-0	1-3	0-1
Plymouth Argyle	1-3	0-2	0-1	0-0	2-2	2-1	1-1	0-0	0-0	1-0	1-5	2-1	2-1	2-0	1-1	0-1	•	0-0	0-4	2-0	1-2	0-1	1-2	0-2
Rotherham United	1-3	4-0	3-0	3-1	0-3	4-3	0-3	1-0	2-0	1-0	3-2	1-1	2-1	0-0	1-1	0-0	3-1	•	0-4	2-2	0-0	2-2	0-0	2-1
Shrewsbury Town	0-2	3-0	0-1	1-2	0-2	1-1	1-1	2-1	1-0	1-0	2-2	2-1	2-3	3-0	1-1	2-2	3-2	1-0	•	2-1	1-2	0-0	2-2	1-0
Stockport County	0-1	3-2	1-0	0-2	0-1	2-0	2-1	2-1	4-1	1-2	3-1	1-1	4-0	0-1	0-2	1-2	2-4	2-0	2-1	•	1-2	0-0	2-2	1-2
Swansea City	0-2	1-0	1-1	0-0	1-1	1-1	1-1	2-1	4-1	0-1	0-1	1-1	2-0	2-0	1-3	2-0	2-1	3-1	0-0	2-0	•	0-2	0-2	2-1
Wrexham	1-1	0-1	1-0	0-0	3-0	2-1	0-0	0-1	0-3	3-1	0-1	2-1	2-0	1-1	3-2	3-3	3-1	3-1	0-1	0-0	4-1	•	4-1	3-0
Wycombe Wanderers	0-3	1-1	1-1	3-1	4-3	0-0	0-0	3-0	3-1	1-0	0-0	2-1	2-2	2-1	1-0	1-2	1-1	2-0	0-1	2-2	1-0	3-0	•	0-0
York City	2-0	4-0	0-0	0-0	2-1	2-1	0-3	2-4	1-0	0-1	1-2	3-1	3-1	4-1	0-2	2-1	1-0	1-3	0-0	2-2	2-4	0-1	0-0	•

ENDSLEIGH INSURANCE LEAGUE THIRD DIVISION

	Barnet	Bury	Carlisle United	Chesterfield	Colchester United	Darlington	Doncaster Rovers	Exeter City	Fulham	Gillingham	Hartlepool United	Hereford United	Lincoln City	Mansfield Town	Northampton	Preston North End	Rochdale	Scarborough	Scunthorpe United	Torquay United	Walsall	Wigan Athletic
Barnet	•	1–1	0–2	4–1	0–1	2–3	0–0	1–1	0–0	1–0	4–0	2–2	2–1	2–2	2–3	2–1	6–2	3–1	1–2	2–0	1–3	1–1
Bury	3–0	•	2–0	2–1	4–1	2–1	2–0	0–0	0–0	3–2	2–0	1–1	2–0	2–2	5–0	0–0	0–1	1–0	0–0	3–1	0–0	3–3
Carlisle United	4–0	3–0	•	1–1	0–0	2–1	1–1	1–0	1–1	2–0	0–1	1–0	1–3	2–1	2–1	0–0	4–1	2–0	2–1	1–0	2–1	2–1
Chesterfield	2–0	0–0	1–2	•	2–2	0–0	2–0	2–0	1–1	2–0	2–0	1–0	1–0	0–1	3–0	1–0	2–2	0–1	3–1	1–0	2–2	0–0
Colchester United	1–1	1–0	0–1	2–3	•	1–0	0–2	3–1	5–2	2–2	2–0	2–2	1–2	0–1	0–1	3–1	0–0	1–0	1–3	1–3	3–2	0–1
Darlington	0–1	0–2	0–2	0–0	1–0	•	0–2	1–0	0–0	1–2	2–0	3–1	0–0	0–0	0–1	0–1	4–0	1–0	1–1	2–1	2–2	1–3
Doncaster Rovers	1–1	1–2	0–0	1–1	1–2	0–0	•	1–0	0–0	1–2	3–0	3–0	3–0	0–2	0–0	2–1	0–1	1–0	2–2	3–0	0–2	5–3
Exeter City	1–2	0–4	1–1	1–2	1–0	0–2	1–5	•	0–1	3–0	2–1	1–1	1–1	2–3	4–1	0–1	0–0	5–2	1–0	1–2	1–3	2–4
Fulham	4–0	1–0	1–1	1–1	1–3	3–1	0–2	4–0	•	1–0	1–0	1–1	1–1	4–2	4–4	2–3	5–0	1–2	1–4	2–1	1–1	2–0
Gillingham	2–1	1–0	0–1	1–1	1–3	2–1	4–2	3–0	4–1	•	1–0	0–0	0–3	0–2	3–1	3–1	1–1	3–1	2–1	1–1	1–3	0–1
Hartlepool United	0–1	1–1	1–5	0–2	3–1	0–0	2–1	2–2	1–2	2–0	•	4–0	0–3	3–2	2–1	0–2	3–1	0–1	3–3	1–1	0–0	1–2
Hereford United	3–2	1–0	0–1	0–2	3–0	0–0	1–0	3–0	1–1	2–1	2–0	•	2–0	0–0	2–1	1–1	1–0	2–1	1–0	2–0	1–1	1–1
Lincoln City	1–2	0–3	1–1	0–1	2–0	3–1	1–0	2–0	2–0	1–1	3–0	2–0	•	3–2	2–2	2–1	0–0	2–0	0–1	0–1	1–1	1–0
Mansfield Town	3–0	0–2	1–2	4–2	2–0	0–1	0–1	1–1	1–1	4–0	2–0	7–1	6–2	•	1–1	2–1	2–2	3–2	1–1	2–0	1–3	4–3
Northampton Town	1–1	1–1	2–1	2–3	1–1	2–1	2–2	2–1	3–2	2–0	1–1	1–3	3–1	0–1	•	2–1	1–0	1–1	1–1	1–1	1–1	1–0
Preston North End	1–0	5–0	1–0	0–0	2–1	1–0	2–0	0–1	1–2	2–1	1–1	4–2	4–0	0–1	2–1	•	1–2	1–1	3–0	3–2	0–1	1–0
Rochdale	2–2	0–3	4–1	4–1	0–0	2–0	2–2	1–1	3–1	0–0	2–2	1–3	1–0	3–3	0–0	0–1	•	1–1	1–1	2–1	0–2	1–0
Scarborough	0–1	1–2	1–2	0–1	0–1	3–1	0–5	3–0	1–2	3–0	0–0	3–1	1–1	2–5	1–1	2–1	2–4	•	2–1	1–0	0–1	1–1
Scunthorpe United	1–0	3–2	2–3	0–1	3–4	2–1	0–1	0–0	2–1	3–1	0–0	1–0	2–0	3–4	2–1	2–1	4–1	3–1	•	1–1	3–2	0–0
Torquay United	1–2	2–2	1–1	3–3	3–3	1–0	0–1	1–0	5–1	2–1	4–1	4–3	2–1	1–0	2–1	2–1	4–1	2–1	1–1	•	1–0	1–1
Walsall	4–0	0–1	1–2	1–3	1–3	2–0	1–0	1–1	1–1	1–0	2–0	0–2	2–1	1–1	1–1	0–2	0–0	4–1	2–1	3–2	•	1–0
Wigan Athletic	1–2	0–3	0–2	2–3	1–2	4–1	3–2	3–2	1–1	0–3	2–0	1–1	0–1	0–4	2–1	1–0	4–0	1–1	0–0	1–1	1–0	•

46 ● LEAGUE CUP WINNERS 1961–1995

Two-legged finals until 1966, all finals after 1966 played at Wembley

Year	Winners		Runners-up	Result
1961	Aston Villa	v	Rotherham United	3–2 (0–2, 3–0 after extra time)
1962	Norwich City	v	Rochdale	4–0 (3–0, 1–0)
1963	Birmingham City	v	Aston Villa	3–1 (3–1, 0–0)
1964	Leicester City	v	Stoke City	4–3 (1–1, 3–2)
1965	Chelsea	v	Leicester City	3–2 (3–2, 0–0)
1966	West Bromwich Albion	v	West Ham United	5–3 (1–2, 4–1)
1967	Queens Park Rangers	v	West Bromwich Albion	3–2
1968	Leeds United	v	Arsenal	1–0
1969	Swindon Town	v	Arsenal	3–1 after extra time
1970	Manchester City	v	West Bromwich Albion	2–1 after extra time
1971	Tottenham Hotspur	v	Aston Villa	2–0
1972	Stoke City	v	Chelsea	2–1
1973	Tottenham Hotspur	v	Norwich City	1–0
1974	Wolverhampton Wanderers	v	Manchester City	2–1
1975	Aston Villa	v	Norwich City	1–0
1976	Manchester City	v	Newcastle United	2–1
1977	Aston Villa	v	Everton	0–0
	Aston Villa	v	Everton	1–1 after extra time replay at Hillsborough
	Aston Villa	v	Everton	3–2 after extra time; 2nd replay at Old Trafford
1978	Nottingham Forest	v	Liverpool	0–0 after extra time
	Nottingham Forest	v	Liverpool	1–0 replay at Old Trafford
1979	Nottingham Forest	v	Southampton	3–2
1980	Wolverhampton Wanderers	v	Nottingham Forest	1–0
1981	Liverpool	v	West Ham United	1–1 after extra time
	Liverpool	v	West Ham United	2–1 replay at Villa Park

as Milk Cup

Year	Winners		Runners-up	Result
1982	Liverpool	v	Tottenham Hotspur	3–1 after extra time
1983	Liverpool	v	Manchester United	2–1 after extra time
1984	Liverpool	v	Everton	0–0 after extra time
	Liverpool	v	Everton	1–0 replay at Maine Road
		v		
1985	Norwich City	v	Sunderland	1–0
1986	Oxford United	v	Queens Park Rangers	3–0

as Littlewoods Cup

Year	Winners		Runners-up	Result
1987	Arsenal	v	Liverpool	2–1
1988	Luton Town	v	Arsenal	3–2
1989	Nottingham Forest	v	Luton Town	3–1
1990	Nottingham Forest	v	Oldham Athletic	1–0

as Rumbelows Cup

Year	Winners		Runners-up	Result
1991	Sheffield Wednesday	v	Manchester United	1–0
1992	Manchester United	v	Nottingham Forest	1–0

as Coca-Cola Cup

Year	Winners		Runners-up	Result
1993	Arsenal	v	Sheffield Wednesday	2–1
1994	Aston Villa	v	Manchester United	3–1
1995	Liverpool	v	Bolton Wanderers	2–1

47 ● COCA-COLA CUP 1994–1995

First Round (Two Legs)

AFC Bournemouth	2;1	v	Northampton Town	0;0
Barnet	4;1	v	Leyton Orient	0;1
Blackpool	1;2	v	Chesterfield	2;4
Bradford City	2;2	v	Grimsby Town	1;1
Brighton & Hove Albion	2;3	v	Wycombe Wanderers	1;1
Bristol Rovers	1;1	v	Port Vale	3;1
Burnley	1;2	v	York City	0;2
Bury	2;1	v	Hartlepool United	0;5
Cardiff City	1;2	v	Torquay United	0;4
Colchester United	0;0	v	Brentford	2;2
Crewe Alexandra	2;0	v	Wigan Athletic	2;0*
Darlington	2;0	v	Barnsley	2;0*
Doncaster Rovers	2;1	v	Wrexham	4;1
Exeter City	2;0	v	Swansea City	2;2
Gillingham	0;0	v	Reading	1;3
Hereford United	0;1	v	West Bromwich Albion	1;0
Hull City	2;0	v	Scarborough	1;2
Lincoln City	2;3	v	Chester City	0;2
Luton Town	1;1	v	Fulham	1;1†
Oxford United	3;1	v	Peterborough United	1;0
Portsmouth	2;3	v	Cambridge United	0;2
Preston North End	1;1	v	Stockport County	1;4
Rochdale	1;0	v	Mansfield Town	2;1
Rotherham United	1;1	v	Carlisle United	0;3
Scunthorpe United	2;0	v	Hartlepool United	1;3
Shrewsbury Town	2;0	v	Birmingham City	1;2
Southend United	0;0	v	Watford	0;1
Walsall	4;1	v	Plymouth Argyle	0;2

Second Round (Two Legs)

Aston Villa	5;3	v	Wigan Athletic	0;0
Barnet	1;1	v	Manchester City	0;4
Blackburn Rovers	2;1	v	Birmingham City	0;1
Brighton & Hove Albion	1;2	v	Leicester City	0;0
Bristol City	0;0	v	Notts County	3;1
Carlisle United	0;0	v	Queens Park Rangers	1;2
Chelsea	1;1	v	AFC Bournemouth	0;0
Chesterfield	1;1	v	Wolverhampton Wanderers	3;1
Everton	2;1	v	Portsmouth	3;1
Fulham	3;0	v	Stoke City	2;1*
Hartlepool United	0;0	v	Arsenal	5;2
Huddersfield Town	0;0	v	Southampton	1;4
Ipswich Town	0;0	v	Bolton Wanderers	3;1
Leeds United	0;0	v	Mansfield Town	1;0
Lincoln City	1;0	v	Crystal Palace	0;3
Liverpool	2;4	v	Burnley	0;1
Millwall	2;1	v	Sunderland	1;1
Newcastle United	2;1	v	Barnsley	1;0
Norwich City	3;0	v	Swansea City	0;1
Nottingham Forest	2;0	v	Hereford United	1;0
Oxford United	1;0	v	Oldham Athletic	1;1
Port Vale	1;0	v	Manchester United	2;2

Reading	3;0	v	Derby County	1;2*
Scarborough	1;1	v	Middlesbrough	4;4
Sheffield Wednesday	2;1	v	Bradford City	1;1
Stockport County	1;0	v	Sheffield United	5;1
Swindon Town	1;4	v	Charlton Athletic	3;1
Tranmere Rovers	1;0	v	Brentford	0;0
Walsall	2;0	v	West Ham United	1;2
Watford	3;3	v	Tottenham Hotspur	6;2
Wimbledon	2;1	v	Torquay United	0;0
Wrexham	1;2	v	Coventry City	2;3

* won on away goals † won on penalty-kicks

Third Round (replays in italics)

Aston Villa	v	Middlesbrough	1–0
Blackburn Rovers	v	Coventry City	2–0
Brighton & Hove Albion	v	Swindon Town	1–1
Swindon Town	*v*	*Brighton & Hove Albion*	*4–1*
Liverpool	v	Stoke City	2–1
Mansfield Town	v	Millwall	0–2
Newcastle United	v	Manchester United	2–0
Notts County	v	Tottenham Hotspur	3–0
Oldham Athletic	v	Arsenal	0–0
Arsenal	*v*	*Oldham Athletic*	*2–0*
Portsmouth	v	Derby County	0–1
Queens Park Rangers	v	Manchester City	3–4
Sheffield United	v	Bolton Wanderers	1–2
Sheffield Wednesday	v	Southampton	1–0
Tranmere Rovers	v	Norwich City	1–1
Norwich City	*v*	*Tranmere Rovers*	*4–2*
West Ham United	v	Chelsea	1–0
Wimbledon	v	Crystal Palace	0–1
Wolverhampton Wanderers	v	Nottingham Forest	2–3

Fourth Round (replays in italics)

Arsenal	v	Sheffield Wednesday	2–0
Blackburn Rovers	v	Liverpool	1–3
Crystal Palace	v	Aston Villa	4–1
Manchester City	v	Newcastle United	1–1
Newcastle United	*v*	*Manchester City*	*0–2*
Norwich City	v	Notts County	1–0
Nottingham Forest	v	Millwall	0–2
Swindon Town	v	Derby County	2–1
West Ham United	v	Bolton Wanderers	1–3

Fifth Round (replays in italics)

Bolton Wanderers	v	Norwich City	1–0
Crystal Palace	v	Manchester City	4–0
Liverpool	v	Arsenal	1–0
Swindon Town	v	Millwall	3–1

Semi-Final (Two Legs)

| Liverpool | 1;1 | v | Crystal Palace | 0;0 |
| Swindon Town | 2;1 | v | Bolton Wanderers | 1;3 |

Final

| Liverpool | v | Bolton Wanderers | 2–1 |

48 ● FA WOMEN'S CUP FINAL 1995

Arsenal 3   Liverpool 2

In June 1993 The Football Association took over responsibility for women's football. The first "FA Women's Challenge Cup" attracted 147 entries and the final, played at Scunthorpe United FC, was won by Doncaster Belles. In the 1994–95 season the holders lost out to Arsenal at the semi-final stage and the North London team went on to win a thrilling final against Liverpool at Tranmere Rovers FC's Prenton Park ground.

Arsenal's status as the top side in the women's game was confirmed two days after their Cup Final success, when a 3–1 win at Red Star Southampton clinched the FA Women's Premier League (National Division) championship. The "double" winners' impressive League record at that stage was: played 16, won 16, goals for 55, goals against 8.

The Cup Final, watched by an appreciative 3,000 crowd, showed the women's game in its best light. There was skill and drama – and some spectacular goals. Classy Liverpool led twice in the match but they were beaten in the end by Marieanne Spacey's brilliant effort nine minutes from time. Marieanne was one of eight England squad members who were playing in the final and it was hoped that she would pack her shooting boots when flying off on World Cup duty in the summer.

Karen Burke, another international, ran onto Harper's pass on 25 minutes to shoot firmly home from 20 yards and put Liverpool in front. They almost went two up ten minutes later when Arsenal goalkeeper Cope had to acrobatically tip Harper's dipping shot over the bar. But on 36 minutes Arsenal drew level as Becky Lonergan netted with an opportunist effort after Pealling's high ball into the box.

Liverpool ended the first half deservedly in the lead once more, Burke firing in from long range, and continued after the break to provide the better passing moves. Then Lonergan levelled with a near-post header and, with Liverpool starting to tire, Spacey took centre stage to shimmy past three defenders and score with a fierce shot that won the Cup.

Arsenal: Cope, Pealling, Curley (Few), Slee, Wylie, Spry, Williams, Britton, Spacey, Lonergan, Churchman (Ball).

Liverpool: Davidson, Taylor, Thomas (Griffiths), Ryde, Easton, Gallimore, Burke, Oldham, Murray, Harper, Hewitt (McQuiggan).

Referee: J. T. Winter (North Riding)

Guest of Honour: Lady Millichip

49 ● FA WOMEN'S CUP 1994–1995

First round – 18 September 1994

(Replays in italics)   *Results*

Blackburn Rovers	v	Brighouse	3–0
Middlesbrough	v	Wakefield	3–0
Huddersfield Town	v	Newcastle	12–0
Wigginton Grasshoppers	v	Oakland Rangers	2–3
Grimsby	v	Bradford City	
(walkover for Bradford City LFC, Grimsby LFC withdrawn)			
City Roses	v	Barnsley	2–5
Preston Rangers	v	Kilnhurst	6–1
South Lakes	v	South Shields	0–6
Sheffield Hallam United	v	Vernon–Carus	5–0
Amble Town	v	Cleveland	0–1
Manchester Belle Vue	v	Manchester City	4–1
Bolton	v	Manchester United	1–4
Rochdale	v	Wigan	1–7
Stockport	v	Tranmere Rovers	1–5
Liverpool Feds	v	Warrington Town	2–5
Stockport County	v	Colls	7–0
Oldham Athletic	v	Port Vale	7–2
Bangor City Girls	v	Leek Town	1–3
Radcliffe Borough	v	Chester City	7–0
Haslingden	v	Wrexham	5–1
Leicester City	v	Birmingham City	3–4
Derby City	v	Chesterfield	4–5
Derby County	v	Rugby	3–1
Pye	v	Calverton MW	0–2
Nettleham	v	Sparta Nottingham	5–0
Rainworth Miners Welfare	v	Notts County	0–2
Peterborough Diamonds	v	Highfield Rangers	0–11
Milton Keynes Athletic	v	Leyton Orient	0–7
Enfield	v	St Germaine	3–3
St Germaine	*v*	*Enfield*	*2–3*
Charlton	v	Milton Keynes United	11–1
Dunstable	v	Mill Hill United	4–6
Queens Park Rangers	v	Redbridge Wanderers	8–1
Fulham	v	Leighton Linslade	7–1
Clapton Orient	v	Slough Town	3–4
Barnet	v	Bedford Belles	1–5
Harlow Town	v	Clacton	3–1
Watford	v	Wycombe Wanderers	6–0
Collier Row	v	Colchester	5–1
Farnborough	v	Teynham Gunners	9–1
Havant	v	St Georges	2–6
Abbey Rangers	v	Binfield	0–7
Pagham	v	Hassocks	4–3
Carterton Town	v	Crowborough Athletic	0–2
Gosport Borough	v	Sutton Athletic	7–2
Comets	v	Eastleigh	0–9
Sittingbourne	v	Reading Royals	3–3
Reading Royals	*v*	*Sittingbourne*	*3–3*
(Reading Royals won on kicks from the penalty mark, 4–2)			
Isle of Wight	v	Surbiton Town	0–6

(Replays in italics)

Chailey Mavericks	v	Chislehurst United	
(walkover for Chailey Mavericks – Chislehurst United amalgamated with Charlton)			
Edenbridge Town	v	Newbury	0–7
Whitehawk	v	Palace Eagles	5–0
Worthing	v	Portsmouth	0–4
Gillingham Girls	v	Lambeth	1–6
Plymouth Pilgrims	v	Cheltenham YMCA	4–2
Swindon Town Spitfires	v	Bournemouth	3–1
Yate Town	v	Torquay United	0–6
Worcester City	v	Exeter Rangers	8–2
Clevedon Town	v	Gloucester Greyhounds	8–1
Dorchester	v	Truro City	
(walkover for Truro City – Dorchester LFC withdrawn)			
Brislington	v	Southampton	1–6
Frome	v	Sturminster Newton	10–1
Bristol Rovers	v	Bristol City	
(walkover for Bristol City LFC – Bristol Rovers LFC withdrawn)			
Swindon Town	v	Weymouth	8–0
Cardiff Institute	v	Tongwynlais	1–3

5 Clubs receiving byes to the Second Round

Colchester Royals	Inter Cardiff	Newsham	Reading	Wilford

Second round – 16 October 1994

Huddersfield Town	v	Barnsley	16–0
Haslingden	v	Bronte	0–5
Wigan	v	Bradford City	2–0
Preston Rangers	v	Middlesbrough	5–2
Oaklands Rangers	v	Radcliffe Borough	1–7
Oldham Athletic	v	Blackburn Rovers	5–1
South Shields	v	Manchester Belle Vue	0–11
Sheffield Hallam United	v	Cowgate Kestrels	2–6
Newsham	v	St Helens/Garswood	3–4
Tranmere Rovers	v	Cleveland	8–0
Warrington Town	v	Manchester United	3–4
Wilford	v	Birmingham City	
(walkover for Birmingham City – Wilford withdrawn)			
Stockport County	v	Calverton MW	1–2
Leek Town	v	Nottingham Argyle	1–4
Bedford Belles	v	Sheffield Wednesday	0–2
Highfield Rangers	v	Solihull Borough	2–3
Chesterfield	v	Villa Aztecs	2–5
Nettleham	v	Kidderminster Harriers	1–6
Notts County	v	Derby County	7–0
Brighton & Hove Albion	v	Reading	14–0
St Georges	v	Surbiton Town	1–2
Colchester Royals	v	Pagham	3–1
Whitehawk	v	Queens Park Rangers	7–0
Harlow Town	v	Watford	2–0
Berkhamsted & Hemel	v	Epsom & Ewell	9–1
Reading Royals	v	Langford	2–4
Leyton Orient	v	Slough Town	25–0
Town & County	v	Chailey Mavericks	22–0
Lambeth	v	Binfield	1–0
Collier Row	v	Enfield	0–2

(Replays in italics)   *Results*

Crowborough Athletic	v	Wimbledon	0 – 7
Mill Hill United	v	Horsham	0 – 1
Fulham	v	Ipswich Town	2 – 5
Maidstone Tigresses	v	Charlton	2 – 1
Brentford	v	Farnborough	6 – 3
Bristol	v	Tongwynlais	

(walkover for Tongwynlais – Bristol disbanded)

Clevedon Town	v	Oxford United	0 – 9
Inter Cardiff	v	Plymouth Pilgrims	2 – 4
Swindon Town	v	Southampton	2 – 1
Portsmouth	v	Newbury	2 – 3
Worcester City	v	Frome	4 – 3
Gosport Borough	v	Bristol City	1 – 8
Swindon Town Spitfires	v	Truro City	3 – 4
Torquay United	v	Eastleigh	4 – 1

Third round – 13 November 1994

Villa Aztecs	v	Huddersfield Town	4 – 4
Huddersfield Town	*v*	*Villa Aztecs*	*4 – 0*

(Match ordered to be replayed – Huddersfield Town played an ineligible player)

Preston Rangers	v	Cowgate Kestrels	1 – 4
Notts County	v	Nottingham Argyle	4 – 2
Oldham Athletic	v	Birmingham City	2 – 1
Wigan	v	Manchester United	4 – 1
Tranmere Rovers	v	Sheffield Wednesday	5 – 5
Sheffield Wednesday	*v*	*Tranmere Rovers*	*2 – 5*
St Helens/Garswood	v	Bronte	4 – 2
Radcliffe Borough	v	Calverton MW	3 – 6
Manchester Belle Vue	v	Solihull Borough	3 – 1
Berkhamsted & Hemel	v	Wimbledon	3 – 4
Maidstone Tigresses	v	Langford	2 – 0
Town & County	v	Brentford	3 – 4
Brighton & Hove Albion	v	Whitehawk	5 – 1
Leyton Orient	v	Lambeth	6 – 1
Enfield	v	Colchester Royals	6 – 1
Harlow Town	v	Surbiton Town	0 – 1
Ipswich Town	v	Horsham	0 – 0
Horsham	*v*	*Ipswich Town*	*0 – 5*
Plymouth Pilgrims	v	Tongwynlais	3 – 1
Oxford United	v	Torquay United	8 – 1
Bristol City	v	Kidderminster Harriers	7 – 1
Truro City	v	Worcester City	2 – 2
Worcester City	*v*	*Truro City*	*2 – 5*
Swindon Town	v	Newbury	3 – 4

Fourth round – 4 December 1994

Brentford	v	Red Star Southampton	2 – 2
Red Star Southampton	*v*	*Brentford*	*2 – 1*
Huddersfield Town	v	Ipswich Town	7 – 3
Tranmere Rovers	v	Leasowe Pacific	1 – 3
Newbury	v	Notts County	1 – 2
St Helens/Garswood	v	Oxford United	2 – 1
Leyton Orient	v	Enfield	7 – 0
Wolverhampton Wanderers	v	Millwall Lionesses	0 – 2

Doncaster Belles	v	Truro City	6–0
Liverpool	v	Surbiton Town	8–0
Wimbledon	v	Cowgate Kestrels	2–0
Ilkeston Town Rangers	v	Brighton & Hove Albion	5–1
Oldham Athletic	v	Croydon	1–7
Manchester Belle Vue	v	Wigan	2–3
Bristol City	v	Plymouth Pilgrims	6–2
Arsenal	v	Maidstone Tigresses	3–0
Calverton MW	v	Wembley	0–12

Fifth round – 15 January 1995

Arsenal	v	Leasowe Pacific	3–1
Liverpool	v	Notts County	5–0
Huddersfield Town	v	Ilkeston Town Rangers	3–1
Leyton Orient	v	Red Star Southampton	3–1
Bristol City	v	Millwall Lionesses	3–2
Wimbledon	v	Croydon	0–5
Wembley	v	Doncaster Belles	3–3
Doncaster Belles	*v*	*Wembley*	*2–1*
Wigan	v	St Helens/Garswood	1–3

Sixth round – 12 February 1995

Liverpool	v	Croydon	3–0
Leyton Orient	v	Arsenal	1–8
Bristol City	v	Huddersfield Town	4–3
Doncaster Belles	v	St Helens/Garswood	4–0

Semi-Finals – 19 March 1995

Doncaster Belles	v	Arsenal	1–3
(at Rotherham United FC)			
Bristol City	v	Liverpool	0–5
(at Mangotsfield United FC)			

50 ● FA WOMEN'S PREMIER LEAGUE – FINAL TABLES 1994–1995

National Division

	P	W	D	L	F	A	GD	Pts
Arsenal	18	17	1	0	60	8	+52	52
Liverpool	18	12	3	3	58	17	+41	39
Doncaster Belles	18	12	2	4	56	24	+32	38
Croydon	18	9	2	7	42	24	+18	29
Wembley	18	8	3	7	34	17	+17	27
Leasowe Pacific	18	5	3	10	36	47	−11	18
Ilkeston Town Rangers	18	4	3	11	20	49	−29	15
Millwall Lionesses	18	4	3	11	25	60	−35	15
Wolverhampton Wanderers	18	4	1	13	23	66	−43	13
Red Star Southampton	18	3	3	12	23	65	−42	12

Red Star Southampton relegated to Southern Division

Northern Division

	P	W	D	L	F	A	GD	Pts
Villa Aztecs	18	11	4	3	59	22	+37	37
Cowgate Kestrels	18	11	3	4	63	30	+33	36
St Helens/Garswood	18	11	3	4	44	26	+18	36
Sheffield Wednesday	18	9	4	5	38	27	+11	31
Ipswich Town	18	8	4	6	33	29	+4	28
Bronte	18	8	3	7	42	28	+14	27
Langford	18	8	0	10	30	40	−10	24
Kidderminster Harriers	18	4	2	12	24	57	−33	14
Nottingham Argyle	18	3	2	13	22	66	−44	11
Solihull Borough	18	4	1	13	22	52	−30	10*

* 3 points deducted

Result (4 June) – Play-Off Final
Tranmere 1   Huddersfield Town 4

Villa Aztecs promoted to National Division

Ipswich Town move to Southern Division

Huddersfield Town (Yorkshire & Humberside League) promoted to Northern Division

No relegation from Northern Division

Southern Division

	P	W	D	L	F	A	GD	Pts
Maidstone Tigresses	14	10	2	2	34	10	+24	32
Berkhamsted & Hemel	14	8	4	2	28	13	+15	28
Oxford United	14	7	3	4	28	28	—	24
Wimbledon	14	6	2	6	28	20	+8	20
Brighton & Hove Albion	14	6	1	7	20	30	−10	19
Town & County	14	5	3	6	22	25	−3	18
Brentford	14	3	4	7	29	41	−12	13
Horsham	14	0	3	11	16	38	−22	3

Result (4 June) – Play-Off Final
Whitehawk 0   Leyton Orient 1

Leyton Orient (Greater London League) promoted to Southern Division

No relegation from Southern Division

51 ● FIFA WORLD CHAMPIONSHIP FOR WOMEN'S FOOTBALL – SWEDEN '95

Date	Venue	Match	Result
1st Phase			
5.6.95	Helsingborg	Sweden v Brazil	0–1
	Karlstad	Germany v Japan	1–0
6.6.95	Karlstad	Norway v Nigeria	8–0
	Helsingborg	England v Canada	3–2
	Gavle	USA v China PR	3–3
	Vasteras	Denmark v Australia	5–0
7.6.95	Helsingborg	Sweden v Germany	3–2
	Karlstad	Brazil v Japan	1–2
8.6.95	Karlstad	Norway v England	2–0
	Helsingborg	Nigeria v Canada	3–3
	Gavle	USA v Denmark	2–0
	Vasteras	China PR v Australia	4–2
9.6.95	Vasteras	Sweden v Japan	2–0
	Karlstad	Brazil v Germany	1–6
10.6.95	Gavle	Norway v Canada	7–0
	Karlstad	Nigeria v England	2–3
	Helsingborg	USA v Australia	4–1
	Vasteras	China PR v Denmark	3–1
Quarter-Finals			
13.6.95	Vasteras	Germany v England	3–0
	Helsingborg	China PR v Sweden	1–1*
	Gavle	USA v Japan	4–0
	Karlstad	Norway v Denmark	3–1
Semi-Finals			
15.6.95	Helsingborg	Germany v China PR	1–0
	Vasteras	USA v Norway	0–1
Match for 3rd/4th place			
17.6.95	Gavle	China PR v USA	0–2
Final			
18.6.95	Stockholm	Norway v Germany	2–0

*China won 4–3 on penalties

52 ● FA SUNDAY CUP WINNERS 1965–1995

Year	Venue	Winners		Runners-up	Result
1965		London	v	Staffordshire	6–2†
1966	Dudley	Unique United	v	Aldridge Fabrications	1–0
1967	Hendon	Carlton United	v	Stoke Works	2–0
1968	Cambridge	Drovers	v	Brook United	2–0
1969	Romford	Leigh Park	v	Loke United	3–1
1970	Corby	Vention United	v	Unique United	1–0
1971	Leamington	Beacontree Rovers	v	Saltley United	2–0
1972	Dudley	Newton Unity	v	Springfield Colts	4–0
1973	Spennymoor	Carlton United	v	Wear Valley	2–1*
1974	Birmingham	Newton Unity	v	Brentford East	3–0
1975	High Wycombe	Fareham Town Centipedes	v	Players Athletic Engineers	1–0
1976	Spennymoor	Brandon United	v	Evergreen	2–1
1977	Spennymoor	Langley Park RH	v	Newton Unity	2–0
1978	Nuneaton	Arras	v	Lion Rangers	2–2
	Bishop's Stortford	Arras	v	Lion Rangers	2–1
1979	Southport	Lobster	v	Carlton United	3–2
1980	Letchworth	Fantail	v	Twin Foxes	1–0
1981	Birkenhead	Fantail	v	Mackintosh	1–0
1982	Hitchin	Dingle Rail	v	Twin Foxes	2–1
1983	Walthamstow	Eagle	v	Lee Chapel North	2–1
1984	Runcorn	Lee Chapel North	v	Eagle	1–1
	Dagenham	Lee Chapel North	v	Eagle	4–3*
1985	Norwich	Hobbies	v	Avenue	1–1
	Birkenhead	Hobbies	v	Avenue	2–2
	Nuneaton	Hobbies	v	Avenue	2–1
1986	Birkenhead	Avenue	v	Glenn Sports	1–0
1987	Birmingham	Lodge Cottrell	v	Avenue	1–0*
1988	Newcastle	Nexday	v	Sunderland Humb Plains	2–0
1989	Stockport	Almithak	v	East Levenshulme	3–1
1990	West Bromwich	Humbledon Plains Farm	v	Marston Sports	2–1
1991	Wigan	Nicosia	v	Ouzavich	3–2*
1992	Reading	Theale	v	Marston Sports	3–2
1993	Chester	Seymour	v	Bedfont Sunday	1–0
1994	Woking	Ranelagh Sports	v	Hartlepool Lion Hotel	2–0
1995	Hull	St Joseph's (Luton)	v	B&A Scaffolding	2–1

* *after extra time*
† *two legs*

53 ● FA SUNDAY CUP 1994–1995

First round – 30 October 1994

(Replays in italics) *Results*

Dock	v	Newfield	1–3
Croxteth & Gilmoss RBL	v	Humbledon Plains Farm	1–3
BRNESC	v	Albion Sports	2–2
Albion Sports	*v*	*BRNESC*	*1–3*
A3	v	Dudley & Weetslade	1–0
Lobster	v	Nenthead	4–1
Baildon Athletic	v	Mode Force Boulevard	1–1
Mode Force Boulevard	*v*	*Baildon Athletic*	*1–0*
Northwood	v	SDV	5–0
Clubmoor Nalgo	v	Etnaward	0–0
Etnaward	*v*	*Clubmoor Nalgo*	*3–0*
East Bowling Unity	v	Mitre	1–2
Boundary	v	Iron Bridge	
(walkover for Boundary – Iron Bridge withdrawn)			
Sandon	v	Hartlepool Staincliffe Hotel	3–2
Waterloo Social Club Blyth	v	Littlewoods Athletic	2–3
Seaton Sluice SC	v	Britannia	1–1
Britannia	*v*	*Seaton Sluice SC*	*3–2*
Queens Park	v	Stockton Roseworth Social	3–2
Salerno	v	Fiddlers Horse 93	7–2
Townley	v	Bolton Woods	5–0
Cork & Bottle	v	Walford Maritime	3–1
Almithak	v	Poets Corner	2–0
Egerton Boys	v	Norwich Busmen	1–1
Norwich Busmen	*v*	*Egerton Boys*	*0–3*
Slade Celtic	v	Clifton Albion	2–1
Elliott Bull & Tiger	v	Poringland Wanderers	5–1
Capel Plough	v	Grosvenor Park	2–1
Greyhound 83	v	Hammer	0–4
Dereham Hobbies	v	Brookvale Athletic	0–1
Leavesden Sports & Social	v	Melton Youth Old Boys	2–2
Melton Youth Old Boys	*v*	*Leavesden Sports & Social*	*2–0*
Hundred Acre	v	Leicester City Bus	0–1
Sawston Keys	v	Continental	2–1
St Joseph's (Sth Oxhey)	v	Altone Steels	0–2
Collier Row Supporters	v	London Boys	
(walkover for London Boys – Collier Row Supporters withdrawn)			
Sandwell	v	Kenwick Dynamo	0–3
Forest Athletic	v	Oakwood Sports	0–2
Fryerns Community	v	Caversham Park	10–0
Courage	v	BRSC Aidan	0–4
Olympic Star	v	Erdington Cosmos	0–2
Sheerness Steel United	v	Charlton Royal 89	3–0
Inter Royalle	v	Shell Club	2–3
Somersett Ambury V&E	v	Oxford Road Social	4–1
Hartley Wintney Sunday	v	Hanham Sunday	0–4
Biddestone (Sun)	v	Evergreen	3–4
Chequers (Herts)	v	Pitsea	2–3
Poole Town Social	v	British Rail SA	2–3
Park Royals	v	St Joseph's AFC (Bristol)	1–1

● 171

St Joseph's AFC (Bristol)		*v*	*Park Royals*	*1–0*
(at Stapleton FC)				
Coach & Horses		v	Gracelands	4–4
Gracelands		*v*	*Coach & Horses*	*3–4*
Vosper Sunday		v	Watford Labour Club	2–3

bye: Sacred Heart

List of 19 clubs receiving exemption

Allerton	Heathfield	Manfast Kirkby	Ouzavich	St Clements Hospital
B&A Scaffolding	Lebeq Tavern	Marston Sports	Ranelagh Sports (*withdrawn*)	St Josephs (Luton)
Bedfont Sunday	Lion Hotel	Nicosia	Reading Borough	Theale Sunday
Hartlepool Lion Hotel	Lodge Cottrell	Oakenshaw	Seymour	

Second round – 20 November 1994

Allerton	v	Cork & Bottle	4–2
Newfield	v	Boundary	2–1
Littlewoods Athletic	v	B&A Scaffolding	0–1
Mode Force Boulevard	v	A3	2–1
Sandon	v	Mitre	5–4
Hartlepool Lion Hotel	v	Salerno	2–0
Nicosia	v	Townley	3–4
Northwood	v	Queens Park AFC	2–4
Lobster	v	BRNESC	1–0
Etnaward	v	Humbledon Plains Farm	1–2
Brittannia	v	Lion Hotel	0–3
Almithak	v	Oakenshaw	2–4
Seymour	v	Manfast Kirkby	3–2
Leicester City Bus	v	Hammer	0–2
Brookvale Athletic	v	Egerton Boys	2–0
Heathfield	v	London Boys	2–3
Ouzavich	v	Sacred Heart	0–4
Lodge Cottrell	v	Fryerns Community	4–0
Marston Sports	v	Slade Celtic	1–3
St Clements Hospital	v	Capel Plough	1–1
Capel Plough	*v*	*St Clements Hospital*	*4–2*
Melton Youth Old Boys	v	St Josephs (Luton)	2–3
Erdington Cosmos	v	Kenwick Dynamo	1–4
Sawston Keys	v	Altone Steels	1–3
Oakwood Sports	v	Elliott Bull & Tiger	2–3
BRSC Aidan	v	Pitsea	0–0
Pitsea	*v*	*BRSC Aidan*	*0–1*
Shell Club	v	Park Royals	2–0
British Rail SA	v	Lebeq Tavern	1–3
Coach & Horses	v	Bedfont Sunday	2–1
Evergreen	v	Watford Labour Club	2–0
Theale Sunday	v	Hanham Sunday	3–0
Reading Borough	v	Somersett Ambury V&E	6–2

bye: Sheerness Steel United FC

Third round – 11 December 1994

Allerton	v	Townley	4–0

(Replays in italics)

Oakenshaw	v	Altone Steels	2–4
B&A Scaffolding	v	Slade Celtic	3–1
Brookvale Athletic	v	Humbledon Plains Farm	0–4
Lion Hotel	v	Newfield	0–2
Seymour	v	Mode Force Boulevard	1–3
Lobster	v	Hartlepool Lion Hotel	0–2
Sandon	v	Queens Park	0–2
Hammer	v	Kenwick Dynamo	3–0
Coach & Horses	v	Reading Borough	7–0
Sacred Heart	v	Theale Sunday	3–0
Sheerness Steel United	v	Shell Club	1–0
Lebeq Tavern	v	London Boys	4–1
Evergreen	v	Lodge Cottrell	0–2
BRSC Aidan	v	St Joseph's (Luton)	1–2
Capel Plough	v	Elliott Bull & Tiger	3–0

Fourth round – 22 January 1995

Hartlepool Lion Hotel	v	Allerton	0–1
Newfield	v	Altone Steels	6–1
Queens Park AFC	v	Humbledon Plains Farm	1–2
B&A Scaffolding	v	Mode Force Boulevard	4–2
Sheerness Steel United	v	Coach & Horses	2–0
Lebeq Tavern	v	Lodge Cottrell	1–0
Hammer	v	Capel Plough	1–2
Sacred Heart	v	St Joseph's (Luton)	0–1

Fifth round – 19 February 1995

Allerton	v	Newfield	3–1
B&A Scaffolding	v	Humbledon Plains Farm	4–0
Lebeq Tavern	v	St Joseph's (Luton)	1–3
Capel Plough	v	Sheerness Steel United	3–2

Semi-Finals – 2 April 1995

Allerton	v	B&A Scaffolding	0–2
(at Marine FC)			
Capel Plough	v	St Joseph's (Luton)	0–0
(at Hadleigh United FC)			
St Joseph's (Luton)	*v*	*Capel Plough*	*1–1*
(at Arlesey Town FC)			

(St Joseph's (Luton) won on kicks from the penalty mark, 4–2)

54 ● FA CHARITY SHIELD WINNERS 1908–1994

Year	Winners		Runners–up	Result
1908	Manchester United	v	Queens Park Rangers	1–1
	Manchester United	*v*	*Queens Park Rangers*	*4–0*
1909	Newcastle United	v	Northampton Town	2–0
1910	Brighton and Hove Albion	v	Aston Villa	1–0
1911	Manchester United	v	Swindon Town	8–4
1912	Blackburn Rovers	v	Queens Park Rangers	2–1
1913	Professionals	v	Amateurs	7–2
1914–18		not played		
1920	West Bromwich Albion	v	Tottenham Hotspur	2–0
1921	Tottenham Hotspur	v	Burnley	2–0
1922	Huddersfield Town	v	Liverpool	1–0
1923	Professionals	v	Amateurs	2–0
1924	Professionals	v	Amateurs	3–1
1925	Amateurs	v	Professionals	6–1
1926	Amateurs	v	Professionals	6–3
1927	Cardiff City	v	Corinthians	2–1
1928	Everton	v	Blackburn Rovers	2–1
1929	Professionals	v	Amateurs	3–0
1930	Arsenal	v	Sheffield Wednesday	2–1
1931	Arsenal	v	West Bromwich Albion	1–0
1932	Everton	v	Newcastle United	5–3
1933	Arsenal	v	Everton	3–0
1934	Arsenal	v	Manchester City	4–0
1935	Sheffield Wednesday	v	Arsenal	1–0
1936	Sunderland	v	Arsenal	2–1
1937	Manchester City	v	Sunderland	2–0
1938	Arsenal	v	Preston North End	2–1
1939–47		not played		
1948	Arsenal	v	Manchester United	4–3
1949	Portsmouth	v	Wolverhampton Wanderers	1–1*
1950	World Cup Team	v	Canadian Touring Team	4–2
1951	Tottenham Hotspur	v	Newcastle United	2–1
1952	Manchester United	v	Newcastle United	4–2
1953	Arsenal	v	Blackpool	3–1
1954	Wolverhampton Wanderers	v	West Bromwich Albion	4–4*
1955	Chelsea	v	Newcastle United	3–0
1956	Manchester United	v	Manchester City	1–0
1957	Manchester United	v	Aston Villa	4–0
1958	Bolton Wanderers	v	Wolverhampton Wanderers	4–1
1959	Wolverhampton Wanderers	v	Nottingham Forest	3–1
1960	Burnley	v	Wolverhampton Wanderers	2–2*
1961	Tottenham Hotspur	v	FA XI	3–2
1962	Tottenham Hotspur	v	Ipswich Town	5–1
1963	Everton	v	Manchester United	4–0
1964	Liverpool	v	West Ham United	2–2*
1965	Manchester United	v	Liverpool	2–2*
1966	Liverpool	v	Everton	1–0
1967	Manchester United	v	Tottenham Hotspur	3–3*
1968	Manchester City	v	West Bromwich Albion	6–1
1969	Leeds United	v	Manchester City	2–1

Year	Winners		Runners–up	Result
1970	Everton	v	Chelsea	2–1
1971	Leicester City	v	Liverpool	1–0
1972	Manchester City	v	Aston Villa	1–0
1973	Burnley	v	Manchester City	1–0
1974	Liverpool	v	Leeds United	1–1†
1975	Derby County	v	West Ham United	2–0
1976	Liverpool	v	Southampton	1–0
1977	Liverpool	v	Manchester United	0–0*
1978	Nottingham Forest	v	Ipswich Town	5–0
1979	Liverpool	v	Arsenal	3–1
1980	Liverpool	v	West Ham United	1–0
1981	Aston Villa	v	Tottenham Hotspur	2–2*
1982	Liverpool	v	Tottenham Hotspur	1–0
1983	Manchester United	v	Liverpool	2–0
1984	Everton	v	Liverpool	1–0
1985	Everton	v	Manchester United	2–0
1986	Everton	v	Liverpool	1–1*
1987	Everton	v	Coventry City	1–0
1988	Liverpool	v	Wimbledon	2–1
1989	Liverpool	v	Arsenal	1–0
1990	Liverpool	v	Manchester United	1–1*
1991	Arsenal	v	Tottenham Hotspur	0–0*
1992	Leeds United	v	Liverpool	4–3
1993	Manchester United	v	Arsenal	1–1†
1994	Manchester United	v	Blackburn Rovers	2–0

each club retained Shield for six months   † *won on penalty-kicks*

55 ● LEAGUE ATTENDANCES

Season	Matches Played	Total (Millions)	Div. 1	Div. 2	Div. 3(S)	Div. 3(N)
1946–47	1848	35.6	15.0	11.1	5.7	3.9
1947–48	1848	40.3	16.7	12.3	6.7	4.6
1948–49	1848	41.3	17.9	11.4	7.0	5.0
1949–50	1848	40.5	17.3	11.7	7.1	4.4
1950–51	2028	39.6	16.7	10.8	7.4	4.8
1951–52	2028	39.0	16.1	11.1	7.0	4.9
1952–53	2028	37.1	16.1	9.7	6.7	4.7
1953–54	2028	36.2	16.2	9.5	6.3	4.2
1954–55	2028	34.1	15.1	9.0	6.0	4.1
1955–56	2028	33.2	14.1	9.1	5.7	4.3
1956–57	2028	32.7	13.8	8.7	5.6	4.6
1957–58	2028	33.6	14.5	8.7	6.1	4.3
1958–59	2028	33.6	14.7	8.6	5.9	4.3
1959–60	2028	32.5	14.4	8.4	5.7	4.0
1960–61	2028	28.6	12.9	7.0	4.8	3.9
1961–62	2015	28.0	12.1	7.5	5.2	3.3
1962–63	2028	28.9	12.5	7.8	5.3	3.3
1963–64	2028	28.5	12.5	7.6	5.4	3.0
1964–65	2028	27.6	12.7	7.0	4.4	3.5
1965–66	2028	27.2	12.5	6.9	4.8	3.0
1966–67	2028	28.9	14.2	7.3	4.4	3.0
1967–68	2028	30.1	15.3	7.5	4.0	3.4
1968–69	2028	29.4	14.6	7.4	4.3	3.1
1969–70	2028	29.6	14.9	7.6	4.2	2.9
1970–71	2028	28.2	14.0	7.1	4.4	2.8
1971–72	2028	28.7	14.5	6.8	4.7	2.7
1972–73	2028	25.4	14.0	5.6	3.7	2.1
1973–74	2027	25.0	13.1	6.3	3.4	2.2
1974–75	2028	25.6	12.6	7.0	4.1	2.0
1975–76	2028	24.9	13.1	5.8	3.9	2.1
1976–77	2028	26.2	13.6	6.3	4.2	2.1
1977–78	2028	25.4	13.3	6.5	3.3	2.3
1978–79	2028	24.5	12.7	6.2	3.4	2.3
1979–80	2028	24.6	12.2	6.1	4.0	2.3
1980–81	2028	21.9	11.4	5.2	3.6	1.7
1981–82	2028	20.0	10.4	4.8	2.8	2.0
1982–83	2028	18.8	9.3	5.0	2.9	1.6
1983–84	2028	18.3	8.7	5.3	2.7	1.5
1984–85	2028	17.8	9.8	4.0	2.7	1.4
1985–86	2028	16.5	9.0	3.6	2.5	1.4
1986–87	2028	17.4	9.1	4.2	2.4	1.7
1987–88	2030	18.0	8.1	5.3	2.8	1.8
1988–89	2036	18.5	7.8	5.8	3.0	1.8
1989–90	2036	19.5	7.9	6.9	2.8	1.9
1990–91	2036	19.5	8.6	6.3	2.8	1.8
1991–92	2064*	20.5	10.0	5.8	3.0	1.7
1992–93	2028	20.7	9.8	5.9	3.5	1.5
1993–94	2028	21.7	10.6	6.5	3.0	1.6
1994–95	2028	21.8	11.2	6.0	3.0	1.6

*NOTE: From Season 1958–59 onwards for Div. 3(S) read Div. 3 and for Div. 3(N) read Div. 4.
From Season 1992–93 onwards for Div. 1 read FA Premier League.*
* Figures include matches played by Aldershot

56 ● THE FOOTBALL ASSOCIATION FIXTURE PROGRAMME 1995–96

* closing dates of rounds † blank weekends for FA Premier League Fixtures

August 1995

9	Wednesday	Euro Competitions Preliminary Round – 1st leg
12	Saturday	Commencement of Football League Season
13	Sunday	Littlewoods Pools FA Charity Shield – Wembley Stadium
16	Wednesday	International Date
		FL Coca-Cola Cup 1st Round – 1st Leg
19	Saturday	Commencement of FA Premier League Season
23	Wednesday	European Competitions Preliminary Round – 2nd Leg
		FL Coca-Cola Cup 1st Round – 2nd Leg
26	Saturday	FA Cup Sponsored by Littlewoods Pools Preliminary Round
28	Monday	Bank Holiday

September 1995

2	Saturday†	FA Carlsberg Vase – 1st Round Qualifying (ex-Extra Preliminary Round)
		Portugal v England (U21)
6	Wednesday	England v Croatia (F)
9	Saturday	FA Cup Sponsored by Littlewoods Pools 1st Round Qualifying (144 ties)
		FA Youth Cup Extra Preliminary Round*
13	Wednesday	European Competitions 1st Round – 1st Leg
16	Saturday	FA Umbro Trophy Preliminary Round (*if required*)
		FA Youth Cup Preliminary Round (72 ties)*
17	Sunday	FA Women's Cup 1st Round (64 ties)
20	Wednesday	FL Coca-Cola Cup 2nd Round – 1st Leg
23	Saturday	FA Cup Sponsored by Littlewoods Pools 2nd Round Qualifying (72 ties)
24	Sunday	FA Sunday Cup Preliminary Round (*if required*)
27	Wednesday	European Competitions 1st Round – 2nd Leg
		FL Auto Windscreens Shield 1st Round – 1st Leg
30	Saturday	FA Carlsberg Vase 2nd Round Qualifying (160 ties) (*ex-Preliminary Round*)

October 1995

4	Wednesday	FL Coca-Cola Cup 2nd Round – Second Leg
7	Saturday†	FA Cup Sponsored by Littlewoods Pools 3rd Round Qualifying (36 ties)
		FA Youth Cup – 1st Round Qualifying (36 ties)*
10	Tuesday	Norway v England (U21)
11	Wednesday	Norway v England (F)
14	Saturday	FA Umbro Trophy 1st Round Qualifying (64 ties)
		FA County Youth Cup 1st Round (12 ties)*
15	Sunday	FA Women's Cup 2nd Round (44 ties)
18	Wednesday	European Competitions 2nd Round 1st Leg
		FL Auto Windscreens Shield 1st Round – 2nd Leg
21	Saturday	FA Cup Sponsored by Littlewoods Pools 4th Round Qualifying (28 ties)
		FA Youth Cup 2nd Round Qualifying (18 ties)
25	Wednesday	FL Coca-Cola Cup 3rd Round
28	Saturday	FA Carlsberg Vase 1st Round Proper (96 ties)
29	Sunday	FA Sunday Cup 1st Round

November 1995

1	Wednesday	European Competitions 2nd Round – 2nd Leg
4	Saturday	FA Umbro Trophy 2nd Round Qualifying (32 ties)
8	Wednesday	FL Coca-Cola Cup 3rd Round Possible Replays
		FL Auto Windscreens Shield 1st Round (3 ties)
11	Saturday†	FA Cup Sponsored by Littlewoods Pools 1st Round Proper (40 ties)
12	Sunday	FA Women's Cup – 3rd Road (22 ties)
14	Tuesday	England v Austria (U21)
15	Wednesday	England v Switzerland (F)
18	Saturday	FA Carlsberg Vase 2nd Round Proper (64 ties)
		FA Youth Cup 1st Round Proper (34 ties)*
19	Sunday	FA Sunday Cup 2nd Round (32 ties)
22	Wednesday	European Competitions 3rd Round – 1st Leg
		FA Cup Sponsored by Littlewoods Pools – 1st Round Possible Replays
25	Saturday	FA Umbro Trophy 3rd Round Qualifying (32 ties)
		FA County Youth Cup – 2nd Round (16 ties)*
29	Wednesday	FL Coca-Cola Cup 4th Round
		Fl Auto Windscreens Shield 2nd Round

December 1995

2	Saturday	FA Cup Sponsored by Littlewoods Pools 2nd Round Proper (20 ties)
3	Sunday	FA Women's Cup 4th Round (16 ties)
6	Wednesday	European Competitions 3rd Round – 2nd Leg
9	Saturday	FA Carlsberg Vase 3rd Round Proper (32 ties)
		FA Youth Cup 2nd Round Proper (32 ties)*
10	Sunday	FA Sunday Cup 3rd Round (16 ties)
12	Tuesday	Draw for Qualifying Competition of 1998 World Cup
13	Wednesday	International Date
		FA Cup Sponsored by Littlewoods Pools 2nd Round Possible Replays
17	Sunday	Euro '96 Draw
20	Wednesday	FL Coca-Cola Cup 4th Round Possible Replays

January 1996

6	Saturday	FA Cup Sponsored by Littlewoods Pools 3rd Round Proper (32 ties)
10	Wednesday	FL Coca-Cola Cup 5th Round
		FL Auto Windscreens Shield – Area Quarter-Finals
13	Saturday	FA Carlsberg Vase 4th Round Proper (16 ties)
		FA Youth Cup 3rd Round Proper (16 ties)*
		FA County Youth Cup 3rd Round (8 ties)*
14	Sunday	FA Sunday Cup 4th Round (8 ties)
17	Wednesday	FA Cup Sponsored by Littlewoods Pools 3rd Round Possible Replays
20	Saturday	FA Umbro Trophy 1st Round Proper (32 ties)
21	Sunday	FA Women's Cup 5th Round (8 ties)
24	Wednesday	International Date (not UEFA)
		FL Coca-Cola Cup 5th Round Possible Replays
27	Saturday	FA Cup Sponsored by Littlewoods Pools 4th Round Proper (16 ties)
31	Wednesday	FL Auto Windscreens Shield – Area Semi-Finals

February 1996

3	Saturday	FA Carlsberg Vase 5th Round Proper (8 ties)
7	Wednesday	International Date (not UEFA)
		FA Cup Sponsored by Littlewoods Pools 4th Round Possible Replays
10	Saturday	FA Umbro Trophy 2nd Round Proper (16 ties)
11	Sunday	FA Sunday Cup 5th Round (4 ties)
		FL Coca-Cola Cup Semi-Final – 1st Leg
14	Wednesday	FL Coca-Cola Cup Semi-Final – 1st Leg

17	Saturday	FA Cup Sponsored by Littlewoods Pools 5th Round Proper (8 ties)
		FA Youth Cup 4th Round Proper (8 ties)*
		FA County Youth Cup 4th Round (4 ties)*
18	Sunday	FA Women's Cup – 6th Round (4 ties)
21	Wednesday	FL Coca-Cola Cup Semi-Final – 2nd Leg
24	Saturday	FA Carlsberg Vase 6th Round Proper (4 ties)
25	Sunday	FL Coca-Cola Cup Semi-Final – 2nd Leg
28	Wednesday	FA Cup Sponsored by Littlewoods Pools 5th Round Possible Replays
		FL Auto Windscreens Shield Area Final – 1st Leg

March 1996

2	Saturday	FA Umbro Trophy 3rd Round Proper (8 ties)
6	Wednesday	European Competitions Quarter-Finals – 1st Leg
9	Saturday	FA Cup Sponsored by Littlewoods Pools 6th Round Proper (4 ties)
		FA Youth Cup 5th Round Proper (4 ties)*
13	Wednesday	FL Auto Windscreens Shield Area Final – 2nd Leg
16	Saturday	FA Carlsberg Vase Semi-Final – 1st Leg
		FA County Youth Cup Semi-Final*
17	Sunday	FA Sunday Cup Semi-Finals
20	Wednesday	European Competitions Quarter-Finals – 2nd Leg
		FA Cup Sponsored by Littlewoods Pools 6th Round Possible Replays
23	Saturday	FA Umbro Trophy 4th Round Proper (4 ties)
		FA Vase Semi-Final – 2nd Leg
24	Sunday	FL Coca-Cola Cup – Final Tie – Wembley Stadium
		FA Women's Cup Semi-Finals
27	Wednesday	International Date
		FA Carlsberg Vase Semi-Final Possible Replays
31	Sunday	FA Cup Sponsored by Littlewoods Pools Semi-Finals

April 1996

3	Wednesday	European Competitions Semi-Finals – 1st Leg
		FA Cup Sponsored by Littlewoods Pools Semi-Finals Possible Replays
6	Saturday	FA Youth Cup Semi-Final*
8	Monday	Easter Monday
13	Saturday	FA Umbro Trophy Semi-Final – 1st Leg
14	Sunday	FL Auto Windscreens Shield Final Tie – Wembley Stadium
17	Wednesday	European Competitions Semi-Finals – 2nd Leg
20	Saturday†	FA Umbro Trophy Semi-Final – 2nd Leg
24	Wednesday	International Date
		FA Umbro Trophy Semi-Final Possible Replays
27	Saturday	FA County Youth Cup Final (*fixed date*)
28	Sunday	FA Women's Cup Final Tie (*venue to be decided*)

May 1996

1	Wednesday	UEFA Cup Final – 1st Leg
4	Saturday	Final matches in FA Premier & Football Leagues
5	Sunday	FA Sunday Cup Final Tie (*venue to be decided*)
8	Wednesday	European Cup Winners' Cup Final (*venue to be decided*)
11	Saturday	FA Cup Sponsored by Littlewoods Pools Final Tie – Wembley Stadium
		FA Youth Cup Final*
12	Sunday	FA Carlsberg Vase Final Tie – Wembley Stadium
		FL Play-off Semi-Final – 1st Leg
14	Tuesday	FA Carlsberg Vase Final Tie Possible Replay
15	Wednesday	UEFA Cup Final – 2nd Leg
		FL Play-off Semi-Final – 2nd Leg
16	Thursday	FA Cup Sponsored by Littlewoods Pools Final Tie Possible Replay (*prov*)
19	Sunday	FA Umbro Trophy Final Tie – Wembley Stadium

22	Wednesday	European Champion Clubs' Cup Final
23	Thursday	FA Umbro Trophy Final Tie Possible Replay
25	Saturday	FL Third Division Play-Off Final – Wembley Stadium
26	Sunday	FL Second Division Play-Off Final – Wembley Stadium
27	Monday	FL First Division Play-Off Final – Wembley Stadium

EURO 96 – JUNE

First Round

8	Saturday	Wembley Stadium	3.00
9	Sunday	Leeds United FC	2.30
		Manchester United FC	5.00
		Sheffield Wednesday FC	7.30
10	Monday	Aston Villa FC	4.30
		Newcastle United FC	7.30
11	Tuesday	Liverpool FC	4.30
		Nottingham Forest FC	7.30
13	Thursday	Aston Villa FC	7.30
		Newcastle United FC	4.30
14	Friday	Liverpool FC	7.30
		Nottingham Forest FC	4.30
15	Saturday	Wembley Stadium	3.00
		Leeds United FC	6.00
16	Sunday	Manchester United FC	3.00
		Sheffield Wednesday FC	6.00
18	Tuesday	Aston Villa FC	7.30
		Newcastle United FC	4.30
		Wembley Stadium	7.30
		Leeds United FC	4.30
19	Wednesday	Liverpool FC	7.30
		Nottingham Forest FC	4.30
		Manchester United FC	7.30
		Sheffield Wednesday FC	4.30

Quarter-Finals

22	Saturday	Liverpool FC	6.30
		Wembley Stadium	3.00
23	Sunday	Manchester United FC	3.00
		Aston Villa FC	6.30

Semi-Finals

26	Wednesday	Manchester United FC	4.00
		Wembley Stadium	7.30

Final

30	Sunday	Wembley Stadium	7.00

56 ● LEAGUE FIXTURES 1995–1996

Saturday, 12 August 1995

Endsleigh Insurance League Division 1

Birmingham City v Ipswich Town ....
Crystal Palace v Barnsley ....
Millwall v Grimsby Town ....
Oldham Athletic v Huddersfield Town ....
Portsmouth v Southend United ....
Stoke City v Reading ....
Sunderland v Leicester City ....
Tranmere Rovers v Wolverhampton Wanderers ...
Watford v Sheffield United ....
West Bromwich Albion v Charlton Athletic ....

Endsleigh Insurance League Division 2

Bradford City v A.F.C. Bournemouth ....
Bristol City v Blackpool ....
Burnley v Rotherham United ....
Carlisle United v Bristol Rovers ....
Hull City v Swindon Town ....
Oxford United v Chesterfield ....
Peterborough v Brighton and Hove
    United   Albion ....
Swansea City v Shrewsbury Town ....
Walsall v Stockport County ....
Wrexham v Notts. County ....
Wycombe Wanderers v Crewe Alexandra ....
York City v Brentford ....

Endsleigh Insurance League Division 3

Chester City v Hartlepool United ....
Colchester United v Plymouth Argyle ....
Doncaster Rovers v Scarborough ....
Exeter City v Darlington ....
Fulham v Mansfield Town ....
Gillingham v Wigan Athletic ....
Hereford United v Barnet ....
Leyton Orient v Torquay United ....
Northampton Town v Bury ....
Preston North End v Lincoln City ....
Rochdale v Cardiff City ....
Scunthorpe United v Cambridge United ....

Sunday, 13 August 1995

Endsleigh Insurance League Division 1

Derby County v Port Vale ....
Luton v Norwich City ....

Saturday, 19 August 1995

FA Carling Premiership

Aston Villa v Manchester United ....
Blackburn Rovers v Queens Park Rangers ....
Chelsea v Everton ....

Liverpool v Sheffield Wednesday ....
Manchester City v Tottenham Hotspur ....
Newcastle United v Coventry City ....
Southampton v Nottingham Forest ....
West Ham United v Leeds United ....
Wimbledon v Bolton Wanderers ....

Endsleigh Insurance League Division 1

Barnsley v Oldham Athletic ....
Charlton Athletic v Birmingham City ....
Grimsby Town v Portsmouth ....
Huddersfield Town v Watford ....
Ipswich Town v Crystal Palace ....
Leicester City v Stoke City ....
Norwich City v Sunderland ....
Port Vale v Millwall ....
Reading v Derby County ....
Sheffield United v Tranmere Rovers ....
Southend United v Luton Town ....

Endsleigh Insurance League Division 2

A.F.C. Bournemouth v Peterborough United ....
Blackpool v Wrexham ....
Brentford v Oxford United ....
Brighton and Hove Albion v Bradford City ....
Bristol Rovers v Swansea City ....
Chesterfield v Carlisle United ....
Notts. County v Wycombe Wanderers ....
Rotherham United v Hull City ....
Shrewsbury Town v Walsall ....
Stockport County v Burnley ....
Swindon Town v York City ....

Endsleigh Insurance League Division 3

Barnet v Colchester United ....
Bury v Chester City ....
Cambridge United v Hereford United ....
Cardiff City v Northampton Town ....
Darlington v Rochdale ....
Hartlepool United v Exeter City ....
Lincoln City v Gillingham ....
Mansfield Town v Leyton Orient ....
Plymouth Argyle v Preston North End ....
Scarborough v Fulham ....
Torquay United v Doncaster Rovers ....
Wigan Athletic v Scunthorpe United ....

Sunday, 20 August 1995

FA Carling Premiership

Arsenal v Middlesbrough ....

Endsleigh Insurance League Division 1

Wolverhampton v West Bromwich
    Wanderers   Albion ....

Monday, 21 August 1995

FA Carling Premiership

Leeds United v Liverpool ....

Tuesday, 22 August 1995

FA Carling Premiership

Bolton Wanderers v Newcastle United ....

Wednesday, 23 August 1995

FA Carling Premiership

Coventry City v Manchester City ....
Everton v Arsenal ....
Manchester United v West Ham United ....
Nottingham Forest v Chelsea ....
Queens Park Rangers v Wimbledon ....
Sheffield Wednesday v Blackburn Rovers ....
Tottenham Hotspur v Aston Villa ....

Saturday, 26 August 1995

FA Carling Premiership

Bolton Wanderers v Blackburn Rovers ....
Coventry City v Arsenal ....
Everton v Southampton ....
Leeds United v Aston Villa ....
Manchester United v Wimbledon ....
Middlesbrough v Chelsea ....
Nottingham Forest v West Ham United ....
Queens Park Rangers v Manchester City ....
Tottenham Hotspur v Liverpool ....

Endsleigh Insurance League Division 1

Birmingham City v Norwich City ....
Crystal Palace v Charlton Athletic ....
Derby County v Grimsby Town ....
Luton Town v Leicester City ....
Millwall v Southend United ....
Oldham Athletic v Sheffield United ....
Portsmouth v Reading ....
Sunderland v Wolverhampton Wanderers ....
Tranmere Rovers v Huddersfield Town ....
Watford v Barnsley ....
West Bromwich Albion v Ipswich Town ....

Endsleigh Insurance League Division 2

Bradford City v Shrewsbury Town ....
Bristol City v Stockport County ....
Burnley v Brentford ....
Carlisle United v Swindon Town ....
Hull City v Blackpool ....
Oxford United v Rotherham United ....
Peterborough United v Notts. County ....
Swansea City v Chesterfield ....
Walsall v Bristol Rovers ....
Wrexham v Brighton and Hove Albion ....
Wycombe Wanderers v A.F.C. Bournemouth ....
York City v Crewe Alexandra ....

Endsleigh Insurance League Division 3

Chester City v Plymouth Argyle ....
Colchester Untied v Lincoln City ....
Doncaster Rovers v Cardiff City ....
Exeter City v Scarborough ....
Fulham v Torquay United ....
Gillingham v Cambridge United ....
Hereford United v Bury ....
Leyton Orient v Darlington ....
Northampton Town v Mansfield Town ....
Preston North End v Wigan Athletic ....
Rochdale v Hartlepool United ....
Scunthorpe United v Barnet ....

Sunday, 27 August 1995

FA Carling Premiership

Sheffield Wednesday v Newcastle United ....

Endsleigh Insurance League Division 1

Stoke City v Port Vale ....

Monday, 28 August 1995

FA Carling Premiership

Blackburn Rovers v Manchester United ....

Endsleigh Insurance League Division 3

Lincoln City v Scunthorpe United ....

Tuesday, 29 August 1995

FA Carling Premiership

Arsenal v Nottingham Forest ....

Endsleigh Insurance League Division 1

Barnsley v Tranmere Rovers ....
Charlton Athletic v Watford ....
Grimsby Town v Luton Town ....
Ipswich Town v Stoke City ....
Port Vale v Sunderland ....
Reading v Millwall ....
Sheffield United v Crystal Palace ....
Southend United v West Bromwich Albion ....

Endsleigh Insurance League Division 2

A.F.C. Bournemouth v Wrexham ....
Blackpool v Peterborough United ....
Brentford v Hull City ....
Brighton and Hove Albion v Wycombe Wanderers
Bristol Rovers v Burnley ....
Chesterfield v York City ....
Crewe Alexandra v Walsall ....
Notts. County v Bradford City ....
Rotherham United v Carlisle United ....
Shrewsbury Town v Bristol City ....
Stockport County v Swansea City ....

Endsleigh Insurance League Division 3

Barnet v Gillingham ....
Bury v Preston North End ....
Cambridge United v Colchester United ....
Cardiff City v Exeter City ....
Darlington v Fulham ....
Hartlepool United v Northampton Town ....
Mansfield Town v Doncaster Rovers ....
Plymouth Argyle v Hereford United ....
Torquay United v Rochdale ....
Wigan Athletic v Chester City ....

Wednesday, 30 August 1995

FA Carling Premiership

Aston Villa v Bolton Wanderers ....
Chelsea v Coventry City ....
Liverpool v Queens Park Rangers ....
Manchester City v Everton ....
Newcastle United v Middlesbrough ....
Southampton v Leeds United ....
West Ham United v Tottenham Hotspur ....
Wimbledon v Sheffield Wednesday ....

Endsleigh Insurance League Division 1

Huddersfield Town v Birmingham City ....
Leicester City v Portsmouth ....
Norwich City v Oldham Athletic ....
Wolverhampton Wanderers v Derby County ....

Endsleigh Insurance League Division 2

Swindon Town v Oxford United ....

Endsleigh Insurance League Division 3

Scarborough v Leyton Orient ....

Saturday, 2 September 1995

Endsleigh Insurance League Division 1

Barnsley v Birmingham City ....
Charlton Athletic v Huddersfield Town ....
Crystal Palace v Tranmere Rovers ....
Grimsby Town v Watford ....
Ipswich Town v Sunderland ....
Leicester City v Wolverhampton Wanderers ....
Luton Town v Derby County ....
Norwich City v Port Vale ....
Portsmouth v Millwall ....
Southend United v Reading ....
Stoke City v Oldham Athletic ....
West Bromwich Albion v Sheffield United ....

Endsleigh Insurance League Division 2

A.F.C. Bournemouth v Rotherham United ....
Bradford City v Wycombe Wanderers ....
Brentford v Swindon Town ....
Brighton and Hove Albion v Notts. County ....
Bristol Rovers v Wrexham ....
Burnley v Walsall ....
Chesterfield v Hull City ....
Oxford United v York City ....

Peterborough United v Bristol City ....
Shrewsbury Town v Blackpool ....
Stockport County v Crewe Alexandra ....
Swansea City v Carlisle United ....

Endsleigh Insurance League Division 3

Barnet v Lincoln City ....
Bury v Plymouth Argyle ....
Chester City v Hereford United ....
Darlington v Cardiff City ....
Doncaster Rovers v Hartlepool United ....
Exeter City v Scunthorpe United ....
Gillingham v Colchester United ....
Leyton Orient v Fulham ....
Preston North End v Cambridge United ....
Rochdale v Northampton Town ....
Scarborough v Wigan Athletic ....
Torquay United v Mansfield Town ....

Saturday, 9 September 1995

FA Carling Premiership

Blackburn Rovers v Aston Villa ....
Bolton Wanderers v Middlesbrough ....
Coventry City v Nottingham Forest ....
Everton v Manchester United ....
Queens Park Rangers v Sheffield Wednesday ....
Southampton v Newcastle United ....
Tottenham Hotspur v Leeds United ....
Wimbledon v Liverpool ....

Endsleigh Insurance League Division 1

Birmingham City v Crystal Palace ....
Derby County v Leicester City ....
Huddersfield Town v Ipswich Town ....
Millwall v Barnsley ....
Oldham Athletic v West Bromwich Albion ....
Port Vale v Portsmouth ....
Reading v Luton Town ....
Sheffield United v Norwich City ....
Sunderland v Southend United ....
Tranmere Rovers v Charlton Athletic ....
Watford v Stoke City ....
Wolverhampton Wanderers v Grimsby Town ....

Endsleigh Insurance League Division 2

Blackpool v Stockport County ....
Bristol City v Brighton and Hove Albion ....
Carlisle United v Burnley ....
Crewe Alexandra v Shrewsbury Town ....
Hull City v Oxford United ....
Notts. County v A.F.C. Bournemouth ....
Rotherham United v Brentford ....
Swindon Town v Chesterfield ....
Walsall v Swansea City ....
Wrexham v Bradford City ....
Wycombe Wanderers v Peterborough United ....
York City v Bristol Rovers ....

Endsleigh Insurance League Division 3

Cambridge United v Barnet ....
Cardiff City v Torquay United ....

Colchester United v Chester City ....
Fulham v Doncaster Rovers ....
Hartlepool United v Darlington ....
Hereford United v Preston North End ....
Lincoln City v Rochdale ....
Mansfield Town v Scarborough ....
Northampton Town v Exeter City ....
Plymouth Argyle v Leyton Orient ....
Scunthorpe United v Gillingham ....
Wigan Athletic v Bury ....

Sunday, 10 September 1995

FA Carling Premiership

Manchester City v Arsenal ....

Monday, 11 September 1995

FA Carling Premiership

West Ham United v Chelsea ....

Tuesday, 12 September 1995

FA Carling Premiership

Middlesbrough v Southampton ....

Endsleigh Insurance League Division 1

Birmingham City v Stoke City ....
Huddersfield Town v Barnsley ....
Oldham Athletic v Ipswich Town ....
Port Vale v Leicester City ....
Reading v Grimsby Town ....
Sheffield United v Charlton Athletic ....
Sunderland v Portsmouth ....
Tranmere Rovers v West Bromwich Albion ....
Watford v Crystal Palace ....

Endsleigh Insurance League Division 2

Blackpool v A.F.C. Bournemouth ....
Bristol City v Brentford ....
Carlisle United v Peterborough United ....
Crewe Alexandra v Brighton and Hove Albion ....
Hull City v Swansea City ....
Notts. County v Stockport County ....
Rotherham United v Bristol Rovers ....
Walsall v Oxford United ....
Wrexham v Shrewsbury Town ....
Wycombe Wanderers v Chesterfield ....
York City v Burnley ....

Endsleigh Insurance League Division 3

Cambridge United v Exeter City ....
Cardiff City v Scarborough ....
Colchester United v Preston North End ....
Fulham v Rochdale ....
Hartlepool United v Torquay United ....
Hereford United v Gillingham ....
Lincoln City v Bury ....
Mansfield Town v Darlington ....
Northampton Town v Leyton Orient ....
Plymouth Argyle v Doncaster Rovers ....

Scunthorpe United v Chester City ....
Wigan Athletic v Barnet ....

Wednesday, 13 September 1995

Endsleigh Insurance League Division 1

Derby County v Southend United ....
Millwall v Luton Town ....
Wolverhampton Wanderers v Norwich City ....

Endsleigh Insurance League Division 2

Swindon Town v Bradford City ....

Saturday, 16 September 1995

FA Carling Premiership

Arsenal v West Ham United ....
Aston Villa v Wimbledon ....
Chelsea v Southampton ....
Leeds United v Queens Park Rangers ....
Liverpool v Blackburn Rovers ....
Manchester United v Bolton Wanderers ....
Middlesbrough v Coventry City ....
Newcastle United v Manchester City ....
Sheffield Wednesday v Tottenham Hotspur ....

Endsleigh Insurance League Division 1

Barnsley v Sheffield United ....
Charlton Athletic v Oldham Athletic ....
Crystal Palace v Huddersfield Town ....
Grimsby Town v Port Vale ....
Ipswich Town v Watford ....
Leicester City v Reading ....
Luton Town v Sunderland ....
Norwich City v Millwall ....
Portsmouth v Derby County ....
Southend United v Wolverhampton Wanderers ...
Stoke City v Tranmere Rovers ....
West Bromwich Albion v Birmingham City ....

Endsleigh Insurance League Division 2

A.F.C. Bournemouth v Crewe Alexandra ....
Bradford City v Bristol City ....
Brentford v Walsall ....
Brighton and Hove Albion v Blackpool ....
Bristol Rovers v Swindon Town ....
Burnley v Hull City ....
Chesterfield v Rotherham United ....
Oxford United v Carlisle United ....
Peterborough United v Wrexham ....
Shrewsbury Town v Notts. County ....
Stockport County v Wycombe Wanderers ....
Swansea City v York City ....

Endsleigh Insurance League Division 3

Barnet v Plymouth Argyle ....
Bury v Cambridge United ....
Chester City v Lincoln City ....
Darlington v Colchester United ....
Doncaster Rovers v Northampton Town ....
Exeter City v Fulham ....

Gillingham v Cardiff City ....
Leyton Orient v Hartlepool United ....
Preston North End v Scunthorpe United ....
Rochdale v Mansfield Town
Scarborough v Hereford United ....
Torquay United v Wigan Athletic ....

Sunday, 17 September 1995

FA Carling Premiership

Nottingham Forest v Everton ....

Saturday, 23 September 1995

FA Carling Premiership

Arsenal v Southampton ....
Aston Villa v Nottingham Forest ....
Blackburn Rovers v Coventry City ....
Liverpool v Bolton Wanderers ....
Manchester City v Middlesbrough ....
Sheffield Wednesday v Manchester United ....
West Ham United v Everton ....
Wimbledon v Leeds United ....

Endsleigh Insurance League Division 1

Barnsley v Derby County ....
Grimsby Town v Norwich City ....
Huddersfield Town v Sheffield United ....
Ipswich Town v Charlton Athletic ....
Leicester City v Southend United ....
Millwall v Sunderland
Oldham Athletic v Crystal Palace ....
Portsmouth v Tranmere Rovers ....
Reading v Port Vale
Stoke City v West Bromwich Albion ....
Watford v Birmingham City ....
Wolverhampton Wanderers v Luton Town ....

Endsleigh Insurance League Division 2

A.F.C. Bournemouth v Brighton and Hove Albion
Blackpool v Crewe Alexandra ....
Bristol Rovers v Brentford ....
Carlisle United v Hull City ....
Chesterfield v Burnley ....
Notts. County v Bristol City ....
Peterborough United v Bradford City ....
Shrewsbury Town v Stockport County ....
Swansea City v Oxford United ....
Swindon Town v Rotherham United ....
Wycombe Wanderers v Wrexham ....
York City v Walsall ....

Endsleigh Insurance League Division 3

Bury v Barnet ....
Chester City v Gillingham ....
Colchester United v Hereford United ....
Darlington v Scarborough
Doncaster Rovers v Rochdale ....
Exeter City v Leyton Orient ....
Fulham v Preston North End ....
Hartlepool United v Cardiff City ....
Lincoln City v Cambridge United ....

Mansfield Town v Scunthorpe United ....
Torquay United v Northampton Town ....
Wigan Athletic v Plymouth Argyle ....

Sunday, 24 September 1995

FA Carling Premiership

Newcastle United v Chelsea ....

Monday, 25 September 1995

FA Carling Premiership

Queens Park Rangers v Tottenham Hotspur ....

Saturday, 30 September 1995

FA Carling Premiership

Bolton Wanderers v Queens Park Rangers ....
Chelsea v Arsenal ....
Coventry City v Aston Villa ....
Leeds United v Sheffield Wednesday ....
Middlesbrough v Blackburn Rovers ....
Nottingham Forest v Manchester City ....
Southampton v West Ham United ....
Tottenham Hotspur v Wimbledon ....

Endsleigh Insurance League Division 1

Birmingham City v Oldham Athletic ....
Charlton Athletic v Barnsley ....
Crystal Palace v Stoke City ....
Derby County v Millwall ....
Luton Town v Portsmouth ....
Norwich City v Leicester City ....
Port Vale v Wolverhampton Wanderers ....
Sheffield United v Ipswich Town ....
Southend United v Grimsby Town ....
Sunderland v Reading ....
Tranmere Rovers v Watford ....
West Bromwich Albion v Huddersfield Town ......

Endsleigh Insurance League Division 2

Bradford City v Blackpool ....
Brentford v Chesterfield ....
Brighton and Hove Albion v Shrewsbury Town ..
Bristol City v Wycombe Wanderers ....
Burnley v Swansea City ....
Crewe Alexandra v Notts. County ....
Hull City v York City ....
Oxford United v Bristol Rovers ....
Rotherham United v Peterborough United ....
Stockport County v A.F.C. Bournemouth ....
Walsall v Carlisle United ....
Wrexham v Swindon Town ....

Endsleigh Insurance League Division 3

Barnet v Darlington ....
Cambridge United v Hartlepool United ....
Cardiff City v Mansfield Town ....
Gillingham v Bury ....
Hereford United v Wigan Athletic ....
Leyton Orient v Doncaster Rovers ....

● 185

Northampton Town v Fulham ....
Plymouth Argyle v Lincoln City ....
Preston North End v Chester City ....
Rochdale v Exeter City ....
Scarborough v Torquay United ....
Scunthorpe United v Colchester United ....

Sunday, 1 October 1995

FA Carling Premiership

Everton v Newcastle United ....
Manchester United v Liverpool ....

Saturday, 7 October 1995

Endsleigh Insurance League Division 1

Barnsley v Leicester City ....
Birmingham City v Southend United ....
Charlton Athletic v Grimsby Town ....
Crystal Palace v Sunderland ....
Huddersfield Town v Port Vale ....
Ipswich Town v Wolverhampton Wanderers ....
Oldham Athletic v Portsmouth ....
Sheffield United v Derby County ....
Stoke City v Norwich City ....
Tranmere Rovers v Luton Town ....
Watford v Millwall ....
West Bromwich Albion v Reading ....

Endsleigh Insurance League Division 2

Brentford v Blackpool ....
Bristol Rovers v A.F.C. Bournemouth ....
Burnley v Wycombe Wanderers ....
Carlisle United v Notts. County ....
Chesterfield v Crewe Alexandra ....
Hull City v Shrewsbury Town ....
Oxford United v Stockport County ....
Rotherham United v Brighton and Hove Albion
Swansea City v Bradford City ....
Swindon Town v Bristol City ....
Walsall v Peterborough United ....
York City v Wrexham ....

Endsleigh Insurance League Division 3

Barnet v Exeter City ....
Bury v Leyton Orient ....
Cambridge United v Cardiff City ....
Chester City v Doncaster Rovers ....
Colchester United v Hartlepool United ....
Gillingham v Rochdale ....
Hereford United v Torquay United ....
Lincoln City v Darlington ....
Plymouth Argyle v Fulham ....
Preston North End v Scarborough ....
Scunthorpe United v Northampton Town ....
Wigan Athletic v Mansfield Town ....

Tuesday, 10 October 1995

Endsleigh Insurance League Division 2

Crewe Alexandra v Bristol City ....

Saturday, 14 October 1995

FA Carling Premiership

Aston Villa v Chelsea ....
Blackburn Rovers v Southampton ....
Bolton Wanderers v Everton ....
Leeds United v Arsenal ....
Liverpool v Coventry City ....
Manchester United v Manchester City ....
Queens Park Rangers v Newcastle United ....
Tottenham Hotspur v Nottingham Forest ....

Endsleigh Insurance League Division 1

Derby County v Ipswich Town ....
Grimsby Town v Oldham Athletic ....
Leicester City v Charlton Athletic ....
Luton Town v West Bromwich Albion ....
Millwall v Tranmere Rovers ....
Norwich City v Barnsley ....
Port Vale v Crystal Palace ....
Portsmouth v Birmingham City ....
Reading v Huddersfield Town ....
Southend United v Sheffield United ....
Sunderland v Watford ....
Wolverhampton Wanderers v Stoke City ....

Endsleigh Insurance League Division 2

A.F.C. Bournemouth v Burnley ....
Blackpool v Chesterfield ....
Bradford City v Bristol Rovers ....
Brighton and Hove Albion v Swindon Town ....
Bristol City v Hull City ....
Crewe Alexandra v Carlisle United ....
Notts. County v Rotherham United ....
Peterborough United v Swansea City ....
Shrewsbury Town v York City ....
Stockport County v Brentford ....
Wrexham v Oxford United ....
Wycombe Wanderers v Walsall ....

Endsleigh Insurance League Division 3

Cardiff City v Barnet ....
Darlington v Gillingham ....
Doncaster Rovers v Hereford United ....
Exeter City v Wigan Athletic ....
Fulham v Bury ....
Hartlepool United v Scunthorpe United ....
Leyton Orient v Chester City ....
Mansfield Town v Plymouth Argyle ....
Northampton Town v Cambridge United ....
Rochdale v Colchester United ....
Scarborough v Lincoln City ....
Torquay United v Preston North End ....

Sunday, 15 October 1995

FA Carling Premiership

Sheffield Wednesday v Middlesbrough ....

Monday, 16 October 1995

FA Carling Premiership

Wimbledon v West Ham United ....

Saturday, 21 October 1995

FA Carling Premiership

Arsenal v Aston Villa ....
Chelsea v Manchester United ....
Coventry City v Sheffield Wednesday ....
Everton v Tottenham Hotspur ....
Manchester City v Leeds United ....
Middlesbrough v Queens Park Rangers ....
Newcastle United v Wimbledon ....
Nottingham Forest v Bolton Wanderers ....
West Ham United v Blackburn Rovers ....

Endsleigh Insurance League Division 1

Barnsley v Port Vale ....
Birmingham City v Grimsby Town ....
Charlton Athletic v Norwich City ....
Crystal Palace v Millwall ....
Huddersfield Town v Sunderland ....
Ipswich Town v Luton Town ....
Oldham Athletic v Reading ....
Sheffield United v Leicester City ....
Stoke City v Derby County ....
Tranmere Rovers v Southend United ....
Watford v Wolverhampton Wanderers ....
West Bromwich Albion v Portsmouth ....

Endsleigh Insurance League Division 2

Brentford v Peterborough United ....
Bristol Rovers v Notts. County ....
Burnley v Brighton and Hove Albion ....
Carlisle United v Bradford City ....
Chesterfield v Shrewsbury Town ....
Hull City v Stockport County ....
Oxford United v Wycombe Wanderers ....
Rotherham United v Blackpool ....
Swansea City v A.F.C. Bournemouth ....
Swindon Town v Crewe Alexandra ....
Walsall v Wrexham ....
York City v Bristol City ....

Endsleigh Insurance League Division 3

Barnet v Rochdale ....
Bury v Scarborough ....
Cambridge United v Darlington ....
Chester City v Fulham ....
Colchester United v Northampton Town ....
Gillingham v Doncaster Rovers ....
Hereford United v Exeter City ....
Lincoln City v Cardiff City ....
Plymouth Argyle v Torquay United ....
Preston North End v Mansfield Town ....
Scunthorpe United v Leyton Orient ....
Wigan Athletic v Hartlepool United ....

Sunday, 22 October 1995

FA Carling Premiership

Southampton v Liverpool ....

Saturday, 28 October 1995

FA Carling Premiership

Aston Villa v Everton ....
Blackburn Rovers v Chelsea ....
Leeds United v Coventry City ....
Liverpool v Manchester City ....
Manchester United v Middlesbrough ....
Queens Park Rangers v Nottingham Forest ....
Sheffield Wednesday v West Ham United ....
Wimbledon v Southampton ....

Endsleigh Insurance League Division 1

Derby County v Oldham Athletic ....
Grimsby Town v Stoke City ....
Leicester City v Crystal Palace ....
Luton Town v Charlton Athletic ....
Millwall v West Bromwich Albion ....
Norwich City v Tranmere Rovers ....
Port Vale v Birmingham City ....
Portsmouth v Watford ....
Reading v Ipswich Town ....
Southend United v Huddersfield Town ....
Sunderland v Barnsley ....
Wolverhampton Wanderers v Sheffield United .....

Endsleigh Insurance League Division 2

A.F.C. Bournemouth v Carlisle United ....
Blackpool v Oxford United ....
Bradford City v Burnley ....
Brighton and Hove Albion v Bristol Rovers ....
Bristol City v Walsall ....
Crewe Alexandra v Brentford ....
Notts. County v Swindon Town ....
Peterborough United v York City ....
Shrewsbury Town v Rotherham United ....
Stockport County v Chesterfield ....
Wrexham v Swansea City ....
Wycombe Wanderers v Hull City ....

Endsleigh Insurance League Division 3

Cardiff City v Colchester United ....
Darlington v Plymouth Argyle ....
Doncaster Rovers v Preston North End ....
Exeter City v Lincoln City ....
Fulham v Hereford United ....
Hartlepool United v Gillingham ....
Leyton Orient v Wigan Athletic ....
Mansfield Town v Bury ....
Northampton Town v Barnet ....
Rochdale v Cambridge United ....
Scarborough v Chester City ....
Torquay United v Scunthorpe United ....

Sunday, 29 October 1995

FA Carling Premiership

Tottenham Hotspur v Newcastle United ....

Monday, 30 October 1995

FA Carling Premiership

Bolton Wanderers v Arsenal ....

● 187

Endsleigh Insurance League Division 3

Doncaster Rovers v Cambridge United ....

Tuesday, 31 October 1995

Endsleigh Insurance League Division 2

A.F.C. Bournemouth v Swindon Town ....
Blackpool v Bristol Rovers ....
Bradford City v Walsall ....
Brighton and Hove Albion v Swansea City ....
Bristol City v Chesterfield ....
Crewe Alexandra v Hull City ....
Notts. County v Brentford ....
Peterborough United v Burnley ....
Shrewsbury Town v Oxford United ....
Stockport County v Rotherham United ....
Wrexham v Carlisle United ....
Wycombe Wanderers v York City ....

Endsleigh Insurance League Division 3

Cardiff City v Scunthorpe United ....
Darlington v Wigan Athletic ....
Exeter City v Gillingham ....
Fulham v Colchester United ....
Hartlepool United v Barnet ....
Leyton Orient v Hereford United ....
Mansfield Town v Lincoln City ....
Northampton Town v Preston North End ....
Rochdale v Chester City ....
Scarborough v Plymouth Argyle ....
Torquay United v Bury ....

Saturday, 4 November 1995

FA Carling Premiership

Arsenal v Manchester United ....
Chelsea v Sheffield Wednesday ....
Coventry City v Tottenham Hotspur ....
Manchester City v Bolton Wanderers ....
Middlesbrough v Leeds United ....
Newcastle United v Liverpool ....
Nottingham Forest v Wimbledon ....
Southampton v Queens Park Rangers ....
West Ham United v Aston Villa ....

Endsleigh Insurance League Division 1

Barnsley v Wolverhampton Wanderers ....
Birmingham City v Millwall ....
Charlton Athletic v Sunderland ....
Crystal Palace v Reading ....
Huddersfield Town v Norwich City ....
Ipswich Town v Grimsby Town ....
Oldham Athletic v Port Vale ....
Sheffield United v Portsmouth ....
Stoke City v Luton Town ....
Tranmere Rovers v Derby County ....
Watford v Southend United ....
West Bromwich Albion v Leicester City ....

Endsleigh Insurance League Division 2

Brentford v Shrewsbury Town ....

Bristol Rovers v Peterborough United ....
Burnley v Notts. County ....
Carlisle United v Brighton and Hove Albion ....
Chesterfield v Bradford City ....
Hull City v Wrexham ....
Oxford United v Bristol City ....
Rotherham United v Crewe Alexandra ....
Swansea City v Wycombe Wanderers ....
Swindon Town v Blackpool ....
Walsall v A.F.C. Bournemouth ....
York City v Stockport County ....

Endsleigh Insurance League Division 3

Barnet v Doncaster Rovers ....
Bury v Darlington ....
Cambridge United v Scarborough ....
Chester City v Torquay United ....
Colchester United v Exeter City ....
Gillingham v Northampton Town ....
Hereford United v Mansfield Town ....
Lincoln City v Hartlepool United ....
Plymouth Argyle v Cardiff City ....
Preston North End v Leyton Orient ....
Scunthorpe United v Rochdale ....
Wigan Athletic v Fulham ....

Sunday, 5 November 1995

FA Carling Premiership

Everton v Blackburn Rovers ....

Wednesday, 8 November 1995

FA Carling Premiership

Newcastle United v Blackburn Rovers ....

Saturday, 11 November 1995

Endsleigh Insurance League Division 1

Derby County v West Bromwich Albion ....
Grimsby Town v Barnsley ....
Leicester City v Watford ....
Luton Town v Oldham Athletic ....
Millwall v Ipswich Town ....
Norwich City v Crystal Palace ....
Port Vale v Sheffield United ....
Portsmouth v Huddersfield Town ....
Reading v Birmingham City ....
Southend United v Stoke City ....
Sunderland v Tranmere Rovers ....
Wolverhampton Wanderers v Charlton Athletic ..

Saturday, 18 November 1995

FA Carling Premiership

Aston Villa v Newcastle United ....
Blackburn Rovers v Nottingham Forest ....
Bolton Wanderers v West Ham United ....
Leeds United v Chelsea ....
Liverpool v Everton ....
Manchester United v Southampton ....

Sheffield Wednesday v Manchester City ....

Tottenham Hotspur v Arsenal ....

Wimbledon v Middlesbrough ....

Endsleigh Insurance League Division 1

Derby County v Charlton Athletic ....

Grimsby Town v West Bromwich Albion ....

Leicester City v Tranmere Rovers ....

Luton Town v Birmingham City ....

Millwall v Huddersfield Town ....

Norwich City v Ipswich Town ....

Port Vale v Watford ....

Portsmouth v Stoke City ....

Reading v Barnsley ....

Southend United v Crystal Palace ....

Sunderland v Sheffield United ....

Wolverhampton Wanderers v Oldham Athletic ....

Endsleigh Insurance League Division 2

A.F.C. Bournemouth v Brentford ....

Blackpool v York City ....

Bradford City v Hull City ....

Brighton and Hove Albion v Walsall ....

Bristol City v Carlisle United ....

Crewe Alexandra v Swansea City ....

Notts. County v Chesterfield ....

Peterborough United v Oxford United ....

Shrewsbury Town v Burnley ....

Stockport County v Swindon Town ....

Wrexham v Rotherham United ....

Wycombe Wanderers v Bristol Rovers ....

Endsleigh Insurance League Division 3

Cardiff City v Bury ....

Darlington v Scunthorpe United ....

Doncaster Rovers v Colchester United ....

Exeter City v Preston North End ....

Fulham v Barnet

Hartlepool United v Plymouth Argyle ....

Leyton Orient v Cambridge United ....

Mansfield Town v Chester City ....

Northampton Town v Wigan Athletic ....

Rochdale v Hereford United

Scarborough v Gillingham ....

Torquay United v Lincoln City ....

Sunday, 19 November 1995

FA Carling Premiership

Queens Park Rangers v Coventry City ....

Monday, 20 November 1995

FA Carling Premiership

Southampton v Aston Villa ....

Tuesday, 21 November 1995

FA Carling Premiership

Arsenal v Sheffield Wednesday ....

Middlesbrough v Tottenham Hotspur ....

Endsleigh Insurance League Division 1

Barnsley v Portsmouth ....

Birmingham City v Derby County ....

Charlton Athletic v Reading ....

Crystal Palace v Wolverhampton Wanderers ....

Huddersfield Town v Leicester City ....

Ipswich Town v Southend United ....

Oldham Athletic v Millwall

Sheffield United v Grimsby Town ....

Tranmere Rovers v Port Vale ....

Watford v Luton Town ....

West Bromwich Albion v Norwich City ....

Wednesday, 22 November 1995

FA Carling Premiership

Chelsea v Bolton Wanderers ....

Coventry City v Manchester United ....

Everton v Queens Park Rangers ....

Manchester City v Wimbledon ....

Nottingham Forest v Leeds United ....

West Ham United v Liverpool ....

Endsleigh Insurance League Division 1

Stoke City v Sunderland ....

Saturday, 25 November 1995

FA Carling Premiership

Chelsea v Tottenham Hotspur ....

Coventry City v Wimbledon ....

Everton v Sheffield Wednesday ....

Manchester City v Aston Villa ....

Middlesbrough v Liverpool ....

Newcastle United v Leeds United ....

Nottingham Forest v Manchester United ....

Southampton v Bolton Wanderers ....

West Ham United v Queens Park Rangers ....

Endsleigh Insurance League Division 1

Barnsley v Luton Town ....

Birmingham City v Leicester City ....

Charlton Athletic v Port Vale ....

Crystal Palace v Derby County ....

Huddersfield Town v Wolverhampton Wanderers

Ipswich Town v Portsmouth ....

Oldham Athletic v Southend United ....

Sheffield United v Reading ....

Stoke City v Millwall ....

Tranmere Rovers v Grimsby Town ....

Watford v Norwich City ....

West Bromwich Albion v Sunderland ....

Endsleigh Insurance League Division 2

Brentford v Bradford City ....

Bristol Rovers v Stockport County ....

Burnley v Wrexham ....

Carlisle United v Wycombe Wanderers ....

Chesterfield v A.F.C. Bournemouth ....

Hull City v Peterborough United ....

Oxford United v Crewe Alexandra ....
Rotherham United v Bristol City ....
Swansea City v Notts. County
Swindon Town v Shrewsbury Town ....
Walsall v Blackpool ....
York City v Brighton and Hove Albion ....

Endsleigh Insurance League Division 3

Barnet v Leyton Orient ....
Bury v Exeter City ....
Cambridge United v Torquay United ....
Chester City v Darlington ....
Colchester United v Mansfield Town ....
Gillingham v Fulham ....
Lincoln City v Northampton Town ....
Plymouth Argyle v Rochdale ....
Preston North End v Hartlepool United ....
Scunthorpe United v Scarborough ....
Wigan Athletic v Doncaster Rovers ....

Sunday, 26 November 1995

FA Carling Premiership

Arsenal v Blackburn Rovers ....

Endsleigh Insurance League Division 3

Hereford United v Cardiff City ....

Saturday, 2 December 1995

FA Carling Premiership

Aston Villa v Arsenal ....
Blackburn Rovers v West Ham United ....
Bolton Wanderers v Nottingham Forest ....
Leeds United v Manchester City ....
Liverpool v Southampton ....
Manchester United v Chelsea ....
Queens Park Rangers v Middlesbrough ....
Tottenham Hotspur v Everton ....

Endsleigh Insurance League Division 1

Derby County v Sheffield United ....
Grimsby Town v Charlton Athletic ....
Leicester City v Barnsley ....
Luton Town v Tranmere Rovers ....
Millwall v Watford ....
Norwich City v Stoke City ....
Port Vale v Huddersfield Town ....
Portsmouth v Oldham Athletic ....
Reading v West Bromwich Albion ....
Southend United v Birmingham City ....
Sunderland v Crystal Palace ....
Wolverhampton Wanderers v Ipswich Town ....

Sunday, 3 December 1995

FA Carling Premiership

Wimbledon v Newcastle United ....

Monday, 4 December 1995

FA Carling Premiership

Sheffield Wednesday v Coventry City ....

Tuesday, 5 December 1995

Endsleigh Insurance League Division 1

Millwall v Charlton Athletic ....

Saturday, 9 December 1995

FA Carling Premiership

Bolton Wanderers v Liverpool ....
Chelsea v Newcastle United ....
Coventry City v Blackburn Rovers ....
Everton v West Ham United ....
Leeds United v Wimbledon ....
Manchester United v Sheffield Wednesday ....
Middlesbrough v Manchester City ....
Southampton v Arsenal ....
Tottenham Hotspur v Queens Park Rangers ....

Endsleigh Insurance League Division 1

Birmingham City v Watford ....
Charlton Athletic v Ipswich Town ....
Crystal Palace v Oldham Athletic ....
Derby County v Barnsley ....
Luton Town v Wolverhampton Wanderers ....
Norwich City v Grimsby Town ....
Port Vale v Reading ....
Sheffield United v Huddersfield Town ....
Southend United v Leicester City ....
Sunderland v Millwall ....
Tranmere Rovers v Portsmouth ....
West Bromwich Albion v Stoke City ....

Endsleigh Insurance League Division 2

Bradford City v Peterborough United ....
Brentford v Bristol Rovers ....
Brighton and Hove Albion v A.F.C. Bournemouth
Bristol City v Notts. County ....
Burnley v Chesterfield ....
Crewe Alexandra v Blackpool ....
Hull City v Carlisle United ....
Oxford United v Swansea City ....
Rotherham United v Swindon Town ....
Stockport County v Shrewsbury Town ....
Walsall v York City ....
Wrexham v Wycombe Wanderers ....

Endsleigh Insurance League Division 3

Barnet v Bury ....
Cambridge United v Lincoln City ....
Cardiff City v Hartlepool United ....
Gillingham v Chester City ....
Hereford United v Colchester United ....
Leyton Orient v Exeter City ....
Northampton Town v Torquay United ....
Plymouth Argyle v Wigan Athletic ....
Preston North End v Fulham ....

Rochdale v Doncaster Rovers ....
Scarborough v Darlington ....
Scunthorpe United v Mansfield Town ....

Sunday, 10 December 1995

FA Carling Premiership

Nottingham Forest v Aston Villa ....

Saturday, 16 December 1995

FA Carling Premiership

Arsenal v Chelsea ....
Aston Villa v Coventry City ....
Blackburn Rovers v Middlesbrough ....
Manchester City v Nottingham Forest ....
Newcastle United v Everton ....
Queens Park Rangers v Bolton Wanderers ....
Sheffield Wednesday v Leeds United ....
West Ham United v Southampton ....
Wimbledon v Tottenham Hotspur ....

Endsleigh Insurance League Division 1

Barnsley v Charlton Athletic ....
Grimsby Town v Southend United ....
Huddersfield Town v West Bromwich Albion ......
Ipswich Town v Sheffield United ....
Leicester City v Norwich City ....
Millwall v Derby County ....
Oldham Athletic v Birmingham City ....
Portsmouth v Luton Town ....
Reading v Sunderland ....
Stoke City v Crystal Palace ....
Watford v Tranmere Rovers ....
Wolverhampton Wanderers v Port Vale ....

Endsleigh Insurance League Division 2

A.F.C. Bournemouth v Stockport County ....
Blackpool v Bradford City ....
Bristol Rovers v Oxford United ....
Carlisle United v Walsall ....
Chesterfield v Brentford ....
Notts. County v Crewe Alexandra ....
Peterborough United v Rotherham United ....
Shrewsbury Town v Brighton and Hove Albion ..
Swansea City v Burnley ....
Swindon Town v Wrexham ....
Wycombe Wanderers v Bristol City ....
York City v Hull City ....

Endsleigh Insurance League Division 3

Bury v Gillingham ....
Chester City v Prseton North End ....
Colchester United v Scunthorpe United ....
Darlington v Barnet ....
Doncaster Rovers v Leyton Orient ....
Exeter City v Rochdale ....
Fulham v Northampton Town ....
Hartlepool United v Cambridge United ....
Lincoln City v Plymouth Argyle ....
Mansfield Town v Cardiff City ....

Torquay United v Scarborough ....
Wigan Athletic v Hereford United ....

Sunday, 17 December 1995

FA Carling Premiership

Liverpool v Manchester United ....

Tuesday, 19 December 1995

Endsleigh Insurance League Division 2

Peterborough United v Stockport County ....

Endsleigh Insurance League Division 3

Hereford United v Scunthorpe United ....

Wednesday, 20 December 1995

Endsleigh Insurance League Division 1

Southend United v Port Vale ....
Stoke City v Sheffield United ....

Friday, 22 December 1995

Endsleigh Insurance League Division 1

Ipswich Town v Barnsley ....

Endsleigh Insurance League Division 2

Brighton & Hove Albion v Chesterfield ....
Carlisle United v York City ....
Notts County v Blackpool ....
Wrexham v Brentford ....

Endsleigh Insurance League Division 3

Doncaster Rovers v Exeter City ....
Leyton Orient v Rochdale ....

Saturday, 23 December 1995

FA Carling Premiership

Coventry City v Everton ....
Liverpool v Arsenal ....
Manchester City v Chelsea ....
Middlesbrough v West Ham United ....
Newcastle United v Nottingham Forest ....
Queens Park Rangers v Aston Villa ....
Sheffield Wednesday v Southampton ....
Tottenham Hotspur v Bolton Wanderers ....
Wimbledon v Blackburn Rovers ....

Endsleigh Insurance League Division 1

Birmingham City v Tranmere Rovers ....
Derby County v Sunderland ....
Grimsby Town v Leicester City ....
Luton Town v Huddersfield Town ....
Millwall v Charlton Athletic ....
Oldham Athletic v Watford ....
Portsmouth v Norwich City ....
Reading v Wolverhampton Wanderers ....

Southend United v Port Vale ....
Stoke City v Sheffield United ....
West Bromwich Albion v Crystal Palace ....

Endsleigh Insurance League Division 2

A.F.C. Bournemouth v Hull City ....
Bradford City v Oxford United ....
Bristol Rovers v Crewe Alexandra ....
Burnley v Bristol City ....
Swansea City v Rotherham United ....
Walsall v Swindon Town ....
Wycombe Wanderers v Shrewsbury Town ....

Endsleigh Insurance League Division 3

Bury v Colchester United ....
Chester City v Barnet ....
Fulham v Cardiff City ....
Mansfield Town v Hartlepool United ....
Plymouth Argyle v Cambridge United ....
Preston North End v Gillingham ....
Scarborough v Northampton Town ....
Torquay United v Darlington ....
Wigan Athletic v Lincoln City ....

Sunday, 24 December 1995

FA Carling Premiership

Leeds United v Manchester United ....

Tuesday, 26 December 1995

FA Carling Premiership

Arsenal v Queens Park Rangers ....
Aston Villa v Liverpool ....
Blackburn Rovers v Manchester City ....
Chelsea v Wimbledon ....
Everton v Middlesbrough ....
Manchester United v Newcastle United ....
Nottingham Forest v Sheffield Wednesday ....
Southampton v Tottenham Hotspur ....
West Ham United v Coventry City ....

Endsleigh Insurance League Division 1

Barnsley v Stoke City ....
Charlton Athletic v Portsmouth ....
Crystal Palace v Luton Town ....
Huddersfield Town v Derby County ....
Leicester City v Ipswich Town ....
Norwich City v Southend United ....
Port Vale v West Bromwich Albion ....
Sheffield United v Birmingham City ....
Sunderland v Grimsby Town ....
Tranmere Rovers v Oldham Athletic ....
Watford v Reading ....
Wolverhampton Wanderers v Millwall ....

Endsleigh Insurance League Division 2

Blackpool v Burnley ....
Brentford v Brighton and Hove Albion ....
Bristol City v Swansea City ....
Chesterfield v Peterborough United ....

Crewe Alexandra v Wrexham ....
Hull City v Notts. County ....
Oxford United v A.F.C. Bournemouth ....
Rotherham United v Walsall ....
Shrewsbury Town v Bristol Rovers ....
Stockport County v Carlisle United ....
Swindon Town v Wycombe Wanderers ....
York City v Bradford City ....

Endsleigh Insurance League Division 3

Barnet v Mansfield Town ....
Cambridge United v Wigan Athletic ....
Cardiff City v Chester City ....
Colchester United v Leyton Orient ....
Darlington v Doncaster Rovers ....
Exeter City v Torquay United ....
Gillingham v Plymouth Argyle ....
Hartlepool United v Scarborough ....
Lincoln City v Fulham ....
Northampton Town v Hereford United ....
Rochdale v Preston North End ....
Scunthorpe United v Bury ....

Wednesday, 27 December 1995

FA Carling Premiership

Bolton Wanderers v Leeds United ....

Saturday, 30 December 1995

FA Carling Premiership

Arsenal v Wimbledon ....
Aston Villa v Sheffield Wednesday ....
Blackburn Rovers v Tottenham Hotspur ......
Bolton Wanderers v Coventry City ....
Chelsea v Liverpool ....
Everton v Leeds United ....
Manchester United v Queens Park Rangers ...
Nottingham Forest v Middlesbrough ....
Southampton v Manchester City ....
West Ham United v Newcastle United ....

Endsleigh Insurance League Division 1

Barnsley v West Bromwich Albion ....
Charlton Athletic v Southend United ....
Crystal Palace v Grimsby Town ....
Huddersfield Town v Stoke City ....
Leicester City v Oldham Athletic ....
Norwich City v Reading ....
Port Vale v Luton Town ....
Sheffield United v Millwall ....
Sunderland v Birmingham City ....
Tranmere Rovers v Ipswich Town ....
Watford v Derby County ....
Wolverhampton Wanderers v Portsmouth .....

Endsleigh Insurance League Division 2

Blackpool v Swansea City ....
Brentford v Wycombe Wanderers ....
Bristol City v Bristol Rovers ....
Chesterfield v Walsall ....

Crewe Alexandra v Peterborough United ....
Hull City v Brighton and Hove Albion ....
Oxford United v Notts. County ....
Rotherham United v Bradford City ....
Shrewsbury Town v Carlisle United ....
Stockport County v Wrexham ....
Swindon Town v Burnley ....
York City v A.F.C. Bournemouth ....

Endsleigh Insurance League Division 3

Barnet v Torquay United ....
Cambridge United v Fulham ....
Cardiff City v Wigan Athletic ....
Colchester United v Scarborough ....
Darlington v Preston North End ....
Exeter City v Chester City ....
Gillingham v Mansfield Town ....
Hartlepool United v Hereford United ....
Lincoln City v Leyton Orient ....
Northampton Town v Plymouth Argyle ....
Rochdale v Bury ....
Scunthorpe United v Doncaster Rovers ....

Monday, 1 January 1996

FA Carling Premiership

Coventry City v Southampton ....
Leeds United v Blackburn Rovers ....
Liverpool v Nottingham Forest ....
Manchester City v West Ham United ....
Middlesbrough v Aston Villa ....
Sheffield Wednesday v Bolton Wanderers ....
Tottenham Hotspur v Manchester United ....
Wimbledon v Everton ....

Endsleigh Insurance League Division 1

Birmingham City v Wolverhampton Wanderers ..
Derby County v Norwich City ....
Grimsby Town v Huddersfield Town ....
Ipswich Town v Port Vale ....
Luton Town v Sheffield United ....
Millwall v Leicester City ....
Oldham Athletic v Sunderland ....
Portsmouth v Crystal Palace ....
Reading v Tranmere Rovers ....
Southend United v Barnsley ....
Stoke City v Charlton Athletic ....
West Bromwich Albion v Watford ....

Endsleigh Insurance League Division 2

A.F.C. Bournemouth v Shrewsbury Town ....
Bradford City v Crewe Alexandra ....
Brighton and Hove Albion v Stockport County ...
Bristol Rovers v Chesterfield ....
Burnley v Oxford United ....
Carlisle United v Blackpool ....
Notts. County v York City ....
Peterborough United v Swindon Town ....
Swansea City v Brentford ....
Walsall v Hull City ....
Wrexham v Bristol City ....
Wycombe Wanderers v Rotherham United ....

Endsleigh Insurance League Division 3

Bury v Hartlepool United ....
Chester City v Northampton Town ....
Darlington v Hereford United ....
Doncaster Rovers v Lincoln City ....
Fulham v Scunthorpe United ....
Leyton Orient v Gillingham ....
Mansfield Town v Cambridge United ....
Plymouth Argyle v Exeter City ....
Preston North End v Cardiff City ....
Scarborough v Barnet ....
Torquay United v Colchester United ....

Tuesday, 2 January 1996

FA Carling Premiership

Newcastle United v Arsenal ....
Queens Park Rangers v Chelsea ....

Endsleigh Insurance League Division 3

Wigan Athletic v Rochdale ....

Saturday, 6 January 1996

Endsleigh Insurance League Division 2

A.F.C. Bournemouth v Bristol City ....
Blackpool v Wycombe Wanderers ....
Brentford v Carlisle United ....
Brighton and Hove Albion v Oxford United ....
Bristol Rovers v Hull City ....
Chesterfield v Wrexham ....
Crewe Alexandra v Burnley ....
Notts. County v Walsall ....
Rotherham United v York City ....
Shrewsbury Town v Peterborough United ....
Stockport County v Bradford City ....
Swindon Town v Swansea City ....

Endsleigh Insurance League Division 3

Barnet v Preston North End ....
Bury v Doncaster Rovers ....
Cambridge United v Chester City ....
Cardiff City v Leyton Orient ....
Darlington v Northampton Town ....
Hartlepool United v Fulham ....
Lincoln City v Hereford United ....
Mansfield Town v Exeter City ....
Plymouth Argyle v Scunthorpe United ....
Scarborough v Rochdale ....
Torquay United v Gillingham ....
Wigan Athletic v Colchester United ....

Saturday, 13 January 1996

FA Carling Premiership

Bolton Wanderers v Wimbledon ....
Coventry City v Newcastle United ....
Everton v Chelsea ....
Leeds United v West Ham United ....
Manchester United v Aston Villa ....
Middlesbrough v Arsenal ....

Nottingham Forest v Southampton ....
Queens Park Rangers v Blackburn Rovers ....
Sheffield Wednesday v Liverpool ....
Tottenham Hotspur v Manchester City ....

Endsleigh Insurance League Division 1

Birmingham City v Charlton Athletic ....
Crystal Palace v Ipswich Town ....
Derby County v Reading ....
Luton Town v Southend United ....
Millwall v Port Vale ....
Oldham Athletic v Barnsley ....
Portsmouth v Grimsby Town ....
Stoke City v Leicester City ....
Sunderland v Norwich City ....
Tranmere Rovers v Sheffield United ....
Watford v Huddersfield Town ....
West Bromwich v Wolverhampton
    Albion   Wanderers ....

Endsleigh Insurance League Division 2

Bradford City v Brighton and Hove Albion ....
Bristol City v Crewe Alexandra ....
Burnley v Stockport County ....
Carlisle United v Chesterfield ....
Hull City v Rotherham United ....
Oxford United v Brentford ....
Peterborough United v A.F.C. Bournemouth ....
Swansea City v Bristol Rovers ....
Walsall v Shrewsbury Town ....
Wrexham v Blackpool ....
Wycombe Wanderers v Notts. County ....
York City v Swindon Town ....

Endsleigh Insurance League Division 3

Chester City v Bury ....
Colchester United v Barnet ....
Doncaster Rovers v Torquay United ....
Exeter City v Hartlepool United ....
Fulham v Scarborough ....
Gillingham v Lincoln City ....
Hereford United v Cambridge United ....
Leyton Orient v Mansfield Town ....
Northampton Town v Cardiff City ....
Preston North End v Plymouth Argyle ....
Rochdale v Darlington ....
Scunthorpe United v Wigan Athletic ....

Saturday, 20 January 1996

FA Carling Premiership

Arsenal v Everton ....
Aston Villa v Tottenham Hotspur ....
Blackburn Rovers v Sheffield Wednesday ....
Chelsea v Nottingham Forest ....
Liverpool v Leeds United ....
Manchester City v Coventry City ....
Newcastle United v Bolton Wanderers ....
Southampton v Middlesbrough ....
West Ham United v Manchester United ....
Wimbledon v Queens Park Rangers ....

Endsleigh Insurance League Division 1

Barnsley v Crystal Palace ....
Charlton Athletic v West Bromwich Albion ....
Grimsby Town v Millwall ....
Huddersfield Town v Oldham Athletic ....
Ipswich Town v Birmingham City ....
Leicester City v Sunderland ....
Norwich City v Luton Town ....
Port Vale v Derby County ....
Reading v Stoke City ....
Sheffield United v Watford ....
Southend United v Portsmouth ....
Wolverhampton Wanderers v Tranmere Rovers .

Endsleigh Insurance League Division 2

A.F.C. Bournemouth v Bradford City ....
Blackpool v Bristol City ....
Brentford v York City ....
Brighton and Hove Albion v Peterborough United ....
Bristol Rovers v Carlisle United ....
Chesterfield v Oxford United ....
Crewe Alexandra v Wycombe Wanderers ....
Notts. County v Wrexham ....
Rotherham United v Burnley ....
Shrewsbury Town v Swansea City ....
Stockport County v Walsall ....
Swindon Town v Hull City ....

Endsleigh Insurance League Division 3

Barnet v Hereford United ....
Bury v Northampton Town ....
Cambridge United v Scunthorpe United ....
Cardiff City v Rochdale ....
Darlington v Exeter City ....
Hartlepool United v Chester City ....
Lincoln City v Preston North End ....
Mansfield Town v Fulham ....
Plymouth Argyle v Colchester United ....
Scarborough v Doncaster Rovers ....
Torquay United v Leyton Orient ....
Wigan Athletic v Gillingham ....

Saturday, 27 January 1996

Endsleigh Insurance League Division 2

Bradford City v Notts. County ....
Bristol City v Shrewsbury Town ....
Burnley v Bristol Rovers ....
Carlisle United v Rotherham United ....
Hull City v Brentford ....
Oxford United v Swindon Town ....
Peterborough United v Blackpool ....
Swansea City v Stockport County ....
Walsall v Crewe Alexandra ....
Wrexham v A.F.C. Bournemouth ....
Wycombe Wanderers v Brighton and Hove Albion
York City v Chesterfield ....

Endsleigh Insurance League Division 3

Chester City v Wigan Athletic ....
Colchester United v Cambridge United ....
Doncaster Rovers v Mansfield Town ....
Exeter City v Cardiff City ....
Fulham v Darlington ....
Gillingham v Barnet ....
Hereford United v Plymouth Argyle ....
Leyton Orient v Scarborough ....
Northampton Town v Hartlepool United ....
Preston North End v Bury ....
Rochdale v Torquay United ....
Scunthorpe United v Lincoln City ....

Saturday, 3 February 1996

FA Carling Premiership

Arsenal v Coventry City ....
Aston Villa v Leeds United ....
Blackburn Rovers v Bolton Wanderers ....
Chelsea v Middlesbrough ....
Liverpool v Tottenham Hotspur ....
Manchester City v Queens Park Rangers ....
Newcastle United v Sheffield Wednesday ....
Southampton v Everton ....
West Ham United v Nottingham Forest ....
Wimbledon v Manchester United ....

Endsleigh Insurance League Division 1

Barnsley v Watford ....
Charlton Athletic v Crystal Palace ....
Grimsby Town v Derby County ....
Huddersfield Town v Tranmere Rovers ....
Ipswich Town v West Bromwich Albion ....
Leicester City v Luton Town ....
Norwich City v Birmingham City ....
Port Vale v Stoke City ....
Reading v Portsmouth ....
Sheffield United v Oldham Athletic ....
Southend United v Millwall ....
Wolverhampton Wanderers v Sunderland ....

Endsleigh Insurance League Division 2

A.F.C. Bournemouth v Wycombe Wanderers ....
Blackpool v Hull City ....
Brentford v Burnley ....
Brighton and Hove Albion v Wrexham ....
Bristol Rovers v Walsall ....
Chesterfield v Swansea City ....
Crewe Alexandra v York City ....
Notts. County v Peterborough United ....
Rotherham United v Oxford United ....
Shrewsbury Town v Bradford City ....
Stockport County v Bristol City ....
Swindon Town v Carlisle United ....

Endsleigh Insurance League Division 3

Barnet v Scunthorpe United ....
Bury v Hereford United ....
Cambridge United v Gillingham ....
Cardiff City v Doncaster Rovers ....
Darlington v Leyton Orient ....

Hartlepool United v Rochdale ....
Lincoln City v Colchester United ....
Mansfield Town v Northampton Town ....
Plymouth Argyle v Chester City ....
Scarborough v Exeter City ....
Torquay United v Fulham ....
Wigan Athletic v Preston North End ....

Saturday, 10 February 1996

FA Carling Premiership

Bolton Wanderers v Aston Villa ....
Coventry City v Chelsea ....
Everton v Manchester City ....
Leeds United v Southampton ....
Manchester United v Blackburn Rovers ....
Middlesbrough v Newcastle United ....
Nottingham Forest v Arsenal ....
Queens Park Rangers v Liverpool ....
Sheffield Wednesday v Wimbledon ....
Tottenham Hotspur v West Ham United ....

Endsleigh Insurance League Division 1

Birmingham City v Huddersfield Town ....
Crystal Palace v Sheffield United ....
Derby County v Wolverhampton Wanderers ....
Luton Town v Grimsby Town ....
Millwall v Reading ....
Oldham Athletic v Norwich City ....
Portsmouth v Leicester City ....
Stoke City v Ipswich Town ....
Sunderland v Port Vale ....
Tranmere Rovers v Barnsley ....
Watford v Charlton Athletic ....
West Bromwich Albion v Southend United ....

Endsleigh Insurance League Division 2

Bradford City v Stockport County ....
Bristol City v A.F.C. Bournemouth ....
Burnley v Crewe Alexandra ....
Carlisle United v Brentford ....
Hull City v Bristol Rovers ....
Oxford United v Brighton and Hove Albion ....
Peterborough United v Shrewsbury Town ....
Swansea City v Swindon Town ....
Walsall v Notts. County ....
Wrexham v Chesterfield ....
Wycombe Wanderers v Blackpool ....
York City v Rotherham United ....

Endsleigh Insurance League Division 3

Chester City v Cambridge United ....
Colchester United v Wigan Athletic ....
Doncaster Rovers v Bury ....
Exeter City v Mansfield Town ....
Fulham v Hartlepool United ....
Gillingham v Torquay United ....
Hereford United v Lincoln City ....
Leyton Orient v Cardiff City ....
Northampton Town v Darlington ....
Preston North End v Barnet ....
Rochdale v Scarborough ....
Scunthorpe United v Plymouth Argyle ....

● 195

Saturday, 17 February 1996

FA Carling Premiership

Arsenal v Manchester City ....
Aston Villa v Blackburn Rovers ....
Chelsea v West Ham United ....
Leeds United v Tottenham Hotspur ....
Liverpool v Wimbledon ....
Manchester United v Everton ....
Middlesbrough v Bolton Wanderers ....
Newcastle United v Southampton ....
Nottingham Forest v Coventry City ....
Sheffield Wednesday v Queens Park Rangers ....

Endsleigh Insurance League Division 1

Barnsley v Huddersfield Town ....
Charlton Athletic v Sheffield United ....
Crystal Palace v Watford ....
Grimsby Town v Reading ....
Ipswich Town v Oldham Athletic ....
Leicester City v Port Vale ....
Luton Town v Millwall ....
Norwich City v Wolverhampton Wanderers ....
Portsmouth v Sunderland ....
Southend United v Derby County ....
Stoke City v Birmingham City ....
West Bromwich Albion v Tranmere Rovers ....

Endsleigh Insurance League Division 2

A.F.C. Bournemouth v Blackpool ....
Bradford City v Swindon Town ....
Brentford v Bristol City ....
Brighton and Hove Albion v Crewe Alexandra ....
Bristol Rovers v Rotherham United ....
Burnley v York City ....
Chesterfield v Wycombe Wanderers ....
Oxford United v Walsall ....
Peterborough United v Carlisle United ....
Shrewsbury Town v Wrexham ....
Stockport County v Notts. County ....
Swansea City v Hull City ....

Endsleigh Insurance League Division 3

Barnet v Wigan Athletic ....
Bury v Lincoln City ....
Chester City v Scunthorpe United ....
Darlington v Mansfield Town ....
Doncaster Rovers v Plymouth Argyle ....
Exeter City v Cambridge United ....
Gillingham v Hereford United ....
Leyton Orient v Northampton Town ....
Preston North End v Colchester United ....
Rochdale v Fulham ....
Scarborough v Cardiff City ....
Torquay United v Hartlepool United ....

Tuesday, 20 February 1996

Endsleigh Insurance League Division 1

Birmingham City v Barnsley ....
Huddersfield Town v Charlton Athletic ....
Oldham Athletic v Stoke City ....

Port Vale v Norwich City ....
Reading v Southend United ....
Sheffield United v West Bromwich Albion ....
Sunderland v Ipswich Town ....
Tranmere Rovers v Crystal Palace ....
Watford v Grimsby Town ....

Endsleigh Insurance League Division 2

Blackpool v Shrewsbury Town ....
Bristol City v Peterborough United ....
Carlisle United v Swansea City ....
Crewe Alexandra v Stockport County ....
Hull City v Chesterfield ....
Notts. County v Brighton and Hove Albion ....
Rotherham United v A.F.C. Bournemouth ....
Walsall v Burnley ....
Wrexham v Bristol Rovers ....
Wycombe Wanderers v Bradford City ....
York City v Oxford United ....

Endsleigh Insurance League Division 3

Cambridge United v Preston North End ....
Cardiff City v Darlington ....
Colchester United v Gillingham ....
Fulham v Leyton Orient ....
Hartlepool United v Doncaster Rovers ....
Hereford United v Chester City ....
Lincoln City v Barnet ....
Mansfield Town v Torquay United ....
Northampton Town v Rochdale ....
Plymouth Argyle v Bury ....
Scunthorpe United v Exeter City ....
Wigan Athletic v Scarborough ....

Wednesday, 21 February 1996

Endsleigh Insurance League Division 1

Derby County v Luton Town ....
Millwall v Portsmouth ....
Wolverhampton Wanderers v Leicester City ....

Endsleigh Insurance League Division 2

Swindon Town v Brentford ....

Saturday, 24 February 1996

FA Carling Premiership

Blackburn Rovers v Liverpool ....
Bolton Wanderers v Manchester United ....
Coventry City v Middlesbrough ....
Everton v Nottingham Forest ....
Manchester City v Newcastle United ....
Queens Park Rangers v Leeds United ....
Southampton v Chelsea ....
Tottenham Hotspur v Sheffield Wednesday ....
West Ham United v Arsenal ....
Wimbledon v Aston Villa ....

Endsleigh Insurance League Division 1

Birmingham City v West Bromwich Albion ....
Derby County v Portsmouth ....
Huddersfield Town v Crystal Palace ....

Millwall v Norwich City ....
Oldham Athletic v Charlton Athletic ....
Port Vale v Grimsby Town ....
Reading v Leicester City ....
Sheffield United v Barnsley ....
Sunderland v Luton Town
Tranmere Rovers v Stoke City ....
Watford v Ipswich Town ....
Wolverhampton Rovers v Southend United ....

Endsleigh Insurance League Division 2

Blackpool v Brighton and Hove Albion ....
Bristol City v Bradford City ....
Carlisle United v Oxford United ....
Crewe Alexandra v A.F.C. Bournemouth ....
Hull City v Burnley
Notts. County v Shrewsbury Town ....
Rotherham United v Chesterfield ....
Swindon Town v Bristol Rovers ....
Walsall v Brentford
Wrexham v Peterborough United ....
Wycombe Wanderers v Stockport County ....
York City v Swansea City ....

Endsleigh Insurance League Division 3

Cambridge United v Bury ....
Cardiff City v Gillingham ....
Colchester United v Darlington ....
Fulham v Exeter City ....
Hartlepool United v Leyton Orient ....
Hereford United v Scarborough
Lincoln City v Chester City ....
Mansfield Town v Rochdale
Northampton Town v Doncaster Rovers ....
Plymouth Argyle v Barnet ....
Scunthorpe United v Preston North End ....
Wigan Athletic v Torquay United ....

Monday, 26 February 1996

Endsleigh Insurance League Division 3

Doncaster Rovers v Fulham ....

Tuesday, 27 February 1996

Endsleigh Insurance League Division 1

Barnsley v Millwall ....
Charlton Athletic v Tranmere Rovers ....
Crystal Palace v Birmingham City ....
Grimsby Town v Wolverhampton Wanderers ......
Ipswich Town v Huddersfield Town ....
Luton Town v Reading ....
Southend United v Sunderland ....
West Bromwich Albion v Oldham Athletic ......

Endsleigh Insurance League Division 2

A.F.C. Bournemouth v Notts. County ....
Bradford City v Wrexham ....
Brentford v Rotherham United ....
Brighton and Hove Albion v Bristol City ......
Bristol Rovers v York City ....
Burnley v Carlisle United ....

Chesterfield v Swindon Town ....
Oxford United v Hull City
Peterborough United v Wycombe Wanderers ......
Shrewsbury Town v Crewe Alexandra ....
Stockport County v Blackpool
Swansea City v Walsall ....

Endsleigh Insurance League Division 3

Barnet v Cambridge United ....
Bury v Wigan Athletic ....
Chester City v Colchester United ....
Darlington v Hartlepool United ....
Exeter City v Northampton Town ....
Gillingham v Scunthorpe United ....
Leyton Orient v Plymouth Argyle ....
Preston North End v Hereford United ....
Rochdale v Lincoln City ....
Scarborough v Mansfield Town ....
Torquay United v Cardiff City ....

Wednesday, 28 February 1996

Endsleigh Insurance League Division 1

Leicester City v Derby County ....
Norwich City v Sheffield United ....
Portsmouth v Port Vale ....
Stoke City v Watford ....

Saturday, 2 March 1996

FA Carling Premiership

Coventry City v West Ham United ....
Leeds United v Bolton Wanderers ....
Liverpool v Aston Villa
Manchester City v Blackburn Rovers ....
Middlesbrough v Everton
Newcastle United v Manchester United ....
Queens Park Rangers v Arsenal ....
Sheffield Wednesday v Nottingham Forest ....
Tottenham Hotspur v Southampton ....
Wimbledon v Chelsea

Endsleigh Insurance League Division 1

Birmingham City v Sheffield United ....
Derby County v Huddersfield Town ....
Grimsby Town v Sunderland ....
Ipswich Town v Leicester City ....
Luton Town v Crystal Palace ....
Millwall v Wolverhampton Wanderers ....
Oldham Athletic v Tranmere Rovers ....
Portsmouth v Charlton Athletic ......
Reading v Watford
Southend United v Norwich City ......
Stoke City v Barnsley ....
West Bromwich Albion v Port Vale ....

Endsleigh Insurance League Division 2

A.F.C. Bournemouth v Oxford United .....
Bradford City v York City
Brighton and Hove Albion v Brentford ....
Burnley v Blackpool ....
Bristol Rovers v Shrewsbury Town .....

● 197

Carlisle United v Stockport County ....
Notts. County v Hull City ....
Peterborough United v Chesterfield ....
Swansea City v Bristol City ....
Walsall v Rotherham United ....
Wrexham v Crewe Alexandra ....
Wycombe Wanderers v Swindon Town ....

Endsleigh Insurance League Division 3

Bury v Scunthorpe United ....
Chester City v Cardiff City ....
Doncaster Rovers v Darlington ....
Fulham v Lincoln City ....
Hereford United v Northampton Town ....
Leyton Orient v Colchester United ....
Mansfield Town v Barnet ....
Plymouth Argyle v Gillingham ....
Preston North End v Rochdale ....
Scarborough v Hartlepool United ....
Torquay United v Exeter City ....
Wigan Athletic v Cambridge United ....

Saturday, 9 March 1996

FA Carling Premiership

Arsenal v Liverpool ....
Aston Villa v Queens Park Rangers ....
Blackburn Rovers v Wimbledon ....
Bolton Wanderers v Tottenham Hotspur ....
Chelsea v Manchester City ....
Everton v Coventry City ....
Manchester United v Leeds United ....
Nottingham Forest v Newcastle United ....
Southampton v Sheffield Wednesday ....
West Ham United v Middlesbrough ....

Endsleigh Insurance League Division 1

Barnsley v Ipswich Town ....
Charlton Athletic v Millwall ....
Crystal Palace v West Bromwich Albion ....
Huddersfield Town v Luton Town ....
Leicester City v Grimsby Town ....
Norwich City v Portsmouth ....
Port Vale v Southend United ....
Sheffield United v Stoke City ....
Sunderland v Derby County ....
Tranmere Rovers v Birmingham City ....
Watford v Oldham Athletic ....
Wolverhampton Wanderers v Reading ....

Endsleigh Insurance League Division 2

Blackpool v Notts. County ....
Brentford v Wrexham ....
Bristol City v Burnley ....
Chesterfield v Brighton and Hove Albion ....
Crewe Alexandra v Bristol Rovers ....
Hull City v A.F.C. Bournemouth ....
Oxford United v Bradford City ....
Rotherham United v Swansea City ....
Shrewsbury Town v Wycombe Wanderers ....
Stockport County v Peterborough United ....
Swindon Town v Walsall ....
York City v Carlisle United ....

Endsleigh Insurance League Division 3

Barnet v Chester City ....
Cambridge United v Plymouth Argyle ....
Cardiff City v Fulham ....
Colchester United v Bury ....
Darlington v Torquay United ....
Exeter City v Doncaster Rovers ....
Gillingham v Preston North End ....
Hartlepool United v Mansfield Town ....
Lincoln City v Wigan Athletic ....
Northampton Town v Scarborough ....
Rochdale v Leyton Orient ....
Scunthorpe United v Hereford United ....

Saturday, 16 March 1996

FA Carling Premiership

Coventry City v Bolton Wanderers ....
Leeds United v Everton ....
Liverpool v Chelsea ....
Manchester City v Southampton ....
Middlesbrough v Nottingham Forest ....
Newcastle United v West Ham United ....
Queens Park Rangers v Manchester United ....
Sheffield Wednesday v Aston Villa ....
Tottenham Hotspur v Blackburn Rovers ....
Wimbledon v Arsenal ....

Endsleigh Insurance League Division 1

Birmingham City v Sunderland ....
Derby County v Watford ....
Grimsby Town v Crystal Palace ....
Ipswich Town v Tranmere Rovers ....
Luton Town v Port Vale ....
Millwall v Sheffield United ....
Oldham Athletic v Leicester City ....
Portsmouth v Wolverhampton Wanderers ....
Reading v Norwich City ....
Southend United v Charlton Athletic ....
Stoke City v Huddersfield Town ....
West Bromwich Albion v Barnsley ....

Endsleigh Insurance League Division 2

A.F.C. Bournemouth v York City ....
Bradford City v Rotherham United ....
Brighton and Hove Albion v Hull City ....
Bristol Rovers v Bristol City ....
Burnley v Swindon Town ....
Carlisle United v Shrewsbury Town ....
Notts. County v Oxford United ....
Peterborough United v Crewe Alexandra ....
Swansea City v Blackpool ....
Walsall v Chesterfield ....
Wrexham v Stockport County ....
Wycombe Wanderers v Brentford ....

Endsleigh Insurance League Division 3

Bury v Rochdale ....
Chester City v Exeter City ....
Doncaster Rovers v Scunthorpe United ....
Fulham v Cambridge United ....

Hereford United v Hartlepool United ....
Leyton Orient v Lincoln City ....
Mansfield Town v Gillingham ....
Plymouth Argyle v Northampton Town ....
Preston North End v Darlington ....
Scarborough v Colchester United ....
Torquay United v Barnet ....
Wigan Athletic v Cardiff City ....

Saturday, 23 March 1996

FA Carling Premiership

Arsenal v Newcastle United ....
Aston Villa v Middlesbrough
Blackburn Rovers v Leeds United ....
Bolton Wanderers v Sheffield Wednesday ....
Chelsea v Queens Park Rangers ....
Everton v Wimbledon
Manchester United v Tottenham Hotspur ....
Nottingham Forest v Liverpool ....
Southampton v Coventry City
West Ham United v Manchester City ....

Endsleigh Insurance League Division 1

Barnsley v Southend United ....
Charlton Athletic v Stoke City ....
Crystal Palace v Portsmouth ....
Huddersfield Town v Grimsby Town ....
Leicester City v Millwall ....
Norwich City v Derby County ....
Port Vale v Ipswich Town ....
Sheffield United v Luton Town ....
Sunderland v Oldham Athletic ....
Tranmere Rovers v Reading ....
Watford v West Bromwich Albion ....
Wolverhampton Wanderers v Birmingham City ..

Endsleigh Insurance League Division 2

Blackpool v Carlisle United ....
Brentford v Swansea City ....
Bristol City v Wrexham ....
Chesterfield v Bristol Rovers ....
Crewe Alexandra v Bradford City ....
Hull City v Walsall ....
Oxford United v Burnley ....
Rotherham United v Wycombe Wanderers ....
Shrewsbury Town v A.F.C. Bournemouth ....
Stockport County v Brighton and Hove Albion ..
Swindon Town v Peterborough United ....
York City v Notts. County ....

Endsleigh Insurance League Division 3

Barnet v Scarborough ....
Cambridge United v Mansfield Town ....
Cardiff City v Preston North End ....
Colchester United v Torquay United ....
Exeter City v Plymouth Argyle ....
Gillingham v Leyton Orient ....
Hartlepool United v Bury ....
Hereford United v Darlington ....
Lincoln City v Doncaster Rovers ....
Northampton Town v Chester City ....
Rochdale v Wigan Athletic ....
Scunthorpe United v Fulham ....

Saturday, 30 March 1996

FA Carling Premiership

Aston Villa v West Ham United ....
Blackburn Rovers v Everton ....
Bolton Wanderers v Manchester City ....
Leeds United v Middlesbrough ....
Liverpool v Newcastle United ....
Manchester United v Arsenal ....
Queens Park Rangers v Southampton ....
Sheffield Wednesday v Chelsea ....
Tottenham Hotspur v Coventry City ....
Wimbledon v Nottingham Forest ....

Endsleigh Insurance League Division 1

Derby County v Stoke City ....
Grimsby Town v Birmingham City ....
Leicester City v Sheffield United ....
Luton Town v Ipswich Town ....
Millwall v Crystal Palace ....
Norwich City v Charlton Athletic ....
Port Vale v Barnsley ....
Portsmouth v West Bromwich Albion ....
Reading v Oldham Athletic ....
Southend United v Tranmere Rovers ....
Sunderland v Huddersfield Town ....
Wolverhampton Wanderers v Watford ....

Endsleigh Insurance League Division 2

A.F.C. Bournemouth v Bristol Rovers ....
Blackpool v Brentford ....
Bradford City v Swansea City ....
Brighton and Hove Albion v Rotherham United ....
Bristol City v Swindon Town ....
Crewe Alexandra v Chesterfield ....
Notts. County v Carlisle United ....
Peterborough United v Walsall ....
Shrewsbury Town v Hull City ....
Stockport County v Oxford United ....
Wrexham v York City ....
Wycombe Wanderers v Burnley ....

Endsleigh Insurance League Division 3

Cardiff City v Cambridge United ....
Darlington v Lincoln City ....
Doncaster Rovers v Chester City ....
Exeter City v Barnet ....
Fulham v Plymouth Argyle ....
Hartlepool United v Colchester United ....
Leyton Orient v Bury ....
Mansfield Town v Wigan Athletic ....
Northampton Town v Scunthorpe United ....
Rochdale v Gillingham ....
Scarborough v Preston North End ....
Torquay United v Hereford United ....

Tuesday, 2 April 1996

Endsleigh Insurance League Division 1

Barnsley v Norwich City ....
Birmingham City v Portsmouth ....
Charlton Athletic v Leicester City ....

Crystal Palace v Port Vale ....
Huddersfield Town v Reading ....
Ipswich Town v Derby County ....
Oldham Athletic v Grimsby Town ....
Sheffield United v Southend United ....
Tranmere Rovers v Millwall ....
Watford v Sunderland ....
West Bromwich Albion v Luton Town ....

Endsleigh Insurance League Division 2

Brentford v Stockport County ....
Bristol Rovers v Bradford City ....
Burnley v A.F.C. Bournemouth ....
Carlisle United v Crewe Alexandra ....
Chesterfield v Blackpool ....
Hull City v Bristol City ....
Oxford United v Wrexham ....
Rotherham United v Notts. County ....
Swansea City v Peterborough United ....
Walsall v Wycombe Wanderers ....
York City v Shrewsbury Town ....

Endsleigh Insurance League Division 3

Barnet v Cardiff City ....
Bury v Fulham ....
Cambridge United v Northampton Town ....
Chester City v Leyton Orient ....
Colchester United v Rochdale ....
Gillingham v Darlington ....
Hereford United v Doncaster Rovers ....
Lincoln City v Scarborough ....
Plymouth Argyle v Mansfield Town ....
Preston North End v Torquay United ....
Scunthorpe United v Hartlepool United ....
Wigan Athletic v Exeter City ....

Wednesday, 3 April 1996

Endsleigh Insurance League Division 1

Stoke City v Wolverhampton Wanderers ....

Endsleigh Insurance League Division 2

Swindon Town v Brighton and Hove Albion ....

Saturday, 6 April 1996

FA Carling Premiership

Arsenal v Leeds United ....
Chelsea v Aston Villa ....
Coventry City v Liverpool ....
Everton v Bolton Wanderers ....
Manchester City v Manchester United ....
Middlesbrough v Sheffield Wednesday ....
Newcastle United v Queens Park Rangers ....
Nottingham Forest v Tottenham Hotspur ....
Southampton v Blackburn Rovers ....
West Ham United v Wimbledon ....

Endsleigh Insurance League Division 1

Barnsley v Sunderland ....
Birmingham City v Port Vale ....
Charlton Athletic v Luton Town ....
Crystal Palace v Leicester City ....

Huddersfield Town v Southend United ....
Ipswich Town v Reading ....
Oldham Athletic v Derby County ....
Sheffield United v Wolverhampton Wanderers .....
Stoke City v Grimsby Town ....
Tranmere Rovers v Norwich City ....
Watford v Portsmouth ....
West Bromwich Albion v Millwall ....

Endsleigh Insurance League Division 2

Brentford v Crewe Alexandra ....
Bristol Rovers v Brighton and Hove Albion ....
Burnley v Bradford City ....
Carlisle United v A.F.C. Bournemouth ....
Chesterfield v Stockport County ....
Hull City v Wycombe Wanderers ....
Oxford United v Blackpool ....
Rotherham United v Shrewsbury Town ....
Swansea City v Wrexham ....
Swindon Town v Notts. County ....
Walsall v Bristol City ....
York City v Peterborough United ....

Endsleigh Insurance League Division 3

Barnet v Northampton Town ....
Bury v Mansfield Town ....
Cambridge United v Rochdale ....
Chester City v Scarborough ....
Colchester United v Cardiff City ....
Gillingham v Hartlepool United ....
Hereford United v Fulham ....
Lincoln City v Exeter City ....
Plymouth Argyle v Darlington ....
Preston North End v Doncaster Rovers ....
Scunthorpe United v Torquay United ....
Wigan Athletic v Leyton Orient ....

Monday, 8 April 1996

FA Carling Premiership

Aston Villa v Southampton ....
Blackburn Rovers v Newcastle United ....
Bolton Wanderers v Chelsea ....
Leeds United v Nottingham Forest ....
Liverpool v West Ham United ....
Manchester United v Coventry City ....
Queens Park Rangers v Everton ....
Sheffield Wednesday v Arsenal ....
Tottenham Hotspur v Middlesbrough ....
Wimbledon v Manchester City ....

Endsleigh Insurance League Division 1

Derby County v Tranmere Rovers ....
Grimsby Town v Ipswich Town ....
Norwich City v Huddersfield Town ....
Port Vale v Oldham Athletic ....
Portsmouth v Sheffield United ....
Reading v Crystal Palace ....
Southend United v Watford ....
Sunderland v Charlton Athletic ....
Wolverhampton Wanderers v Barnsley ....

Endsleigh Insurance League Division 2

Blackpool v Rotherham United ....

Bradford City v Carlisle United ....
Bristol City v York City ....
Crewe Alexandra v Swindon Town ....
Peterborough United v Brentford
Stockport County v Hull City ....
Wrexham v Walsall ....
Wycombe Wanderers v Oxford United ....

Endsleigh Insurance League Division 3

Cardiff City v Lincoln City ....
Darlington v Cambridge United ....
Doncaster Rovers v Gillingham ....
Exeter City v Hereford United ....
Fulham v Chester City ....
Hartlepool United v Wigan Athletic ....
Leyton Orient v Scunthorpe United ....
Mansfield Town v Preston North End ....
Northampton Town v Colchester United ....
Rochdale v Barnet ....
Torquay United v Plymouth Argyle ....

Tuesday, 9 April 1996

Endsleigh Insurance League Division 1

Leicester City v West Bromwich Albion ....
Luton Town v Stoke City ....

Endsleigh Insurance League Division 2

A.F.C. Bournemouth v Swansea City ....
Brighton & Hove Albion v Burnley ....
Notts. County v Bristol Rovers ....
Shrewsbury Town v Chesterfield ....

Endsleigh Insurance League Division 3

Scarborough v Bury ....

Wednesday, 10 April 1996

Endsleigh Insurance League Division 1

Millwall v Birmingham City ....

Saturday, 13 April 1996

FA Carling Premiership

Arsenal v Tottenham Hotspur ....
Chelsea v Leeds United ....
Coventry City v Queens Park Rangers ....
Everton v Liverpool ....
Manchester City v Sheffield Wednesday ....
Middlesbrough v Wimbledon ....
Newcastle United v Aston Villa ....
Nottingham Forest v Blackburn Rovers ....
Southampton v Manchester United ....
West Ham United v Bolton Wanderers ....

Endsleigh Insurance League Division 1

Barnsley v Reading ....
Birmingham City v Luton Town ....
Charlton Athletic v Derby County ....
Crystal Palace v Southend United ....
Huddersfield Town v Millwall ....
Ipswich Town v Norwich City ....

Oldham Athletic v Wolverhampton Wanderers ....
Sheffield United v Sunderland ....
Stoke City v Portsmouth
Tranmere Rovers v Leicester City ....
Watford v Port Vale ....
West Bromwich Albion v Grimsby Town ......

Endsleigh Insurance League Division 2

Brentford v Notts. County ....
Bristol Rovers v Blackpool ....
Burnley v Peterborough United ....
Carlisle United v Wrexham ....
Chesterfield v Bristol City ....
Hull City v Crewe Alexandra ....
Oxford United v Shrewsbury Town ....
Rotherham United v Stockport County ....
Swansea City v Brighton and Hove Albion ....
Swindon Town v A.F.C. Bournemouth ....
Walsall v Bradford City ....
York City v Wycombe Wanderers ....

Endsleigh Insurance League Division 3

Barnet v Hartlepool United ....
Bury v Torquay United ....
Cambridge United v Doncaster Rovers ....
Chester City v Rochdale ....
Colchester United v Fulham ....
Gillingham v Exeter City ....
Hereford United v Leyton Orient ....
Lincoln City v Mansfield Town ....
Plymouth Argyle v Scarborough ....
Preston North End v Northampton Town ......
Scunthorpe United v Cardiff City ....
Wigan Athletic v Darlington ....

Saturday, 20 April 1996

Endsleigh Insurance League Division 1

Derby County v Birmingham City ....
Grimsby Town v Sheffield United ....
Leicester City v Huddersfield Town ....
Luton Town v Watford ....
Millwall v Oldham Athletic ....
Norwich City v West Bromwich Albion ....
Port Vale v Tranmere Rovers ....
Portsmouth v Barnsley ....
Reading v Charlton Athletic ....
Southend United v Ipswich Town ....
Sunderland v Stoke City ....
Wolverhampton Wanderers v Crystal Palace ....

Endsleigh Insurance League Division 2

A.F.C. Bournemouth v Walsall ....
Blackpool v Swindon Town ....
Bradford City v Chesterfield ....
Brighton and Hove Albion v Carlisle United ....
Bristol City v Oxford United ....
Crewe Alexandra v Rotherham United ....
Notts. County v Burnley ....
Peterborough United v Bristol Rovers ....
Shrewsbury Town v Brentford ....
Stockport County v York City ....
Wrexham v Hull City ....
Wycombe Wanderers v Swansea City ....

Endsleigh Insurance League Division 3

Cardiff City v Plymouth Argyle ....
Darlington v Bury ....
Doncaster Rovers v Barnet ....
Exeter City v Colchester United ....
Fulham v Wigan Athletic ....
Hartlepool United v Lincoln City ....
Leyton Orient v Preston North End ....
Mansfield Town v Hereford United ....
Northampton Town v Gillingham ....
Rochdale v Scunthorpe United ....
Scarborough v Cambridge United ....
Torquay United v Chester City ....

Saturday, 27 April 1996

FA Carling Premiership

Aston Villa v Manchester City ....
Blackburn Rovers v Arsenal ....
Bolton Wanderers v Southampton ....
Leeds United v Newcastle United ....
Liverpool v Middlesbrough ....
Manchester United v Nottingham Forest ....
Queens Park Rangers v West Ham United ....
Sheffield Wednesday v Everton ....
Tottenham Hotspur v Chelsea ....
Wimbledon v Coventry City ....

Endsleigh Insurance League Division 1

Derby County v Crystal Palace ....
Grimsby Town v Tranmere Rovers ....
Leicester City v Birmingham City ....
Luton Town v Barnsley ....
Millwall v Stoke City ....
Norwich City v Watford ....
Port Vale v Charlton Athletic ....
Portsmouth v Ipswich Town ....
Reading v Sheffield United ....
Southend United v Oldham Athletic ....
Sunderland v West Bromwich Albion ....
Wolverhampton Wanderers v Huddersfield Town

Endsleigh Insurance League Division 2

A.F.C. Bournemouth v Chesterfield ....
Blackpool v Walsall ....
Bradford City v Brentford ....
Brighton and Hove Albion v York City ....
Bristol City v Rotherham United ....
Crewe Alexandra v Oxford United ....
Notts. County v Swansea City ....
Peterborough United v Hull City ....
Shrewsbury Town v Swindon Town ....
Stockport County v Bristol Rovers ....
Wrexham v Burnley ....
Wycombe Wanderers v Carlisle United ....

Endsleigh Insurance League Division 3

Cardiff City v Hereford United ....
Darlington v Chester City ....
Doncaster Rovers v Wigan Athletic ....
Exeter City v Bury ....
Fulham v Gillingham ....
Hartlepool United v Preston North End ....
Leyton Orient v Barnet ....

Mansfield Town v Colchester United ....
Northampton Town v Lincoln City ....
Rochdale v Plymouth Argyle ....
Scarborough v Scunthorpe United ....
Torquay United v Cambridge United ....

Saturday, 4 May 1996

FA Carling Premiership

Arsenal v Bolton Wanderers ....
Chelsea v Blackburn Rovers ....
Coventry City v Leeds United ....
Everton v Aston Villa ....
Manchester City v Liverpool ....
Middlesbrough v Manchester United ....
Newcastle United v Tottenham Hotspur ....
Nottingham Forest v Queens Park Rangers ....
Southampton v Wimbledon ....
West Ham United v Sheffield Wednesday ....

Endsleigh Insurance League Division 1

Barnsley v Grimsby Town ....
Birmingham City v Reading ....
Charlton Athletic v Wolverhampton Wanderers ..
Crystal Palace v Norwich City ....
Huddersfield Town v Portsmouth ....
Ipswich Town v Millwall ....
Oldham Athletic v Luton Town ....
Sheffield United v Port Vale ....
Stoke City v Southend United ....
Tranmere Rovers v Sunderland ....
Watford v Leicester City ....
West Bromwich Albion v Derby County ....

Endsleigh Insurance League Division 2

Brentford v A.F.C. Bournemouth ....
Bristol Rovers v Wycombe Wanderers ....
Burnley v Shrewsbury Town ....
Carlisle United v Bristol City ....
Chesterfield v Notts. County ....
Hull City v Bradford City ....
Oxford United v Peterborough United ....
Rotherham United v Wrexham ....
Swansea City v Crewe Alexandra ....
Swindon Town v Stockport County ....
Walsall v Brighton and Hove Albion ....
York City v Blackpool ....

Endsleigh Insurance League Division 3

Barnet v Fulham ....
Bury v Cardiff City ....
Cambridge United v Leyton Orient ....
Chester City v Mansfield Town ....
Colchester United v Doncaster Rovers ....
Gillingham v Scarborough ....
Hereford United v Rochdale ....
Lincoln City v Torquay United ....
Plymouth Argyle v Hartlepool United ....
Preston North End v Exeter City ....
Scunthorpe United v Darlington ....
Wigan Athletic v Northampton Town ....

© *The FA Premier League*
© *The Football League*